The New Politics of the Old South

The New Politics of the Old South

An Introduction to Southern Politics

Fourth Edition

Edited by
Charles S. Bullock III and Mark J. Rozell

ROWMAN & LITTLEFIELD PUBLISHERS, INC.
Lanham • Boulder • New York • Toronto • Plymouth, UK

Published by Rowman & Littlefield Publishers, Inc.
A wholly owned subsidiary of The Rowman & Littlefield Publishing Group, Inc.
4501 Forbes Boulevard, Suite 200, Lanham, Maryland 20706
http://www.rowmanlittlefield.com

Estover Road, Plymouth PL6 7PY, United Kingdom

British Library Cataloguing in Publication Information Available

Library of Congress Cataloging-in-Publication Data
The new politics of the old South : an introduction to Southern politics / edited
by Charles S. Bullock III and Mark J. Rozell. — 4th ed.
     p.   cm.
  Includes bibliographical references and index.
  ISBN 978-0-7425-7020-7 (cloth : alk. paper) — ISBN 978-0-7425-7021-4
(pbk. : alk. paper) — ISBN 978-1-4422-0018-0 (electronic)
  1. Southern States—Politics and government—1951– I. Bullock, Charles S.,
1942– II. Rozell, Mark J.
  F216.2.N49 2010
  320.975—dc22

                                                                2009012363

∞™ The paper used in this publication meets the minimum requirements of
American National Standard for Information Sciences—Permanence of Paper for
Printed Library Materials, ANSI/NISO Z39.48-1992.

Printed in the United States of America

Contents

Introduction

Southern Politics in the Twenty-first Century

Charles S. Bullock III

When V. O. Key (1949) published *Southern Politics*, the region was solidly Democratic. No Republican had been elected U.S. senator or governor in decades, and a generation had passed since a Republican collected a single Electoral College vote. For most of a century after Reconstruction, the South provided the foundation on which the national Democratic Party rested. When the party was in eclipse in the rest of the country, little more than the southern foundation could be seen. During periods of Democratic control of the presidency and Congress, as in the New Deal era, the South made a major contribution. The 2004 election reduced the Democratic Party in the South to its weakest position in more than 130 years as Republicans swept the region's Electoral College votes and held all but four senators and almost two-thirds of the House delegation.

Key's South had an electorate in which Republicans were rare and blacks even scarcer. While he observed that "In its grand outlines the politics of the South revolves around the position of the Negro" (1949, p. 5), it was not a commentary on black political influence, which was nonexistent, but rather an acknowledgment that the region expended so much political capital to keep African Americans away from the levers of power. Since implementation of the 1965 Voting Rights Act, black votes have become the mainstay of the Democratic Party—the vote without which few Democrats can win statewide. The votes cast by African Americans have helped elect a black governor (Virginia's Douglas Wilder), as many as eighteen members of Congress, hundreds of legislators and local officials, and were critical to Barack

1

Obama's nomination and later his success in carrying Virginia, Florida, and North Carolina.

Partisan change and black mobilization have not been continuous but have come at different paces in various locales and for different offices. Nonetheless, the changes have been massive. The chapters that follow delineate the nature of the changes for each of a dozen southern states. This introductory chapter sketches broadly the patterns of the South's politics for which the state chapters provide rich details.

PRESIDENCY

For generations southern politicians had no chance to become president because they opposed equal opportunities for African Americans. This prohibition ended when Lyndon Johnson succeeded John Kennedy in 1963. Since the assassination in Dallas, southerners have usually occupied the White House. Ronald Reagan and Barack Obama are the only presidents without southern ties since Jimmy Carter's 1976 victory. The 1992 Democratic ticket marked the first time a major party had two southerners, and the first election in which both parties' nominees had held office in the South. George W. Bush became the fourth southern governor to advance to the presidency within the span of a quarter of a century. In contrast, 2008 marked the first time since 1972 when neither major party ticket included a southerner.

Even before southerners could reasonably hope to become president, the region's partisan identity began changing. Presidential elections, the first office in which Republicans initially flexed electoral muscles, remain the ones in which southern whites give their most enthusiastic support to Republicans.

As a bit of history, only twice from 1876 through 1948 did a Republican presidential nominee carry even one southern state. In 1920, Tennessee and Oklahoma responded to Warren Harding's call for a return to normalcy. Eight years later, these states, along with Florida, North Carolina, Texas, and Virginia, rejected the Democratic nominee: NewYork–bred, Catholic, anti-prohibition Al Smith. These exceptions from the 1920s had no lasting impact as the South stayed in the Democratic fold throughout the Roosevelt era. However, 1944 marked the last hurrah for the Solid Democratic South. In 1948, Alabama, Louisiana, Mississippi, and South Carolina broke with the Democratic Party over its antidiscrimination planks and supported the Dixiecrat candidacy of South Carolina governor Strom Thurmond.

In 1952, the Deep South united behind Adlai Stevenson even as all Rim South states except Arkansas rallied to Dwight Eisenhower.[1] Four years later, Louisiana became the first Deep South state to vote for a Republican, making Eisenhower the first GOP nominee to carry the bulk of the South's electoral votes since 1872. The Eisenhower years also saw the first Republicans elected to the U.S. House in decades from Florida, North Carolina, Texas, and Virginia.

Partisan change began in the Deep South immediately after the 1964 Civil Rights Act extended federal protections to public accommodations, school desegregation, and employment opportunities. Senator Barry Goldwater (AZ), one of a few Republicans to break with his party's traditional support for civil rights, rejected the 1964 act as an unconstitutional invasion of states' rights. His stand coupled with President Lyndon Johnson's outspoken support for the bill prompted all five Deep South states to vote Republican for the first time (Carmines and Stimson 1989). Goldwater's popularity also elected the first Deep South Republicans to the House from Alabama, Georgia, and Mississippi.

Since 1972, the bulk of the South has voted for Republican presidential candidates, with the exception of 1976. In the initial post-Watergate election and the first with a Deep South candidate in more than a century, the region almost resurrected its solid Democratic voting pattern as all of the states of the Confederacy except for Virginia rallied behind Jimmy Carter. The reconciliation proved short-lived, and during the three elections of the 1980s, the only Democratic success came in 1980 when Georgia stood by its former governor but lost Georgia.

While the South has been the most Republican region since the 1990s, Democrats made a comeback when their ticket boasted not one but two southerners. In both presidential elections of the decade, the home states of the presidential and vice-presidential nominees (Arkansas and Tennessee, respectively) voted Democratic. Among Deep South states only Louisiana supported the Clinton-Gore ticket in both elections. Democrats narrowly carried Georgia in 1992; in 1996 Democrats took Florida for only the second time in more than a quarter century but lost Georgia.

The new millennium saw a reemergence of the solidly Republican South of the 1980s. Unlike in Florida, where Bush's 2000 victory was measured in hundreds of votes, the GOP decisively carried the rest of the region. In a stinging rebuke, Al Gore lost his home state of Tennessee 51 percent to 47 percent. Clinton's Arkansans went for the Republican by a similar margin.

Despite having North Carolina senator John Edwards on the 2004 ticket, Democrats got no traction in the South. Early in the fall some thought that the Kerry-Edwards ticket might be competitive in Arkansas, Louisiana, North Carolina, Tennessee, and Virginia in addition to Florida. But as election day drew nigh, Democratic troops pulled out of the South except for Florida. Even though midday exit poll results showed Kerry carrying Florida and winning the presidency, the final result held no suspense as Bush beat Kerry by three hundred and eighty thousand votes. Among southern states, only Florida (52.1 percent), Arkansas (54.4 percent), and Virginia (53.7 percent) did not give Bush a landslide victory (i.e., more than 55 percent). North Carolina abandoned its senator, giving him and Kerry 43.6 percent of the vote, which matched Al Gore's 2000 performance.

Both of Bush's elections depended on the South, which provided the bulk of his Electoral College votes. Had he not swept the region in 2000, he would have completed his second term as Texas governor. In 2004, his 286 Electoral College vote total could have withstood the defection of any southern state except Florida or Texas, but various combinations of two defections would also have proven fatal. Bush carried the South's popular vote by 5.5 million votes while losing the other thirty-eight states and the District of Columbia by 2.5 million votes. While today's South is not nearly as solidly Republican as Key's solid Democratic South, when the nation is closely divided, the South provides decisive support.

In 2008 the South provided support critical for Obama's nomination but proved irrelevant in November. Obama's appeal succeeded in winning three states worth fifty-five Electoral College votes, the most won by a Democrat since 1976. He became the first Democrat to carry Virginia since 1964 and the first non-southern Democrat to win any southern state since John Kennedy. Massive support from African Americans, many of whom had recently registered, proved critical to Obama's stronger performance than Kerry's in the South.

CONGRESS

GOP presidential success is now being paralleled in Congress, although overcoming the Civil War–induced antipathy toward the GOP took longer in congressional than presidential elections and has been less sweeping. Since 1972, the South has been at least as Republican as the rest of the nation in presidential elections, with the sole exception of 1976 (Bullock 1988, 225). In Congress, however, southern Republicans lagged their northern cousins, in part due to the many Democratic incumbents (Black and Black 2002), who could often convince voters that they shared the region's values and were far more conservative than most northern Democrats (Lublin 2004).

As shown in figure I.1, not until 1993 did the GOP share of southern Senate seats (46 percent) outpace their proportion in the remainder of the nation (42 percent). In the next two elections, the southern advantage increased so that in 1997, Republicans had 71 percent of the seats from the twelve southern states compared with half the remaining seats.

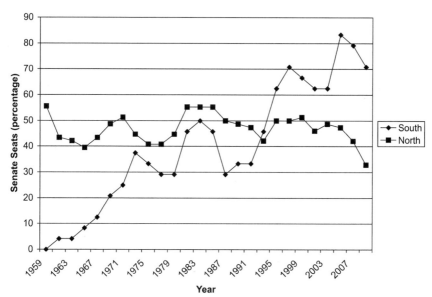

Figure I.1.   U.S. Senate Seats Held by Republicans from the South and Non-South, 1959–2009

The 2004 Senate elections gave Republicans their biggest boost—a twenty-one percentage point gain. Democrats had to defend open seats in Florida, Georgia, Louisiana, North Carolina, and South Carolina. Oklahoma had the only seat in the region from which a Republican retired. All of the open seats proved competitive except in Georgia, where Democrats failed to field a quality candidate. While none of the other five winners broke 54 percent, the thrust all went in the same direction as Republicans swept the region's open seats. David Vitter became Louisiana's first popularly elected Republican ever sent to the Senate. Florida had the most competitive race where the presidential opponents spent millions of dollars and they and their surrogates campaigned extensively. Former Bush cabinet member Mel Martinez, whom the White House encouraged to run, won a plurality victory over former university president Betty Castor. Only Arkansas incumbent Blanche Lincoln won a seat for the Democrats. Gaining five seats gave Republicans 83 percent of the region's seats.

GOP victories in 2004 established their high water mark. Democrats took back one Virginia seat in 2006 and easily won the second in 2008. Kay Hagen ousted North Carolina's Elizabeth Dole to increase Democrats to seven southern senators in 2009.

Broadening GOP House holdings in the South coincides with Republican breakthroughs in presidential voting. GOP House success came initially in

urban areas like Charlotte, St. Petersburg, Tulsa, and Dallas in the 1950s and
1960s. After 1964, as figure I.2 shows, the GOP's share of southern House
seats trended upward but with setbacks in the 1974, 1982, and 1986 midterm
elections when Republicans held the White House.

Even in taking control of the House, Newt Gingrich's fellow southerners trailed the northern wing of the GOP. Only after four disaffected Democrats followed Nathan Deal's (GA) lead and shifted partisan allegiance
did Republicans have a slightly larger share of the southern House seats
(56 percent) than the non-southern (53 percent). From 1997 to 2007, Republican House control rested on the South. The 104th Congress is
the only time in the last thirty years when Republicans have held most of
the non-southern seats in the House.

In the twelve-state South, Republicans registered substantial gains in
1992 (nine seats), 1994 (nineteen seats) and 1996 (eight seats when
midterm partisan changes are included). In the next two elections, the
parties held their own as Republicans, who had picked most of the low-
hanging fruit, controlled 57 percent to 58 percent of the House seats. The
post-2000 congressional reapportionment beefed up the South, already
the nation's most populous region. Florida, Georgia, and Texas each received two additional seats while North Carolina gained one. Since slow-
growing Mississippi lost a seat, the region boasted 136 seats in the first

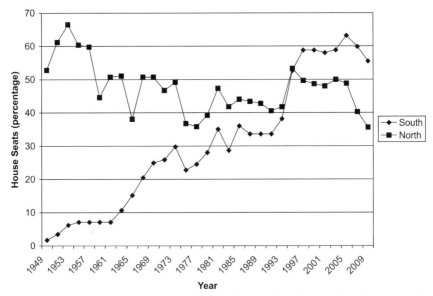

**Figure I.2.   U.S. House Seats Held by Republicans from the South and Non-South,
1949–2009**

decade of the new millennium. Following reapportionment, several states adopted extraordinary gerrymanders. Georgia Democrats sought to transform an eight-to-three Republican advantage into a seven-to-six Democratic delegation through what national elections expert Stuart Rothenberg described as "an example of partisanship and common sense run amuck" (2005). Florida Republicans enhanced their party's influence by designing the two new seats to favor Republicans and to defeat a Democratic incumbent. In Texas, no map got drawn, as the Democrats who controlled the House checked the ambitions of Republicans who controlled the Senate and governorship. A federal court drew the Texas map, and while the GOP got the two new seats, sitting Democrats continued to benefit from the gerrymander designed by their party a decade earlier.

Democratic ambitions in Georgia were only partially realized, as Republicans retained eight seats while Democrats picked up the two new seats allocated to the state. In Florida, Republicans gained three seats for an eighteen-to-seven advantage. Democrats maintained a seventeen-to-fifteen majority in the Texas delegation even though Republican candidates continued to poll a majority of the congressional votes cast in the state. Republicans came out ahead in Mississippi, where the delegation shrank from five to four and a Republican incumbent beat a Democratic incumbent. Democrats won the new seat awarded to North Carolina and took a seat away from Republicans in Oklahoma and Tennessee.

With most states using redistricting to eliminate partisan competition, few seats are marginal. In 2004 a disproportionate share of the fifteen seats that changed partisan hands occurred in the South. The disruptive influence came from Texas. House Majority Leader Tom DeLay wanted to increase his party's margin in the chamber. Moreover, Texas Republicans continued to chafe under the plan that Representative Martin Frost (D) had designed in 1991. Republicans, who after the 2002 elections controlled both chambers of the Texas legislature and the governorship, redrew the congressional districts in 2003 and targeted seven white Democrats. When the 109th Congress convened in 2005, only Chet Edwards and Lloyd Doggett survived GOP machinations. One Democrat switched to the GOP, contributing to a net gain for the party of six seats. The gains in Texas coupled with the loss of a seat in Georgia increased the GOP share of southern seats from 58 to 63 percent.

After twelve years in the minority, Democrats regained control of the House in 2006. While the bulk of the seats they picked up came from outside the South, wins in North Carolina, Florida, and Texas contributed to the margin. As in the Senate, the erosion in GOP strength begun in 2006 continued in 2008. The drop in the Republican share of House seats across those two elections shown in figure I.2 is one of the most dramatic in the time series. Democrats picked up Republican seats in each state Obama won, taking three in Virginia, two in Florida, and one in North Carolina. Partially offsetting these gains was a Republican victory in Florida where a freshman Democrat, who had multiple mistresses in addition to a wife, lost. Republicans also reclaimed the seat formerly held by Majority Leader DeLay and won two additional Louisiana seats. In one of the most surprising upsets of the year, the first Vietnamese American candidate, who is a Republican, upset William Jefferson in a 64 percent black district. The eighteen-year veteran had been indicted by federal authorities on charges of bribery.

GOVERNORSHIPS

As early as 1972, Republicans' percentage of southern governorships approximated the share outside the region, with about a third of all chief executives being Republicans. After the 1994 election, Republicans led six southern states, which increased to eight in 1996. Democrats made a comeback in 1998 when their nominees defeated incumbents in Alabama and South Carolina based on promises to earmark funds from a Georgia-style lottery for college scholarships. GOP efforts to win an open governorship failed in Georgia, but in Florida, Jeb Bush won the open seat. Ronnie Musgrove reclaimed the Mississippi governorship for Democrats in 1999 when that seat came open, and the next year Mike Easley retained North Carolina's governorship for Democrats so that by 2001, the South had five Democratic chief executives—all the Deep South states except Louisiana, plus North Carolina.

Republicans enjoyed an extraordinary year in 2002 which, in retrospect, foreshadowed their Senate successes two years later. The GOP reclaimed the Alabama and South Carolina governorships, but their most unexpected success came in Georgia, where Sonny Perdue astonished everyone—including himself and Democratic incumbent Roy Barnes—to become the state's first GOP chief executive since 1872. After former Republican National Committee chief Haley Barbour made Ronnie Musgrove a one-termer in Mississippi, the GOP led seven states.

As recently illustrated by Mississippi, Oklahoma, Tennessee, and Virginia, Republicans continue to struggle with a problem that has plagued them since their first gubernatorial victories in 1966. They have difficulty retaining the governorship following the retirement of an incumbent of their party. In more than four decades since the first modern Republican governor won in the Confederate South, there have been only six instances in which a Republican succeeded an incumbent Republican governor. Half of these occurred in Virginia (1973, 1977, and 1997), the only state to limit its chief executive to a single term. Other instances came in

South Carolina in 1994 and Florida in 2006. In Texas, Rick Perry succeeded George W. Bush when he moved on to the presidency and has won two full terms in his own right.[2] Currently seven states, including the five Deep South states, have GOP leadership.

Term limits for governors—a factor except in Texas—make it easier for the out-party to regain that office than a seat in Congress. Democratic gubernatorial candidates who have had careers in state politics can avoid embracing policies endorsed by their party at the national level that are out of step with southern preferences. By avoiding the national forces that push southern Democrats in Congress to the left, gubernatorial candidates can maintain centrist positions that appeal to southern voters (Black and Black 2002).

As the GOP matures, it may become more successful at retaining high-profile offices. Although its success has often seemed to percolate downward with the party's initial successes coming in presidential elections and the share of GOP congressional seats exceeding the share of state legislative seats, a strong party requires grassroots nourishment (Lublin 2004). The growing ranks of Republican legislators and local officials mean both that the GOP has larger numbers of experienced candidates who can compete for higher offices and that the ranks of possible Democratic candidates get reduced.

STATE LEGISLATURES

In keeping with the trickle-down theory of partisan realignment, success in state legislatures has proven more elusive to the GOP than have higher offices (Bullock 1988, 235; Bullock et al. 2006). Not until 1984 did Republicans fill more than twenty percent of the seats in lower chambers of the South, a figure only about half as large as their share of U.S. Senate seats at that time. Growth in state senates has come more slowly than in state lower chambers.

The 1994 elections marked a breakthrough as Republicans gained majorities in the Florida and Tennessee senates and the lower chambers of North and South Carolina. In 1996 Republicans claimed majorities in the Florida House and Texas Senate, but Democrats retook the Tennessee Senate. The success in Florida marked the first time since Reconstruction that Republicans controlled both chambers of a southern legislature. Jeb Bush's gubernatorial victory in 1998 marked the first time since the 1870s that the GOP controlled a southern legislature and governorship. Redistricting that cleared away the gerrymander barricades erected by Democrats to protect their majorities resulted in Republicans consolidating control of the Texas legislature in 2002 and in Georgia in 2004. In 2009,

Republicans won control of thirteen of the region's legislative chambers with complete control of six states, while Democrats dominated five states. In Virginia, each party claimed one house. Republicans have majorities in nine of fourteen Rim South chambers while Democrats organized six of ten Deep South states' chambers. In Louisiana, Democrats still have a comfortable majority in the Senate but in the House, neither party has a majority since Democrats have fifty-two seats, Republicans control fifty, and the remaining three are filled by independents. In 2009, the two parties hold an almost equal number of southern legislative seats. Democrats hold 252 Senate seats and Republicans hold 250. In the Houses, Republicans have a 711 to 707 advantage. Republicans are at their strongest ever in both sets of chambers, despite Obama's greater appeal than the two previous Democratic presidential nominees. Two chambers have the narrowest possible Republican majorities, as the GOP has a one-seat advantage in the Tennessee and Texas houses. Democrats' majorities in the senates of Mississippi and Virginia are also narrow, being two seats each in chamber. Except for the 1974 Watergate backlash, Republican strength in state legislatures has generally grown (Bullock et al. 2006). The rate of growth has varied but the arrow has been almost relentlessly upward. In keeping with this pattern, Democrats have infrequently regained majorities in chambers once Republicans win control, with their rebounds limited to the North Carolina House, Virginia Senate (2007), and the Tennessee Senate, although the last one proved temporary.

PARTISANSHIP IN THE ELECTORATE

Partisan shifts in the ranks of southern officeholders have outpaced changes in reported voter partisanship. As a carryover from the era of one-party politics, most states in the region do not require voters to pledge loyalty to a party when registering to vote. States without party registration allow voters to choose either party's primary ballot. In states with partisan registration, like Florida and North Carolina, the GOP has gone far toward eliminating the Democratic advantage, but even that does not match GOP gains in congressional and state legislative elections.

Where party registration figures are unavailable, surveys help fill the gap. Table I.1 presents exit poll results from the last three presidential elections. These figures show that southwide, 38 percent of the electorate identified with the Democrats. The proportion of Democrats in 2008 returns to the figure of eight years earlier, an increase of two points from 2004. Republican identifiers fell to their lowest figure, 36 percent, across the three elections after peaking at 43 percent in 2004. Louisiana, North Carolina, Oklahoma, and Mississippi had the highest proportions of

Democrats, with around 40 percent in each state. Alabama, Mississippi, and Oklahoma had the highest proportion of Republicans, each at about 45 percent. Obviously, party identification is more widespread in Mississippi and Oklahoma than in most states since these two each scored among the top states in terms of identification for each party. Seven states had Democratic pluralities although in several, as well as across the region, the partisan differences fall within or near the margin of error. The three states that voted for Obama underwent dramatic shifts. In Virginia, the Democratic share of the electorate increased by four points while Republicans lost six points. In Florida, while Democrats held constant with 37 percent of the voters, Republicans experienced a seven point decline. In North Carolina, Democratic identifiers increased by three points while Republican identifiers fell by nine. Democrats had their largest advantage in North Carolina (eleven points), followed by Virginia at six points. Republicans lost ground in every state except Arkansas and Oklahoma, where their one-point gains are within the margin of error. Democrats registered gains of more than one point in six states, while in five states no change occurred between 2004 and 2008. The 2008 exit polls show that the drift toward the GOP that had been under way in most states had halted if not been reversed.

In 1996, the mean percentage of Republican identifiers in the Deep South states (Alabama, Georgia, Louisiana, Mississippi, and South Carolina) was 35, while in the Rim South it was 37.9. Twelve years later, the average for the Rim South had dipped to 34.4 percent, down from 39.6 percent in 2004. Democrats once again outnumbered Republicans in the Rim South by a narrow margin of 37.1 to 34.4 percent. In the Deep South, Republicans stood at 40.8 percent, down four points from 2004 but still slightly above the 39 percent of Democratic identifiers. The Deep South, which began the shift toward the GOP roughly a decade later than the Rim South, has become the more Republican subregion in partisan identification. Despite continuing growth of the GOP, in no state does either party command the loyalty of most voters who turned out to choose between Obama and McCain. To win elections, each party must mobilize its adherents but also attract a share of independents or voters who weakly identify with the opposition party.

Party loyalties have weakened substantially in the last forty years and the numbers of independents have grown. Even many southerners who acknowledge a partisan tie nonetheless split their tickets. Changes in voting behavior have come quicker than changes in professed party loyalty, so Republican nominees for major offices such as president, governor, and senator usually secure larger shares of the vote than predicted by party identification data. These gaps have been greatest and were first observed in presidential elections. When Richard Nixon swept the South in 1972,

Table I.1. Party Identification at the Time of the 2000, 2004, and 2008 General Elections (in percentages)

	2000		2004		2008	
	Democrat	*Republican*	*Democrat*	*Republican*	*Democrat*	*Republican*
South	38	41	36	43	38	36
Alabama	41	37	32	50	37	45
Arkansas	42	25	41	31	36	32
Florida	40	38	37	41	37	34
Georgia	41	37	34	42	38	35
Louisiana	48	34	42	41	42	38
Mississippi	40	42	38	47	40	45
North Carolina	41	38	39	40	42	31
Oklahoma	42	44	40	43	41	44
South Carolina	33	39	33	44	38	41
Tennessee	39	37	32	40	32	33
Texas	35	42	32	43	33	34
Virginia	35	37	35	39	39	33

Source: Compiled from exit polls.

fewer than one southerner in five identified with the GOP (Stanley and Castle 1988, 239). In 1984 when Ronald Reagan repeated the feat, Republican Party identifiers remained well below 25 percent. In 2004, Bush got about 58 percent of the vote in the South, well above the 43 percent of the exit poll voters who identified with the GOP.[3] A disparity, albeit a less dramatic one, also exists on the Democratic side, where Kerry got 42 percent of the southern vote compared with the 36 percent of the electorate that identified as Democrats. In 2008, Obama's vote share exceeded the proportion of Democratic identifiers in the exit polls by eight percentage points.

Focusing on the party identification or voting preferences of the southern electorate obscures a growing chasm running along the racial fault line. African Americans support Democratic nominees up and down the ticket at rates of 80 percent and higher. Black Democratic nominees do even better among African American voters, and Obama got more than 90 percent of the black vote in each southern state. White support for Republicans, while not nearly as uniform as black voting for Democrats, has increased. Figure I.3 shows that across the seven most recent presidential elections, Democrats have polled about a third of the white vote in the South. Kerry and Obama slumped to only 29 percent of the white vote. The varied appeal of Democratic nominees in the rest of the nation is not reflected among southern whites, who found Clinton and Obama no more attractive than Kerry or even Michael Dukakis.

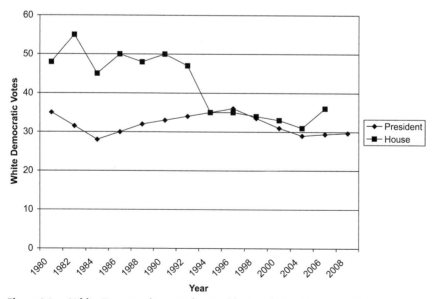

Figure I.3.   White Democratic Votes for President and U.S. House, 1980–2008

Until the mid-1990s, southern Democratic candidates for Congress did relatively well among whites even as their party's presidential nominees struggled. Recently, however, the appeal of southern congressional Democrats has sagged to the level of their party's presidential candidates. Figure I.3 shows that Democratic House nominees now perform only marginally better among white voters in the region than the party's presidential candidates. The up-and-down, off-year to presidential-year oscillation that had marked white congressional voting since 1980 ceased in 1994. After seven elections in which between 45 and 55 percent of the whites voted Democratic, support fell to barely a third and has yet to rise (also see Bullock et al. 2005). In 2004, Democratic congressional candidates in the South stumbled along with the support of 31 percent of the white voters but boasted support from 90 percent of African Americans. In 2006, an excellent year for Democrats nationwide and one in which they picked up a handful of congressional seats in the South, they improved their share of the white vote only to 36 percent.

Republican senatorial candidates have also attracted most of the white voters. In only six of thirty-nine southern U.S. Senate elections from 1996 to 2008 for which exit polls exist did the Democratic nominee poll a majority of the white vote. Two of these were incumbents and have since left Congress, but Mark Pryor (AR) and Mark Warner (VA) each won in 2008 with the bulk of the whites on their side.[4] Warner's success with white voters is especially notable since he did not have the advantage of incumbency. In less than a third of the contests, however, did the Democrat exceed 40 percent of the white vote, according to exit polls.

BLACK MOBILIZATION

At about the same time that Republicans began to score their first successes in the region, the civil rights movement began striking off the shackles of racism. Martin Luther King Jr. and the Montgomery bus boycott, court orders invalidating racially segregated facilities premised on the separate-but-equal doctrine, and numerous marches and protests demanding equal access to voting booths, quality education, and well-paying jobs pricked the conscience of the nation and ultimately persuaded Congress to act.

The 1965 Voting Rights Act banned the use of literacy tests and good character tests and provided alternative methods to register when local election officials discriminated against prospective black voters. Shortly after implementation of this legislation, black registration jumped from only 29 percent of the region's adult blacks being registered in 1962 to more than 60 percent in 1968 (Rodgers and Bullock 1972, 25). The most pronounced changes came in states that had been most repressive, with the share of age-eligible blacks registered rising from 19 to 52 percent in Alabama and from 7 to 60 percent in Mississippi. In recent years, registration and turnout rates among blacks have almost equaled those of whites (Bullock and Gaddie 2009).

In addition to supporting white Democrats, the black electorate has helped increase the number of African American officeholders. Figure I.4 shows the increase in the number of black legislators in the South from a scant thirty-five in 1969, of whom fourteen served in Georgia. In 2007, more than 300 African Americans sat in southern legislatures. Increases often followed a redistricting that created additional heavily black districts (Handley and Grofman 1994). Two-thirds of the growth in black representation occurred within two elections of the 1970, 1980, and 1990 censuses.

Creating districts with black concentrations also opened the way for the first black Democrats in Congress from the South. In 1972, Atlanta and Houston districts redrawn to be over 40 percent black elected Andrew Young and Barbara Jordan, respectively. Two years later Harold Ford Sr. won a 47 percent black Memphis district. The 1980s saw the election of Mike Espy from the Mississippi Delta, and when Lindy Boggs retired, William Jefferson succeeded to her New Orleans district. The 1992 redistricting sent a dozen new black members to Congress. The quantum leap in 1992 resulted from demands by the U.S. Department of Justice that

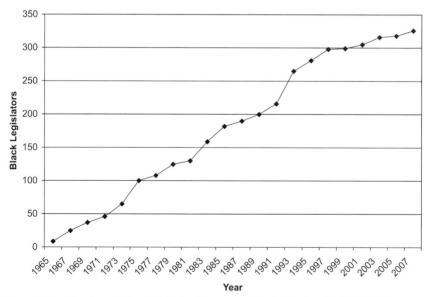

Figure I.4.   Number of Black State Legislators Serving in the South, 1965–2007

states maximize their numbers of majority-black districts. And while the Supreme Court found many of these districts to be unconstitutional, caus- ing their black percentages to be reduced, all continue to elect African Americans, except in Louisiana where Cleo Fields opted to seek the governorship.

The post-2000 redistricting had less impact but did result in additions to the Congressional Black Caucus. Georgia became the first southern state represented by four African Americans when David Scott won a metro-Atlanta district barely 40 percent black. After Texas Republicans implemented a mid-decade redistricting in 2003, Al Green defeated the incumbent in the Democratic primary in a 38 percent black district to be- come the third African American in that state's delegation. Recently the number of black members of Congress from the South has declined from its peak of eighteen achieved following the 2004 election. In 2006, Stephen Cohen became the first white member of Congress from Memphis since 1974 when he won a plurality in the Democratic primary against a large field of African Americans. Two years later, William Jefferson lost the majority-black New Orleans district to a Republican following the Demo- crat's federal indictment on charges of bribery.

RACE, PARTY, AND POLITICAL CONSEQUENCES

Blacks have succeeded in winning congressional districts that are only about 40 percent black in population because of the cohesiveness of the African American vote. Today's South, in which nine in ten blacks often vote Democratic and most whites back Republicans, gives each party ad- vantages in distinctive types of constituencies. As reported in table I.2, Re- publicans hold two-thirds of the congressional seats in districts less than 10 percent black and three-fourths of the seats in districts 10–19.9 percent black. If we exclude the seven heavily Hispanic Texas districts repre- sented by Democrats, then Republicans have 78 percent of the seats less than 20 percent black. At the other end of the scale, Democrats represent all but one district at least 40 percent black, and all but one of these Dem- ocrats are African American. Only one Republican represented a district that had a 2000 population more than 34 percent black. The rapidity with which Republicans have come to dominate heavily white districts is ap- parent since as recently as 1991, Democrats still had most of the seats even in the districts less than 10 percent black. The kinds of districts in which white Democrats most often won, that is, districts with black populations between 20 and 39.9 percent, shrank from fifty in 1991 to thirty-two today, which helps explain the drop in southern Democratic members of Con- gress. The redistricting plans of the early 1990s designed to increase the

Table I.2.　District Racial Composition (N) and GOP House Seats (%), Controlling for Racial Composition of the District, 1991, 2005, and 2009

Percent Black	2009 (%)	2005 (%)	N	1991 (%)	N
0–9.9	67.9	77.4	51	44.4	36
10–19.9	77.8	81.8	33	36.7	30
20–29.9	31.8	55.0	20	21.4	28
30–39.9	50.0	60.0	10	36.4	22
40–49.9	0	0	7	0	2
>50	9.1	0	11	0	4

number of majority-black districts resulted not only in more heavily black districts but many more heavily white districts, with fewer districts in the 20–40 percent black range.

Table I.2 shows that overwhelming shares of the congressional districts at either end of the spectrum are won by a single party. A review of election returns for individual districts reveals that in the South like the rest of the nation, hotly contested races are rare. In 2004, only five winners got less than 55 percent of the vote. The 2008 elections proved far more competitive as Democrats scored a number of gains and their stronger performance resulted in sixteen districts being won with less than 55 percent of the vote.

U.S. Senate and gubernatorial elections are more likely than U.S. House races to be competitive. In 2002, seven of nine southern senators who faced opposition won less than 55 percent of the vote.[5] However, six years later, only a third of the southern Senate contests were competitive.

Open seats can be especially competitive; the 1996 Louisiana contest ended in almost a dead heat and Max Cleland (D-GA) won with a plurality that year. The 2002 election had three open seats in the South while in 2004 there were six; only one winner got more than 55 percent of the vote. While incumbents usually fare better, from 1998 to 2008 Chuck Robb (D-VA), George Allen (R-VA), Elizabeth Dole (R-NC), Max Cleland (D-VA), and Tim Hutchinson (R-VA) lost close reelection bids. During this period, Paul Coverdell (R-GA), Saxby Chambliss (R-GA), and Fritz Hollings (D-SC) had close calls but won additional terms.

With the bulk of the white vote going to Republicans, successful Democrats depend on strong showings among minority voters. The bulk of Bill Clinton's 1996 votes in Georgia, Louisiana, Mississippi, and South Carolina came from blacks. In 2000, exit polls indicate that blacks provided most of the votes for Al Gore in each Deep South state and, Southwide, about 40 percent of Gore's votes came from African Americans. Without overwhelming black support Obama would not have won the three southern states he carried. Blacks also accounted for about three of every eight votes won by a Democratic congressional candidate in the region.

Even when black votes are insufficient to elect an African American, successful white Democrats depend heavily on this component of their electorates. This reliance makes Democratic legislators more responsive to black policy concerns and has largely eliminated the traditional southern conservative Democrat from Congress. As more conservative voters participate in GOP primaries, Democratic voters have rejected conservative candidates and become ideologically more like their northern cousins. At the same time, now that the GOP has become competitive, it provides a more attractive environment for conservative candidates.

The transformation in Congress has been accompanied by a similar change in Democratic primaries. With large numbers of whites participating in GOP primaries, the Democratic primary electorate now has a much higher black percentage than the general election turnout. One consequence is the nomination of more African Americans. Most southern states have seen African Americans nominated for major statewide offices, with blacks competing against Republican incumbent senators in 2008 in Alabama and Mississippi. African Americans have won major executive positions in Virginia, Georgia, and North Carolina, and statewide judicial positions in a number of states. Obama won the presidential primaries in seven southern states. Outside of his home state of Illinois and the District of Columbia, Obama's largest victories came in Georgia, Virginia, and Mississippi.

Down ticket, even if a black candidate is not nominated, the likelihood of nominating more liberal candidates or of pulling candidates to the left in search of votes increases. The risk for Democrats is that if their nominees stake out positions further to the left in order to secure support from blacks—the most reliable component of the Democratic Party—these stands can drive additional whites to the GOP, rendering the Democratic primary electorate even more liberal.

The importance of Democrats establishing moderate credentials is underscored in recent exit polls showing less than a fifth of the southern electorate being liberal, with the remainder almost evenly divided between conservatives and moderates. The small share of the southern electorate that considers itself liberal explains why Republicans so frequently characterize their Democratic opponents as liberals. In statewide southern contests, if Republicans succeed in attaching the liberal label to the Democratic nominee, that will determine the outcome.

Earl and Merle Black, leading students of southern politics, observed years ago that when Democrats offered candidates who were moderate conservatives or conservative moderates, these candidates usually won (1987). More recently they report that conservatives have forsaken the

Democratic Party, and, with their exodus near complete, moderates have joined in the move to the GOP (2002). Massive departures from the Democratic Party make it increasingly difficult for Democrats to win—as already documented in this chapter. Inept or ideologically-driven GOP politicians, some of whom took positions too far to the right, account for recent but short-lived Democratic successes in the late 1990s, when they won governorships in Alabama, Georgia, Mississippi, and South Carolina. Even more vulnerable than state officials are Democratic moderates who go to Congress and vote too often with the Democratic Party. Saxby Chambliss succeeded in convincing Georgians that Senator Max Cleland (D), a Vietnam triple amputee, had forgotten Georgia values and become too willing to support the initiatives of the national Democratic Party and therefore should be denied a second term.

Democrats who succeed in the South are often toward the right end of their party's continuum. For example, in 2007 the ideological rankings computed by the *National Journal* show Mary Landrieu (LA) and Mark Pryor (AR) to be two of the three most conservative Democrats in the Senate (Cohen and Friel 2008). Of southern Democratic senators, only Florida's Bill Nelson failed to vote conservatively at least a third of the time. In the House, eleven of the fifteen Democrats who voted conservatively more often than liberally came from the South. Establishing moderate records enabled these Democrats to withstand the rising tide of Republicanism in the region. While moderate Democrats remain, no southern Democrats come from the conservative end of the continuum today.

Religious conservatives are southern Republicans' most loyal supporters, both in primaries and general elections, and come from the right end of the political spectrum. In general elections, Republicans often win three-fourths of the ballots cast by voters who identify themselves as evangelicals while losing the remainder of the vote. The temptation to appeal to religious conservatives carries risks both in the region and nationally. Southern Republicans who have provided much of the congressional leadership over the last fifteen years and who are moving up the seniority rosters have pulled the party rightward. Contributing to the party's swing to the right has been the decimation of its moderates, as demonstrated by the elimination of Republican representatives from New England, finalized in 2008, and the reduction of GOP ranks in the New York delegation to three members.

Although southern Republicans tend to be conservative, there are limitations on how conservative a candidate can be and succeed. Those seen as out of the mainstream struggle to win statewide. For example, those who would allow abortions *only* to save the life of the mother rarely win statewide offices while those who take less restrictive stands, even though they are to the right of most Democratic candidates, succeed. Republicans closely identified with Christian conservatives succeed less often in the South than do more secular Republicans (Bullock and Smith 2005).

With the decline of southern conservative Democrats, Congress lost an important counterweight. Democratic Party success in Congress stemmed in no small part from its ability to appear liberal in the North but moderate to conservative in the South. Maintaining this Janus-like image required that northerners allow southerners to march to the beat of a different drum and vice-versa. In the words of Speaker Sam Rayburn, "You have to go along to get along." This orientation often produced moderately progressive legislation that both northern liberals and southern conservatives could tolerate although neither group saw it as ideal. Democrats' loss of Congress in the mid-1990s resulted at least in part from the demands that southerners be "good Democrats" (i.e., liberal) if they hoped to achieve influence and status within the party.[6] To secure promotion to exclusive committees like Appropriations or Ways and Means, Democrats had to support national party goals. Southerners who placed responsiveness to their conservative constituents above adherence to the party line foreclosed the prospects of achieving a seat on a power committee and risked eligibility to lead even subcommittees of lesser committees. In this hostile climate, conservative senator Richard Shelby (AL), Representative Billy Tauzin (LA) and Representative Nathan Deal (GA) changed parties, others retired, and those whom constituents saw as too supportive of Clinton policies lost in 1994 (Black and Black 2002).

The weakness of the South among congressional Democrats is further shown by the inability of a white southerner—even a liberal one—to attain a leadership position since Speaker Jim Wright (TX) resigned in 1989. Southerners always had at least one of the top three positions among House Democrats as long as the party leader appointed the whip. Since the mid-1980s, the Democratic Caucus has chosen the whip responsible for lining up members behind the party's policy positions. The whip has been the stepping stone for the higher positions of party leader and, when Democrats are in the majority, the speakership, so the inability of southerners to have one of their own as whip foreclosed party leadership offices to the region. The absence of southerners has also meant that no one in the senior councils advocated a more moderate course.

When Democrats took over the House in 2007, James Clyburn (SC) became whip, the first southerner to hold that position in a generation. While a moderate among members of the Congressional Black Caucus, Clyburn's voting record places him in the top third of the Democratic Party in terms of liberalism.

As southerners lost influence within the Democratic Caucus, their stock rose in the GOP leadership. Following the Republican takeover of the House in 1994, Georgia's Newt Gingrich became speaker and his two chief lieutenants, Majority Leader Dick Armey and Whip Tom DeLay, came from Texas. In the Senate, Mississippi's Trent Lott served as Majority Leader from 1996 to 2001, followed by Bill Frist from Tennessee from 2003 to 2007. More recently, southerners' hold on the Republican congressional leadership has declined, and as of 2009, the only Republican leader in either chamber from the South was House Whip Eric Cantor (VA).

While there are southern urban districts, often represented by blacks or Latinos, in which the representative can take stands in line with the policy preferences of the national Democratic Party, it would be suicidal for a Democrat to seek statewide office in the South by embracing the policies articulated by Democratic leaders in Congress. Georgia's former Democratic senator Zell Miller (2000–2005), who campaigned for the reelection of President Bush in 2004, castigated his party for taking stands so alien to his fellow partisans in the South and stated that party leaders like Hillary Clinton, Ted Kennedy, or Nancy Pelosi would be unwelcome interlopers for most southern Democratic candidates. Franklin Roosevelt, in a Depression-era reference to the South, observed that "I see one-third of a nation ill-housed, ill-clad, ill-nourished." Miller recast this statement charging that today the Democratic Party's attitude toward the South is, "I see one-third of a nation and it can go to hell" (Miller 2003, 9).

If congressional Democrats continue to be well to the left of the GOP, Republican efforts to recruit good candidates and win more offices in the South may be helped, since many white southerners equate the Democratic Party with failed liberal reforms, as evidenced by their rejection of Democratic presidential nominees since 1976. The last thing that Democrats in the South need are actions and pronouncements from the congressional wing of the party that underscore such perceptions.

A GLIMMER OF HOPE FOR DEMOCRATS

Recent elections have found Democrats competitive in some Rim South states. They have turned the tide in the Senate and House, reclaiming seats in each of the last two elections. As of 2009, Democrats held both Virginia Senate seats, had elected consecutive governors in the Old Dominion, narrowly reclaimed the state Senate and voted for a Democrat for president for the first time in forty-four years. In North Carolina, Obama won the electoral votes, and Democrats won their fifth consecutive gubernatorial election and defeated Elizabeth Dole to take a Senate seat. Florida, after narrowly voting Republican for president in 2000 and 2004, went for Obama, and two Republican incumbents lost House seats. Changing demographics, more specifically the in-migration of less conservative voters from the North, contributed significantly to these recent Democratic advances.

In these states plus Texas and Georgia, other demographic changes could imperil GOP hegemony. Republicans have succeeded by relying almost exclusively on white voters. But as whites constitute smaller shares of the electorate, Republican future prospects will grow dimmer unless they develop appeals to a more diverse electorate. If the growing Latino and Asian American voters join with African Americans, then to succeed, Republicans will have to win ever larger proportions of a white electorate that constitutes a smaller share of all voters.

The chapters dealing with individual states will more fully explore the themes set out in this chapter. Each state, of course, has it own unique features so that no two have taken the same path toward greater participation of minority groups and the emergence of two-party competition.

NOTES

1. The South is often divided into five Deep South states (Alabama, Georgia, Louisiana, Mississippi, and South Carolina). The remainder of the region is referred to as the Rim South or Peripheral South—the term preferred by the Blacks (1992).

2. Republicans won three consecutive Alabama gubernatorial elections (1986–1994) but did not govern throughout that period since Lieutenant Governor Little "Big Jim" Folsom, a Democrat, succeeded Guy Hunt upon the latter's removal and sentencing to community service plus a fine.

3. Exit polls have often underestimated Republicans in the electorate, since prior to 2008 Republicans were more likely than Democrats to cast early or absentee ballots.

4. The sponsors of the surveys did not consider exit data for 2002 to be reliable, and those elections are excluded from our analyses. Although no exit poll data were released for Mark Pryor's (AR) 2008 reelection, since he won with 79 percent of the vote it is safe to assume that most whites supported him.

5. No Democrat challenged Trent Lott (R-MS) or John Warner (R-VA).

6. For an alternative perspective that argues that Democrats can be a majority without doing well in the South, see Schaller (2006).

REFERENCES

Black, Earl, and Merle Black. 1987. *Politics and Society in the South*. Cambridge, MA: Harvard University Press.

———. 1992. *The Vital South: How Presidents Are Elected*. Cambridge, MA: Harvard University Press.

———. 2002. *The Rise of Southern Republicans*. Cambridge, MA: Harvard University Press.

Brady, David W., and Charles S. Bullock III. 1980. "Is There a Conservative Coalition in the House?" *Journal of Politics* 42:549–559.

Bullock, Charles S., III. 1983. "The Effects of Redistricting on Black Representation in Southern State Legislatures." Presented at the annual meeting of the American Political Science Association.

———. 1984. "Racial Crossover Voting and the Election of Black Officials." *Journal of Politics* 46 (February): 238–251.

———. 1988. "Creeping Realignment in the South." In *The South's New Politics: Realignment and Dealignment*, ed. Robert H. Swansbrough and David M. Brodsky, 220–237. Columbia: University of South Carolina Press.

———. 1991. "The Nomination Process and Super Tuesday." In *The 1988 Presidential Election in the South*, ed. Laurence W. Moreland, Robert P. Steed, and Tod A. Baker, 3–19. New York: Praeger.

———. 1995. "The Evolution of Redistricting Plans in Georgia in the 1990s." Presented at the annual meeting of the Association of American Geographers.

Bullock, Charles S., III, and Ronald Keith Gaddie. 2009. *The Triumph of Voting Rights in the South*. Norman: University of Oklahoma Press.

Bullock, Charles S., III, Ronald Keith Gaddie, and Donna Hoffman. 2005. "Consolidation of the White Southern Congressional Vote." *Political Research Quarterly* (June).

Bullock, Charles S., III, Donna R. Hoffman, and Ronald Keith Gaddie. 2006. "Regional Variations in the Realignment of American Politics, 1944–2004." *Social Science Quarterly* 87 (September): 494–518.

Bullock, Charles S., III, and Mark J. Rozell. 1998. "Southern Politics at Century's End." In *The New Politics of the Old South*, ed. C. S. Bullock III and M. J. Rozell, 3–21. Lanham, MD: Rowman & Littlefield.

Bullock, Charles S., III, and Mark C. Smith. 2005. "The Religious Right and Electoral Politics in the South." In *Politics and Religion in the White South*, ed. Glenn Feldman. Lexington: University Press of Kentucky.

Carmines, Edward G., and James A. Stimson. 1989. *Issue Evolution: Race and the Transformation of American Politics*. Princeton, NJ: Princeton University Press.

Cohen, Richard E., and Brian Friel. 2008. "The New Center." *National Journal* 40 (March 8): 20–62.

Handley, Lisa, and Bernard Grofman. 1994. "The Impact of the Voting Rights Act on Minority Representation: Black Officeholding in Southern State Legislatures and Congressional Delegations." In *Quiet Revolution in the South*, ed. Chandler Davidson and Bernard Grofman. Princeton, NJ: Princeton University Press.

Key, V. O., Jr. 1949. *Southern Politics in State and Nation*. New York: Alfred A. Knopf.

Lublin, David. 2004. *The Republican South*. Princeton, NJ: Princeton University Press.

Miller, Zell. 2003. *A National Party No More*. Atlanta: Stroud and Hall.

Rodgers, Harrell R., Jr., and Charles S. Bullock III. 1972. *Law and Social Change*. New York: McGraw-Hill.

Rothenberg, Stuart. 2005. "Mid-Decade Redistricting: What's Appropriate?" *Roll Call*, January 24.

Schaller, Thomas F. 2006. *Whistling Past Dixie: How Democrats Can Win Without the South*. New York: Simon & Schuster.

Stanley, Harold W., and David S. Castle. 1988. "Partisan Changes in the South: Making Sense of Scholarly Dissonance." In *The South's New Politics: Realignment and Dealignment*, ed. Robert H. Swansbrough and David M. Brodsky, 238–252. Columbia: University of South Carolina Press.

1

THE DEEP SOUTH STATES

1

South Carolina

The New Politics of the Palmetto State

Cole Blease Graham Jr., Laurence Moreland, and Robert P. Steed

V.O. Key's analysis of South Carolina politics at the middle of the twentieth century described a state that illustrated, often in sharp detail, most of the significant characteristics of the region as a whole (Key 1949, chap. 7). The foundation of the state's politics was an overriding concern with race and the maintenance of white supremacy that suppressed competing tendencies toward a class-based populist politics and shaped South Carolina politics into patterns congruent with Daniel Elazar's traditionalistic political culture, with its emphasis on paternalism, elitism, social hierarchy, a limited role for government, and conservatism characterized by strong defense of the status quo (Elazar 1972, 99–102).[1] During the first half of the twentieth century and into the post–World War II period, South Carolina's political system was marked by one-party politics, low voter turnout, a large percentage of disenfranchised African Americans in the population, white political leaders willing to use the race issue for their benefit, and a malapportioned state legislature (Key 1949, chap. 7; Bass and DeVries 1976, chap. 11).

By the end of the 1950s and into the 1960s, however, regional changes were under way that would dramatically alter South Carolina politics over the next decades. Increased urbanization and industrialization, economic development and diversification, the pressures of the civil rights movement, and a more heterogeneous population were accompanied by a decline in racist rhetoric on the part of candidates and public officials, an enlarged (and eventually integrated) electorate, and a reduction in the political influence of rural areas (Bass and DeVries 1976; Barone and

Ujifusa 1995; Kuzenski 1998; Woodard 2006, chaps. 3–4). In this altered environment, the South Carolina party and political systems began a marked transformation as well.

In this partisan transformation, South Carolina paralleled the larger South. A solidly one-party Democratic state prior to World War II and on into the early 1960s, it began to become more competitive with the slow growth of the Republican Party in the mid-1960s. The key factor in this increasingly competitive partisan battleground was the growth of Republican electoral strength, first at the presidential level and later at the congressional and state/local levels. Closely connected to these electoral developments were the organizational structures developed by both parties; these organizational structures were sufficiently institutionalized by the 1990s to perform a variety of functions within the state's political system.

PARTY AND ELECTORAL PATTERNS, 1960–2004[2]

Background

During the first half of the twentieth century the Democratic Party dominated South Carolina politics. At the presidential level, for example, Democrats won every election from 1900 to 1964 with the single exception of 1948 (when favorite son Strom Thurmond carried the state as the States' Rights Party candidate). Not only did the Democrats consistently win, prior to the 1950s they won impressively, dropping below 90 percent of the vote only once during this period (at 87 percent in 1944). Similarly, prior to the 1960s there were no Republican successes—and often no Republican candidates—in senatorial, congressional, gubernatorial, or state legislative elections.

One of the earliest and clearest manifestations of the crack in the state's Democratic solidarity came with its support of Strom Thurmond in 1948. Although the state returned to the Democratic fold in the next three presidential elections, it was by razor-thin margins unheard of in the preceding half century—51 percent of the vote for Adlai Stevenson and John F. Kennedy in 1952 and 1960, respectively, and only a plurality of 45 percent for Stevenson in 1956 (with the remaining 55 percent going to incumbent Dwight Eisenhower or to independent Harry Byrd). Thus, as presaged by presidential electoral patterns, by 1960 the state was poised for significant change.

Electoral Patterns, 1960–2004

In 1964, Senator Thurmond made a dramatic switch from the Democratic Party to the Republican Party and endorsed Barry Goldwater's presidential candidacy. Later that year, the state cast 59 percent of its votes for Goldwater. The events surrounding Goldwater's strong showing in the state (and in the Deep South generally) were important to Republican Party development not only because they added Deep South states' electoral votes to the Republican column for the first time in modern history, but also because they underscored the importance of race in the region's partisan transformation. Whereas Republican support in the 1950s had been largely based on conservative economic concerns among a growing white middle class located mainly in developing urban areas (see, e.g., Strong 1955, 1960), support for Goldwater was rooted mainly in those segments of the southern population—often blue collar and rural—who were most concerned with defending the Jim Crow system of racial segregation (Cosman 1966, 66–67; Bartley and Graham 1975, 105–110; Kuzenski 1998). Goldwater had cast a vote in the U.S. Senate against the 1964 Civil Rights Act, and this was widely interpreted as an indicator of his presumed opposition to the civil rights movement itself.

In a related development, Second District Congressman Albert Watson, who supported Goldwater, was stripped of his seniority by House Democrats, resigned, and switched parties. Watson regained his vacant seat in a special election in 1965, thus becoming the first Republican elected to Congress in the state since Reconstruction. The following year both Watson and Thurmond won reelection to their respective seats. Also, in 1966 the Republican Party's first gubernatorial candidate in decades (Joseph Rogers) won a respectable 42 percent of the vote and carried three counties, an unexpectedly strong showing accompanied by Republican victories in contests for 16 seats (of 124) in the lower house of the state legislature.

Over the next fifteen years, the Republican Party established itself as a viable electoral party by consistently winning one, and sometimes two, of South Carolina's six seats in the U.S. House of Representatives and Thurmond's seat in the U.S. Senate. Additionally, Republicans constituted a persistent minority in the state legislature, and the party broke through with a close gubernatorial victory in 1974 (although this was largely attributable to a series of internal problems in the Democratic Party relating to the legal disqualification of the primary-winning candidate and the subsequent bitter feelings related thereto). At the presidential level the only Republican loss between 1964 and 1980 was to fellow southerner Jimmy Carter in 1976.

Earl and Merle Black (2002) have discussed the importance to regional Republican growth of Ronald Reagan's 1980 and 1984 presidential election victories in the South; Reagan's importance in South Carolina was no different. Mirroring this general pattern, Reagan won South Carolina's electoral vote in 1980 and thereby helped launch a slow but steady movement toward a competitive two-party system in the state over the final two decades of the century. During this period, the Republican Party won every presidential election in the state, won three of five gubernatorial elections (with the 1990 win being a true landslide), continued to split the state's two U.S. Senate seats, and won half or more of the state's seats in the U.S. House of Representatives in eight of eleven elections (see table 1.1). As in many other southern states, the 1994 congressional elections marked an especially important breakthrough for Republicans in South Carolina as they established control of two-thirds of the House seats, control they have maintained in every election since.

The state legislative elections in 1994 were also important for Republican growth. After steadily pushing their share of state House seats up during the 1980s and early 1990s, a combination of additional victories and party switches in and around the 1994 elections gave Republicans a majority in the lower chamber for the first time in this century. (The 1994 elections also saw Republicans winning seven of the state's nine constitutional offices, including the governorship.) In the state Senate their share of seats rose above 40 percent between 1992 and 1996 as well.

In this changed political environment, the South Carolina Democratic Party found it progressively more difficult to compete with an increasingly vigorous Republican Party. Indeed, by the mid-1990s, it appeared that Democrats at the statewide level had become an endangered species. Republican momentum was slowed, however, in the 1998 statewide elections when the Democrats were able to take advantage of several short-term factors to achieve some surprise victories.

Most importantly, in 1998, incumbent seventy-six-year-old senator Ernest F. ("Fritz") Hollings was persuaded by the Democrats to head the ticket by running for reelection. Democrats, especially Democratic gubernatorial candidate Jim Hodges, were also aided by a series of missteps by Governor David Beasley. Foremost among these was his stance on an issue almost unique to South Carolina—whether the Confederate battle flag should continue to fly atop the statehouse, an issue on which Beasley reversed his earlier position and called for its removal, much to the surprise and disgust of many fellow Republicans in the state legislature and across the state. Other important short-term factors included the infusion of money into the campaign from the video-poker industry, which feared that moralistic Republicans would seek to ban such gambling, and a clever move by Democrat Jim Hodges to connect two popular issues— improvements in education and the creation of a state lottery (which he said would provide money for his proposed educational improvements). The result was that about 20 percent of self-professed Republicans crossed party lines and voted for Hodges. The Democrats were thus able to elect Hodges (with 53 percent of the vote), three other candidates for statewide

Table 1.1.   Republican Strength in South Carolina, 1960–2000 (in percentages)

Year	Vote for President	Vote for Governor	Vote for U.S. Senator	U.S. House Delegation	State House Delegation	State Senate Delegation
1960	48.8	0.0	0.0	0.0	0.0	
1962		0.0	42.8	0.0	0.0	0.0
1964	58.9	0.0	0.0	0.0		
1966		41.8	62.2/48.7*	16.6	13.7	
1968	38.1**		38.1	16.6	4.0	16.0
1970		45.6		16.6	8.9	
1972	70.8		63.3	33.3	16.9	6.5
1974		50.9	28.6	16.6	13.7	
1976	43.1			16.6	9.7	
1978		37.8	55.6	33.3	12.9	
1980	49.6**		29.6	66.6	13.7	10.9
1982		30.2		50.0	16.1	
1984	63.6		66.8	50.0	21.8	21.8
1986		51.1	35.6	33.3	25.8	
1988	61.5			33.3	29.8	23.9
1990		69.5	64.2	33.3	33.3	
1992	48.0**		46.9	50.0	40.3	34.8
1994		50.4		66.6	48.3***	
1996	49.8**		53.4	66.6	56.5	43.5
1998		45.2	45.7	66.6	53.2	
2000	56.8			66.6	56.4	50.0***
2002		52.9	55.2	66.6	58.1	
2004	58.0	53.7	66.6	59.6	56.5	
2006		55.1		66.6	58.8	
2008	53.9		57.5	66.6	57.3	58.6

Source: South Carolina State Elections Commission Reports for the selected elections.
*Special election to fill unexpired term of office.
**Three-way contests:
   a. In 1968: Republican Richard M. Nixon won with 38.1 percent to American Independent Party candidate George C. Wallace's 32.3 percent and Democrat Hubert H. Humphrey's 29.6 percent;
   b. In 1980: Republican Ronald Reagan won with 49.8 percent to Democrat Jimmy Carter's 48.1 percent and Independent John Anderson's 1.6 percent;
   c. In 1992: Republican George H. W. Bush won with 48.0 percent to Democrat Bill Clinton's 40.5 percent and Independent Ross Perot's 10.1 percent;
   d. In 1996: Republican Bob Dole won the state with 49.8 percent to Democratic incumbent Bill Clinton's 44.0 percent and Reform Party candidate Ross Perot's 5.6 percent.
***Party switching by Democrats after the election resulted in increases in the Republican percentage; after the 1994 election, the Republican Party held 52 percent of the state House seats and 43.4 percent of the state Senate seats; after the 2000 elections, such a switch gave Republicans 52.2 percent of the state Senate seats.

constitutional offices, and reelect Hollings (also with 53 percent of the vote).

The 1998 elections enthused Democrats and stunned Republicans. The 2000 state party conventions reflected these reactions, as Democrats predicted a party resurgence in the state while Republicans, in a rare show of dissension, pointed fingers and engaged in a struggle over party leadership.

An attempt to dump the state party chair, Henry McMaster, who seemed too closely identified with the 1998 losses, eventually failed in a very close vote, but only after a number of emotional convention speeches revealed the depth of Republican concerns.

Whether the 1998 election results were interpreted as a sign of Democratic revitalization or as a fluke grounded in short-term issues and events, few expected much impact on the 2000 election in the state. The strength and consistency of Republican support in presidential elections was so firmly established by 2000 that most considered it a lock to vote for George W. Bush. The major importance of South Carolina in the presidential election process had shifted during the 1990s to its increased significance as an early primary state, and this was certainly the case in 2000. In a brutal—even nasty—campaign, George W. Bush defeated John McCain, a win that provided a strong boost to his eventual nomination and demonstrated his popularity among South Carolina voters. Still, some Democratic Party leaders, such as Bob Coble, mayor of Columbia, gamely insisted that the state was winnable for Al Gore (Bandy 2000). Both candidates, however, saw South Carolina as being in the Bush column from the start, and neither spent any time in the state during the campaign. No member of either candidate's campaign team visited South Carolina during the campaign, nor did either campaign even buy television time in the state.

The results were consistent with the predictions. Bush carried the state handily with just under 57 percent of the vote, improving on his father's 48 percent in 1992 and Dole's 50 percent in 1996. This improvement was expected inasmuch as Ross Perot's presence in the two previous elections had cut into Republican support; what was not expected was Al Gore's poor showing. Despite Bill Clinton's unpopularity in the state (he regularly took a drubbing in newspaper editorial pages across the state and on local talk radio), Gore failed to improve appreciably on Clinton's vote, winning only 41 percent of the vote, barely better than Clinton's 40 percent in 1992 against an incumbent and less than Clinton's 44 percent in 1996. In short, the 2000 election confirmed the Republican hold on South Carolina's presidential vote. For the eighth time out of the previous nine presidential elections, and for the sixth consecutive time, the Republican ticket took the state's eight electoral votes.

Going into the 2002 election season, both parties had reason for optimism. The Democrats were buoyed by success in state elections four years earlier and by their enjoyment in having the incumbent governor, James Hodges, running for reelection. Republicans, still largely convinced that the 1998 elections were a fluke, saw the results of the 2000 elections as further evidence of their growing strength in the state. Additionally, South Carolina Republicans were optimistic about holding the U.S. Senate seat vacated by Strom Thurmond, who had served just under a half century in that chamber.

Following a spirited multicandidate primary contest, the Republicans nominated former congressman Mark Sanford to oppose Hodges for governor. Republican Lindsay Graham, a member of Congress who had gained some national name recognition with his role as a House manager in the impeachment of President Bill Clinton, won the Republican nomination for Thurmond's U.S. Senate seat. He ran against former South Carolina Supreme Court justice and college president Alex Sanders.

The two major issues which had benefited the Democrats in the 1998 gubernatorial election—the Confederate battle flag placement and the education lottery—were largely settled and, hence, no longer very salient to South Carolina voters in 2002. In the end, the advantages of incumbency were not enough to save Jim Hodges in an increasingly Republican state. In fact, not only did Mark Sanford win, his 53 percent majority was the second highest Republican gubernatorial vote percentage in modern history, surpassed only by Carroll Campbell's landslide 70 percent in 1990. Sanford's vote fit the pattern of Republican voting strength in the state as he ran strongest in the three vote-rich urban corridors centered around Greenville-Spartanburg in the north, Columbia's suburbs in the midlands, and Charleston in the coastal low country. Hodges only carried two of the fifteen counties in these urban areas, and even though he won 53 percent of the vote in the remaining counties (mostly rural and small town with only about one-third of the state's electorate), this was clearly insufficient to overcome Sanford's advantage in the urban-suburban Republican strongholds. These geographic patterns also reflected a continuing racial divide within the South Carolina electorate, with whites voting strongly Republican and African Americans voting even more strongly Democratic (Steed and Moreland 2007).

In the Senate race, Lindsay Graham defeated Alex Sanders by an even larger margin, 54 percent to 44 percent (the presence of two third-party candidates apparently affected the Democratic candidate disproportionately). As in the gubernatorial election, Graham ran strongest in the urban corridors (with 57 percent of the vote to Sanders's 41 percent), but he also beat Sanders in the remaining counties by 48 percent to 47 percent.

In the elections for other state constitutional offices, the news for the Democrats was not any better, as they won only two: State Treasurer and Superintendent of Education. Similarly, Republicans won four of the six congressional races to maintain their two-thirds majority in the state's congressional delegation for the fifth consecutive election, and they maintained control of both chambers of the state legislature. In short, the 2002 elections suggested strongly that the Democratic successes of 1998 were aberrations and that the Republican Party had established itself as the majority party in South Carolina state politics as well as in South Carolina presidential politics.

Although South Carolina Democrats were staggered by the 2002 election results, they were still clearly in a competitive position, at least in state and local elections. As the 2004 election campaigns opened, there was additional hope that a national ticket could be constructed that would aid state Democratic candidates even if it could not carry the state. Inasmuch as South Carolina's Democratic presidential primary was scheduled early in the delegate selection process, there was some hope that it would be able to influence such an outcome. In this vein, then, it was encouraging to state Democrats that Senator John Edwards of neighboring North Carolina (and a native of South Carolina) won the South Carolina primary in a multicandidate field. In the final analysis, of course, the presidential nomination went to John Kerry, but his selection of Edwards as his running mate was certainly aimed at strengthening the ticket's appeal in the South—and in South Carolina. In fact, even though Kerry was from Massachusetts, usually enough to condemn a candidate in the Palmetto State, he possessed strong military credentials that state Democrats hoped would blunt such condemnation. While few thought the Kerry-Edwards ticket would carry the state, there was some guarded optimism that it would not overly hurt state and local Democrats.

As the campaign unfolded, it quickly became apparent that Kerry and Edwards themselves had largely written South Carolina off as a potential source of electoral votes. There was no television campaign by either party's ticket, and surrogates largely made what few campaign visits there were to the state (e.g., Laura Bush visited in mid-September, but even that visit was primarily to stump for the Republican senatorial candidate, Jim DeMint). Both presidential campaigns expected a Bush-Cheney victory and, consequently, concentrated their time and resources in other states.

The major race thus became the race for the open seat in the U.S. Senate created by the retirement of Democrat Ernest F. Hollings. South Carolina Republicans saw this as an excellent opportunity to gain a seat historically held by the Democrats, while the Democrats considered retaining control of the seat to be highly important to their continued viability in the state. A hard-fought Republican contest ended in the run-off nomination of Congressman Jim DeMint.

In sharp contrast to the Republicans, who had numerous attractive candidates vying for their nomination, and reflecting the reduced strength of the Democratic Party in the state, the key problem the Democrats faced was finding a viable candidate to run for the seat. The nomination ultimately went to Inez Tenenbaum, the State Superintendent of Education and one of the two remaining Democrats holding statewide office. With

76 percent of the primary vote, Tenenbaum was by far the strongest candidate in the field.

The Tenenbaum-DeMint race quickly became highly heated and contentious. Both candidates crisscrossed the state, flooded the media with ads, engaged in a series of debates in various venues in different parts of the state, and collected and spent huge sums of money by South Carolina standards (for more detailed discussion of this race, see Steed and Moreland 2007).

Most other campaigns in the state paled in comparison with the white-hot Senate race. The expectations were that the Republicans would win the presidential election in South Carolina, that the congressional seats would remain distributed at four to two in favor of the Republicans, and that the Republicans would retain control of the state legislature. As the campaign unfolded, the only real question concerned the Senate race. Surveys revealed a race close enough to give Democrats real hope of victory.

The election results were a real disappointment for the Democrats. As expected, Bush and Cheney won an easy victory in the presidential election with 58 percent of the vote, Republicans retained their four-to-two margin in congressional seats, and they retained majorities in both houses of the state legislature. The stunning blow to the Democrats came with Tenenbaum's loss to DeMint in the Senate race. Not only did Tenenbaum lose, she lost by a 54 percent to 44 percent margin, no real improvement over the Democrats' 2002 showing with a less vigorous campaign and a less active (and less visible) candidate.

In both key races, Republican support again tended to be greatest in the state's urban areas. Bush again ran strongest in the three urban corridors, a pattern mirrored by DeMint in the Senate race. Perhaps of even greater concern for South Carolina Democrats, Bush also defeated Kerry in the state's remaining counties by a 7 percent margin. While Tenenbaum managed to hold the non-urban counties, the margin was a thin 50 percent to 48 percent of the total vote cast.

Exit polls revealed that Bush led Kerry among most of the standard demographic and socioeconomic groups in the state: men (63 percent) *and* women (55 percent), *all* age groups (ranging from 51 percent of those between the ages of eighteen and twenty-nine linearly upward to 61 percent of those sixty or older), all income categories from $30,000 per year and up, Protestants (75 percent) *and* Catholics (62 percent), and so on. The only major exceptions to the pattern were Kerry's success among low income groups and especially among African Americans. Indeed, the racial divide that has characterized South Carolina voting since the late 1960s again was the most prominent dividing line within the electorate; Bush received 78 percent of the white vote in the state while Kerry received 85 percent of the black vote.

Party Organizational Development, 1960–2004

As might be expected, party organizational development in South Carolina changed in accordance with the transformation of electoral patterns described above.

Prior to the 1960s, party organization in South Carolina was virtually nonexistent: there were so few Republicans that there was nothing to organize and, consequently, there was no need for Democratic organization either. (See Moore 1983; Jordan 1962; Key 1949.) With the increased electoral competition in the early 1960s described in the previous section, both parties began to give increased attention to their respective organizations. This was especially the case for the Republicans. Between 1962 and 1965 Republican state chair J. Drake Edens Jr., regarded by many as the father of the modern Republican Party in South Carolina, built the state's first genuine party organization (Moore 1983; Bass and DeVries 1976, 24). This, combined with the modest electoral gains of the mid-1960s and the significant financial support of South Carolinian Roger Milliken, president of the third-largest textile corporation in the world, gave the Republican Party a small but active nucleus interested in organizational development. By 1966, the Republicans had established a well-structured, multidivisional headquarters with a cadre of full-time salaried administrators (*Standard Operating Procedures of the South Carolina Republican Party State Headquarters* 1966).

Largely because the Democrats were still dominant in the 1960s, their response to the Republican organizing effort was slow. The focus of the State Executive Committee was less on competing with the Republicans than on administering the electoral system, especially the party's primaries. While the Democrats began to take some notice of the emerging Republican threat and moved to improve fundraising and other candidate support activities, their main concern related to changes occurring within the Democratic Party itself.

Specifically, the South Carolina Democratic Party found itself wrestling with a tangle of changes in election law (e.g., the 1965 Voting Rights Act) and party rules related to the civil rights movement's attack on laws denying African Americans the right to vote and on party rules excluding them from participating in party activities. (See, e.g., Crotty 1983; Price 1984, chap. 6; Polsby 1983; and Steed and McGlennon 1990.) At the same time, and in a related matter, South Carolina Democrats struggled to deal with what many considered to be unwelcome changes in the national party: an increasingly liberal image (and policy positions), often reflected in the nomination of locally unpopular presidential candidates such as George McGovern. The challenge was one of remaining a part of the national organization without alienating South Carolina voters to the detriment of state and local Democratic candidates.

During the 1970s the Republican Party continued its organizational development at the local level, especially in the state's urban centers, even though its main campaign involvement was still at the presidential level. The election of Republican James B. Edwards to the governorship in 1974 helped to spur further organizational development over the next two decades. Through the 1970s and on into the 1980s the Republican Party continued to operate a permanent, well-staffed headquarters in Columbia, succeeded in getting a county chair in almost every county, worked to expand local organizations, and regularly organized well-attended, efficient state conventions.

By the 1980s, as the turmoil of adjusting to new national party rules and the entry of African Americans into the party organization diminished, the South Carolina Democratic Party began to concentrate more of its organizational effort on meeting the growing Republican threat, particularly as Republican success in presidential elections began to trickle down to state and local elections. It was especially important that the Democrats find a way to hold together a fragile biracial coalition. Black voters were important to the party's electoral chances, and black party activists were becoming more and more important to the party's organizational operations as well. By the late 1980s, African Americans were well represented in state conventions, even constituting a majority of delegates in 1988 (when Jesse Jackson was a candidate for the Democratic presidential nomination), and they were a growing presence in precinct organizations (though still a relatively small minority at this level as late as 1992). Unfortunately for the party, many white Democratic activists were still having problems accepting blacks who did not share their ideological and issue orientations, and the party, therefore, faced a significant threat to internal cohesion on platforms, candidates, and election campaign strategy. (See Steed and McGlennon 1990; Steed, Moreland, and Baker 1995a.) To their credit, state Democratic leaders worked through these shoals and steered the organization into the 1990s intact.

By the end of the twentieth century, both parties in South Carolina had established well-organized party operations. Both maintained and operated permanent headquarters in Columbia, and both had a full slate of administrators and staff. Both state parties were primarily concerned with advancing party interests in the state, providing campaign assistance to the party's candidates for state and national office, and serving as a liaison between the national and local parties. A related activity concerns the development and maintenance of local organizations throughout the state. In this regard, the state party acts as a general service agency assisting local parties in fundraising, candidate recruitment, general communications, and the like. For both parties, the heavy reliance on volunteers and interns and the frequent turnover of key staff personnel have often posed problems related to continuity and organizational memory, both of which hinder organizational efficiency. However, in both parties this has begun to be addressed with more careful attention to record keeping and staff retention.

Clearly, then, the development of a competitive electoral system in South Carolina in the post–World War II period was accompanied by the development of stronger, more active party organizations. One last indicator of the sweep of party change in the state can be found in data on delegates to the parties' state conventions and data on local party officials. These data show that both parties not only succeed in attracting activists at various organization levels, they also attract activists who differ on a number of variables in ways that are congruent with the interparty differences found among activists outside the South. For example, supporters of the Religious Right are primarily found among Republican Party activists while African Americans are primarily found within the ranks of Democratic activists (for fuller discussion of these data, see Steed and Moreland 2000; Steed and Moreland 2001; Steed and Moreland 2003). Similarly, an ideological party sorting has occurred in the state as Republicans have become strongly conservative and Democrats have become increasingly less conservative and more liberal over the last two decades of the century (see Steed and Moreland 1999; Steed and Moreland 2007). At the beginning of the new century, then, South Carolina had developed a highly competitive two-party system that structured politics in the state in ways unheard of a half century earlier.

CONTEMPORARY SOUTH CAROLINA ELECTORAL AND PARTISAN POLITICS

The Elections of 2006

The gubernatorial election was the 2006 centerpiece of two-party competition in South Carolina. Late in 2005, incumbent Republican governor Mark Sanford, along with Louisiana governor Kathleen Blanco and Ohio governor Bob Taft, had been named as one of the three worst governors in America (*Time* 2005), opening the door for primary and general election opposition. Sanford's critics highlighted his poor relations with the General Assembly. Sanford's primary opponent, Oscar Lovelace, appealed to disappointed Republicans with proposals for health care reform and job creation. He opposed Sanford's advocacy of school vouchers. Undaunted by critics, Sanford ignored an invitation to debate Lovelace on state educational television and, in a light Republican primary turnout (247,281 votes), was nominated with 65 percent of the vote. After the primary, in mid-2006, one Republican state senator, angered over the governor's rejection of proposed development of the hospital in his district, gathered enough signatures to run as a petition candidate, but then did not.

In a more up-tempo primary campaign to nominate a candidate for lieutenant governor, incumbent Republican Andre Bauer defeated former governor Carroll Campbell's son, Mike, in a runoff by 51 percent. By comparison to Governor Sanford, Bauer brought some energy to his campaign by getting a speeding ticket from a state trooper, crashing his airplane, and depending on his grass-roots groundwork.

The Democratic primary was a contest between a veteran state senator from the midlands, Tommy Moore of Aiken County, and Florence mayor Frank Willis from the Pee Dee region. Moore criticized Willis's contributions to Republican candidates, including President George W. Bush. Willis defended himself as a crime-fighter and successful ambassador for economic development. Moore took 64 percent of the almost one hundred and thirty thousand Democratic primary participants.

Moore promoted his candidacy as a moderate along with extensive experience in state government. He called for active recruitment of new business and aggressive development of rural infrastructure. He wanted an increase in the state's lowest-in-the-nation cigarette tax to help small businesses finance employee health insurance. Sanford held to his earlier proposals to restructure state government to make it less costly and to cut taxes. He also stuck with his support for tuition tax credits to finance school choice, a policy that was sharply opposed by public school advocates. Sanford raised extensive campaign funds, about $8 million, compared to Moore's approximately $3 million. Sanford steadily led in the polls, and Moore was not able to mobilize any television advertising until just weeks before the vote.

Sanford carried the November general election with 55 percent of the vote. Overall turnout was 1,102,700, or 45 percent of registered voters. Sanford's main strongholds continued to be the long-established upstate and coastal urban Republican corridors. He won upstate Greenville and Pickens counties and coastal Dorchester County by more than 65 percent. His margin was over 60 percent in upstate Oconee, Spartanburg, and York counties and coastal Horry, Berkeley, and Beaufort counties. Moore's strongest support came from primarily rural Williamsburg, Orangeburg, Bamberg, Allendale, and Hampton counties.

In other significant statewide races, incumbent lieutenant governor Andre Bauer narrowly defeated Democratic challenger Robert Barber with just over 50 percent of the vote. A veteran incumbent Democratic constitutional officer, State Treasurer Grady Patterson, was defeated by Thomas Ravenel, a Charleston real estate developer and son of a former congressman. With strong support from his home area, Ravenel got 52 percent of the vote and was considered a rising star among future statewide Republican candidates until involvement in drug-law violations in 2007 ultimately led to his removal from office and a federal prison sentence.

Democrats did not change Republican dominance in either the Congressional delegation or the General Assembly. Defeats notwithstanding and with ample room to be more successful, Democrats continued to be well organized and to anticipate two-party competition in the 2008 statewide elections as well as the Congressional and state legislative ones.

The Elections of 2008

The presidential election was the focus in 2008. The nominating primaries began early in 2007. A long list of Republican presidential aspirants saw potential in South Carolina. Arizona Republican senator John McCain won the endorsement of Senator Lindsey Graham, who, along with now-governor Mark Sanford, had led McCain's 2000 primary campaign in South Carolina. Massachusetts governor Mitt Romney sought the approval of business leaders and gained the support of Senator Jim DeMint. Tennessee senator and actor Fred Thompson had appeal but really never campaigned. South Carolina evangelicals were courted by Arkansas governor Mike Huckabee, who made a direct appeal to them and to ordinary South Carolinians (Sheinin 2007).

McCain consistently seemed to be the front-runner and did win the primary, but with a disappointing 33 percent plurality. Huckabee was a significant challenger with 30 percent. Thompson and Romney trailed the divided field with 15 percent each. Another Republican disappointment was former New York Mayor Rudy Giuliani's performance at 2 percent, less than Texas Congressman Ron Paul's 4 percent. According to exit polls, McCain was more attractive to voters over forty-four years of age; Huckabee was more popular in the eighteen to forty-four age group. Huckabee won 41 percent of weekly churchgoers and led McCain among native Republican voters 36 percent to 32 percent, while McCain did slightly better among non-natives, with 34 percent to 26 percent (CNN 2008).

Democrats used the presidential nominating primary to underscore their potential prominence and competitiveness. They hosted the first debate for the national Democratic Party candidates. John Edwards, 2004 vice-presidential candidate, entered but did not do well. The primary centered on New York senator Hillary Clinton, who had been third in the Iowa caucuses and who had won the New Hampshire primary. Should she take the South Carolina primary, the speculation was that she would sweep away opposition and become the national party's nominee.

Enter Illinois senator Barack Obama. He had come in first in Iowa and, according to some South Carolina political observers, had crossed a significant political barrier in that victory, making it acceptable for a white person to vote for an African American who could potentially become president.

The intense competition between Clinton and Obama was something unexpected for South Carolina Democrats. Clinton stumbled early with a very traditional campaign that hired established party leaders as consultants. Maintaining their support became an expenditure drain, up to $7 million, compared to Obama's more controlled and sophisticated voter mobilization approach. In summer 2007, the Obama camp had begun a long-term voter identification project that targeted many younger voters. The energy of the Obama campaign surged with younger voter interest and well-attended public events as the Clinton campaign simultaneously sagged.

President Bill Clinton tried to help his wife by campaigning across the state. He had a good reputation among African Americans, who were expected to make up approximately 60 percent of Democratic primary voters, but his constant criticism of Obama turned President Clinton into a negative influence.

Obama's increasingly professional image ran beyond the usually limited appeal to African American voters by an African American candidate. Now Obama could count on support not only from younger voters, but from many white moderates and reformers as well as his African American base. Senator Obama won 55 percent of the vote and thirty-three out of forty-five convention delegates; Senator Clinton had 27 percent and twelve delegates; and Senator Edwards 18 percent with no delegates. Obama got 54 percent of the male vote (39 percent overall) and a similar percentage of female voters (61 percent overall). He also won 55 percent or more in each age category between eighteen and fifty-nine years. Among white voters, Obama won 51 percent of the eighteen to twenty-nine age group (5 percent overall). Edwards did best among middle-aged groups and tied Senator Clinton in the sixty years and over category with 42 percent (16 percent overall). Fifty-four percent of Democratic primary voters were black, and Obama exceeded 70 percent support in each category (CNN 2008).

South Carolina's 2008 primaries were significant, since both winners eventually were nominated by their national party for president. Significant for South Carolina Democrats, more voters participated in their primary than in the Republican one. Over five hundred and thirty thousand Democrats voted on January 26, 2008, compared to about four hundred and forty-five thousand Republicans on January 19. Few observers, however, translated this fact into a November Democratic victory.

With a record turnout of almost 2 million voters (a rate of approximately 75 percent of registered voters and approximately 58 percent of voting-age population), the November general election went to McCain with 54 percent over Obama's 45 percent. McCain had led all pre-election polls, typically by about 10 percent. Today, the upstate urban corridor contains about 28 percent of voters; the midlands contains about 24 percent, and the coastal and Pee Dee urban areas have another 25 percent, leaving approximately 23 percent scattered among the remaining rural counties. Only the rural areas, with half the number of counties and about one-fourth the population, are predominately Democratic. This pattern has not changed substantially since the 1970s.

Obama won the rural part of South Carolina by a plurality of slightly over 49 percent to McCain's just under 49 percent. McCain won a dominant 61 percent average in six upstate counties. The largest shares were in Pickens (71 percent) and Anderson (65 percent) counties. Suburban Lexington County was the most Republican county in the midlands (68 percent). Horry County, in the Pee Dee and with only 14 percent registered nonwhite voters, went for McCain by 62 percent. Dorchester County gave McCain the highest proportion in the low country, with 56 percent.

With respect to race, approximately 70 percent of registered voters are white, and McCain won 73 percent of them. Obama received 96 percent support among black voters, but only 27 percent of white voters. White men supported McCain at a higher rate than white women (76 percent to 70 percent), and white women supported Obama more than white men (29 percent to 23 percent). Obama had overwhelming support from black men (97 percent) and black women (96 percent) (MSNBC 2008).

Among age categories, McCain had his highest level of support among the sixty-five and over group (66 percent) and his lowest among the forty-five to sixty-four group (39 percent). Obama was stronger among younger voters. In income categories, Senator McCain had an average of 63 percent support among exit poll respondents making from $50,000 to over $100,000 annually. Obama's greatest share was 60 percent support from the 20 percent of respondents making less than $30,000 per year. There was about an even split, 48 percent for McCain and 51 percent for Obama, for the income group in the $30,000–50,000 category (MSNBC 2008).

The ideological split so evident in the nation (Black and Black 2007) is also present in South Carolina. Self-identified liberals (17 percent overall) supported Obama by 84 percent, while self-identified conservatives (40 percent overall) supported McCain at a rate of 86 percent. Moderates (42 percent overall) gave Obama a solid advantage over McCain (58 percent to 42 percent) (MSNBC 2008). By this measure, South Carolina Republicans did not do their usually successful job of neutralizing moderates.

Throughout the primaries and the campaign, much was made of the influence of evangelicals. Forty percent of whites identified with the Christian Right, and 85 percent of them supported McCain. Notwithstanding, the state of the economy emerged as the central issue. Eighty-seven percent of respondents reported being "worried about the direction of the economy next year," and 58 percent of them endorsed McCain. Obama was more convincing while discussing the war in Iraq as an issue, but only 11 percent of voters thought it mattered most, and Obama split their support with McCain (64 percent to 36 percent) (MSNBC 2008).

Incumbent U.S. senator Lindsey Graham was reelected by a typical Republican margin in South Carolina: 58 percent to 42 percent over his Democratic rival, Bob Conley. Graham increased his electoral margin by over 3 percent above his 2002 election to succeed Strom Thurmond. Graham received 73 percent in Lexington County and over 70 percent in hometown counties Oconee (73 percent) and Pickens (72 percent). The Democrat, Conley, won fifteen counties, primarily in rural, smaller populated areas. For example, Conley carried small, largely African American Allendale County with 73 percent to only 27 percent for Graham.

South Carolina's congressional delegation has four Republicans and two Democrats, all of whom were reelected in 2008. Among Republicans, First District incumbent Republican Henry Brown defeated a strong Democratic challenger, Linda Ketner, 52 percent to 48 percent, a surprisingly close margin and perhaps a wake-up call for an otherwise comfortable incumbent. Republican incumbent Joe Wilson had an 8 percent margin over Democratic competitor and Iraq veteran Rob Miller in the Second District. Third District incumbent Gresham Barrett defeated a female Democratic opponent, Jane Ballard Dyer, 65 percent to 35 percent. Returning Republican Bob Inglis won 60 percent in the Fourth District against two rivals, C. Faye Walters of the Green Party and Paul Corden, a Democrat.

Incumbent Democrat John Spratt won the Fifth District with 62 percent over 37 percent for Albert F. Spencer, a Republican, and 1 percent for Constitution Party candidate Frank Waggoner. Spratt is the Democrat whom the Republicans oppose frequently but can never seem to defeat. Incumbent Democrat and U.S. House Majority Whip, James Clyburn, maintained his dominance of the Sixth District with 68 percent against Republican Nancy Harrelson's 32 percent. The district was created in 1992 as a black majority district under the Voting Rights Act.

With few Democratic challengers or upsets, Republican domination continues in the General Assembly. There are seventy-one House Republicans to fifty-two Democrats (57 percent with one vacancy) and twenty-seven Republican senators to nineteen Democrats (59 percent). South Carolina has the lowest rate of women legislators in the country. There are seventeen women in the House (14 percent) and no women in the state Senate. Among House members there are twenty-nine African Americans (23 percent) and nine black senators (20 percent). Three black Republicans ran for House seats, one of whom had no opposition and became the state's first African American House Republican in over a century.

CONCLUSION

South Carolina's major importance in recent presidential politics has come at the nomination stage of the process, as it has often been a key early presidential primary state with highly competitive races. The 2008 election was no different since both McCain and Obama solidified their campaigns and shed significant rivals in the South Carolina primaries. As in the past, however—and despite an energizing presidential nominating primary for the Democrats—the state took a backseat in the broader general election campaign as both candidates accepted the reality of South Carolina's strong presidential Republicanism. This was a reality that was confirmed by the final vote tally, as Obama did only marginally better than John Kerry in 2004.

The long-term future of South Carolina politics turns on the question of whether South Carolina Republicans are a dominant party or whether more politically competitive outcomes will emerge from the better-organized two-party system that has developed in the state since 1960. Holding the first national debate among the contenders for the nomination and the "First in the South" Democratic primary in 2008 were concessions by the Democratic National Committee to give more prominence to South Carolina and to boost the state Democratic Party organization. Unfortunately for the Democrats, there is little evidence that such efforts have yet borne fruit. Not only did Republicans carry the state's presidential electoral votes for the eighth consecutive time, as of 2008 they also held the governorship, all statewide elected offices except the state superintendent of education, both U.S. Senate seats, two-thirds of the congressional delegation (four Republicans to two Democrats), and majorities in both chambers of the General Assembly.

Moreover, there is certainly no guarantee that Obama's national election victory will help renew and reinvigorate the Democratic Party in South Carolina. While this is a possibility, given Obama's performance in the state's presidential primary, the increase (though slight) in the Democratic proportion of the popular vote in the 2008 presidential election, and Obama's personal appeal, there are longer-term (and potent) factors at work as well.

In recent elections, Democrats have found it very difficult to win more than about 41 to 45 percent of the statewide vote. While the African American vote (nonwhites constituted slightly over 30 percent of those registered to vote in 2008) typically runs 90 percent or better in favor of the Democrats, white voters strongly favor Republicans for reasons related to the state's traditionalistic political culture, the high proportion of religious and social conservatives among whites, and many of the social and demographic factors at work in the state (such as South Carolina's attractiveness to relatively affluent retirees from outside the state—both military and otherwise—and its high proportion of gun owners). Democrats typically win only about 20 percent of the white vote, and until that percentage routinely approaches at least a third of white voters, statewide electoral success will remain elusive for Democrats. This is especially true in presidential elections, where South Carolina remains an undisputed part of the Republicans' (largely southern) base. Moreover, even Obama's strong appeal to African Americans in South Carolina could possibly be blunted by an approach to the presidency, already apparent in many of his pre-inaugural actions, that emphasizes performance, professionalism, merit, and effective governance over established Democratic policies responding to racial, gender, or ethnic needs.

In short, absent significant events that run counter to political trends with roots stretching back nearly five decades, Republicans seem well positioned to maintain control of the state's politics for the immediate future. While Democrats will continue to win a number of local offices and to hold a significant number of seats in the state legislature (particularly from districts with high concentrations of African Americans), Republicans will likely remain the dominant party for the foreseeable future.

NOTES

1. This pattern is generally consistent with Earl and Merle Black's analysis for the South generally that Daniel Elazar's concept of traditionalistic political culture provides a useful context for understanding much of the South's political history (Black and Black 1987, esp. chap. 2). Although variants of individualistic political culture occasionally manifested themselves in populism and entrepreneurial individualism, they argue that traditionalism most fully captured the essence of the southern political system.

2. The summary overview of this period of South Carolina electoral history is taken from Fowler 1966; Moore 1983; Moreland, Steed, and Baker 1986; Graham 1988; Moreland, Steed, and Baker 1991; Steed, Moreland, and Baker 1992; Steed, Moreland, and Baker, 1995b; Broach and Bandy 1999; Moreland and Steed 2002; Steed and Moreland 2003; Moreland and Steed 2005; and Steed and Moreland 2007.

REFERENCES

Bandy, Lee. 2000. "Gore Can Win in South Carolina, Coble Says." *The (Columbia) State*. September 9:B1.

Barone, Michael, and Grant Ujifusa. 1995. *The Almanac of American Politics 1996*. Washington, DC: National Journal.

Bartley, Numan V., and Hugh D. Graham. 1975. *Southern Politics and the Second Reconstruction*. Baltimore: Johns Hopkins University Press.

Bass, Jack, and Walter DeVries. 1976. *The Transformation of Southern Politics*. New York: Basic Books.

Black, Earl, and Merle Black. 1987. *Politics and Society in the South*. Cambridge, MA: Harvard University Press.

———. 2002. *The Rise of Southern Republicans*. Cambridge, MA: Harvard University Press.

———. 2007. *Divided America: The Ferocious Power Struggle in American Politics*. New York: Simon & Schuster.

Broach, Glen T., and Lee Bandy. 1999. "South Carolina: A Decade of Rapid Republican Ascent." In *Southern Politics in the 1990s*, ed. Alexander P. Lamis. Baton Rouge: Louisiana State University Press.

CNN. 2008. Exit Polls for Republican and Democratic Primaries. January 14; January 25. http://www.cnn.com/ELECTION/2008/primaries/results/epolls/#val=SCREP and http://www.cnn.com/ELECTION/2008/primaries/results/epolls/#val=SCDEM.

Cosman, Bernard. 1966. *Five States for Goldwater: Continuity and Change in Southern Presidential Voting Patterns*. Tuscaloosa: University of Alabama Press.

Crotty, William. 1983. *Party Reform*. New York: Longman.

Elazar, Daniel J. 1972. *American Federalism*. New York: Thomas Y. Crowell.

Fowler, Donald L. 1966. *Presidential Voting in South Carolina, 1948–1964*. Columbia: University of South Carolina Bureau of Governmental Research and Service.

Graham, Cole Blease, Jr. 1988. "Partisan Change in South Carolina." In *The South's New Politics: Realignment and Dealignment*, ed. Robert H. Swansbrough and David M. Brodsky. Columbia: University of South Carolina Press.

Jordan, Frank E., Jr. 1962. *The Primary State: A History of the Democratic Party in South Carolina 1876–1962*. Columbia: South Carolina Democratic Party.

Key, V. O., Jr. 1949. *Southern Politics in State and Nation*. New York: Alfred A. Knopf.

Kuzenski, John C. 1998. "South Carolina: The Heart of GOP Realignment in the South." In *The New Politics of the Old South*, ed. Charles S. Bullock III and Mark J. Rozell. Lanham, MD: Rowman & Littlefield.

Moore, William V. 1983. "Parties and Electoral Politics in South Carolina." In *Politics in the Palmetto State*, ed. Luther F. Carter and David S. Mann. Columbia: University of South Carolina Bureau of Governmental Research and Service.

Moreland, Laurence W., and Robert P. Steed. 2002. "South Carolina: Republican, Primarily." In *The 2000 Presidential Election in the South: Partisanship and Southern Party Systems in the 21st Century*, ed. Robert P. Steed and Laurence W. Moreland. Westport, CT: Praeger.

———. 2005. "South Carolina: Republican Success, Democratic Decline." *American Review of Politics* 26:109–130.

Moreland, Laurence W., Robert P. Steed, and Tod A. Baker. 1986. "South Carolina." In *The 1984 Presidential Election in the South: Patterns of Southern Party Politics*, ed. Robert P. Steed, Laurence W. Moreland, and Tod A. Baker. New York: Praeger.

———. 1991. "Different Cast, Same Drama in the Palmetto State." In *The 1988 Presidential Election in the South: Continuity Amidst Change in Southern Party Politics*, ed. Laurence W. Moreland, Robert P. Steed, and Tod A. Baker. New York: Praeger.

MSNBC. 2008. Exit Poll for South Carolina. http://www.msnbc.msn.com/id/25384430.

Polsby, Nelson W. 1983. *Consequences of Party Reform*. New York: Oxford University Press.

Price, David E. 1984. *Bringing Back the Parties*. Washington, DC: Congressional Quarterly Press.

Sheinin, Aaron Gould. 2007. "Arizona Senator Leads Most S.C. GOP Polls, but Nine Others Are Hoping to Knock Him Off." *The (Columbia) State*. May 13:A22.

Standard Operating Procedures of the South Carolina Republican Party State Headquarters. 1966. Howard H. "Bo" Calloway Collection, Richard B. Russell Memorial Library, The University of Georgia.

Steed, Robert P. 1997. "South Carolina." In *State Party Profiles: A 50-State Guide to Development, Organization, and Resources*, ed. Andrew M. Appleton and Daniel S. Ward. Washington, DC: Congressional Quarterly Press.

Steed, Robert P., and John McGlennon. 1990. "A 1988 Postscript: Continuing Coalitional Diversity." In *Political Parties in the Southern States: Party Activists in Partisan Coalitions*, ed. Tod A. Baker, Charles D. Hadley, Robert P. Steed, and Laurence W. Moreland. New York: Praeger.

Steed, Robert P., and Laurence W. Moreland. 1999. "Ideology, Issues, and the South Carolina Party System, 1980–1996." *The American Review of Politics* 20:49–74.

———. 2000. "Black Political Activists and the South Carolina Party System, 1986–2000." Paper presented at the 2000 annual meeting of the Southern Political Science Association, Atlanta, GA, November.

———. 2001. "The Group Bases of Southern Parties, 1984–2000: The Case of South Carolina." Paper presented at the 2001 annual meeting of the Southern Political Science Association, Atlanta, GA, November.

———. 2003. "South Carolina: Party Development in the Palmetto State." *The American Review of Politics* 24:91–108.

Steed, Robert P., and Laurence W. Moreland. 2007. "Change and Continuity in the Palmetto State." In *The New Politics of the Old South*, 3rd ed., ed. Charles S. Bullock III and Mark J. Rozell. Lanham, MD: Rowman & Littlefield.

Steed, Robert P., Laurence W. Moreland, and Tod A. Baker. 1992. "The South Carolina Party System: Toward a Two-Party System." In *Government in the Palmetto State: Toward the 21st Century*, ed. Luther F. Carter and David S. Mann. Columbia: The University of South Carolina Institute of Public Affairs.

———. 1995a. "Party Sorting at the Local Level in South Carolina." *The National Political Science Review* 5:181–196.

———. 1995b. "South Carolina: Toward a Two-Party System." In *Southern State Party Organizations and Activists*, ed. Charles D. Hadley and Lewis Bowman. Westport, CT: Praeger.

Strong, Donald. 1955. *The 1952 Presidential Election in the South*. Tuscaloosa: University of Alabama Bureau of Public Administration.

———. 1960. *Urban Republicanism in the South*. Tuscaloosa: University of Alabama Press.

Time. 2005. "*Time* Names the Five Best Governors in America." November 13. http://www.time.com/time/press_releases/article/0,8599,1129509,00.html.

Woodard, J. David. 2006. *The New Southern Politics*. Boulder, CO: Lynne Rienner.

2

Georgia

A Study of Party and Race

Charles S. Bullock III

In less than twenty years, Georgia has gone from the most Democratic state in the South to a solidly Republican one. In 1991, Republicans held none of the statewide offices, only one congressional seat, and less than one-fifth of the state legislative seats. In 2009, Republicans occupied twelve of fifteen statewide posts, including the governorship, held seven of thirteen congressional seats, and controlled both houses of the legislature. While Barack Obama performed better than any recent non-incumbent Democratic nominees for national or statewide offices, he failed to break the Republican hold on the Peach State.

Improving Republican fortunes accompanied dramatic population growth. The 2000 census revealed that Georgia's population had soared by more than 26 percent, the largest percentage gain east of the Mississippi River. Georgia's growth continued into the twenty-first century as it overtook New Jersey to become the ninth most populous state, with an estimated population of 9.7 million in 2008. More than five million people live in metro Atlanta, where they have to deal with the nation's longest average commutes to work. Georgia has long since moved beyond the "Rule of the Rustics" that V. O. Key (1949) described.

BACKGROUND

Rural Democratic dominance continued unchecked until the U.S. Supreme Court's one person, one vote decisions of the early 1960s. Each

of Georgia's 159 counties had at least one House seat. As a slight genu-
flection to population differences, the eight most populous counties received two additional seats while the next thirty largest counties got a second seat, for a total of 205 representatives. A rotational system ensured
that even the least populous county got to select a state senator every
third term.

Georgia not only gave rural areas exceptional influence in the legislature, but also gave rural voters greater control over statewide offices than
in other states. In Democratic primaries for statewide offices—and no Republican won a statewide election until 1980—and often congressional
contests, county unit votes rather than popular votes determined the victor. The best analogy here is the presidential Electoral College, with the
most popular candidate in a county getting all its unit votes. Each
county's unit vote equaled twice its number of seats in the state House, so
that Fulton County, which includes most of Atlanta, had six votes. Three
tiny counties with a few hundred voters each could easily offset the Atlanta vote, and in the days of boss-controlled counties, manipulating the
rural vote took less effort than winning large urban counties. A statewide
official from that era observed, "Give me five good men in 100 rural counties and I could run the state under the county unit system" (Campbell
1983). Until the Supreme Court mandated equal population districts, as
little as 25 percent of the population could elect a majority of the legislature and determine the outcome in statewide Democratic primaries. The
rural bias led the foremost practitioner of rustic politics, three-term governor Eugene Talmadge, to assert that he never wanted to carry a county
with a streetcar line. As witnessed in the 2000 presidential election, popular vote outcomes can differ from results based on winning political units,
and Talmadge won his fourth gubernatorial contest although another candidate got more popular votes. A judicial challenge invalidated the
county unit system just before the 1962 election.

Close behind the demise of the county unit system came court decisions
establishing one-person, one-vote for legislative districts. These orders
produced a more immediate racial impact in Georgia than elsewhere in
the South. Atlanta's large black population ensured the creation of majority black legislative seats once districts had equal populations. In 1962,
Leroy Johnson won a Senate seat to become the first African American to
serve in a southern state legislature in modern times. When the House
was redrawn to eliminate counties as the basis for representation, African
Americans entered that chamber, as shown in table 2.1.

Redistricting also opened the door for Republicans. A couple of north
Georgia counties, like the mountain areas of Tennessee and North Carolina, had sent Republicans to the legislature, but the minority party
could have caucused in a phone booth. Once urban counties got more

Table 2.1. **Partisan and Racial Makeup of the General Assembly and Congressional Delegation, 1963–2009 (in percentages)**

Year	GOP Members		Black Members		U.S. House	
	House	Senate	House	Senate	GOP	Black
1963	1.0	5.6	0	1.9	0	0
1965	11.2	16.7	3.4	3.7	10.0	0
1967	10.2	14.8	4.4	3.7	20.0	0
1969	13.8	12.5	5.9	3.7	20.0	0
1971	11.3	10.7	6.3	3.7	20.0	0
1973	16.1	14.3	7.8	3.6	10.0	10.0
1975	13.3	8.9	10.6	3.6	0	10.0
1977	13.3	7.1	11.7	3.6	0	10.0
1979	11.7	8.9	11.7	3.6	10.0	0
1981	13.3	8.9	11.7	3.6	10.0	0
1983	13.3	12.5	11.7	7.1	10.0	0
1985	13.3	16.1	11.7	10.7	20.0	0
1987	15.6	17.9	13.3	10.7	20.0	10.0
1989	20.0	19.6	13.9	12.5	10.0	10.0
1991	19.4	19.6	15.0	14.3	10.0	10.0
1993	28.9	26.9	17.2	16.1	36.4	27.3
1995	36.7	37.5	17.8	17.9	72.7	27.3
1997	41.1	39.3	18.3	19.6	72.7	27.3
1999	43.3	39.3	18.3	19.6	72.7	27.3
2001	42.2	42.9	20.0	19.6	72.7	27.3
2003	40.0	53.6	21.7	17.9	61.5	30.8
2005	55.0	60.7	21.7	19.6	53.8	30.8
2007	58.9	60.7	24.2	21.4	53.8	30.8
2009	58.3	60.7	24.2	21.4	53.8	30.8

than the three-seat maximum awarded by the county unit system, upscale suburban neighborhoods began electing Republicans. In 1964, Barry Goldwater became the first Republican to carry the state's electoral votes, and his coattails contributed to the election of the first GOP member of Congress since Reconstruction and a jump in Republican state legislators.

GOP STRUGGLES

The GOP crop sown by Goldwater seemed destined to produce a bountiful harvest in 1966, when Democrats nominated Lester Maddox, a restaurateur known for his racist rantings in the *Atlanta Journal-Constitution* and for chasing off prospective black customers with an ax handle, for governor. Republicans countered with Bo Callaway, heir to a textile fortune who epitomized country club Republicans. Maddox ran an underfunded campaign, but his attacks on blacks and Communists stirred the same rural passions that had elected the Talmadges (Bartley 1970, 69–72).

Unlike in Arkansas and Florida, where Republican gubernatorial candidates capitalized on the racial conservatism of their 1966 Democratic opponents, Callaway refused to reach out to African Americans, explaining that to do so "would be playing politics." The frustrated adviser who had urged seeking black support responded, "What the hell do you think you're playing, Bo?" An attack on the outgoing governor, several of whose lieutenants had worked covertly for Callaway, drove away more potential supporters and spawned a write-in campaign for progressive former-governor Ellis Arnall (1943–1947), who had lost the runoff to Maddox. Callaway eked out a 3,039-vote plurality, but because of the Arnall write-ins, no majority. In the absence of a majority, the choice fell to the General Assembly, which elected Maddox.

As often happens in the South, Georgia Republicans won their first significant sub-presidential election in the midst of Democratic disarray. In 1980, Senator Herman Talmadge sought a fifth term following a highly publicized divorce, bouts of alcoholism, and a Senate reprimand for financial misconduct. Talmadge failed to replenish his campaign treasury after an expensive primary runoff victory over Lieutenant Governor Zell Miller. He also refused to debate his opponent despite the challenger's weak speaking skills. By the time Congress adjourned and Talmadge returned home, the momentum had switched to Republican Mack Mattingly, a little-known IBM salesman. Even majority-black Fulton County (Atlanta) rejected the Democrat, casting 57 percent of its votes for Mattingly. The Talmadge dynasty, founded by the man who never wanted to carry a county with a streetcar, ended in the urban and suburban counties he had ignored with the coup de grace administered by African Americans in repayment for Eugene Talmadge's race baiting. Herman Talmadge's twenty-seven-thousand-vote defeat came despite President Carter's 236,000 majority in the one southern state to give electoral votes to a Democrat during the 1980s. Georgians had learned to split their ballots.

The Mattingly victory provided a rare down-ticket bright spot for the GOP. The landslide victories by Reagan in 1984 and Bush in 1988 had short coattails in Georgia. Sandwiched between Reagan's 362,000 majority and Bush's slightly larger margin was Mattingly's 1986 reelection defeat. Underscoring the GOP's inability to make down-ticket headway, Joseph Aistrup (1989) showed Georgia Republicans to be the weakest in the region.

Democrats' success sprang from their ability to unite black and white voters. Legislative leaders took pains to keep issues that might prove racially divisive off the agenda while working to improve the state's education system, an effort that paid dividends to both races. The deference given to seniority in the General Assembly allowed black legislators to assume larger roles as their service lengthened. The numbers of African American public officials continued to increase, and by 1990 blacks held thirty-five seats in the 236-member legislature.

AWAKENING FROM DORMANCY

Rip Van Winkle slept in the Hudson Valley for twenty years, a brief nap compared to the 121 years that elapsed from the time redeemer Democrats drove Republican Rufus Bullock from Georgia's governorship in 1871 until the emergence of the GOP as a serious competitor statewide. The breakthrough came via Georgia's majority vote requirement, which had saved the Democrats in 1966. Libertarian candidates captured slivers of the vote, which forced general election runoffs in 1992 for a renegade Democrat running for the Public Service Commission (PSC) and for Senator Wyche Fowler, who had unseated Mattingly.

Having lost the state to President Bill Clinton by 13,714 votes, Republicans sought revenge in the runoffs. An all-star team of national Republicans campaigned for Paul Coverdell and deluged the state with money. Coverdell, who had come up thirty-five thousand votes short in the general election, reversed fortunes and retired Fowler, while Republicans captured the PSC seat by an even larger margin (Fenno 1996; Bullock and Furr 1997).

The 1992 election also saw Republicans add three House seats to the one held by Newt Gingrich since 1979, giving the GOP its largest share of the delegation since 1874. The minority party also surged to more than a quarter of the state legislative seats, making its biggest single-election gains since the Goldwater election.

REDISTRICTING 1990s STYLE, OR HOW THE DEMOCRATS GOT MUGGED BY JUSTICE

Republican gains in Congress and the General Assembly could not have been achieved without the assistance of the U.S. Department of Justice (DOJ). Georgia, like all southern states except Arkansas, Oklahoma, and Tennessee, must have districting plans approved by the DOJ or the federal district court sitting in the District of Columbia. Congress placed this requirement in section 5 of the 1965 Voting Rights Act (VRA) to keep southern governments from erecting new barriers to black political participation once old ones were eliminated. By 1992, Congress had amended the VRA to bar election practices that resulted in minorities having less opportunity than others to participate in the political process or to elect their preferred candidates. The DOJ used this new provision to demand that jurisdictions *maximize* the number of districts in which blacks constituted a majority of the voting age population.

The DOJ refused to approve Georgia's congressional districting plan until it increased the number of majority-black districts from one to three. Meeting the DOJ's demands necessitated bleaching adjacent districts. Concentrating black voters, the most loyal Democrats, in three districts left neighboring districts whiter and more Republican (Lublin 2004). In districts made more favorable to Republicans, stronger candidates came forward to carry the GOP banner. In 1992, GOP state legislators gave up secure seats to win election in two congressional districts. The third Republican gain came when John Linder, who had lost by nine thousand votes in 1990, eked out a 2,676-vote victory. Had DeKalb County not been split along racial lines in order to make the Eleventh District 64 percent black, it would have been easy to keep the Fourth District black enough to elect a Democrat but not threaten black ambitions in the Eleventh.

Racial gerrymandering influenced the 1994 results in districts Eight and Ten as Republicans won another three seats. The percentage of blacks in the Eighth District dropped from 35 to 21 in 1992 and declined from 25 to 18 in the Tenth District. The other GOP pick up occurred in the Seventh District, which shifted parties as a result of growing suburbanization with new, affluent voters who had little attachment to the senior Democratic incumbent. The GOP tide lapped higher in April 1995 when Nathan Deal of the Ninth District became the first of five southern House Democrats to change parties during the 104th Congress. Deal's defection left no white Democrats in Georgia's delegation.

The redistricting battle of the 1990s did more than simply create whiter districts in which stronger Republican candidates triumphed. The prolonged struggle to satisfy DOJ demands for more black districts moved racial issues to the forefront in the General Assembly. The Democrats' biracial coalition faced unprecedented pressures, as black members thought whites unfairly blocked black ambitions for more seats. White Democrats saw black members, who aligned with Republicans in the redistricting battles, as disloyal to the party. Republicans, who fully appreciated that they would benefit to the extent that blacks secured new districts, provided technical assistance to the black legislators who had a special relationship with the DOJ staff. After the redistricting efforts that involved submission of three sets of maps to the DOJ, other issues took on racial overtones for the first time.

PARTISAN BALANCE

Statewide election results showed a very competitive state during the 1990s. In 1992 Bill Clinton won the state by fewer than fourteen thousand votes, the closest outcome in the nation. Four years later, Georgia was among the few states to shift parties, giving Bob Dole a twenty-seven-thousand-vote plurality. Narrow victories also characterized several high profile contests in the mid-1990s. In 1996 Max Cleland (D) reversed Bob Dole's fortunes for a thirty thousand vote plurality to fill Sam Nunn's (D) Senate seat. Competitiveness characterized 1994, when the first Republicans narrowly won constitutional offices. Three Republicans supplanted Democratic incumbents for down-ticket offices, with each victor taking 51 percent of the vote or less. Governor Zell Miller (D) won reelection with 51 percent of the vote, saved by the popular HOPE scholarships which enabled him to cut into GOP majorities in suburbia.[1]

DEMOCRATS' LAST HURRAH

Their unprecedented success in statewide, congressional, and state legislative seats fueled Republican expectations that in 1998 they would win the governorship, pick up additional constitutional offices, and perhaps take a majority in at least one chamber of the legislature. They realized none of these hopes, as Republicans fell before a record black turnout. African American voters had multiple motivations, including intemperate statements made by the GOP nominee for lieutenant governor and the presence of three African Americans among statewide Democratic nominees—two of whom won. Finally, Democrats tapped black support for Bill Clinton, who faced impeachment and removal from office, by targeting a recorded telephone call from the embattled president to each black voter's household.[2] These efforts boosted black turnout to a record 23 percent of all voters, up substantially from four years earlier, and African Americans continued casting 90 percent of their votes for Democrats.[3]

As black participation rose, Republicans' core support group shrank in 1998. As table 2.2 shows, white evangelicals constituted the smaller share of the electorate since polling began on this group. Evangelical whites regularly give more than 70 percent of their votes to GOP nominees while the remainder of the electorate votes for Democrats. In 1998, Republicans' strongest supporters withdrew from participation while the Democratic base expanded.

Georgia's 2000 elections resembled those of 1998 in that little changed. George Bush coasted to a three-hundred-thousand-vote majority while

Table 2.2. Proportion of Georgia's General Election Voters That Belong to the Parties' Core Constituencies and Their Voting Preferences (in percentages)

	1992	1994	1996	1998	2000	2004	2006	2008
Blacks								
Exit Polls	20	16	24	29	26	25	16	30
Verified by Secretary of State	NA	NA	21	23	23	25	24	NA
Support for Democratic Nominees								
President	87	—	92	—	91	88	—	98
Governor	—	90	—	90	—	—	81	—
U.S. Senator	86	—	83	89	93	87	—	91
White/Evangelicals								
Support for Republican Nominees	NA	26	22	19	20	35	35	37
President	NA	—	89	—	87	84	—	90
Governor	—	77	—	73	—	—	84	—
U.S. Senator	NA	—	78	85	64	87	—	85

Source: Exit poll data and estimates of support from Voter News Service except as noted.

former governor Zell Miller, who had been appointed to the Senate in July when Paul Coverdell died, polled 58 percent of the vote against a field of six in the non-partisan special election.[4] Each party retained a seat on the five-person PSC, with the successful Democrat being the first African American to serve on this body. Only modest changes occurred in the state legislature. Republicans concentrated their efforts in the Senate, where they needed seven seats in order to block Democratic gerrymanders in the upcoming redistricting battles. The GOP knocked off two incumbents and claimed that they came within 5,500 votes of their goal (Johnson 2000).

Even though Democrats did well in 2000, a major problem loomed on the horizon. State legislative contests underscored the extent of the Democratic bias in the districting scheme. In 1996, seventy-five thousand more voters preferred Republican than Democratic state Senate candidates even though the Democrats emerged with a thirty-four-to-twenty-two edge in the chamber (Baxter 1996). The pattern recurred in 1998 as Republicans secured 52 percent of the statewide vote for the Senate but only 39 percent of the seats and 53 percent of the state House votes compared with 43 percent of the seats. Republicans' inability to win even a majority of the seats despite taking sizable majorities of the vote runs counter to the usual practice where the party that attracts a majority of the vote gets a bonus in its share of the seats.

REPUBLICAN COMING OF AGE

In 2002, Republicans completed the long march out of political obscurity that began with Goldwater in 1964. After fifty consecutive gubernatorial elections won by Democrats, former state senator Sonny Perdue pulled off what some saw as that year's most startling upset (Sabato 2003). Although outspent by more than six to one and struggling to even get on television, Perdue thwarted Roy Barnes's reelection bid.

Perdue added to the Republican base by exploiting Barnes's unpopular actions. To satisfy repeated demands from the Legislative Black Caucus and avoid threatened boycotts of Georgia convention sites, Barnes convinced the legislature to adopt a flag that dramatically shrank the size of the St. Andrews Cross of the Confederate flag, which had dominated the Georgia flag. The change infuriated heritage groups like the Sons of Confederate Veterans. Barnes's education reform alienated teachers. Teachers supported his call for smaller classes, but he lost their support when it appeared to them that he thought them to be largely incompetent and uncaring. Leaders in rural counties that had heretofore been kept intact in a single district turned on the governor when his new districting maps split their counties. Elected officials risk alienating some supporters when they make decisions. Most incumbents, however, augment the ranks of their initial backers by attracting new support. Barnes failed to do so despite millions of dollars in television advertising.

Barnes's underfunded challenger ran a grassroots campaign that concentrated on seventy counties that in 1998 had supported Barnes for governor but voted to reelect Republican senator Paul Coverdell. Perdue reasoned that if he could add the counties that had split their votes in 1998 to counties that consistently voted Republican, he would win. If one were to grade the Perdue campaign, he would earn an "A" since he carried sixty-five of the seventy swing counties.

The Republican surge included Saxby Chambliss, who upset Senator Max Cleland's reelection bid. Cleland's defeat also resulted from alienating key constituents. His narrow 1996 victory relied on moderates who expected their new senator to follow in the footsteps of the retiring Sam Nunn. By the time that Cleland got to the Senate, the conservative southern Democratic contingent that had frequently held the balance of power in the chamber beginning in the 1940s had been decimated. With no senior role models from his region, Cleland fell under the spell of national Democrats who emphasized party loyalty and staked out positions far to the left of most Georgia voters.

President Bush's proposal for a Department of National Security provided the final piece in the GOP campaign to depict Cleland as "too liberal for Georgia." Senator Miller quickly embraced the president's position while Cleland stood by the Democratic alternative, which guaranteed employees of the new department the right to unionize. Republicans attacked Cleland, charging that he placed protection of unions above national defense. Georgia, a right-to-work state, has been inhospitable to union activity, thus making the Republican charges all the more lethal. To drive home their claim that Cleland's opposition to the president's proposal threatened national security, a Republican television ad juxtaposed pictures of Cleland and Osama Bin Laden.

The relationship between race and voting in 2002 was striking. Perdue won all but three of the 113 counties in which blacks constituted less than a third of the registrants. Chambliss almost matched Perdue's feat by carrying 105 of these counties. The strong showing among white voters enabled the Republicans to carry many rural south Georgia counties that in the past had formed part of the Democratic coalition. The outcomes of recent state Senate elections also correlate with race. Republicans have won all thirty-three Senate districts in which blacks constituted less than 30 percent of the registrants. Democrats retained all but one of the more heavily black districts. The remarkable success of Republicans in winning districts more than a quarter black in registration was less striking in the

House, where a few long-time Democratic incumbents have managed to hold on.

The white voters who abandoned Democratic state Senate candidates provided little support for Democrats at the top of the ticket in 2004. John Kerry and Democratic Senate nominee Denise Majette got less than a quarter of the white vote according to exit polls and lost by more than half a million votes. The presence of Majette as the Democratic nominee underscored the problems plaguing the once-dominant party, which failed to convince better-known officeholders to contest the Senate seat. A constitutional amendment prohibiting gay marriage helped mobilize conservative voters. The presence of this amendment may account for the jump in evangelical voters who, as reported in table 2.2, constituted 35 percent of the white electorate in 2004. These elements combined to make Georgia one of the states with the greatest increase in turnout, and the GOP benefited from the heightened voter interest.

MOPPING UP

In contrast with national trends that favored Democrats in 2006, Georgia Democratic losses continued to mount in 2006 when their top two prospects, Lieutenant Governor Mark Taylor and Secretary of State Cathy Cox, competed for the gubernatorial nomination. Taylor's nomination relied on strong support in the African American community, which cast almost half the votes in the Democratic primary. Wounds inflicted in the primary festered, which prevented Taylor from uniting his party. In the general election he managed only 38 percent of the vote, the poorest showing by a major party gubernatorial nominee in a generation. While popular among African Americans, exit polls put Taylor's support among whites at 27 percent, only four percentage points better than John Kerry had done two years earlier. In addition to failing to regain the governorship, Democrats lost the two positions vacated by their gubernatorial hopefuls, a seat on the Public Service Commission, and seven seats in the state House. Two members of Congress came closer to losing reelection than any other Democratic incumbents in the nation as John Barrow held on to his seat by less than 900 votes, while Jim Marshall won a third term with 51 percent of the vote.

Taylor's rejection by whites is more striking than the 2004 results. That white southerners would not support a Massachusetts liberal for president or a largely unknown black nominee for the Senate was hardly surprising. But Taylor had been lieutenant governor for eight years, had long service in the state Senate, and came from conservative south Georgia. He had none of the handicaps of the Democrats who led their ticket in 2004; nonetheless, he had the same minimal appeal to white Georgians.

2008

The presidential primary found Georgia Republican and Democratic voters at opposite ends of the ideological spectrum. Democrats, a majority of whom were African Americans, the first time such a scenario existed, cast 66 percent of their votes for Barack Obama, the highest percentage he obtained in any state on his way to the Democratic nomination. He drew the support of 87 percent of black voters along with 40 percent of whites. Republicans supported the most conservative of their major candidates as Mike Huckabee (34 percent) narrowly defeated John McCain (32 percent) and Mitt Romney (30 percent) in the winner-take-all contest. Huckabee benefited from extraordinary levels of participation by religious conservatives, who cast 62 percent of the GOP vote.

The 2008 general election saw Georgia once again largely ignored by the two presidential candidates, who only ventured into the Peach State for fundraisers. Nonetheless, in the last two weeks of the campaign, Georgia suddenly emerged as a battleground state. The shift from scarlet to pink resulted from changes in the registered electorate. In the last nine and a half weeks before registration books closed for the general election, 323,000 new voters signed up, with African Americans constituting almost half. The surge in black registration far exceeded the 30 percent black share of the adult population and indicates the success of Obama's get-out-the-vote effort.

Not only did the Obama effort, with its thirty-three campaign offices, more than fifty paid staff, and almost five thousand trained volunteers, encourage new registrants, it succeeded in getting these new voters to the polls. Georgia extended no-excuse early voting to begin forty-five days prior to November 4. Most Georgians took advantage of these opportunities to cast ballots prior to Election Day, and of the more than 2 million early voters, the secretary of state reported that 35 percent were black. White turnout exceeded that for African Americans on Election Day; nonetheless the figures on turnout from the secretary of state show blacks casting 30 percent of all votes, which indicates a record black participation and equals their share of registrants. In previous elections, blacks turned out at lower rates than they registered.

To carry Georgia, Obama needed not simply enthusiastic black support but a larger share of the white vote than recent Democratic candidates for statewide office or the presidency had managed. He came up short on this dimension, with exit polls showing him getting the same share of white voters (23 percent) as had supported John Kerry. But with higher black participation, Obama substantially improved on Kerry's performance, losing Georgia by only two hundred thousand votes in contrast to Kerry's massive rejection by five hundred and fifty thousand votes. Although improving on Kerry's showing, Obama had less appeal for Georgia's young electorate than elsewhere. While he won the youth vote nationally by more than 2:1, he narrowly lost it in Georgia. Obama also did somewhat less well among first-time voters in Georgia than nationwide, although he did get most of their votes. As elsewhere, by overwhelming margins, Georgians identified the economy as the most significant issue. However, while those most concerned about the economy favored Obama nationwide, in Georgia, McCain polled a narrow majority among these voters. In a countermovement to Obama's strength among African Americans, table 2.2 shows that the core constituency of the GOP also mobilized in record numbers. White evangelicals cast a record 37 percent of the vote, with 90 percent of their support going to John McCain.

The increased black participation stimulated by the Obama campaign helped other Democrats. Saxby Chambliss, who had a double-digit lead in early September polls, suddenly found himself hard pressed by former state representative Jim Martin. Three factors contributed to the evaporation of the Chambliss advantage. Besides the addition of new black voters, Chambliss's vote for the $700 billion rescue package alienated a number of white conservatives. This reminded conservatives that they had questioned Chambliss's commitment previously, when he supported President Bush's immigration reform and the pork-laden farm bill. Finally, Chambliss ignored a basic rule of politics. He failed to go on television and define his largely unknown opponent, despite having a massive war chest. Chambliss's hesitation allowed Martin to have unchallenged dominance in the television ad wars for more than two weeks, during which he introduced himself to Georgians. Prior to the Martin ad buy, 45 percent of Georgians knew so little about the challenger they offered no evaluation of him. After his television advertising, almost all likely voters knew who Martin was, and his favorable-to-unfavorable ratings increased dramatically. Once Martin demonstrated political viability, the Democratic Senatorial Campaign Committee began purchasing television ads on his behalf.

The same requirement that Georgia winners secure a majority of the vote, which had opened the way for Coverdell's Senate victory in 1992, tripped up Chambliss. The election showed the polls to have been accurate, as Chambliss led Martin by three percentage points, but the incumbent came up 9,200 votes short of a majority, which necessitated a December 2 runoff.

During the four weeks leading up to the runoff, top Republicans from across the nation campaigned for Chambliss. All of the major presidential contestants from 2004 came to the state, with the visit by Sarah Palin on the day before the election inspiring Republican crowds in four cities. Democrats tried to counter by bringing in Bill Clinton and Al Gore. On the day before the election, while Palin spoke for Chambliss, Martin appeared with rap artists Ludacris, Young Jeezy, and T.I. in an effort to pump up the black participation critical for Democratic success. As in previous general election runoffs, Republicans had far greater success in getting their voters back to the polls. Chambliss increased his vote share across the state in both Democratic and Republican counties and handily defeated Martin by taking 57 percent of the vote. A key element of the Chambliss campaign warned that should Martin win, Senate Democrats might then have the sixty votes needed to prevent Republicans from filibustering liberal initiatives.

BASES OF PARTISAN SUPPORT

Traditionally, when Democrats got overwhelming African American support along with 40 percent of the white vote, they could fashion a statewide majority. African Americans remain overwhelmingly supportive of Democrats up and down the ticket. Democratic congressional candidates consistently get more than 90 percent of the black vote (Bullock and Dunn 1996).

In 1988 and 1990, state-level Democrats got about half the white vote and won by what would now be considered to be comfortable margins. An analysis of Governor Zell Miller's 1994 reelection done by Democratic campaign consultants Alan Secrest and Mike Sanelli (1995) showed that 41 percent of the white vote provided a sufficient bulwark for Democrats. Roy Barnes replicated Miller's showing among whites in 1998. Democrat Max Cleland won a plurality in the 1996 Senate election with 39 percent white support, thanks to a Libertarian who siphoned off 4 percent of the vote.

Presidential candidates have struggled to attract white support, and in the last seven elections the Democrat has failed to exceed a third of the white vote. This is insufficient in a two-person contest, but in 1992, when Ross Perot took 13 percent of the state's ballots, Clinton got just enough white votes to squeeze out a plurality.

In the new century, only Democratic incumbents have retained enough white support to win statewide contests. The bad news for Democrats began in 2002, when Governor Barnes lost reelection with only 31 percent of the white vote. Even that figure looks good by comparison with more recent performances. In the last two presidential elections, Kerry and Obama each managed just 23 percent of the white vote according to exit polls. In 2006 Mark Taylor, the Democratic nominee for governor, did little better with 26 percent of the white vote, a figure just slightly above what Jim Martin, the Democratic nominee for the Senate, received in

November 2008. With blacks casting 30 percent of the vote in the 2008 presidential election, Obama could have carried Georgia had he managed 31 percent of the white vote, but he came nowhere close to that figure.

In addition to race, Georgia's electorate also divides geographically. Republicans do better in north Georgia. In 1992, Clinton carried only half a dozen counties north of Atlanta. Two years later Governor Zell Miller won eight counties in that area, and that included his home county and one of its neighbors. Miller's inability to win his own part of the state stands in stark contrast to the friends-and-neighbors pattern Key (1949) identified. Democrats do best in urban counties and in the diagonal swath of the Black Belt cutting across the middle of the state. All but six of the counties carried by Al Gore in 2000 were in the Black Belt, and of these exceptions, three were at the center of Atlanta's metropolitan area, and the University of Georgia dominated a fourth. The Gore pattern emerged again in the 2002 gubernatorial and Senate contests, the 2004 presidential and Senate elections, and the 2006 gubernatorial election. In 2008, with the help of higher black turnout and growing diversity in some close-in suburban counties, Obama managed to win six metro Atlanta counties, doubling the number that had supported Democrats earlier in the decade. He also carried additional suburban counties in the Augusta, Columbus, and Macon areas.

As Republicans achieved unprecedented electoral success beginning in the 1990s, exit polls showed their share of the electorate also expanding. As table 2.3 shows, in 1992, Georgians responding to the exit poll gave Democrats an eight-point advantage over Republicans. The Democratic advantage shrank to four points in 1994 as Republicans began winning statewide constitutional offices, and remained at that level through 2000. Unfortunately the 2002 exit polls had so many problems that they have never been released, meaning we lack an indication of partisan preferences in the year in which Republicans first won the governorship. However, by 2004, the partisan distribution shows the reverse of 1992, with the electorate now 42 percent Republican. Table 2.3 registers further Republican gains in 2006 as the GOP consolidated its hold on the state House, defeated the last Democrat on the Public Service Commission, and, for the first time, won the offices of lieutenant governor and secretary of state.

Table 2.3.   Party Identification of Georgia Voters Over Time (in percentages)

	1992	1994	1996	1998	2000	2004	2006	2008
Democrats	42	40	38	40	41	34	32	38
Republicans	34	36	34	37	37	42	44	35

Source: Exit polls.

The exit polls for 2008 show a startling turnaround, with the partisan makeup of the electorate being almost identical to that of a dozen years earlier. Democrats regained plurality status with a 38 to 35 percent advantage over Republicans. While the dramatic increases in black registration account for part of the change, the nine-point drop in Republican identifiers indicates some switch in party allegiance, while still other Republicans now considered themselves to be independents. Democrats could draw some pleasure in outnumbering Republicans, but their improved fortunes did not translate into significant political successes. Their nominees for the U.S. Senate and one seat on the Public Service Commission held the Republicans below a majority, and the Democratic PSC candidate emerged with a twenty-three-thousand-vote lead. However, both Democrats lost in December runoffs. A fuller test of the swing toward the Democratic Party will come in 2010. The first part of the test will be whether Democrats can hold their advantage, and the second part of the test will be whether Democrats can add to their three statewide constitutional offices even if they do outnumber Republicans.

As another indicator of the development of two-party competition, participation in the GOP primary has grown. The GOP held its first statewide primary in 1970, but until the 1990s, no more than one in ten voters helped choose Republican nominees. Table 2.4 shows that as recently as 1990, participants in the Democratic primary outnumbered Republicans 9:1. Most voters continue to ask for the Democratic ballot at the open primaries, but in recent years just under half the voters participated in the GOP primary. Although total primary participation had changed little since 1990, the Democratic primary attracted five hundred thousand fewer voters in 2008 than in 1990. Virtually no African Americans vote in the GOP primary, which means that rising Republican turnout results from whites leaving the Democratic Party. Because of these defections, blacks cast a larger share of the Democratic votes. Until 1998, blacks accounted for less than a quarter of the Democratic primary vote, except in the extremely low-interest 1994 primary. In recent regular primaries, just under half the Democrats were African Americans. In the 2008 presidential primary, Barack Obama's appeal prompted blacks to cast 55 percent of the Democratic ballots. While blacks did not dominate the 2008 regular primary as they had the presidential primary, that year marks the first regular primary in which whites failed to cast a majority of the votes. Of the ballots cast in the summer Democratic primary, African Americans cast 48.2 percent, compared with 49.4 percent cast by whites.

The enthusiasm engendered by the presidential contest failed to carry over to the July primary, which had one million fewer participants across the two parties than had shown up in February. The overall turnout rate of 21.3 percent was the lowest by a narrow margin in the last twenty years.

Table 2.4. Participation in Georgia Primaries, 1990–2008

	Total Turnout	Democrat Total	% Black	GOP	GOP % of Turnout	Turnout as % of Registrants
1990	1,171,131	1,053,013	24.6	118,118	10.1	43.5
1992	1,151,971	875,149	22.1	276,822	24.0	40.1
1994	761,371	463,049	39.2	298,322	39.2	25.8
1995	1,182,168	717,302	22.5	474,866	40.2	33.7
1998	905,383	486,841	36.4	418,542	46.2	23.7
2000	960,414	613,884	31.3	340,001	35.6	26.7
2002	1,102,611	575,533	45.2	527,078	47.8	28.6
2004	1,418,838	731,111	47.2	71,961	47.4	35.4
2006	912,358	485,748	46.5	426,610	46.8	21.4
2008 Presidential Primary	2,014,544	1,056,251	55.4	958,293	47.6	44.8
2008 General Primary	1,011,199	552,651	48.2	458,548	45.3	21.3

Source: Georgia Secretary of State.

REDISTRICTING 2001:
DEMOCRATS TAKE GERRYMANDERING TO NEW EXTREMES

The Atlanta metro area added almost a million people in the 1990s as Georgia overtook North Carolina to become the nation's tenth most populous state and earned two more seats in the U.S. House. This exceptional growth continued a trend begun in the 1980s, when Georgia picked up an eleventh seat in Congress. Atlanta suburban growth also necessitated relocating state legislative seats from south Georgia to north Georgia and from central cities to surrounding areas, which boded well for Republicans, who dominated north Georgia and newer suburbs.

In the redistricting struggles of the early 1980s and 1990s, Republicans joined forces with African Americans (Holmes 1998). The coalition could be easily outvoted by white Democrats and consequently achieved its objectives only when the U.S. attorney general, operating under section 5 of the Voting Rights Act, refused to preclear the legislature's plans. In 2001, a coalition of African Americans and Republicans would constitute a majority in both legislative chambers. While the GOP invited its old partner back, blacks, seeing how much Republicans had gained from past collaborations, assigned higher priority to maintaining Democratic majorities in the legislature than to maximizing the number of black seats. An ideological coalition of Republicans and conservative white Democrats like the one that emerged in 1995 in the Senate during unsuccessful efforts to redraw congressional districts after *Miller v. Johnson* also failed to materialize, leaving Republicans with no partners.

Since Republicans had been consistently winning most of the votes statewide in House and Senate contests, and since the state's growth areas tended to vote Republican, Democrats faced a stiff challenge in their efforts to maintain legislative majorities. If Republicans captured a majority in a legislative chamber, Governor Barnes might become Georgia's first governor to experience the challenge of divided government. With the stakes so high, Barnes played an unprecedented role during the 2001 special sessions to redraw Georgia's districts.

Under Barnes's watchful eye, Georgia legislative districts became less compact as Democrats strung together often far-flung Republican enclaves (Gaddie and Bullock 2007). A Republican Senate district that consisted of five counties on the north side of Atlanta was overpopulated by twenty-one thousand. One might have expected it to become smaller as it shed the additional population in order to meet the one-person, one-vote requirement. The redesign, however, stretched it 200 miles, running across more than half the state's northern border (at points less than two thousand feet wide) as it went from Atlanta's suburbs to South Carolina after brushing past Tennessee and North Carolina. A six-county Senate district that came within 653 people of being exactly at the state population mean was redone to include five entire counties and parts of another eleven counties.

Democrats also sought to gain congressional seats. In their congressional plan the two new seats earned through population growth had black voting age populations of just under 40 percent. With hundreds of thousands of whites participating in the Republican primary (see table 2.4), these districts would likely have a majority black electorate in the Democratic primary, and given their black concentrations, the Democratic nominee would almost certainly win in November. When redrawing existing districts, Democrats paired two Republican incumbents in each of two districts, thereby creating two more open districts, both of which had voting histories that indicated a strong likelihood of electing Democrats. If 2002 elections followed past results, the new plan would elect seven Democrats and six Republicans.

Designing districts to help Democrats more than double their ranks in the congressional delegation required creative cartography. In the early 1990s, use of geographic information systems that integrated demographic and political data led to new extremes in gerrymandering. A decade after using these techniques to meet Department of Justice demands for additional majority-black districts, Democrats carefully split counties and even precincts along partisan lines. These partisan ploys, which gave less deference to the boundaries of counties and cities, produced less compact districts.

Democrats' gerrymandering fell short of its objectives. They won the two new congressional seats, but Republicans held on to an eight-to-five majority in the delegation. Republicans managed to retain two seats as a result of poor choices made in the Democratic primaries. In the more blatant case, a 40 percent African American district became the most heavily black district in the nation to elect a Republican. Max Burns won this district when the Democratic nominee's arrest record turned out to be longer than his political record. He had five arrests but had never held public office.

In the state Senate, Democrats believed their plan would increase their membership by five. Instead, Republicans scored a net gain of three. Although the 2002 election returned a Democratic majority, it slipped away when four newly elected Democrats succumbed to the appeals of GOP governor-elect Perdue and changed parties, giving Republicans a thirty-to-twenty-six majority. Only in the state House did Democrats score a majority, although the plan designed to add fifteen seats to the Democrats' majority netted them only four additional seats.

Both the House and Senate plans came apart in 2004 when a federal court found that they violated the Equal Protection Clause requirement of equal populations among districts. Democrats explained that they had drawn the misshapen districts in order to underpopulate districts in South Georgia and Atlanta while overpopulating districts in suburbia and North Georgia. The federal district court ruled this behavior unconstitutional under the *Baker v. Carr* precedent established in 1962. Thus the careful Democratic effort to soak up Republicans by overpopulating their districts by 4 percent or more while underpopulating Democratic districts by like numbers was struck down. When the legislature failed to take corrective action, the court had plans drawn that brought all districts to within $+/-1$ percent of the ideal population.

The 2004 elections demonstrated the degree to which Democrats had gerrymandered the invalidated plans. Republicans gained four more Senate seats, and in the House, their share of the seats increased by 15 percentage points (as reported in table 2.1), which gave them their first House majority since Reconstruction.

Republicans, who controlled both legislative chambers and the governorship, carried out a mid-decade congressional redistricting. The main objective of Georgia's 2005 plan was to shore up the district of a Republican. Only one district held by a Democrat became more vulnerable in the new map and it narrowly elected the incumbent in 2006.

CONCLUSION

The GOP grew slowly in Georgia. Sixteen years elapsed from the initial Republican presidential success to the first statewide victory (a Senate seat). Another twelve years passed before Republicans won a statewide office as opposed to a federal office. By the mid-1990s, the GOP finally dominated Georgia's congressional delegation, held most statewide offices, and occupied 40 percent of the state legislative seats. But at that point the GOP stagnated, and by 2001, Democrats had taken back a U.S. Senate seat, a Public Service Commission seat, reclaimed the post of attorney general, and picked up several state House seats. Despite these setbacks, Republican candidates for the state House and Senate had polled a majority of the votes cast for the state legislature in recent elections, even as they struggled to win 40 percent of the seats in these chambers. Despite frequent changes in election laws (Bullock 1998) and an extraordinary set of gerrymanders, Democrats' prolonged control of state government finally collapsed early in the new century. Like weary workers stacking sandbags in the face of a flood, Georgia Democrats' efforts failed to stem the GOP tide. Once the GOP breached the critical bulwark, it quickly pushed its share of Senate seats to 60 percent and won a House majority in 2004 thanks to fairer electoral districts. Two years later Republicans won the office of lieutenant governor and secretary of state, and dispatched the last Democratic PSC member. The only three Democrats surviving in statewide offices won reelections as incumbents in 2006.

Race and party increasingly run parallel in Georgia. Republicans attract tiny shares of the black vote. In 2006 and 2008, African Americans cast only 2 percent of the votes in the Republican primary. Exit polls show Republican candidates struggling to attract even a tenth of the black vote. Black Republican officeholders are rare, with the two highest profile individuals serving in the state House. While Democrats do better among whites than Republicans do among blacks, one could make the case that the Democratic Party is on the way to becoming a predominately African American party. African Americans cast almost half the votes in regular Democratic primaries and dominated the 2008 presidential primary on the Democratic side. Of three statewide Democratic officeholders, two of them, the attorney general and labor commissioner, are black. Moreover, most Democratic state legislators are African Americans, as are four of the six members of Congress.

Current legislative maps and partisan preferences make it unlikely that Democrats can retake either chamber in 2010. In 2008 Democrats did little to capitalize on Obama's charisma, as they failed to recruit challengers to Republican legislators even in districts with substantial black minorities. Democratic recruitment efforts came up so far short that for them to win a majority in the House, they would have had to win ninety-one of the ninety-nine districts in which they had nominees. Even with their short list of candidates, Democrats unseated four Republicans in suburban areas experiencing racial change. Republicans partially offset the Democratic gains by defeating two north Georgia Democrats.

County officeholders remain overwhelmingly Democratic. More than 62 percent of the almost 800 county commissioners in Georgia were Democrats in 2007. While Republicans win additional local offices with each election, Georgia's multitude of counties, most of which remain untouched by urban development, provide refuge for the declining numbers of "yellow-dog Democrats." Rural white electors, who eagerly vote Republicans for president on down through state legislator, retain traditional partisan loyalties when choosing sheriffs and county commissioners. The tradition of Democratic dominance in many communities remains so strong that, like a taboo, it goes unchallenged. The ambitious do not seriously consider running as Republicans in many counties (Lublin 2004). In some counties that regularly vote Republican in top-of-the-ticket contests, the local Republican Party remains small and inactive. A student, after attending a Republican meeting in a county where the GOP racks up majorities in statewide contests but has yet to score a victory locally, observed, "I was the only one there with any teeth."

The opposite pattern exists in a smaller number of suburban counties. Here Republicans dominate the ranks of local officeholders sometimes to the exclusion of Democrats. While there are relatively few Republican counties, a large share of the state's population lives in these suburban counties (Lublin 2004). As counties around Atlanta and other metropolitan areas develop, Republicans win local offices. A pattern that has frequently been repeated is for a county to elect a few Republicans to the county commission or school board and then, once the newcomers outnumber the natives, the county will have an all-Republican slate of officers.

In older Atlanta suburbs, yet another transformation is under way as Democrats have eliminated most Republicans from offices in DeKalb and Clayton counties, both of which were majority black in 2000, and have even made gains in Cobb and Gwinnett counties, which had been the most Republican bastions in the state in the early 1990s but are becoming more racially diverse.

Despite a lingering loyalty to Democrats in rural counties, Democratic claims on white voters have shrunk dramatically. The 2008 exit polls show the first reversal as Democrats gained adherents. The uptick in Democrats did not suffice for the party to make major gains. The 2010 elections will be critical for Democrats. If they win the governorship, then they can block Republican redistricting plans, and that may be a first step toward increasing the competitiveness of the Democratic Party. If Republicans retain control of the governorship, then for the first time in history the GOP will draw Georgia's legislative districts, and the likely result will be a Republican legislature for the next decade. Was the improved position of Democrats in 2008 an ephemeral response to the charismatic Obama or does it signal the beginning of a political turnaround?

NOTES

1. HOPE, funded by the state lottery—the creation of which had been the major plank in Miller's 1990 campaign—pays for tuition and books at state-supported colleges and technical schools for all Georgia high school grads with B averages who maintain those grades in college. HOPE has proven very popular with middle-class parents, who save tens of thousands of dollars.

2. Georgia registration materials indicate the race of the voter, which facilitates targeting black registrants.

3. The 1998 exit poll estimated that blacks cast 29 percent of the vote, while the 23 percent figure comes from the voter validation done by Georgia's secretary of state. The state did not undertake voter validation efforts until 1996, so we rely on exit polls for earlier years.

4. Candidates in Georgia special elections run without party designations. However, voters knew Miller, who had stepped down as governor in 1999 to be a

Democrat. His leading challenger, Mack Mattingly, had served as a Republican senator from 1981 to 1987.

REFERENCES

Aistrup, Joseph A. 1989. "Top-Down Republican Party Development in the South: A Test of Schlesinger's Theory." Presented at the annual meeting of the Midwest Political Science Association, Chicago, IL.

Bartley, Numan C. 1970. *From Thurmond to Wallace: Political Tendencies in Georgia, 1948–1968.* Baltimore: Johns Hopkins University Press.

Baxter, Tom. 1996. "Rapid Suburban Growth Undercuts 'One Man, One Vote.'" *Atlanta Journal*, December 3: C2.

Bullock, Charles S., III. 1995. *Georgia Political Almanac, 1995–1996.* Atlanta: Cornerstone Publishing.

———. 1998. "Georgia: Election Rules and Partisan Conflict." In *The New Politics of the Old South*, ed. Charles S. Bullock III and Mark J. Rozell. Lanham, MD: Rowman & Littlefield.

Bullock, Charles S., III, and Richard Dunn. 1996. "Election Roll-Off: A Test of Three Explanations." *Urban Affairs Review* 32 (September): 71–86.

Bullock, Charles S., III, and Robert P. Furr. 1997. "Race, Turnout, Runoff and Election Outcomes: The Defeat of Wyche Fowler." *Congress and the Presidency* 24 (Spring): 1–16.

Campbell, J. Phil. 1983. Interview by Charles S. Bullock III. March 1.

Fenno, Richard F., Jr. 1996. *Senators on the Campaign Trail: The Politics of Representation.* Norman: University of Oklahoma.

Gaddie, Ronald Keith, and Charles S. Bullock III. 2007. "From *Ashcroft* to *Larios*: Recent Redistricting Lessons from Georgia." *Fordham Urban Law Review* 34 (April): 997–1048.

Holmes, Robert A. 1998. "Reapportionment Strategies in the 1990s: The Case of Georgia." In *Race and Redistricting in the 1990s*, ed. Bernard Grofman. Bronx, NY: Agathon Press.

Johnson, Eric. 2000. Election e-mail memo.

Key, V. O., Jr. 1949. *Southern Politics in State and Nation.* New York: Alfred A. Knopf.

Lublin, David. 2004. *The Republican South.* Princeton, NJ: Princeton University Press.

Miller v. Johnson, 115 S.Ct. 2475 (1995).

Sabato, Larry. 2003. *Mid-Term Madness.* Lanham, MD: Rowman & Littlefield.

Secrest, Alan, and Mike Sanelli. 1995. "A Precinct-Level Analysis of Racial Voting Patterns in Georgia's 1994 General Election for Governor." Alexandria, VA: Cooper & Secrest Associates.

Williams, Clint. 2000. "Contest's Price Tag a Record." *Atlanta Journal-Constitution.* November 25: G1.

3

———◦◉◦———

Alabama

From One Party to Competition, and Maybe Back Again

Patrick R. Cotter

In the days of the "old" South, relatively few Alabama citizens participated in the state's politics. Those who did were whiter, more male, and
better off than the public as a whole. Most notably, African American citizens were almost totally excluded from the state's elections, despite the
fact that race was a central concern of Alabama's politics. What did dominate the state was a disorganized, multifactional Democratic Party. Year
after year, Democratic candidates from president to the most local of offices won the support of large majorities of the state's voters. Meanwhile,
the Republican Party was largely, but not totally, absent from the state as
a political organization, among officeholders, and in the hearts and minds
of Alabama's voters.

Now Alabama's politics are quite different. The state has a larger and
more representative electorate. African Americans actively participate in
all parts of Alabama's politics and government. In the last several
decades, party competition has emerged, developed, and matured in the
state. Both Democrats and Republicans are found among Alabama officeholders. Both parties can also claim the allegiance of a significant number
of the state's citizens. Indeed, Republicans now are not only competitive
in Alabama, but they may be the state's dominant party.

Other southern states have experienced similar political changes since
the days of the old South. The pace and process of Alabama's political
transformation is, however, unique. The same may be true for the state's
political future.

PARTICIPATION

During the first half of the 1900s, voting turnout in Alabama was low, even compared to other southern states (Key 1949, 492). Then, generally less than one in five of the state's voting-age population participated in Alabama elections (figure 3.1).[1] This low participation rate was due in part to the generally low levels of education and income of Alabamians during that time. The absence of competitive parties mobilizing the state's voters also contributed to the low voter turnout. Perhaps most important, however, was the structural barriers to registering and voting erected by the state's 1901 (and still current) constitution (McMillan 1955). Alabama was not alone in using disfranchising devices such as lengthy residency requirements, a literacy test, a permanent ban on voting by anyone convicted any of a long list of felonies, a poll tax, and a white primary. Alabama's suffrage restrictions, and particularly its cumulative poll tax, were, however, especially effective (Porter 1918; Lewinson 1963; Kousser 1974; Keyssar 2000; Perman 2001).

The region's mid-1900s "Second Reconstruction" slowly removed or reduced many of the structural barriers to registration and voting found within the state. Alabama's political leaders mostly resisted efforts to reduce voting barriers. Ultimately, however, a combination of internal and external forces overcame this resistance. As a consequence, turnout in the state's general elections increased following the granting of women's suffrage in 1920, the 1944 U.S. Supreme Court's decision outlawing the white primary, the ending of the cumulative feature of the state's poll tax in 1953, and the passage of the 1965 Voting Rights Act.[2]

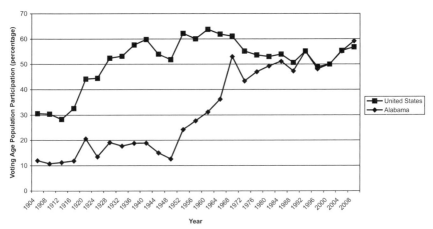

Figure 3.1.   Voting Turnout in Presidential Elections, Alabama and the United States, 1904–2008

With the higher rate of turnout in the state's elections, voting participation in Alabama has for the last twenty years or so been quite close to the national average. Indeed, in the recent 2008 presidential election, the estimated turnout rate among Alabama's voting age population (59.2 percent) exceeded that found in the nation as a whole (56.8 percent).

Not only was voting turnout low in the old South, but also those who did participate were quite unrepresentative of the population as a whole. With the increase in voting participation since the mid-1900s, Alabama's electorate, like its regional neighbors, has become more representative. In particular, research shows that racial differences in participation have largely disappeared within the state (Cohen, Cotter, and Coulter 1983).

One byproduct of the state's more representative electorate is an increasing number of African Americans holding elected office within the state. In the days of the old South, Alabama had virtually no black elected officials. Now, African Americans fill about 17 percent of the roughly 4,400 elected government positions within the state (Bositis 2003). African Americans currently hold an even larger proportion, about 25 percent, of the seats in the state legislature. Alabama is the only state in which the proportion of African Americans in the state legislature is equal to the percentage of blacks in the population as a whole (Bositis 2003).

An African American has held one of the state's seven congressional seats since 1992. Democrat Artur Davis, the state's current African American congressional representative, won his seat in 2002 when he defeated incumbent Earl Hilliard. Davis, a friend and early supporter of Barack Obama, has become a visible and influential figure in the state's politics (Dean 2008a, 2008b; Evans 2008). This rise in prominence has at least somewhat marginalized the influence of some of the state's older, civil rights–era African American political leaders. Furthermore, following the 2008 presidential election, Davis has clearly signaled his intention to run for governor in 2010 (Lyman 2008; Gordon 2008).

PRESIDENTIAL POLITICS

In the days of the old South, Alabama's electoral politics were solidly Democratic. While there was some Republican presence in parts of the state, overall the GOP had little influence (Webb 1997). Instead, as figures 3.2 and 3.3 show, only a small percentage of Alabama voters typically supported Republican presidential or gubernatorial candidates during the first half of the 1900s.

Republicans did enjoy a temporary increase in support in 1928 when the state's Democrats split over the presidential nomination of Al Smith, the Catholic, anti-prohibition governor of New York. This split continued

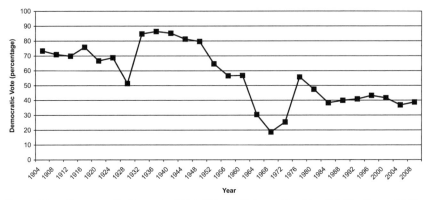

Figure 3.2. Democratic Percent of Total Vote, Alabama Presidential Elections, 1904–2008

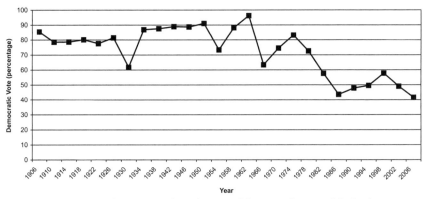

Figure 3.3. Democratic Percent of Total Vote, Alabama Gubernatorial Elections, 1906–2006

into the 1930 state elections. However, the Depression, the election of Franklin Roosevelt, and the popularity of his New Deal programs resulted in both a return of party unity and an increase in the already high level of Democratic support (Thornton 1968).

In the post–World War II years, Democratic dominance in Alabama declined while Republican strength grew. A 1948 split among both national and state Democrats over civil rights, labor, and other issues was a major catalyst to this partisan shift (Barnard 1974; Frederickson 2001). President Harry Truman was not even listed on the Alabama ballot in that year's election. Instead, the States' Rights or Dixiecrat presidential candidate, Strom Thurmond, appeared under the Democratic label and won almost 80 percent of Alabama's vote.

Dwight Eisenhower in 1952 and 1956, and then Richard Nixon in 1960 each received about 40 percent of the presidential vote in Alabama— roughly double the support received by any other Republican presidential candidate in the preceding twenty years. This increase in GOP support was aided by the state's growing urban population and economic development; by the policy positions taken by the national parties, which resulted in some of the state's young business leaders becoming active within the GOP; and by continuing splits among Alabama Democratic leaders over both civil rights and economic issues (Strong 1972; Barnard 1974).

The 1964 presidential election introduced a period of political volatility in Alabama politics. Republicans achieved a major breakthrough in that year's presidential contest when Barry Goldwater won almost 70 percent of the state's vote. The GOP also won five of the state's congressional seats in 1964. Republican (and Democratic) support plummeted in 1968, when Alabama's own George Wallace was an independent party presidential candidate. In the 1972 contest, GOP strength rebounded when Richard Nixon won more than 70 percent of the vote against George McGovern. Jimmy Carter reclaimed Alabama for Democrats in 1976. As of this date, however, 1976 was the last time that Democrats won a presidential contest in the state. Instead, Ronald Reagan's narrow victory against Carter in 1980 began an era in which Republicans have dominated the state's presidential elections. The GOP's margin of victory in some of these contests has been relatively small. Still, Alabama has voted more Republican than has the nation as a whole in each presidential election since 1984.

One result of the continuing GOP success in Alabama is that both parties have generally ignored the state in recent presidential general elections. Indeed, no major-party presidential candidate has made a post-convention campaign stop in Alabama since 1996, when both Bill Clinton and Bob Dole came to the state on the same day (Cotter 1997).

The practice of ignoring Alabama continued in the 2008 election. Neither Barack Obama nor John McCain made a post-convention campaign appearance in the state. On Election Day, McCain easily carried Alabama, defeating Obama by a 60.4 percent to 38.8 percent margin. In only four other states (Idaho, Oklahoma, Utah, and Wyoming) did McCain receive more support. Similarly, despite his victory nationwide, Obama received about the same level of support in Alabama as Al Gore (41.6 percent) in 2000 or John Kerry (36.8 percent) in 2004.

Voting patterns in the 2008 presidential election parallel those found in other post-1980 statewide elections. In particular, analyses of these elections show that Democratic support is higher in counties with relatively large African American populations. In 2008, the relationship between support for Obama and percentage African American was particularly strong (r = .96). Conversely, Republican support increases as a county's income level rises (r = .65). There is, however, little relationship (r = .04) between Democratic Party support and the proportion of a county's population living in an urban setting. Instead, Democratic candidates, including Obama in 2008, tend to do relatively well in both the state's rural, black belt counties and in its largest urban centers.[3]

What was different in 2008 was, first, the amount of attention Alabama received during each party's presidential nomination contests. In recent election cycles, Alabama had held its presidential primary in June, well after the winners of the nomination contests had been identified. In 2008, however, Alabama moved its presidential primary to February. This, combined with the extended nomination contests among both Democratic and Republican candidates, resulted in a relatively large amount of attention being given to the state. In particular, all the leading presidential hopefuls made appearances in the state in the weeks leading to the primary. In the primary itself, Obama won the Democratic contest, defeating Hillary Clinton by a 56.0 percent to 41.6 percent margin. In the GOP primary, former Arkansas governor Mike Huckabee (41.2 percent) won over John McCain (37.1 percent) and former Massachusetts governor Mitt Romney (17.8 percent).

A second difference in 2008 was the level of voter involvement in the election. Turnout in the state's 2008 presidential primaries doubled that of four years earlier.[4] Similarly, turnout in the general election increased in all sections of the state. Altogether, the number of votes cast increased by more than two hundred thousand between the 2004 and the 2008 general elections.

GUBERNATORIAL POLITICS

Republican strength has also grown in Alabama below the office of president. However, while the direction has been the same, the pace of partisan change at the state level has been slower, even when compared to other parts of the South. One source of this distinctiveness is the political career of George Wallace. (For discussions of Wallace's political career, see, for example, Carter 1995; Permaloff and Grafton 1995; Frederick 2007.)

When Key (1949) wrote about Alabama politics during the days of the old South, he noted the general absence of organization and continuity in the state's electoral politics. Alabama then lacked a durable faction, such as the Byrd organization in Virginia, or the Crump machine in Tennessee. Alabama also had no spectacular political figure, such as Eugene Talmadge in Georgia, who personally dominated the state's politics over the course of several elections.

George Wallace's almost thirty-year-long career changed this situation. Indeed, when Wallace finally retired from electoral politics in 1986 it was noted that for Alabamians, "His endurance as a political figure is such that no voter younger than fifty can recall participating in a gubernatorial election in which George Wallace was not a candidate or at least a controlling influence" (Schmidt 1986).

Wallace's longevity (he was elected governor in 1962, 1970, 1974, and 1982, and his wife Lurleen was elected governor in 1966) was based on a number of factors. First, throughout his career Wallace successfully portrayed himself as a spokesperson and a protector of Alabama's interests, particularly against what he argued was an intrusive and unresponsive national government. He also pursued distributive public policies. In Alabama these are best remembered in the form of free textbooks for public school students and an extensive system of community colleges located throughout the state. Finally, Wallace was adaptable. Better than most politicians, Wallace altered the themes he emphasized or the issue positions he took in response to changes in either the public's mood or the political context.

Wallace's adaptability is perhaps best illustrated by his shifting position on the race issue. He was a strong segregationist when he won his first election to governor in 1962. Then he told one campaign rally, "As governor of your state I will stand strong for segregation. Some people say you are too strong, but how can you be too strong in what you believe? There is no middle ground. You are either for it or against it" (*Anniston Star* 1962). Later, after the racial composition of Alabama's electorate had changed, Wallace's position shifted. Then he apologized for his segregationist stance, claiming that the motivation behind his actions had been misinterpreted. "Our actions in being anti–big government were translated into being racist" (*Anniston Star* 1982).

Wallace's blend of issue positions made him a difficult candidate to run against. In particular, Alabama Republicans found that they could not outflank Wallace on social or racial issues, but were themselves easy targets for his populist appeals as a representative of the average Alabamian. As a consequence, as long as Wallace remained active in Alabama's politics, GOP strength in state elections remained relatively weak.

Wallace's retirement from state politics during the early stages of the 1986 gubernatorial election set off a rancorous conflict over control of the Democratic Party. (For a discussion of this campaign, see Cotter and Stovall, forthcoming.) Eventually this fight developed into a contest between Lieutenant Governor Bill Baxley, supported by education, civil rights, and labor groups within the Democratic Party, and Attorney General Charlie

Graddick, supported by business and conservative interests. Graddick barely defeated Baxley (by a 8,756 vote margin out of more than 900,000 votes cast) in the Democratic runoff. Baxley, however, refused to concede defeat. Instead, Graddick was soon challenged in federal court over whether, as attorney general, he had violated the preclearance provision of the 1965 Voting Rights Act by issuing an order nullifying an existing Democratic Party rule prohibiting Republican primary voters from "crossing-over" and voting in the Democratic runoff election. After a series of hearings, the court supported this challenge. Graddick was thus denied the nomination. Instead, a party committee named Baxley as the Democratic gubernatorial candidate. The uproar this decision caused led many of the state's voters to support, and ultimately elect, the heretofore unknown and ignored Republican candidate, Guy Hunt.

Hunt's victory altered political patterns within Alabama. In the eyes of the state's media and campaign contributors, winning the Democratic primary was no longer tantamount to victory in the general election. Nor, for potential candidates, was it any longer necessary to be a Democrat in order to have a reasonable chance of winning elections. Furthermore, by using his appointment power to fill vacancies, Hunt could give some Republican candidates the advantage of incumbency.

In 1990, Hunt won a narrow reelection campaign against Paul Hubbert, the head of the powerful Alabama Education Association. Shortly into his second term, Hunt was charged with violating the state's ethics laws regarding his personal use of funds donated to his first inauguration. When he was convicted of these charges, Hunt was removed from office and replaced by the Democratic lieutenant governor, Jim Folsom Jr.

In the 1994 gubernatorial election, Folsom, the son of a former two-time Alabama governor, faced Fob James. James had first come onto the state's political scene in 1978. In that year, George Wallace was constitutionally barred from seeking a third consecutive term as governor. In what was then seen as the end of the Wallace era, James, a one-time Republican official, entered the crowded Democratic gubernatorial primary. In a well-financed and effective media campaign, James portrayed himself as a successful businessman not tied to the state's existing political patterns or interests. James won the Democratic nomination and then easily defeated the token Republican gubernatorial candidate (future governor Guy Hunt) in the general election.

For a variety of reasons, not all of which were under his control, James proved to be a very unpopular governor. This unpopularity set the stage for Wallace's final election as governor in 1982.

In 1994, after unsuccessful reelection efforts as a Democrat in 1986 and 1990, James switched back to the Republican Party and won the GOP's nomination for governor. That year's nationwide GOP landslide resulted in a number of Republican victories in Alabama. One of these was Fob James's narrow win (50.3 percent to 49.4 percent) over Folsom in the race for governor.

In office, James once again proved to be a controversial and unpopular governor. As a result, he faced several serious candidates in the 1998 GOP primary. Ultimately, this led to a runoff election between James, who, as a vocal advocate for issues such as school prayer, had strong support among social conservatives, and Winton Blount, a Montgomery business-man and son of "Red" Blount, one of the pioneering members of the state's postwar Republican Party (Strong 1972). James won this primary contest but had little remaining resources or support to draw upon in the general election. Thus it was no surprise when James was defeated by a convincing margin (57.2 percent to 42.1 percent) in November by Demo-cratic lieutenant governor Don Siegelman. In his campaign, Siegelman had focused on the need for Alabama to have a state lottery. The proceeds of a lottery, he argued, would address the problems facing the state's pub-lic schools.

As governor, Siegelman succeeded in getting his lottery proposal (mod-eled on the plan used in Georgia) through the state legislature and, in 1999, a constitutional referendum was held on the issue. In the referen-dum campaign, Siegelman and his allies spent considerable resources telling voters of the benefits, such as college scholarship and preschool programs, that would result from adopting the "education lottery." Op-ponents of the measure raised three general objections. First, they argued that state-supported gambling was immoral. Second, they raised ques-tions about which students would actually receive the lottery-funded col-lege scholarships. Finally, opponents said that the lottery would lead to government corruption (Cason 1999a).

In the end, voters rejected Siegelman's lottery proposal by a 45.8 to 54.2 percent margin. The lottery's failure indicates the political power of reli-gious conservatives in the state. It also indicates the distrust that Al-abamians have of the state government. As Jim Cooper, the head of Citi-zens Against Legalized Lottery, explained, part of his group's message to Alabama voters was that "you can't trust politicians" (Cason 1999b).

Alabama's pattern of competitive gubernatorial elections continued in 2002. Incumbent Don Siegelman easily won renomination in the Demo-cratic primary. On the Republican side, Congressman Bob Riley, with the apparent support of much of the party's leadership, easily won the GOP gubernatorial primary.

In his general election campaign, Siegelman pointed to the achieve-ments of his administration. He also revived the idea of a state lottery. Throughout the last part of his administration, however, Siegelman was dogged by allegations of corruption regarding state contracts and programs. Riley's campaign focused on these allegations, arguing to the state's voters that, as a new face in state government, he represented "honest change" (Cason 2002). In the end, Riley won the governorship, defeating Siegelman by an extremely narrow 49.2 percent to 48.9 percent margin.

As a member of Congress, Bob Riley had never wandered from the Republican antitax orthodoxy. Thus it was somewhat of a surprise when, shortly after becoming governor, Riley proposed a state constitutional amendment involving a massive $1.2 billion tax reform and government accountability plan.

In the campaign leading to a vote on the amendment, the governor argued that his reform plan was needed to address a looming state budget crisis and to remedy shortcomings in the state education system. Riley also appealed to voters to support his program on moral grounds, arguing that the plan would correct the inequities and unfairness of the state's current tax system (Cason 2003).

Some of the state's business and religious organizations supported Riley's plan, while others opposed it. Most Democratic officeholders and groups endorsed the proposal. Alabama's Republicans, however, were split, with a narrow majority of the party's state executive committee voting to oppose the governor's proposal. Opponents of Riley's plan argued that reduced spending was a better solution to the state's budget problems. They also pointed out that the taxes raised by the proposal were not earmarked for education and could in fact be used for any purpose by state officeholders.

Alabama voters overwhelmingly rejected Riley proposal, 67.5 percent to 32.5 percent. Its defeat was attributed to citizens' opposition to higher taxes, the ineffectiveness of the pro-reform campaign, and Alabamians' general distrust of state government.

The defeat of Riley's plan made him potentially vulnerable in seeking reelection in 2006. This vulnerability was increased by the results of another constitutional referendum campaign, this one occurring in 2004. The issue then involved a proposal to remove segregationist-era language from the state constitution. Among the specific clauses to be eliminated by the proposed amendment was one that said, "Nothing in this Constitution shall be construed as creating or recognizing any right to education." Governor Riley and many other state leaders supported the amendment.

Among the opponents to the constitutional change was Roy Moore. Moore had first attracted widespread attention when he was a circuit court judge in Etowah County. There Moore was involved in a protracted civil liberties–related controversy involving his courtroom display of the Ten Commandments and his practice of starting court sessions with a prayer. In 2000, Moore used this attention to get elected as the Chief Justice of the Alabama Supreme Court. Once in office, he had a 5,280-pound granite block inscribed with the Ten Commandments and placed in the rotunda of the state judicial building. Eventually a federal judged ordered Moore to remove the Ten Commandments monument. When Moore refused to obey the court order, the other justices on the court had the monument taken from the building. Later, because of his refusal to obey the court order, Moore was himself removed from office. (For more information about Moore, see Fisher 2004; Johnson 2004.)

In the 2004 constitutional referendum campaign, Moore opposed the Riley-backed proposal, saying that removing the clause regarding the state's obligation regarding education would open the door to court mandated tax increases to support education. On Election Day, the Riley-backed proposed amendment was narrowly defeated, 49.9 percent to 50.1 percent.

As a result of his apparent electoral support and the incumbent's vulnerability, Moore challenged Riley in the 2006 GOP gubernatorial primary. By the time of the primary, however, the governor had repaired his party ties, and Moore's challenge failed to generate much intensity or interest. Riley won the primary over Moore by a 66.7 percent to 33.3 percent margin (Gordon 2006).

On the Democratic side in 2006, the contest over the gubernatorial nomination was between Lieutenant Governor Lucy Baxley (the former wife of previous lieutenant governor and Democratic gubernatorial candidate Bill Baxley) and former governor Don Siegelman. In an interesting twist, Siegelman spent much of the primary campaign in a federal courtroom defending himself against corruption charges.[5] Baxley eventually defeated Siegelman, 59.8 percent to 36.4 percent (Davis 2006).

Compared to earlier gubernatorial contests, the 2006 general election was a low-key affair. In his campaign, Riley emphasized the state's good economy, improved standardized test scores for public school students, his scandal-free administration, and his leadership ability, as illustrated by Alabama's response to the problems resulting from Hurricane Katrina. His campaign also argued that Lucy Baxley was "too liberal" for Alabama. Baxley disputed this claim and in turn argued that Riley's tax policies had hurt the state's schools (Dean 2006; Faulk 2006; Chandler and Dean 2006a, 2006b). In the end, Riley (58.0 percent) easily defeated Baxley (42.0 percent).

Below the level of governor, the number of Republican officeholders has also grown. Here, however, Democrats still remain relatively strong, though at a level of dominance far less than found during the days of the Solid South. In particular, Democrats continue to hold a substantial

Table 3.1.   Partisan Makeup of Alabama State Legislature, 1954–2008 (in percentages)

	Democrat*	
	State House	*State Senate*
1954	100	100
1956	100	100
1958	100	100
1960	100	100
1962	98	100
1964	98	100
1966	100	97
1968	100	97
1970	98	100
1972	98	100
1974	100	100
1976	98	97
1978	96	100
1980	95	100
1982	92	91
1984	83	80
1986	85	86
1988	81	80
1990	78	80
1992	78	77
1994	70	66
1996	69	63
1998	68	63
2000	60	66
2002	61	71
2004	60	69
2006	60	71
2008	59	66

Source: Statistical Abstract of the United States.
*The state House has 105 members. Before 1974, it had 106 members. The state Senate has 35 members. Percentages are based upon total membership (including vacancies).

majority of the seats in both houses of the state legislature (table 3.1). During the 2008 legislative session, Democrats held about 59 percent of House seats and almost 66 percent of the Senate seats.

Also, despite losing (sometimes by narrow margins) five of the last six gubernatorial elections, Democrats have consistently managed to split control over other state constitutional offices with the GOP. Both the state's current lieutenant governor and commissioner of agriculture are Democrats. Alabama's current secretary of state, treasurer, auditor, and attorney general are, however, Republicans.

CONGRESSIONAL POLITICS

Republican strength has also increased in Alabama's congressional delegation. Currently both of Alabama's U.S. senators are Republicans. One of these, Richard Shelby, was initially elected as a Democrat. He switched parties the day after the 1994 election—a contest in which Republicans gained a majority of seats in Congress. Shelby faced no serious opposition in winning reelection in either 1998 or 2004. Alabama's other senator, Jeff Sessions, was elected (with 52.5 percent of the total vote) to an open seat in 1996. He was reelected in 2002 and 2008, in each year defeating a serious (but underfunded) Democratic opponent by a comfortable margin.

In 1994 Republicans gained a five to two majority in the state's U.S. House seats. This partisan balance continued through 2008. Indeed, among the incumbent congressmen, only the Third District's Republican Mike Rogers (who took over the seat in 2002 when Bob Riley decided to run for governor) faced any serious electoral challenge during this period.

The 2008 election, however, did change the state's congressional delegation. In particular, shortly after the 2006 election (when Democrats gained a national majority of U.S. House seats) two veteran Alabama representatives—Democrat Bud Cramer and Republican Terry Everett—announced their retirements. These two open seats resulted in contested nomination battles within each party. Eventually, Democratic state senator Parker Griffith faced businessman Wayne Parker to replace Cramer in the Fifth District, while Montgomery mayor Bobby Bright, a Democrat, faced Republican state legislator Jay Love in the Second District. In their campaigns, both Griffith and Parker portrayed themselves as pro-life, pro-gun, pro-traditional marriage, "mainstream" Democrats (Kitchen 2008; McCarter and Stephens 2008). Also, unlike most other recent Democratic congressional candidates in Alabama, Griffith and Parker received financial assistance from the party's national campaign committee. On Election Day, Griffith retained the Democratic seat, defeating Parker 51.8 percent to 48.2 percent. Meanwhile, Bright (50.3 percent) defeated Love (49.7 percent), thus becoming the first Democrat to hold the Second District seat since 1964.

PARTY IDENTIFICATION

Finally, measures of party identification show that, unlike in earlier years, there is now a rough parity in the number of Democratic and Republican identifiers in Alabama (table 3.2). Analysis of current party identification data shows, as is the case elsewhere in the country, that African Americans in Alabama are overwhelmingly Democratic in their party attachments.

Table 3.2.　Party Identification in Alabama, 1981–2005 (in percentages)

	Strong+ Weak Republican	Independent Republican	Independent	Independent Democrat	Strong+ Weak Democrat	Partisan Balance*
1981	24	10	9	11	47	23
1982	18	9	8	10	55	37
1983	20	10	10	11	50	30
1984	27	12	9	6	45	18
1985	29	10	6	11	44	15
1986	27	12	10	9	40	13
1987	30	14	6	8	43	13
1988	30	16	10	8	36	6
1989	38	11	6	9	36	−2
1990	26	12	13	10	39	13
1991	28	15	10	10	37	9
1992	30	16	12	8	34	4
1993	31	10	11	10	37	6
1994	31	14	8	11	36	5
1995	38	12	8	10	33	−5
1996	35	12	8	9	36	1
1997	32	15	10	12	31	−1
1998	32	12	8	10	38	6
1999	32	11	10	10	36	4
2001	37	10	10	5	38	1
2003	38	9	7	6	39	1
2005	38	8	7	8	38	0

Source: University of Alabama/Southern Opinion Research surveys.
*Partisan balance 1 = Strong/Weak Democrats = Strong/Weak Republicans

Conversely, white Alabamians are more likely to identify with the Republican than the Democratic Party. Furthermore, among whites in Alabama, males and more educated citizens are more likely than others to be Republicans (Cotter and Stovall 1996; Cotter 2002).[6]

CONCLUSION

Again, Alabama's politics today are far different from the low participation, unequal involvement, one-party patterns found in the state fifty to one hundred years ago. Political participation in Alabama is now both widespread and relatively robust. Further, Democratic dominance over the state has ended while Republican strength has grown. As a result, Alabama's party politics are now more balanced in terms of both office holding and party affiliations. In sum, Alabama is now a politically active and competitive state.

It is not difficult to imagine that Alabama will continue to be a politically competitive state. However, given the general direction of political change since the days of the old South, it is also not difficult to see Republicans becoming the state's dominant party.[7]

Which of these outcomes—continued competitiveness or Republican dominance—occurs in Alabama will undoubtedly be influenced by a variety of factors. One of these is the conduct of partisan politics at the national level. As was the case for other presidents, the general successes and failures of the Obama administration will undoubtedly affect partisan politics in Alabama. Furthermore, the chance of Republican domination in Alabama is probably enhanced if Democratic presidential candidates continue to ignore the state. In terms of fundraising, organizational development, and candidate recruitment, it is difficult to see how the Alabama Democratic Party can maintain itself if it experiences a landslide defeat every four years. At the congressional level, the 2008 results show that with "mainstream" Alabama candidates and adequate financial support, Democrats can be successful in the state. However, without such outside support, even the most electable Democratic congressional candidate is unlikely to succeed.

The state's partisan future will also be influenced by political activities taking place within Alabama. Perhaps particularly important here is the potential for serious conflict within the GOP. Alabama's Republicans have experienced some internal divisions in recent years, as illustrated by the James-Blount primary fight in 1994, the divisions over Governor Riley's tax reform plan in 2003, and the conflict over the 2004 constitutional amendment concerning the state's obligation for public education. The growth of these divisions is likely to hurt the GOP and help Alabama's Democrats. Just as the 1986 Democratic conflict between Graddick and Baxley opened the door for Republicans at the state level, a similar split among Republicans may work to maintain the current competitiveness of the state's politics.

Finally, another factor that may contribute to continued competition is the lack of trust Alabamians express towards state government. This cynicism/alienation, earlier noted by both Key (1949) and Strong (1972), was recently manifested in the outcome of the 1999 lottery referendum and the 2003 tax reform amendment. Partisan competitiveness, at least in the form of rotation in office, may remain in Alabama if the state's alienated and cynical voters continue their recent pattern of frequently replacing one party's group of "rascals" with another.

The upcoming 2010 gubernatorial election has the potential for resolving some of the uncertainty about Alabama's future partisan politics. It has been nearly two decades since the state has had a gubernatorial election without an incumbent candidate. The early indicators are that both

Democrats and Republicans will have contested primaries involving, for each party, multiple serious candidates. If, as expected, Congressman Artur Davis enters the Democratic primary and thus becomes the first African American to have a realistic chance of winning the governorship of Alabama, much national attention and many resources will likely flow to the state. Given these conditions, plus the fact that both Democrats and Republicans can use recent elections to identify winning strategies, the 2010 gubernatorial election is likely to be hard fought, colorful, intense, and meaningful for Alabama's political future.

NOTES

1. The turnout figures through the 1996 election come from Rusk (2001). The results for more recent contests come from the "United States Election Project" website created by Professor Michael McDonald at George Mason University (elections.gmu.edu).

2. McWhorter (2001) and Thornton (2002) examine some of the important civil rights activities that took place in Alabama during the Second Reconstruction. See, for example, Foster (1949), Norrell (1985), and Strong (1956) for discussions of efforts to resist increases in voting participation within Alabama. For examinations of the women's suffrage movement in Alabama, see Thomas (1992) and Schuyler (2006). An interesting account of the successful effort to remove the cumulative component of Alabama's poll tax is presented by Wilkerson-Freeman (2002). Despite the settlement of many suffrage-related questions, the right of ex-felons to vote remains a contentious issue within Alabama (Chandler 2008a, 2008b).

3. In recent statewide elections, the relative strength of Democratic candidates has increased in both black belt counties and in the state's largest urban places. At the same time, relative Republican strength has increased in the predominantly white counties of the Tennessee Valley section of Alabama. This pattern of shifting partisan strength, which was not disrupted by the 2008 election, complicates the task of determining what role race played in support for Obama.

4. The increased turnout in the 2008 presidential primary runs counter to the general trend found within the state. In particular, the development of party competition within Alabama has been associated with a general decline in primary election turnout. Some of the decline in Democratic primary turnout has been offset by an increase in the number of voters participating in the Republican primary. Indeed, since 1998 GOP primary turnout has roughly equaled that found in the Democratic primary. Still, total primary turnout in recent year has been less than that found earlier, including years before the passage of the Voting Rights Act. In 1986, for example, about one-third of Alabama's voting-age population participated in the Democratic primary. However, in total less than one-fourth (23.5 percent) of the state's voting-age population participated in the 2006 primary, even though both Democrats (12.9 percent) and Republicans (10.6 percent) had contested gubernatorial elections.

5. Siegelman was eventually convicted and imprisoned on these corruption charges. After nine months in prison, he was released on appeal. One issue in his appeal is whether Republican political leaders unduly influenced the decision to prosecute Siegelman. This question has also been the subject of a congressional investigation (Nossiter 2008).

6. The findings of the Southern Grassroots Party Activist Project provide another indication of current competitiveness of Alabama's partisan politics. In particular, this study found that organizationally the two parties are about evenly matched within Alabama. For the specific findings of the Grassroots Party Activists study, see Clark and Prysby 2003, 2004.

7. Even if the GOP gains dominance over Alabama's electoral politics, the increased size and heterogeneity of the state's electorate makes it unlikely that Republicans will achieve the same level of uncontested control that Democrats enjoyed during the period of the old South.

REFERENCES

Anniston Star. 1962. "Jefferson voters asked by Wallace." May 16:1A.

Anniston Star. 1982. "Wallace defends his reputation." October 21:7.

Barnard, William D. 1974. *Dixiecrats and Democrats: Alabama Politics, 1942–1950*. Tuscaloosa: University of Alabama Press.

Bositis, David A. 2003. *Black Elected Officials: A Statistical Survey, 2001*. Washington, DC: Joint Center for Political and Economic Studies.

Carter, Dan T. 1995. *The Politics of Rage: George Wallace, the Origins of the New Conservatism, and the Transformation of American Politics*. New York: Simon & Schuster.

Cason, Mike. 1999a. "Lottery Battle Nears End." *Montgomery (AL) Advertiser*, October 10:1A.

———. 1999b. "Lottery Fails." *Montgomery (AL) Advertiser*, October 13:1A.

———. 2002. "Riley Awaits Final Count." *Montgomery (AL) Advertiser*, November 6:1A.

———. 2003. "Alabama Governor Hears Message from Voters: Cuts to Come." *Montgomery (AL) Advertiser*, September 10:A1.

Chandler, Kim. 2008a. "ACLU Challenges State Denial of Felons' Vote." *Birmingham (AL) News*, July 22:1B.

———. 2008b. "Confusion Reigns in Alabama over Ex-felons' Ability to Vote." *Birmingham (AL) News*, October 6:1A.

Chandler, Kim, and Charles J. Dean. 2006a. "Riley, Baxley Sound Familiar Themes on Tour." *Birmingham (AL) News*, November 3:1A.

———. 2006b. "Baxley, Riley Take Final Aim at Undecideds." *Birmingham (AL) News*, November 5:1A.

Clark, John A., and Charles Prysby. 2003. "Introduction: Studying Southern Political Party Activists." *American Review of Politics* 24:1–19.

———. 2004. *Southern Political Party Activists: Patterns of Conflict and Change, 1991–2001*. Lexington: University Press of Kentucky.

Cohen, Jeffrey E., Patrick R. Cotter, and Philip B. Coulter. 1983. "The Changing Structure of Southern Political Participation: Matthews and Prothro 20 Years Later." *Social Science Quarterly* 64:536–549.

Cotter, Patrick R. 1997. "Alabama: The Elephants Trumpet." In *The 1996 Presidential Election in the South*, ed. Laurence W. Moreland and Robert P. Steed. Westport, CT: Praeger.

———. 2002. "Alabama: A 'Small Time' Election." In *The 2000 Presidential Election in the South*, ed. Robert P. Steed and Laurence W. Moreland. New York: Praeger.

Cotter, Patrick R., and James G. Stovall. 1996. "Party Identification and Political Change in Alabama: A Mid-1990s Update." *The American Review of Politics* 17:193–211.

———. Forthcoming. *After Wallace: The 1986 Contest for Governor of Alabama.* Tuscaloosa: University of Alabama Press.

Davis, John. 2006. "Governor's Race a Wild One." *Montgomery (AL) Advertiser*, June 4:1A.

Dean, Charles J. 2006. "Riley Kicks Off Bus Tour of State in Last Week of Campaign." *Birmingham (AL) News*, November 1:9A.

———. 2008a. "Obama Victory Enhances Davis." *Birmingham (AL) News*, February 8:1A.

———. 2008b. "The Rise and Stall of Politico Joe Reed." *Birmingham (AL) News*, June 22:1A.

Evans, Ben. 2008. "Rep Artur Davis Forms Rival Committee on Appointees." *Tuscaloosa (AL) News*, December 10:3B.

Faulk, Kent. 2006. "Baxley Criticizes Tax Cut Plan as Taking Funds from Education." *Birmingham (AL) News*, November 1:1A.

Fisher, Samuel H., III. 2004. "Judge Roy Moore: Moore May Be Less." Paper presented at the 2004 Southern Political Science Association Meeting, New Orleans.

Foster, Vera Chandler. 1949. "'Boswellianism': A Technique in the Restriction of Negro Voting." *Phylon* 10:26–37.

Frederick, Jeff. 2007. *Stand Up for Alabama: Governor George Wallace.* Tuscaloosa: University of Alabama Press.

Frederickson, Kari. 2001. *The Dixiecrat Revolt and the End of the Solid South, 1932–1968.* Chapel Hill: University of North Carolina Press.

Gordon, Tom. 2006. "Strong Economy, Absence of Scandal Help Incumbent." *Birmingham (AL) News*, June 7:1A.

———. 2008. "Davis: A Black Candidate Can Win in Alabama." *Birmingham (AL) News*, November 6:1B.

Johnson, Bob. 2004. "Judge Details Display Fight in New Book *Ten Commandments*." *Mobile (AL) Register*, December 30:2A.

Key, V. O., Jr. 1949. *Southern Politics in State and Nation.* New York: Alfred A. Knopf.

Keyssar, Alexander. 2000. *The Right to Vote: The Contested History of Democracy in the United States.* New York: Basic Books.

Kitchen, Sebastian. 2008. "Bright Claims Victory in Close District 2 Race." *Montgomery (AL) Advertiser*, November 5:1A.

Kousser, J. Morgan. 1974. *The Shaping of Southern Politics: Suffrage Restrictions and the Establishment of the One-Party South, 1880–1910.* New Haven, CT: Yale University Press.

Lewinson, Paul. 1963. *Race, Class and Party: A History of Negro Suffrage and White Politics in the South*. New York: Russell & Russell.

Lyman, Brian. 2008. "Artur Davis Sticks to Center." *Mobile (AL) Press-Register*, September 15:1A.

McCarter, Patricia C., and Challen Stephens. 2008. "Democrats Take Seat Vacated by Cramer." *Huntsville Times*, November 5:B1.

McMillan, Malcolm Cook. 1955. *Constitutional Development in Alabama, 1798–1901: A Study in Politics, the Negro, and Sectionalism*. Chapel Hill: University of North Carolina Press.

McWhorter, Diane. 2001. *Carry Me Home: The Climatic Battle of the Civil Rights Revolution*. New York: Simon & Schuster.

Norrell, Robert J. 1985. *Reaping the Whirlwind: The Civil Rights Movement in Tuskegee*. New York: Alfred A. Knopf.

Nossiter, Adam. 2008. "Appeal Hearing in Ex-Governor's Conviction." *New York Times*, December 10:A28.

Permaloff, Anne, and Carl Grafton. 1995. *Political Power in Alabama: The More Things Change* . . . Athens: University of Georgia Press.

Perman, Michael. 2001. *Struggle for Mastery: Disfranchisement in the South, 1888–1908*. Chapel Hill: University of North Carolina Press.

Porter, Kirk H. 1918. *A History of Suffrage in the United States*. Chicago: University of Chicago Press.

Rusk, Jerrold G. 2001. *A Statistical History of the American Electorate*. Washington, DC: CQ Press.

Schmidt, William E. 1986. "Ending an Era, Wallace Announces He Will Retire." *New York Times*, April 3:1A.

Schuyler, Lorraine Gates. 2006. *The Weight of Their Votes: Southern Women and Political Leverage in the 1920s*. Chapel Hill: University of North Carolina Press.

Strong, Donald S. 1956. *Registration of Voters in Alabama*. University of Alabama Bureau of Public Administration.

———. 1972. "Alabama: Transition and Alienation." In *The Changing Politics of the South*, ed. William C. Havard. Baton Rouge: Louisiana State University Press.

Thomas, Mary Martin. 1992. *The New Woman in Alabama: Social Reforms and Suffrage, 1890–1920*. Tuscaloosa: University of Alabama Press.

Thornton, J. Mills, III. 1968. "Alabama Politics, J. Thomas Heflin, and the Expulsion Movement of 1929." *Alabama Review* 21:83–112.

———. 2002. *Dividing Lines: Municipal Politics and the Struggle for Civil Rights in Montgomery, Birmingham, and Selma*. Tuscaloosa: University of Alabama Press.

Webb, Samuel L. 1997. *Two-Party Politics in the One-Party South: Alabama's Hill Country, 1874–1920*. Tuscaloosa: University of Alabama Press.

Wilkerson-Freeman, Sarah. 2002. "The Second Battle for Woman Suffrage: Alabama White Women, the Poll Tax, and V. O. Key's Master Narrative of Southern Politics." *Journal of Southern History* 68:333–374.

4

———◦———

Mississippi

Emergence of a Modern Two-Party State

David A. Breaux and Stephen D. Shaffer

The Magnolia state has come a long way from the days depicted by V. O. Key (1949), when the Democratic Party was so dominant that most voters were regarded as "Yellow Dog" Democrats, people so partisan that in the general election they would vote for anyone nominated by Democrats, even a "yellow dog," and when Republicans were so rare that even they joked that they could almost hold their party meetings in a phone booth or closet. Today, Republicans have become so strong in federal elections that not since 1976 has a Democratic presidential candidate carried the state's electoral votes, and not since 1988 has even one of the state's two U.S. senators been a Democrat. Republicans have even gained an advantage in statewide elections, winning most of the gubernatorial and lieutenant governorship elections since 1991 (inclusive), half of *all* state offices elected statewide in 2003, and all except one of these statewide races in 2007. Yet Democrats remain a powerful force, clinging to numerical control of both houses of the state legislature, and in 2008 winning back the third of the state's four U.S. House seats. Mississippi in the twenty-first century has emerged as a genuine two-party state, as white conservatives over the past few decades have moved to the GOP.

GROWING REPUBLICANISM IN FEDERAL ELECTIONS

Historically, white Mississippians were so obsessed with race that they voted overwhelmingly against the Republican Party, the anti-slavery party that had championed Radical Reconstruction after the Civil War. As late as Franklin D. Roosevelt's final reelection in 1944, Mississippians voted over 90 percent Democratic for president. Even when Republicans offered war hero Dwight Eisenhower, the Democratic loser nationally still garnered 60 percent and 58 percent of Mississippi's vote in 1952 and 1956, respectively. Only when the national Democratic Party began to advocate federal protection of the civil rights of African Americans did whites desert the party's candidates. The state voted for the States' Rights candidacy of South Carolina governor Strom Thurmond in 1948, backed an independent Democratic slate of electors in 1960, and supported the racially and socially conservative independent, Alabama governor George Wallace, in 1968. Indeed, white Mississippians even voted Republican in 1964 after the party of Lincoln nominated an ideologically pure conservative who had opposed the 1964 Civil Rights Act as a matter of ideological principle (table 4.1).

Mississippi finally began to change in the 1970s, as many whites made their peace with the inevitability of racial integration, and as the state's large African American population was enfranchised after the 1965 Voting Rights Act. Party politics began moving from a nearly all-white, Democratic Party hegemony into a more competitive two-party political environment, such as existed outside of the South. The Magnolia State had finally entered the national mainstream, as it backed every presidential winner from 1972 through 1988. More conservative than the nation as a whole on not only racial but also national defense, crime, and morality issues, Mississippi overwhelmingly backed Republicans Nixon in 1972, Reagan in 1984, and Bush in 1988, rejecting liberal northern Democrats McGovern, Mondale, and Dukakis, respectively. Only with a born-again Southern Baptist, Georgian Jimmy Carter, as the Democratic nominee were the presidential contests hotly contested, as Mississippi narrowly helped to elect the Democrat in 1976 and voted narrowly to unseat him four years later.

This period also ushered in a competitive two-party era in congressional elections. Nixon's coattails in 1972 helped elect Republicans Thad Cochran and Trent Lott to the Fourth (the state capital of Jackson) and Fifth (Gulf Coast) districts, respectively. Both Republicans capitalized on the retirement of Democratic incumbents, were personally popular (Lott had been the incumbent's administrative assistant), and were helped by divisive Democratic primaries contested by six or ten candidates. Though both Republicans began to win easy reelections, conservative Democrats such as Sonny Montgomery and Jamie Whitten also continued to be reelected to Congress. Even the U.S. Senate elections became very competitive and soon split between the parties, as the Republican Representative Cochran in 1978 won the seat vacated by con-

Table 4.1. Two-Party Competition in Federal Elections, 1960–2008

Year	% Dem. Vote for President	% Rep. Vote for President	% Dem. Vote for U.S. Senate	% Rep. Vote for U.S. Senate	No. of Dem. U.S. House Members	No. of Rep. U.S. House Members
1960[a]	36.3	24.7	91.8	8.2	6	0
1962	—	—	—	—	5	0
1964	12.9	87.1	100.0	0	4	1
1966	—	—	65.6	26.7	5	0
1968[b]	23.0	13.5	—	—	5	0
1970	—	—	88.4	0	5	0
1972	19.6	78.2	58.1	38.7	3	2
1974	—	—	—	—	3	2
1976	49.6	47.7	100.0	0	3	2
1978[c]	—	—	31.8	45.1	3	2
1980	48.1	49.4	—	—	3	2
1982	—	—	64.2	35.8	3	2
1984	37.4	61.9	39.1	60.9	3	2
1986	—	—	—	—	4	1
1988	39.1	59.9	46.1	53.9	4	1
1990	—	—	0	100.0	5	0
1992[d]	40.8	49.7	—	—	5	0
1994	—	—	31.2	68.8	4	1
1996[e]	44.1	49.2	27.4	71.0	2	3
1998	—	—	—	—	3	2
2000	40.7	57.6	31.6	65.9	3	2

(continued)

Table 4.1. (continued)

Year	% Dem. Vote for President	% Rep. Vote for President	% Dem. Vote for U.S. Senate	% Rep. Vote for U.S. Senate	No. of Dem. U.S. House Members	No. of Rep. U.S. House Members
2002	—	—	0	84.6	2	2
2004	39.8	59.5	—	—	2	2
2006	—	—	34.9	63.6	2	2
2008f	43.0	56.2	41.8	58.2	3	1

Source: America Votes series, Congressional Quarterly Publisher, Washington, D.C., editions 6–25. Edited by Richard M. Scammon, with Alice V. McGillivray starting with edition 12, joined also by Rhodes Cook starting in edition 22. Results for the years 2004 and 2006 are from the Secretary of State's website.

Note: Percentages do not total 100 percent across rows due to minor candidates, some of whom are listed below.

aAn unpledged Independent Democratic presidential slate received 39.0 percent of the vote.

bWallace's American Independent Party won 63.5 percent of the presidential vote.

cBlack Independent Charles Evers won 23.1 percent of the U.S. Senate vote.

dRoss Perot received 8.7 percent of the presidential vote in 1992.

eThe Reform party received 5.8 percent of the presidential vote in 1996.

fRepublicans won both of the 2008 U.S. Senate elections (61.4–38.6 percent in the regular election and 55.0–45.0 percent in the special election); the table entry averages the percentages.

servative Democrat James Eastland, while Democratic incumbent John Stennis in 1982 won his final reelection by defeating Republican Haley Barbour. Republicans scored a further breakthrough in 1988, picking up the state's second Senate seat when Stennis retired and was replaced by Representative Lott. Lott had adroitly used his massive campaign war chest to run a series of visually appealing television ads that defused claims he was too conservative by painting him as a supporter of Social Security, college student loans, the environment, and federal highway spending (Shaffer 1991).

The 1990s ushered in a period when Republicans became dominant in presidential elections, though Democrats remained competitive in congressional races. Mississippi bucked the national trend by voting to reelect President Bush in 1992 and to unseat President Clinton in 1996, and by subsequently giving George W. Bush two generous victories. State Republicans repeatedly hung the unpopular "liberal" label on the Democrats. Republican governor Kirk Fordice in 1992 blasted Clinton as a "liberal, Democrat, draft-dodger, philanderer," and in 1996 attacked the Democrat's anti–Vietnam War posture shown by his going "on foreign soil in time of war" to "demonstrate against his own country" (first quote in Shaffer 1994, 72; other quotes in Shaffer and Burnside 1997, 99). Republican governor Haley Barbour in 2004 mocked John Kerry as "Teddy Kennedy's ideological twin. Kerry is just the taller, thinner version" (Shaffer, Breaux, and Patrick 2005, 92). Indeed, sometimes national Democrats appeared to help the Republicans make their case, as John Kerry in a campaign stop equated discrimination against gays to historic racial discrimination. Consequently, Mississippi voters repeatedly perceived Democratic presidential hopefuls as "somewhat liberal," while viewing Republicans as "somewhat conservative," thereby perceiving the GOP candidates as being very much in line with their own "somewhat" conservative views.

Democrats remain much more competitive in U.S. House contests, where their party's broad tent that even today includes all ideologies permits them to select candidates that reflect the views of the local constituency. The creation of a majority-black Mississippi River "Delta" district in the 1980s eventually produced liberal African American congressmen, such as Mike Espy in 1986 and Bennie Thompson in a 1993 special election. Thompson skillfully united his African American constituency against his GOP opponent in his first election by claiming that "If you vote for my opponent, it's like the chicken voting for Colonel Sanders" (Glaser 1996, 163). The 1989 special election of conservative white Democrat Gene Taylor in Trent Lott's old Gulf Coast district temporarily gave Democrats control of all five of the state's House districts. The retirement of Boll Weevil (i.e. moderate-to-conservative) Democrats Jamie Whitten in

1994 and Sonny Montgomery in 1996 saw them replaced by conservative Republicans Roger Wicker and Chip Pickering in districts that had been voting Republican for president since at least 1984. Accused by his Democratic opponent of being a "player" for controversial conservative GOP House Speaker Newt Gingrich, Pickering skillfully linked the Democrat to the liberal national Democratic Party by retorting that: "I guess the choice is sending Bill and Hillary another player" (Shaffer and Burnside 1997, 102). Republicans temporarily gained a third congressional seat when moderate conservative Democrat Mike Parker switched to the GOP in 1996, but his retirement two years later to run unsuccessfully for governor was followed by the election of moderate Democrat Ronnie Shows.

The Magnolia State's loss of one House seat after reapportionment set up a titanic struggle in 2002 between two popular incumbents, Democrat Shows and Republican Pickering. We deal at length with this election campaign because it illustrates so well the dramatic differences in campaign themes and approaches of the two parties in modern Mississippi. After a state legislative stalemate over how to redraw the state's district lines, a three-judge panel of Republican-appointed federal judges drew up a map that retained a larger percentage of Pickering's former district than Shows's and that reduced the black voting-age population of the district from 37 percent to 30 percent. In what turned out to be the fifth most expensive congressional seat in the 2002 midterm election and the most expensive congressional campaign in the state's history, Pickering defeated Shows, 64 percent to 35 percent, in this new district that had cast 64 percent of its vote for George W. Bush two years earlier.

Both Chip Pickering and Ronnie Shows took conservative positions on key social issues, being pro-life, anti-gun control, pro-veterans' rights, and supportive of a strong military. Their conservative credentials earned both support from the National Right to Life Committee, the National Rifle Association, and the Family Research Council. They differed on the North American Free Trade Agreement (NAFTA), which Pickering had voted for and Shows, claiming that it would result in a loss of jobs for the state, had voted against. They also differed on tort reform, or capping the amount of money an individual could receive because of "pain and suffering," which Pickering campaigned for while Shows had argued against. They also differed over Social Security, which Pickering had initially favored privatizing, though he later changed his position because of the hard economic times, the unstable stock market, and the possibility of war; Shows favored stashing Social Security funds in a "lock box" to prevent the government from raiding it. Overall, some ideological differences were evident, as the American Conservative Union gave Pickering a lifetime rating of ninety-six out of one hundred, the highest conservative rating in the Mississippi delegation, while Shows received sixty-six out of one hundred, ranking him as the second most "liberal" member in the Mississippi delegation (Breaux 2003).

As in other state and federal campaigns in modern Mississippi, the candidates clearly differed in the extent to which they were willing to be identified with their national parties. Pickering embraced his party's president, congressional leaders, and policies. In August, President Bush visited the state and attended a $1,000 per person fundraising luncheon in Jackson that was slated to raise $500,000 for Pickering. On the other hand, Shows was extremely uncomfortable running as a Democrat and never talked about his party's last president or its congressional leaders. Pickering capitalized on this throughout the campaign by constantly reminding voters that the first vote cast by the new representative would be for the leader of the House of Representatives, and that while he would vote for a conservative speaker, Shows would vote for a liberal one (Breaux 2003).

The 2008 federal elections reinforced these themes and the portrait of Mississippi as a "safe Republican" state in presidential elections but a relatively competitive one in congressional contests. As early as April 2008 the average Mississippian viewed Democrat Barack Obama as "somewhat liberal" in ideology as compared to John McCain's perceived "moderate-to-somewhat conservative" philosophy, a position virtually identical to that of the average voter's (see website: http://www2.msstate .edu/~kauai/poll/Results08.htm). State Republicans skillfully tarred Obama with the "liberal" label when former state GOP chair Jim Herring asserted that "Mississippi remains a conservative state and we are confident Obama's brand of socialism will not be successful in his effort to win Mississippi in November" (WAPT.com 2008). Indeed, the presidential contest had become so invisible in the state, seeing as the national parties fully expected Republicans to win yet again, that Republican governor Barbour and former Democratic governor Ray Mabus spent the closing days of the campaign touting their party's standard-bearer in the more competitive state of Virginia (Associated Press 2008)! Republican McCain went on to earn a landslide 56.2 percent of the vote in Mississippi while losing nationally.

The parties split the 2008 congressional elections, with Republicans winning both of the state's U.S. Senate elections and Democrats picking up a U.S. House seat, giving them a majority of Mississippi's House delegation for the first time since the titanic 2002 Shows-Pickering contest. Since veteran Senate incumbent Cochran was viewed as a shoo-in for reelection, as were Democratic congressmen Thompson and Taylor and the Republican successor to the retiring congressman Pickering, the only "real" contests revolved around the special Senate election to fill Senator Lott's unexpired term after his unexpected midterm retirement, as well as the First Congressional District special and regular elections necessitated by the governor's appointment of Representative Roger Wicker as interim senator. To oppose Wicker, Democrats offered former Governor Ronnie Musgrove. Musgrove was most known to voters for enacting a multiyear teacher pay raise for public school teachers, for unsuccessfully trying to change the state flag to remove the symbol of the old Confederacy, and for losing reelection as governor during tough economic times. Exit polls showed Republicans outnumbering Democrats by 6 percent (46 percent Republicans to 40 percent Democrats with 14 percent independents), and with McCain winning Mississippi by a 13 percentage point margin, and with over 80 percent of voters backing the Senate candidate of the same party as their own party identification or the party of their presidential favorite, Wicker went on to a comfortable 10 percent victory margin (see website: http://www.cnn.com/ELECTION/2008/results/polls/#val=MSS02p1).

Turning to the other most hotly contested congressional race, the battle for Wicker's old congressional seat, Democrats benefited from a bitter Republican primary runoff battle, the scars of which never healed. The Democratic victor was longtime County Chancery Clerk Travis Childers, who appealed to rural constituents, had cast himself in the mold of Jamie Whitten, and was backed by the fiscally conservative Democratic Blue Dog Coalition of the U.S. House.

PARTY IDENTIFICATION SHIFTS IN THE ELECTORATE

Not only have Republicans made great gains in federal elections over the past few decades, but also the electorate's basic psychological identifications have shifted away from the Democratic Party and toward the GOP. As late as 1975, only 6 percent of voters in one survey regarded themselves as Republicans while 51 percent viewed themselves as Democrats (Bass and DeVries 1977, 216). Though Republicans made some gains among whites, even as late as 1982, when for the last time a Democratic U.S. senator, John Stennis, was being reelected, a majority of whites remained Democratic in partisanship (table 4.2). Since then, Democrats have suffered steady losses among white Mississippians, though African Americans generally remain over 80 percent Democratic. From 1984 through 1990, as Democratic support among whites dropped into the 40 percent range and as whites became equally divided between the two parties, popular Republicans were able to seize control of both of the U.S. Senate seats. By 1992, a majority of whites were now calling themselves Republicans, and the party's candidates began making inroads in state elected offices such as governor, lieutenant governor, and the state legis-

Table 4.2. Party Identification of Adult Mississippians, Whites and Blacks, 1981–2008

	Among Whites Only				Among Blacks Only			
Year	Dem. %	Ind. %	Rep. %	N Size	Dem. %	Ind. %	Rep. %	N Size
1981	51.0	9.0	40.0	(420)	87.8	1.2	11.0	(164)
1982	53.0	13.3	33.7	(570)	89.0	2.0	8.9	(246)
1984	46.2	14.3	39.4	(398)	82.6	7.6	9.8	(184)
1986	42.4	9.1	48.5	(396)	82.1	6.6	11.2	(196)
1988	43.9	10.5	45.6	(419)	82.2	5.6	12.2	(180)
1990	45.2	5.6	49.2	(394)	84.8	2.9	12.3	(171)
1992	36.9	7.1	56.0	(352)	84.1	2.4	13.4	(164)
1994	29.0	13.4	57.7	(411)	88.4	4.2	7.4	(189)
1996	31.1	11.9	57.0	(386)	82.7	8.4	8.9	(179)
1998	31.0	11.7	57.3	(393)	79.2	8.7	12.0	(183)
1999	34.5	12.5	53.0	(417)	84.2	7.1	8.7	(196)
2000	35.4	8.4	56.1	(367)	90.4	1.7	7.9	(178)
2002	28.1	6.3	65.7	(367)	77.2	10.4	12.4	(193)
2004	22.2	12.9	65.0	(311)	81.8	6.9	11.3	(159)
2006	30.1	5.1	64.8	(349)	84.2	6.4	9.4	(171)
2008	30.9	10.1	59.0	(324)	79.3	6.5	14.2	(169)

Source: The Mississippi Poll project, Social Science Research Center, Mississippi State University.

lature. Republican identification among whites further increased after the turn of the century, but then dipped slightly to 59 percent in 2008. Only the overwhelmingly Democratic orientation of the 36 percent of the state population that is African American has kept the aggregated electorate closely divided in partisanship. Indeed, in the latest (April 2008) poll, 48.1 percent of all adult Mississippians called themselves Democrats, 43.1 percent were Republicans, and 8.8 percent were pure independents (though the higher turnout of Republicans essentially erases that small deficit).

The primary reason for Republican gains among white Mississippians was their conservative values, evident on a variety of issues, not merely racial considerations. Examining five issues asked from 1992 through 2008 by the Mississippi Poll project in a multiple regression equation, the party identification ties of whites were most related to ideological self-identification; an economic issue scale (incorporating health care, public jobs, and good living standards items) was second in importance, and a racial issues scale (including affirmative action and the federal government improving the conditions of blacks and other minorities items) was only third in importance. Furthermore, most whites perceived that the Republican Party was the party most likely to "reduce crime" and to "maintain traditional values," and these perceptions were much more likely to shape their partisan identifications than was the perception that Democrats were the party more concerned with "protecting African American interests" (Shaffer, Cotter, and Tucker 2000, 143). Table 4.3 illustrates the dramatic gains that Republicans have made among self-identified white conservatives, who in the early 1980s were only 52 percent Republican, but who became steadily more Republican as the years passed, reaching a 78 percent mark in 2006 and 2008. Democrats, whose ranks thirty years earlier had furnished such conservative elected leaders as Senators John Stennis and James Eastland, and Representatives Jamie Whitten and Sonny Montgomery, had by the turn of the century become a more ideologically narrow party. In 2006 and 2008, only 17 percent of conservative white Mississippians called themselves Democrats.

To make up for the conservative white exodus to the GOP, Mississippi Democrats must assemble a biracial coalition that includes many white liberals and moderates and the great majority of African Americans. Though Republicans have made gains among white moderates, Democrats are nearly as numerous as the GOP among them. Furthermore, Democrats have lost little support among the small group of self-identified white liberals, where they retain a majority and hold a clear advantage over Republicans (table 4.3). Therefore, even with Republican gains among conservative whites, Democrats today are still able to assemble a biracial, ideologically diverse coalition to win many state and local elections.

Table 4.3. Party Identification of White Mississippians, by Ideological Self-Identification Groups and by Time Periods

Years	Dem. %	Ind. %	Rep. %	N Size
Among Self-Identified Liberals				
1981–1982	57.3	16.0	26.7	(75)
1984–1990	51.7	8.3	40.0	(145)
1992–2000	51.8	11.7	36.5	(394)
2002–2004	47.9	8.3	43.8	(96)
2006–2008	52.4	19.6	28.0	(82)
Among Self-Identified Moderates				
1981–1982	55.6	11.3	33.1	(284)
1984–1990	50.2	9.6	40.2	(759)
1992–2000	41.5	15.5	43.0	(718)
2002–2004	35.8	15.0	49.2	(187)
2006–2008	46.1	7.3	46.6	(178)
Among Self-Identified Conservatives				
1981–1982	39.1	8.7	52.2	(312)
1984–1990	32.3	7.2	60.5	(517)
1992–2000	19.8	7.3	72.9	(1118)
2002–2004	11.9	6.9	81.2	(361)
2006–2008	17.4	4.6	78.0	(386)

Source: The Mississippi Poll project, Social Science Research Center, Mississippi State University.
Note: Years have been combined or pooled to maximize the numbers of people analyzed and minimize the sample error. The years are logically combined based on the changing numbers of the two parties' identifiers in the electorate.

REPUBLICAN GAINS FILTER DOWN TO STATEWIDE OFFICES

The historic ruling Democratic Party was so strong that Republicans failed to even field a candidate for lieutenant governor in four of the six elections from 1963 through 1983, and failed to elect any Republican in any of the sixty-one statewide elections held for state offices during these years (table 4.4). Republican hopes began to improve in 1987, when progressive Tupelo businessman and chairman of the state Board of Education Jack Reed garnered a post-Reconstruction GOP high of 47 percent of the vote in a losing gubernatorial race to Democratic auditor Ray Mabus. Republicans achieved post–Reconstruction era firsts in the recession year of 1991 as voters, tired of two years of budget cuts that included popular elementary, secondary, and higher education programs, ousted the incumbent governor and lieutenant governor. Both Democrats were ousted in the general election after narrowly surviving bitter party primary battles. Elected as the first Republican governor and lieutenant governor since Reconstruction were a little known construction executive, conservative Kirk Fordice, and Democrat-turned-Republican state senator and reformer Eddie Briggs (Shaffer, Sturrock, Breaux, and Minor 1999, 257).

Table 4.4. Two-Party Competition in State Offices

Year	Popular Vote for Governor		Popular Vote for Lieutenant Governor		Party Control of Eight Statewide Offices	
	Dem. %	Rep. %	Dem. %	Rep. %	Dems.	Reps.
1963	61.9	38.1	74.0	26.0	11	0
1967	70.3	29.7	100.0	0	11	0
1971[a]	77.0	0	100.0	0	11	0
1975[b]	52.2	45.2	69.5	30.5	11	0
1979	61.1	38.9	100.0	0	9	0
1983[c,d]	55.1	38.9	64.3	0	8	0
1987[e]	53.4	46.6	73.4	17.7	8	0
1991[f]	47.6	50.8	41.5	49.5	6	2
1995	44.4	55.6	52.7	47.3	6	2
1999[g]	49.6	48.5	52.9	47.1	7	1
2003	45.8	52.6	37.1	61.0	4	4
2007	42.1	57.9	41.4	58.6	1	7

Source: Mississippi Official and Statistical Register, 1964–1968 through 2000–2004, Secretary of State of Mississippi. The results for 2007 are from the Secretary of State's website.

Note: Eight offices that are elected statewide in Mississippi include governor, lieutenant governor, attorney general, secretary of state, treasurer, auditor, insurance commissioner, and agriculture commissioner. (Prior to 1983, the superintendent of public education was also elected statewide. Prior to 1979, the Supreme Court clerk and state land commissioner were also elected.) These elections, as well as elections for all state legislators, occur every four years in the November before the presidential election year. Percentages do not total 100 percent across rows due to minor candidates, some of whom are listed below.
[a]Black Independent Charles Evers won 22.1 percent in the 1971 governor's race.
[b]Black Independent Henry Kirksey won 2.7 percent in the 1975 governor's race.
[c]Black Independent Charles Evers won 4.1 percent in the 1983 governor's race.
[d]Gil Carmichael ran as an independent for lieutenant governor in 1983, winning 35.7 percent.
[e]Black Independent Henry Kirksey won 8.9 percent in the lieutenant governor's race in 1987.
[f]Black Independent Henry Kirksey won 9.0 percent in the lieutenant governor's race in 1991.
[g]The Democratic gubernatorial candidate in 1999, lacking a majority, was selected by the state legislature.

The newly competitive state Republicans now faced their own bitter intraparty conflicts. Some GOP lawmakers joined Democrats to override Governor Fordice's veto of a tax increase needed to prevent more cuts in education, prompting the outspoken Fordice to angrily denounce his own party members as "pseudo-Republicans" who should be sent home by voters. Though Fordice was reelected in 1995 because of voter satisfaction during a time of a booming economy, Lieutenant Governor Eddie Briggs, who had been accused by some conservative Republicans of not being pro-life enough, was defeated by Democratic state senator and education committee chair Ronnie Musgrove. Only the subsequent resignation of the state auditor and Fordice's appointment of Republican state representative Phil Bryant kept two of the state's eight statewide elected offices Republican. The last state election of the twentieth century was even worse for Republicans, as Democrat-turned-Republican ex-congressman Mike Parker, sitting on his lead, lost a narrow gubernatorial contest to Musgrove, who had unveiled an effective television ad of his accomplishments as lieutenant governor in improving public elementary and secondary education. Moderate Amy Tuck retained the lieutenant governorship for the Democrats, reducing Republicans to holding only one statewide office, that of state auditor.

The seesaw of which party could hurt itself the most in intraparty infighting in this modern era of competitive two-party politics now tilted back to the Democrats. Governor Musgrove delivered on his pledge to enact a six-year plan to raise public elementary and secondary teachers' salaries to the southeast average, but this expensive program, coupled with a post–9/11 recession, produced years of cuts in other state programs, including higher education. Blasting his 2003 GOP opponent, former RNC chair Haley Barbour, as a "Washington lobbyist" whose firm did business with tobacco companies that "poison our kids," Musgrove lost reelection to Barbour, who had decried the sizable state deficit and had promised that "we can do better" (Shaffer, Breaux, and Patrick 2005).

Meanwhile Lieutenant Governor Amy Tuck, who had taken progressive positions on such key issues as the massive teacher pay raise and urging early (pre-kindergarten) education, resisted pressure from partisan and liberal Democrats to back a congressional redistricting plan that would have maximized Ronnie Shows's chances of beating Chip Pickering. Also reeling from Democratic criticism of her support for tort reform, Tuck switched to the GOP before seeking reelection. To oppose Tuck in 2003, Democrats nominated state senator Barbara Blackmon, a liberal African American. Irritated by the divorced Tuck's claim to be pro-life, Blackmon challenged the lieutenant governor to sign an oath that she had never had an abortion. As newspaper editors denounced Blackmon's getting too personally intrusive in the contest, and as state GOP leaders and the business community rallied to Tuck, the Democrat-turned-Republican officeholder won a landslide reelection. Republicans also won an open seat for treasurer, as Tate Reeves's spending advantage over the well qualified Gary Anderson, another African American Democrat, translated into greater name visibility. Reelecting Phil Bryant as auditor once again, Republicans now held an unprecedented four statewide offices (table 4.4), tying the Democrats in number of offices. Democrats won the open attorney general contest and reelected their party's secretary of state, insurance commissioner, and agriculture commissioner (Shaffer, Breaux, and Patrick 2005).

Haley Barbour's landslide reelection in the 2007 state elections completed the Democratic meltdown, as Democrats won only one statewide office, reelecting Attorney General Jim Hood, though they did retain control of both chambers of the state legislature. In the governor's race, Democratic social conservative John Arthur Eaves had stressed his backing of school prayer and kept promising to throw the "money changers" out of the state capital, but Barbour's inspirational leadership after Hurricane Katrina had garnered him *Governing* magazine's prestigious award for Public Official of the Year, and a *Clarion-Ledger* endorsement praised his bringing new jobs into the state by helping to land a new Toyota plant (*Clarion-Ledger* 2007a). Even Mississippi's first African American congressman since Reconstruction, Mike Espy, ended up backing Barbour, as did such Democratic former officeholders as Lieutenant Governor Brad Dye and Governor Bill Waller (Rupp 2007, 1A, 6A).

Especially chilling for Democrats was that the GOP won every open contest for statewide office, as Auditor Phil Bryant moved up to the lieutenant governorship vacated by Tuck due to term limits, and well-qualified Republican candidates won the offices of secretary of state, auditor, and insurance commissioner. Republicans also reelected incumbents for treasurer and agriculture commissioner, the latter a recent party switcher who had survived a tough GOP primary challenge. Contributing to the GOP tidal wave was the aggressive state Republican Party's financial backing of their statewide candidates, as they contributed the following sums to party candidates: $450,000 for insurance commissioner, $287,500 for attorney general, $137,000 for auditor, $120,000 for secretary of state, $100,000 for agriculture commissioner, and $65,000 for lieutenant governor. The only Democrat successful in attracting such a large sum was the victorious Attorney General Jim Hood, who received $850,000 over the year from the national Democratic Attorney General Association (see Mississippi secretary of state website: http://www.sos.state.ms.us). Democrats had also shot themselves in the foot when their state party executive committee sought to deny incumbent Democratic insurance commissioner George Dale a place on the primary ballot because he had publicly supported Republican President Bush in 2004. Dale found himself in court fighting to have his ballot position restored, only to be knocked off by voters in the Democratic primary election.

Instrumental in the Republican wave of statewide victories was that they had finally become such a mature party and therefore were able to offer such well-qualified candidates that even major state newspapers ended up endorsing them. For example, the *Clarion-Ledger* endorsed state auditor Phil Bryant for lieutenant governor over three-term state representative Jamie Franks, praising the Republican's non-partisan operation of his office and his stress on accountability and consensus-seeking (*Clarion-Ledger* 2007b). The paper also backed attorney and businessman Delbert Hosemann for secretary of state over veteran Democratic lawmaker Rob Smith, touting the Republican's businesslike approach focused on promoting openness in government and combating voter fraud (*Clarion-Ledger* 2007c). Also, the Biloxi and Gulfport–based *Sun Herald* endorsed four-term legislative veteran Mike Chaney over Democratic state chief fiscal officer Gary Anderson for insurance commissioner, praising the Republican's pledge to hold the insurance companies accountable and to fight for affordable insurance coverage throughout the state, even on the hurricane-plagued Gulf Coast (*Sun Herald* 2007).

Republicans have come a long way from the dismal days of the 1960s and the early 1970s when they failed to even offer a candidate in thirty of thirty-three statewide contests (table 4.5). Beginning with progressive Gil Carmichael's 1975 gubernatorial bid, Republicans began to challenge roughly half of statewide races through the 1983 elections. The next four elections saw the GOP challenging a majority of contests, including all eight in 1995 and six of the eight in 1999. The 2003 elections that resulted in Barbour becoming governor saw a historic reversal of party fortunes, as Republicans ran candidates in all eight offices and Democrats contested only seven races, declining to challenge incumbent auditor Phil Bryant, while in 2007 both parties offered candidates for every statewide office.

Democrats retain an advantage in turnout in the Democratic primary, since the great majority of county and local officials remain Democratic. Even as late as 2007, 69 percent of the votes cast in the first gubernatorial primary were cast in the Democratic rather than Republican primary.

Table 4.5. First Gubernatorial Primary Turnout and State Offices Contested by the Major Parties

	Votes Cast in First Primary for Governor				No. of Statewide Offices Contested in Gen. Election	
Year	Dem.	Rep.	% of Total Cast in Dem. Primary	% of Total Cast in Rep. Primary	Dem.	Rep.
1963	474,414	0	100.0	0	11	2
1967	684,005	0	100.0	0	11	1
1971	762,987	0	100.0	0	11	0
1975	789,894	0	100.0	0	11	8
1979	737,131	32,452	95.8	4.2	9	4
1983	828,211	0	100.0	0	8	3
1987	807,990	18,853	97.7	2.3	8	7
1991	726,465	63,561	92.0	8.0	8	3
1995	514,649	126,018	80.3	19.7	8	8
1999	545,555	153,142	78.1	21.9	8	6
2003	517,345	190,223	73.1	26.9	7	8
2007	446,722	197,647	69.3	30.7	8	8

Source: Mississippi Official and Statistical Register, 1964–1968 through 2000–2004, Secretary of State of Mississippi. Figures for the years 2003 and 2007 are from the Secretary of State's website.

However, Democrats no longer retain their overwhelming turnout advantage, which before the 1990s was reflected in over 90 percent of the votes being cast in the Democratic rather than GOP first primary.

AN ERA OF PARTISAN POLITICS
IN THE STATE LEGISLATURE EMERGES

Prior to the 1965 Voting Rights Act, the state legislature was an all-white and nearly all-Democratic institution. Robert Clark, a Freedom Democrat leader, was elected to the state House as an independent in 1967, and for eight years he was the sole African American lawmaker in a bicameral legislature of 174 members. As African Americans won lawsuits challenging legislative districting schemes as discriminatory, their numbers in the legislature rose. Beginning in 1979 when the number of black lawmakers jumped, all were getting elected as Democrats. That year the numbers of GOP lawmakers also began a slow rise. The 1987 and 1991 elections contested by popular GOP gubernatorial candidates Jack Reed and Kirk Fordice saw Republican legislative numbers rise dramatically from nine to sixteen and then to thirty-two, outnumbering black lawmakers by 1991. White Democrats remained the dominant faction, however, outnumbering blacks and Republicans combined by a two-to-one margin (table 4.6).

Court-ordered redistricting that promoted the creation of more black majority districts, as well as the rising strength of the GOP in Mississippi, produced dramatic change in the legislature's composition after 1991. The number of African Americans rose from twenty-one to thirty-six in the state House and from four to thirteen in the state Senate in this 1991–2007 era. Republican gains were even more dramatic, doubling in the House from twenty-three to forty-seven and more than doubling in the Senate from nine to twenty-five. Though Democrats continued to control both chambers of the legislature after the 2003 and 2007 elections, Republicans (all of whom were white) now constituted the single largest faction in both chambers. The rising numbers of blacks and Republicans were of course accompanied by a big slide in the numbers of white Democrats. Already declining from their near-monopoly of political power in 1963 with 120 representatives and 51 senators, white Democratic numbers between the 1991 and 2007 elections fell from 77 to 39 in the House, and from 39 to only 14 in the Senate (table 4.6).

The need for Democrats to maintain a racially unified party produced some real gains for black lawmakers in terms of legislative leadership positions and even victories on important bills and nominations. After the 1991 elections, veteran Black Caucus Representative Robert Clark was

Table 4.6. Race and Party Composition of State Legislature

	State House of Representatives			State Senate		
Year	Black Democrats	White Democrats	White Republicans	Black Democrats	White Democrats	White Republicans
1963	0	120	2	0	51	1
1967	1[a]	121	0	0	52	0
1971	1[a]	119	2	0	50	2
1975	4[b]	115	3	0	50	2
1979	15	102	4	2	46	4
1983	18	98	6	2	47	3
1987	20	93	9	2	43	7
1991	21	77	23	4	39	9
1992	30	63	27	10	29	13
1995	35	50	34	10	24	18
1999	35	51	33	10	24	18
2003	36	40	46	11	18	23
2007	36	39	47	13	14	25

Source: Figures from *Politics in the New South: Representation of African Americans in Southern State Legislatures*. Edited by Charles E. Menifield and Stephen D. Shaffer. SUNY Press, 2005.
"Political Parties in Modern Mississippi," by Stephen D. Shaffer, in *Politics in Mississippi*, 2nd edition. Edited by Joseph B. Parker. Sheffield Publishing Co., Salem, WI: 2001, p. 297. *Mississippi Official and Statistical Register*, 1964–1968 through 2000–2004, Secretary of State of Mississippi. Figures for 2007 are from the state legislature's website, accessed October 15, 2008.
Note: The legislature consists of 122 house members and 52 senators. Rows may fail to reach that total due to white independents. The special legislative election in 1992 was required by court-ordered redistricting.
[a]Representative Robert Clark, an African American and a leader of the Freedom Democrats, was elected as an independent.
[b]Representative Douglas Anderson, an African American, was elected as an independent.

elected to the number two leadership post in the House, Speaker Pro Tempore. Newly elected Lieutenant Governor Ronnie Musgrove elevated blacks to chair such powerful Senate committees as Judiciary, Constitution, Elections, and Universities and Colleges in 1996. Though two white Democrats were selected to the two top positions in the state House after the 2003 election, for the first time an African American was appointed to chair the powerful Ways and Means Committee, a position that he retained after the 2007 elections. Committee chairmanships also translated into some important legislative victories for the Black Caucus. Republican governor Fordice's effort in 1996 to place four white male businessmen on the state College Board was defeated by one vote in the Senate Universities and Colleges Committee, forcing him to nominate one black and one woman along with only two white males (Menifield and Shaffer 2005). Republican governor Barbour's effort in a 2004 special session to save money by restricting a bond bill solely to promoting economic development was stymied when Ways and Means Committee chairman Percy Watson invited university and community college leaders to testify about their "needs," leading to a bond bill of $456 million that included a diverse range of state needs in place of Barbour's mere $108 million bill.

White Democrats have tended to remain an important swing faction on roll call votes. Generally voting with African American Democrats to enact landmark education measures in the 1990s, even those requiring a tax increase, white Democrats would then break party ranks and join with Republicans to enact tough anti-crime measures. Democrats of both races successfully overrode Fordice's vetoes of a 1992 tax hike for education, a 1992 higher education bond bill, and the 1997 Adequate Education Act. White Democrats even joined with their African American colleagues to override Fordice's 1995 veto of a telecommunications bond bill that included racial set asides. Black Democrats, though, lost out to a bipartisan, overwhelmingly white coalition that voted on measures to crack down on school violence (1994) and street gangs (1996). Losing to a majority of whites of both parties who enacted longer prison terms (a 1995 Truth in Sentencing law), African Americans attracted a majority of white Democrats in 2001 to limit this law by providing early parole for first-time, nonviolent offenders. And though a majority of whites of both parties backed a cut in the income tax in the Fordice reelection year of 1995, unified African American opposition doomed the tax cut to failure by preventing it from achieving the 60 percent margin constitutionally needed for revenue legislation, thereby providing state programs such as education with the funds that they needed to operate effectively (Menifield and Shaffer 2005).

Mississippi's history of one-partyism has minimized the type of divisiveness that exists between the parties in Washington. As Republicans gained legislative seats, Democratic House speakers and lieutenant governors appointed a few as committee chairs. (Under Senate rules, the lieutenant governor, whatever his or her party, makes committee assignments.) Republican lieutenant governors have continued this bipartisan tradition. Many landmark bills have been enacted with majority support by both parties and races, including the 1982 Education Reform Act, the 1987 highway bill to four-lane one thousand miles of roads, the 2000 multi-year teacher pay raise, and the 2002 settlement of the Ayers higher education desegregation lawsuit. The parties do not yet organize as caucuses. The entire chamber membership votes for the House speaker, House speaker pro tempore, and Senate president pro tempore. Finally, though Republicans continue to lack numeric control of the state House or Senate, after the 2003 and 2007 elections popular Republican lawmakers Travis Little and Billy Hewes were elected president pro tempore of the Senate.

CONCLUSION

V. O. Key would hardly recognize today's Mississippi, given the state's sizable legislative Black Caucus that exerts a decisive impact on some public policies, and the Republican Party's dominance in presidential and U.S. Senate elections. Yet in some respects the state has not changed all that much— it still remains an essentially conservative place. Mississippi's conservatism is reflected in a 2001 statewide election where 64 percent of Mississippians voted to keep their 1894 state flag, which includes the Confederate battle emblem (Breaux and Menifield 2003). However, today that conservatism has changed its home from that of the southern Democratic Party to that of the national Republican Party. The conservatism of today's Mississippi Republican Party fits so well with the national party that some state Republicans rise to national leadership positions, such as Haley Barbour's RNC chairmanship, Trent Lott's Republican Senate leadership posts, and Roger Wicker's chairmanship of the 1995 GOP House freshman class.

Yet V. O. Key, in detailing the conflict between the poor whites in the hills and the conservative Delta planters, also pointed out that the Magnolia State has a Populist strain. The enfranchisement of African Americans, who comprise 36 percent of the state's population, dramatically increases the size of the state electorate's more progressive element even further. Legislative overrides of Fordice's vetoes reflect the limits of a policy of unbridled conservatism promoted by any GOP leader. Democratic comebacks in the 1999 statewide elections and their pickup of a U.S. House seat in 2008 illustrate how fleeting GOP gains in any one election may be. It seems unlikely that the state will ever turn 180 degrees about from its Democratic heritage and become a solidly Republican state. Intensely competitive two-party politics is a far more likely scenario.

REFERENCES

Associated Press. 2008. "Mabus, Barbour Stumping for Candidates." *The Clarion-Ledger*, October 23:3B.

Bass, Jack, and Walter DeVries. 1977. *The Transformation of Southern Politics: Social Change and Political Consequence Since 1945*. New York: New American Library.

Biloxi-Gulfport (MS) Sun Herald. 2007. "Mike Cheney Has Best Approach to Solving Insurance Crisis." November 4:8A.

Breaux, David A. 2003. "The Mississippi 3rd Congressional District Race." In *The Last Hurrah: Soft Money and Issue Advocacy in the 2002 Congressional Elections*, ed. David B. Magleby and Quin Monson. Brigham Young University: Center for the Study of Elections and Democracy.

Breaux, David A., and Charles E. Menifield. 2003. "Mississippi: A Study in Change and Continuity." In *The New Politics of the Old South*, 2nd ed., ed. Charles S. Bullock III and Mark J. Rozell. Lanham, MD: Rowman & Littlefield.

Glaser, James M. 1996. *Race, Campaign Politics, and the Realignment in the South*. New Haven, CT: Yale University Press.

Jackson (MS) Clarion-Ledger. 2007a. "Gov: Barbour Best Choice Nov. 6." November 4:4G.

Jackson (MS) Clarion-Ledger. 2007b. "Lt. Gov: Bryant Best Choice Nov. 6." November 4:4G.

Jackson (MS) Clarion-Ledger. 2007c. "Sec'y of State: Hosemann Best Choice Nov. 6." October 31:8A.

Key, V. O., Jr. 1949. *Southern Politics in State and Nation*. New York: Alfred A. Knopf.

Menifield, Charles E., and Stephen D. Shaffer, eds. 2005. *Politics in the New South: Representation of African Americans in Southern State Legislatures*. Albany: State University of New York Press.

Rupp, Leah. 2007. "Big-Name Dem Throws Support to Barbour Side." *Jackson (MS) Clarion-Ledger*, October 18:1A, 6A.

Shaffer, Stephen D. 1991. "Mississippi: Electoral Conflict in a Nationalized State." In *The 1988 Presidential Election in the South: Continuity Amidst Change in Southern Party Politics*, ed. Laurence W. Moreland, Robert P. Steed, and Tod A. Baker. New York: Praeger.

———. 1994. "Mississippi: Friends and Neighbors Fight the 'Liberal' Label." In *The 1992 Presidential Election in the South: Current Patterns of Southern Party and Electoral Politics*, ed. Robert P. Steed, Laurence W. Moreland, and Tod A. Baker. Westport, CT: Praeger.

Shaffer, Stephen D., and Randolph Burnside. 1997. "Mississippi: GOP Consolidates Its Gains." In *The 1996 Presidential Election in the South: Southern Party Systems in the 1990s*, ed. Laurence W. Moreland and Robert P. Steed. Westport, CT: Praeger.

Shaffer, Stephen D., David A. Breaux, and Barbara Patrick. 2005. "Mississippi: Republicans Surge Forward in a Two-Party State." *American Review of Politics* 26:85–107.

Shaffer, Stephen D., Patrick R. Cotter, and Ronnie B. Tucker. 2000. "Racism or Conservatism: Explaining Rising Republicanism in the Deep South." *Southeastern Political Review* 28:133–148.

Shaffer, Stephen D., David E. Sturrock, David A. Breaux, and Bill Minor. 1999. "Mississippi: From Pariah to Pacesetter?" In *Southern Politics in the 1990s*, ed. Alexander P. Lamis. Baton Rouge: Louisiana State University Press.

WAPT.com. 2008. "Democrats Rally to Rock the Vote: Obama Supporters Seek Big Turnout in Mississippi." October 19. http://www.wapt.com/news/17757721/detail.html.

5

Louisiana

African Americans, Republicans, and Party Competition

Wayne Parent and Huey Perry

On paper, Louisiana looks remarkably similar to its sister states in the Deep South. However, Louisiana politics at the beginning of the twenty-first century remain distinct. Disasters, both natural and political, had a disproportionate impact on elections throughout the first decade of the twenty-first century. While generally the first years of the new century saw a continued movement toward the Republicans, Hurricanes Katrina and Rita in 2005 and Hurricanes Gustav and Ike in 2008 had dramatic political effects. In addition, a political scandal involving the state's only African American member of Congress, and an admission of a "very serious sin" by the state's first and only Republican elected to the U.S. Senate had both direct and indirect consequences for election outcomes.

While in the 1990s Louisiana was host to an erratic, often unpredictable, certainly uneven evolution from Democratic dominance to Republican parity and from virtually white-only participation to genuine black political power, by 2008 Republicans had both consolidated their gains and made some significant and substantial advances. In 2008, following a landslide victory in 2007 for Republican Bobby Jindal as governor, Louisiana elected six Republicans to the seven-member Congressional delegation and was one of the few states in the union to see Republican support increase in the 2008 presidential election, giving Republicans three straight decisive victories at the top. Democrats could find solace in the reelection of U.S. senator Mary Landrieu, who was considered the most vulnerable Democratic senator in 2008, their tentative hold on both houses of the legislature, and some gains in local offices in urban areas.

But the overall trend was clearly Republican. And on the surface, at least, the political landscape looked very similar to Mississippi and Alabama to the east.

This chapter will address the reasons for the partisan shift by closely examining the transition years of the last decades of the twentieth century. In addition the chapter will consider the emergence of blacks in power and as key players in power politics. Even though in 2008 Louisiana's only African American member of Congress was defeated and the statewide Republican trends put African Americans increasingly on the losing side in statewide elections, there were some noteworthy, more localized gains.

THE ERRATIC EMERGENCE OF THE REPUBLICAN PARTY

Republican gains in Louisiana came later than in most states of the Deep South, but were quite impressive nonetheless. The Republican trend began in earnest in 1995 when Louisianans elected Republican Mike Foster governor by a wide margin. In 1996 U.S. Senate candidate Louis "Woody" Jenkins came within six thousand votes of becoming Louisiana's first Republican elected to that body. In the 1990s, Republicans began increasing their numbers in the state legislature and winning significant numbers of elections at all levels of government. Republican voter registration surged from less than 1 percent in 1960 to over 20 percent. By 2000, Republicans had clearly established themselves as an equal partner in this obviously two-party state. Tables 5.1 and 5.2 illustrate the erratic growth of Republican strength in the state legislature and in voter registration during this time.

The agents of change away from the hundred years of Democratic dominance in Louisiana are similar to those of other states in the South. In 1956, Dwight Eisenhower became the first Republican to carry Louisiana (and, in the Deep South, only Louisiana) with a pro-business "establishment" Republican message that attracted middle-to-upper income suburbanites. In 1964, Louisiana followed the pattern that established Republican success in the remainder of the Deep South when Republican Barry Goldwater's message of racial and cultural conservatism attracted enough middle-to-lower income whites to carry the state; Republican Ronald Reagan's similar message of strong defense and social conservatism not only carried the state in 1980 and 1984 but helped George H. W. Bush win, although by his smallest margin in the South, in 1988. Republican congressional candidates began winning in the (mostly white) suburban areas surrounding New Orleans, Shreveport, and Baton Rouge, and then eventually in (mostly white) rural areas as well.

Table 5.1.   Partisan Makeup of the Louisiana Legislature, 1962–2008

	House of Representatives		Senate	
	Democrat	*Republican*	*Democrat*	*Republican*
1962	101	0	39	0
1964	103	2	39	0
1966	103	2	39	0
1968	105	0	39	0
1970	104	1	38	1
1972	101	4	38	1
1976	101	4	38	1
1978	96	9	38	1
1980	95	10	39	0
1982	93	11	38	1
1984	91	14	38	1
1986	87	15	34	5
1988	86	17	34	5
1990	89	16	34	5
1992	88	16	34	5
1994	89	16	33	6
1996	77	27	25	14
2000	70	33	26	13
2002	71	34	26	13
2004	69	36	26	13
2006	64	41	24	15
2008	55	50	24	15

There are two fairly distinct aspects of Republican appeal. First, as was evident in the Eisenhower victory, is the pro-business, economic appeal to middle-class white suburbanites. Louisiana's higher proportion of urban centers than Mississippi, Alabama, and South Carolina provides a fertile ground for these suburban political messages that obviously resonated in some of Louisiana's consistently strongest Republican parishes. Republicans have been quite successful around Louisiana's largest urban areas of Jefferson Parish (i.e., county) and St. Tammany Parish in suburban New Orleans, and the areas in and around Shreveport (Caddo and Bossier parishes), Baton Rouge (East Baton Rouge and Livingston parishes), and Lafayette (Lafayette Parish).

The second aspect of Republican appeal was more evident in the Goldwater victory. Republicans carried rural white parishes, especially in Protestant north Louisiana, for the first time. These voters were attracted to Goldwater's opposition to the Civil Rights Act. These conservative policy positions were precursors to other socially conservative positions on such issues as gun control and prayer in public schools in that they appealed to a similar voter. This second type of Republican voter is now

Table 5.2.   Louisiana Voter Registration by Party, 1960–2008 (in percentages)

Year	Democrat	Republican
1960	98.6	0.9
1961	98.7	0.9
1962	98.7	0.9
1963	98.5	1.0
1964	98.1	1.5
1965	97.7	1.6
1966	97.9	1.6
1967	97.8	1.6
1968	97.4	1.9
1969	97.4	1.9
1970	97.2	2.1
1971	96.7	2.2
1972	96.0	2.8
1973	96.0	2.8
1974	95.9	2.8
1975	95.2	3.0
1976	93.3	3.8
1977	92.9	4.0
1978	91.8	4.4
1979	89.5	5.3
1980	86.5	7.5
1981	86.0	8.0
1982	85.0	8.4
1983	83.5	9.1
1984	82.2	10.0
1985	79.3	12.8
1986	78.1	13.6
1987	77.5	14.0
1988	75.4	16.4
1989	74.8	17.2
1990	74.1	17.7
1991	73.5	18.1
1992	71.5	19.0
1993	71.1	19.2
1994	70.6	19.4
1995	68.4	20.0
1996	65.4	21.0
1997	63.5	21.4
1998	62.4	21.5
1999	61.1	21.6
2000	59.9	22.2
2001	58.6	22.8
2002	57.9	23.1
2003	56.7	23.4
2004	55.3	24.0
2005	54.7	24.3
2006	53.6	24.6
2007	53.0	24.7
2008	52.5	25.3

Source: Louisiana Commissioner of Elections/Louisiana Secretary of State.

often categorized by using the all-too-limited term "Christian Right." These social/cultural conservatives have formed the second part of the foundation of the Republican coalition in Louisiana.

When Republicans can combine the two appeals of pro-business conservatism and social/cultural conservatism, they are almost impossible to stop. The combination of suburban and rural parishes is a healthy one. Ronald Reagan was probably most adept at combining these messages. Mike Foster, who became only the second Republican elected governor in Louisiana and the first to be re-elected, became the prototype of Republican success. If Republicans field candidates that both groups—the "establishment" business conservatives and the "populist" cultural conservatives—find attractive, Republicans will win often in Louisiana.

THE TENACITY OF THE DEMOCRATIC PARTY

The continued appeal of the Democrats is quite naturally to groups other than those described above. When, in 1964, the Republican presidential candidate appealed to conservative whites with opposition to the Civil Rights and Voting Rights Act, black Louisianans of all demographic backgrounds began voting overwhelmingly Democratic. Before the Voting Rights Act, Louisiana's blacks were registered at low rates, due mainly to the restrictions on black voting that were later remedied by that act. Black turnout was higher in south Louisiana than in much of the rest of the Deep South, but still tellingly low. Black votes are concentrated in urban areas (notably Orleans Parish) and many rural parishes along the Mississippi River Delta.

The first significant statewide breakthrough for a black/white Democratic coalition came in the election of Edwin Edwards to the governorship in 1971 after he campaigned hard for black support. He rewarded that support by appointing blacks to visible positions and by backing black legislators for leadership positions on reapportionment and important policy positions on education, health, and welfare legislation. Many Democrats, like senators John Breaux and Bennett Johnston, followed this successful strategy. However, in 1995, when the first major black candidate for governor made the runoff for governor, a friction between black and white Democrats began to show. In that race, which will be covered extensively below, African American Congressman Cleo Fields did not receive the endorsement from many of the same white Democratic officeholders whom he and many black leaders had supported in previous years.

While black support for the Democratic Party is most noticeable, many whites continued to support the Democratic Party throughout the Republican realignment beginning in the 1960s. The parishes that straddle the Mississippi River between Baton Rouge and New Orleans are home to a vast chemical industry as well as a shrinking demographic group: southern white labor union Democrats. The parishes of Assumption, Ascension, Iberville, St. John the Baptist, and St. Charles are predominately white and core Democratic parishes. The Catholic, French-Acadian parishes of especially southwest Louisiana also are part of the Democratic base. This area, which covers roughly the Seventh Congressional District through the past several decades of redistricting, was the congressional home base of four-term governor Edwin Edwards and former Democratic senator John Breaux, who retired in 2004.

THE UNIQUENESS OF THE RULES:
LOUISIANA'S OPEN ELECTION SYSTEM

A brief explanation of Louisiana's unique election system must precede any discussion of Louisiana's contemporary electoral politics. In 1975 the Louisiana legislature, at the urging of Governor Edwin Edwards, adopted an electoral system that was seen as benefiting both the governor and incumbent legislators (Hadley 1985). The system is unique but straightforward. All candidates for office, regardless of party affiliation, run in one election, and any candidate who receives a majority of votes cast is elected. If no candidate receives a majority, the top two candidates, regardless of party affiliation, compete in a runoff. Unlike the newly adopted California system and similar systems in other states, the Louisiana system allows two Democrats or two Republicans to compete in the final election.

Governor Edwards proposed and legislators supported the new system because under it they would often hold an advantage. Incumbents could win outright in the first election, thereby avoiding the cost and unpredictability of running in a general election against an opponent of the other party who, even if not well known, could depend on party support or coattails in a general election. In 2005, the state legislature voted to continue this election system for all state offices but to return to a party primary and general election system for U.S. Senate and House of Representatives elections.

ALMOST "DUKED" OUT:
THE FRAGILE PARTY COALITIONS OF THE 1990s

As the 1996 elections approached, the two parties in Louisiana were in similar positions. Each had a coalition that was formidable when united, but highly vulnerable when divided. Perhaps stated oversimply, the Republicans were an uneasy coalition of suburban business conservatives and more rural cultural conservatives; the Democrats were a coalition of most blacks, some labor, and a small number of socially liberal urban whites. Even though the form of the coalitions is similar to those nationally, the proportions and opportunities for disruption differ.

The gubernatorial elections of 1991 and 1995 are particularly instructive. In 1991, in perhaps the most spectacular election in a state with a history of spectacular elections, Louisianans were faced with three major candidates for governor. The first and early favorite was incumbent governor Charles "Buddy" Roemer, who was elected in 1987 as a Democrat and had become a Republican while in office after having alienated the conservative wing by not signing a restrictive abortion bill. The second was three-term former Democratic governor Edwin Edwards. Edwards, as noted above, was initially elected with a black/labor/Cajun coalition that was a winning combination for the Democrats in the 1970s. Edwards had enjoyed wildly enthusiastic and high approval ratings until he was tried for racketeering in the middle of his second term; although he was acquitted, the trial tainted his image and his effectiveness and approval ratings plummeted. Finally, the ballot included Republican David Duke, known internationally as the former Grand Wizard of the Ku Klux Klan (KKK). He had won a seat in the Louisiana House of Representatives and had garnered a striking 40 percent of the vote in his 1990 race for the U.S. Senate against incumbent Bennett Johnston. In the first election, Edwards ran first with solid support of black voters and some labor support. Duke ran second with a strong showing especially in the rural white areas of north Louisiana. Roemer, who had the support of Democrats who had turned against Edwards after his trial and pro-business Republicans, finished out of the running. Since no one got a majority of the votes, Edwards and Duke were in a runoff.

The Duke-Edwards race offered two choices that were widely disdained by a large proportion of the voters. Democrat Edwards had become unpopular because of perceived unethical and even criminal behavior. Republican Duke's association with the KKK and use of racist rhetoric caused him to be despised by much of the electorate. Almost all prominent Republican officials refused to support Duke and even endorsed Democrat Edwards. In the end, a bumper sticker summed up the sentiments of much of the electorate: "Vote for the Crook: It's Important." After an election that created an international media circus, Edwards easily won the runoff. The Republican Party in the state had not only lost an election, but had to cope with having David Duke as its most visible politician.

The 1995 governor's race illustrated the fact that Republicans were not alone in confronting potentially fatal splits. In that year, several well-known Democrats faced only two Republicans. The Republicans appeared to be in a state of disarray: The candidate endorsed at the state

convention, suburban New Orleans state representative Quentin Das-
tugue, chose not run, which left only former governor "Buddy" Roemer
and little-known Democratic state senator Mike Foster, who switched his
party affiliation the day he filed to run for office. The same ballot featured
four well-known and well-funded Democrats who would have been
"firsts" as governors of Louisiana: two women, Lieutenant Governor
Melinda Schweggman and state treasurer Mary Landrieu, and African
American members of Congress Cleo Fields and William Jefferson.

Even though Roemer had lost support from the Christian Right, he was
expected to run well based on name recognition. Among the Democrats,
Landrieu, who had announced her candidacy a year earlier, a move that
angered incumbent governor Edwards (who had not yet announced his
own intentions), was seen as the most likely to make a runoff. A Roemer-
Landrieu runoff, however, was not to be.

Foster eventually emerged as the choice of the Christian Right. In a bril-
liant campaign move, he ran as a "Christian and a gun owner" in ads that
had this millionaire businessman wearing a welder's cap. In the last few
weeks of the campaign, Foster surged to the top of the opinion polls.
Fields, who benefited from the other black congressman's exit from the
race , moved into second place, edging out Landrieu and leaving Roemer
behind in fourth place.

The days and weeks of the Foster-Fields runoff proved to be a night-
mare for Democratic cohesion. A feud between Fields and Landrieu
erupted as the result of a very heated contest to make the runoff. Fields
became upset because Landrieu and others in her campaign allegedly
warned African American voters that Fields could not win in the runoff
election and that Landrieu could. In effect, the allegation was that African
Americans should not waste their vote to achieve symbolic satisfaction
when they could help elect someone who would be just as mindful of
their interests as Fields would.

Fields attacked Landrieu for that allegation, and Landrieu had to pub-
licly deny that her campaign had made such statements. Fields's public
criticism of Landrieu probably mobilized enough African American support to place second in the election and thus qualify for the runoff. Landrieu blamed her failure to make the runoff on Fields's public attack and
vented her frustration by not endorsing his candidacy. In the runoff,
Fields lost to Mike Foster by a landslide.

As Louisiana entered the 1996 elections for president, an open U.S. Senate seat, and all seven seats in the U.S. House of Representatives, both
parties had reason to be concerned about party unity. Democrats had reason for concern after the Fields/Landrieu conflict in the governor's race
because now it was Fields's turn to be upset. Landrieu entered the U.S.
Senate race less than a year after the gubernatorial election and was im-

mediately anointed by the polls as the front-runner. Although she slipped to second place in the first election, Landrieu made it into the runoff against Republican state senator Woody Jenkins. Public opinion polls throughout the runoff period indicated an evenly contested campaign. Initially, Fields refused to endorse Landrieu. Although several prominent African American political leaders endorsed Landrieu, including Congressman William Jefferson and New Orleans Mayor Marc Morial, the majority of African Americans appeared to be taking their cue from Fields. Until Fields decided to endorse Landrieu, African Americans faced a very uncomfortable choice: either vote for Jenkins or abstain.

The Democratic Party leadership was in no position to negotiate between Fields and Landrieu. Fields was upset with the party's white leaders for refusing to endorse him in the gubernatorial election but enthusiastically endorsing Landrieu in the Senate runoff. Fields believed that this double standard was due to his race. It is difficult to argue that Fields's belief is not meritorious. Ultimately, the National Democratic Party, in the person of Vice President Al Gore, had to intervene to settle the dispute between Fields and Landrieu. The Louisiana contest had national implications, as President Clinton was attempting to reestablish Democratic control of the U.S. Senate. Gore convinced Fields to endorse Landrieu, but Fields's endorsement was not enthusiastic.

If the Fields/Landrieu conflict was simply a personality clash, it would be difficult to derive any lasting meaning that would facilitate scholarly understanding of Louisiana politics, since personality clashes often occur in American politics. We believe that in the Fields/Landrieu struggle there is an underlying basis to the feud that helps to illuminate scholarly understanding of Louisiana politics.

The Fields/Landrieu feud represents a growing tension between African Americans and moderate and liberal whites, currently the two mainstays in the Democratic Party's coalition. This tension is erupting in southern politics faster than elsewhere because growing Republicanization of political leadership has siphoned away conservative party leaders from the Democratic Party. This development has made it possible for African Americans and moderate and liberal whites to vie for leadership positions in the Democratic Party in the South for the first time since African Americans became active players in the South in the mid-1960s. The split would return again and again and cost Democrats some seats and some loyal following.

Republicans had problems of their own. Despite the tension in the Democratic Party, Republicans were unable to win the seat. In the first election, two Democrats were leading the pack and appeared likely to squeeze the Republicans out of the runoff. In the final weeks of the first election, key Republican leaders began endorsing Jenkins, who was consistently polling best among the Republican contenders. By the final days of the first election, the Republican strategy had worked and Jenkins roared into first place, with Landrieu second.

Jenkins, who clearly represented the more rural conservative wing of the party, had trouble gaining support that might have gone to more suburban conservatives and barely lost the election to Landrieu. Indeed, in the ABC exit poll, 66 percent of self-described "moderates" voted for Landrieu. Although Landrieu was widely criticized by the Jenkins campaign for being an extremist primarily because of her pro-choice stance, in the end, it was Jenkins who lost the support of the middle. The Republicans, by fielding a candidate who was perceived as too conservative by moderates, missed a golden opportunity to capture an open Senate seat.

At the end of 1996, both parties were in a state of conflict and were also highly competitive. Democrats had successfully brought blacks and whites together for a resounding win for President Clinton, but had barely found a way to hold on to the Senate seat, even with probably reluctant but strong black support for Mary Landrieu. The Republicans had almost pulled together behind a candidate with visible ties to the conservative wing of the party, but found themselves just short of a victory. This race illustrates well the splits in both parties and suggests that in years to come, success for one party may well depend on failure of the opposite party to heal its divisions. But perhaps more importantly, the closeness of the race suggested that Republicans, even with a candidate perceived to be out of the mainstream, were becoming a more and more powerful force.

A NEW EQUILIBRIUM: INCUMBENCY AND REPUBLICAN ADVANTAGE

The nine years between the 1996 Landrieu win and the 2005 hurricanes were an oddly stable interlude in Louisiana politics. Incumbency, moderate stances, and healthy two-party competition marked by an emerging Republican Party were the hallmark of those years. Incumbent Democratic senator John Breaux was easily reelected in 1998, incumbent Republican governor Mike Foster was easily reelected in 1999, Louisiana voters helped reelect Republican George W. Bush in 2000, and in 2002 Democratic senator Mary Landrieu was reelected in a close election. In 2003, Louisiana elected its first female governor, former lieutenant governor Kathleen Blanco, a Democrat, over a young Indian American health administrator, Republican Bobby Jindal. Both were seen as moderate, reform candidates in a truly historic election. In 2004, Republican muscle began to show more clearly. Republican congressman David Vitter easily beat two well-known Democrats to become Louisiana's first elected Republican in the U.S. Senate. and incumbent Republican president George W. Bush easily won the state.

The partisan shift was most pronounced in the formerly more competitive French-Catholic parishes in south Louisiana, or as Louisianans know it, "Acadiana." Social issues, especially abortion, seemed to drive Republican votes steadily higher among these voters. This trend in this part of the state played a significant role in helping Republicans win a congressional seat, the Senate seat, and two presidential elections in the years 2000 and 2004. The increasingly visible emphasis of the Catholic Church on the abortion issue appears to be the force behind the trend. That stance is clearly associated with the Republican Party nationally and is one that Louisiana Democrats have a difficult time distancing themselves from, even if their own position on the issue is the same as Republicans'. This issue may well have tipped the partisan balance in Louisiana from "leans Democratic" to "leans Republican." It was the 1996 U.S. Senate race that was barely won by the Democrat over a weak Republican that exposed the strength of the issue.

Those nine years in Louisiana led most analysts to conclude that the dynamics of Louisiana's politics were beginning to take shape as a fairly stable system, where incumbents and Republicans were at a slight advantage. Then scandals hit, rules changed, and hurricanes intruded. Republicans and incumbents still had the advantage, but the dynamics of individual elections were extraordinarily affected by these extraneous causes.

HURRICANES, SCANDALS, AND REPUBLICAN CONSOLIDATION IN 2008

In 2005, Hurricane Katrina and, to a much lesser extent, Hurricane Rita hit the political landscape with almost the same fury as they hit the physical one. Governor Kathleen Blanco, fairly or unfairly, received the brunt of the blame and decided not to run for reelection. Former Democratic senator John Breaux spoke of running, freezing the fundraising of any other possible Democratic candidate. When Breaux finally decided against the run, Republican congressman Bobby Jindal found himself alone in a field of relatively unknown Democratic opponents and was swept into office in 2007 with a large mandate. He instantly became a towering figure in Louisiana politics, a Republican who had successfully combined the business-oriented Republican supporters in the suburbs with the more rural cultural conservatives throughout the state. His successes brought him national attention, and his name is regularly mentioned as a future contender for the Republican presidential nomination.

If the hurricanes had destroyed Governor Blanco's chances for reelection, they had the opposite effect on Louisiana's other prominent female Democratic officeholder, U.S. senator Mary Landrieu. Her performance during the two years after the hurricanes, in very visibly garnering resources in Congress for rebuilding both the mainland and the coast, helped her push aside all of the national press talk of her being the most vulnerable Democratic U.S. senator in the 2008 election cycle, and she comfortably won reelection to a third term by securing strong support in the heavily Republican parishes surrounding New Orleans that were affected by the hurricanes.

While the impact of Hurricane Katrina is widely understood to have helped elect Republican Bobby Jindal and reelect Democratic senator Mary Landrieu, the impact of the two hurricanes of 2008, Gustav and Ike, is less widely known. Hurricane Gustav struck Louisiana on the weekend when Louisiana's party primaries were to be held for congressional elections, and the elections were postponed. This postponement pushed runoffs to November 4; the national general election and the congressional general elections in two districts were held a month later. With President Barack Obama on the November 4 ballot, reliably Democratic African American turnout was high, but without him on the ballot a month later, it fell, leaving Republicans at an advantage thanks to the timing. Indeed, Republicans won a highly competitive open seat in northwest Louisiana, and, in a stunner, were able to defeat Louisiana's only African American congressman, scandal-plagued William Jefferson, in New Orleans.

The Hurricane Gustav election postponement was not the only bad news for Democratic congressional candidates in 2008. Democrat Don Cazayoux, who had won a special election to replace Republican congressman Richard Baker in the Baton Rouge area, found himself in a race for reelection with not only a Republican candidate but an African American state representative who ran against him in the Democratic primary. When Cazayoux won renomination, the African American challenger switched to become an independent in the fall 2008 election, effectively ceding the race to the Republican.

Democratic senator Mary Landrieu won the most prominent race in Louisiana in 2008. However, 2008 was generally a banner year for Republicans. Republican presidential candidate John McCain won by an even larger margin than President Bush had four years earlier, and six of the seven congressional seats were now in Republican hands.

With a presidential win, a governor, a U.S. senator, and six of seven congressional seats, Louisiana for the first time appeared to be a dominant Republican state. However, Democrats still barely controlled both houses of the state legislature and the other U.S. Senate seat, as well as a host of local offices. The future of the partisan balance in the state will remain uncertain, with Republican U.S. senator David Vitter, who admitted to a "very serious sin" in a prostitution scandal, running for reelection in 2010 and a congressional reapportionment that is almost certain to remove one seat from Louisiana's seven-member delegation.

THE DEVELOPMENT OF BLACK POLITICS IN LOUISIANA

The ascent of the Republican Party is only half of the story of Louisiana politics in the last few decades. Equally dramatic is the emergence of African Americans as a potent political force. Blacks in Louisiana, similar to the situation in most southern states, began to reemerge politically in the immediate post–World War II years. As a result of the well-known and successful efforts by southern states to formally suppress black political participation between 1890 and 1910 (see Kousser 1974), the substantial black political participation that had ensued from the Reconstruction era was eventually reduced to a bare minimum between 1910 and 1945 in most southern states. The nation's participation in World War II unleashed a confluence of political, social, and economic forces that opened opportunities for southern blacks to begin redeveloping a political presence. This political reemergence took the form of increased voter registration by blacks, as seen in table 5.3.

Table 5.3.   Black Voter Registration in Louisiana, 1910–1964

Year	Black Registration	Estimated Black Population	Percentage of Black Population Registered to Vote
1910	730	174,211	0.4
1920	3,533	359,351	0.9
1928	2,054	359,251	0.5
1932	1,591	415,047	0.3
1936	1,981	415,047	0.4
1940	886	473,562	0.1
1944	1,672	473,562	0.3
1948	28,177	473,562	5
1952	107,844	481,284	22
1954	112,789	481,284	23
1956	152,578	481,284	31
1960	158,765	514,589	30
1962	150,878	514,589	29
1964	164,717	514,589	32

Source: James Bolner, ed. *Louisiana Politics: Festival in a Labyrinth*. Baton Rouge: Louisiana State University Press, 1982, p. 299. The data for 1910 are for black males only. Women were not allowed to vote prior to the ratification of the Nineteenth Amendment to the United States Constitution in 1920.

The white primary essentially denied blacks effective participation in the political process, since the dominance of the Democratic Party meant that the only viable electoral competition occurred in the Democratic primary. The Democratic nominee always won the general election because the Republican Party was not strong enough to mount a serious challenge. Realizing the white primary system was denying them political participation, most blacks were not inspired to attempt to overcome other formal as well as informal efforts to suppress their political participation during this period. After the elimination of the white primary by *Smith v. Allwright*, black voter registration in Louisiana increased considerably in the 1950s and the first half of the 1960s (see table 5.4).

The Voting Rights Act of 1965 accelerated the rate of black political participation in the state as it did in the entire South. African Americans in 1997 comprised 30 percent of the registered voters in the state. There were two major consequences of the significant increase in black voter registration following the enactment of the 1965 Voting Rights Act. One was an increase in the number of moderate and liberal white Democrats elected to office with the help of black voters. The other consequence has been a significant increase in the number of black elected officials. These two developments occurred chronologically in the order in which they are presented in this discussion. One of us (Perry 1990a, 1983) has suggested elsewhere that this sequence has occurred with enough regularity in the development of black politics to be considered a pattern of black political participation.

Turning to the first impact, the earliest consequence of significantly increased black political participation usually results in the election of first moderate and then liberal white candidates (Perry 1990b, 1983). The election of Moon Landrieu, a white liberal and father of Mary Landrieu, as mayor of New Orleans in 1967 occurred precisely in this manner. Similarly, in 1971, black voters exerted a critical impact on the election of Edwin W. Edwards, a U.S. congressman from southwest Louisiana, to the governorship. Edwards defeated state senator Bennett Johnston in the Democratic primary principally because of the overwhelming support he received from black voters.

In the general election, Edwards received 202,055 black votes, as compared to only 10,709 for Republican Dave Treen (Prestage and Williams 1982). Since Edwards's margin of victory was about 160,000 votes, black support constituted the critical difference. That black voters were able to cast decisive voter support for Edwards was attributable to the fact that Edwards and Treen split the white vote, with Edwards receiving 30,000 fewer white votes than Treen (Prestage and Williams 1982, 307–308).

In 1972, state senator Johnston ran successfully for the U.S. Senate seat, receiving the majority of the black vote. Johnston defeated former governor John J. McKeithen. In the 1967 Landrieu election, the 1971 Edwards/

Table 5.4. Black Voter Registration in Louisiana, 1965–2008

Year	Total Voter Registration	Black Registration (LA Board of Registration)	Percentage of Black Registered Voters (LA Board of Registration)
1965	1,190,122	163,414	13.7
1966	1,281,919	238,356	18.6
1967	1,285,933	245,275	19.1
1968	1,411,071	279,468	19.8
1969	1,422,900	291,547	20.5
1970	1,438,727	298,054	20.7
1971	1,633,181	347,098	21.3
1972	1,704,890	397,158	22.3
1973	1,712,850	380,490	22.2
1974	1,726,693	391,666	22.7
1975	1,798,032	408,696	22.7
1976	1,866,117	420,697	22.5
1977	1,787,031	413,178	23.2
1978	1,821,026	429,231	23.6
1979	1,831,507	431,196	23.5
1980	2,015,402	465,005	23.0
1981	1,942,941	454,988	23.4
1982	1,965,422	474,238	24.1
1983	1,968,898	476,618	24.2
1984	2,133,363	533,526	25.0
1985	2,175,264	550,225	25.3
1986	2,141,263	549,916	25.7
1987	2,139,861	551,263	25.8
1988	2,190,634	572,133	26.1
1989	2,113,867	552,781	26.2
1990	2,121,302	561,379	26.5
1991	2,103,334	569,603	27.1
1992	2,241,949	626,678	27.9
1993	2,294,043	636,018	27.7
1994	2,257,080	628,578	27.8
1995	2,400,086	689,046	28.7
1996	2,518,896	724,831	28.8
1997	2,628,778	758,113	28.8
1998	2,686,560	773,935	28.8
1999	2,720,573	785,813	28.9
2000	2,725,473	788,685	28.9
2001	2,763,121	803,017	29.1
2002	2,719,540	794,915	29.2
2003	2,786,940	820,373	29.4
2004	2,924,895	871,541	29.8
2005	2,842,443	846,252	29.8
2006	2,893,674	862,857	29.8
2007	2,831,831	845,163	29.8
2008	2,940,985	902,160	30.7

Sources: Data for 1965 to 1979 were taken from James Bolner, ed. *Louisiana Politics: Festival in a Labyrinth*. Baton Rouge: Louisiana State University Press, 1982, p. 305. Data for 1980 to 1996 were provided by the Office of the Louisiana Commissioner of Elections, Baton Rouge. Data for 1997 through 2008 were provided by the Louisiana Secretary of State Office, Baton Rouge.

Johnston gubernatorial election, and the 1972 Johnston/McKeithen U.S. Senate election, black voters cast the decisive vote for the more progressive candidates. Edwards's 1971 gubernatorial victory and Johnston's 1972 U.S. Senate victory established these two men as fixtures in Louisiana politics for the next twenty-five years. Edwards and Johnston won easy reelection to office in 1976 and 1978, respectively, both receiving substantial support from black voters.

The influence of black Louisianans in the 1980 state election was mixed. In the gubernatorial race that year, Edwards could not run for a third term because the state's constitution prohibits a governor from serving more than two consecutive terms. This was the year that Louisiana's new open elections system went into effect. Republican Treen defeated the Democratic candidate, Louis Lambert, despite strong African American support.

African Americans had a more positive influence on the 1986 U.S. Senate race. Russell Long, the senior U.S. senator, had earlier announced that he was going to retire from the Senate at the end of the term. John Breaux, a young Democratic U.S. congressman, won this race with substantial support from African Americans.

In 1983, Edwards ran for governor against the incumbent Republican governor Treen. This was an evenly contested campaign from start to finish, and in the end Edwards won a narrow victory over Treen with overwhelming support from African American voters. This was a disappointing defeat for Treen because he had appointed three African Americans to major positions in his administration and had openly sought the African American vote in the 1983 campaign.

The 1986 U.S. Senate race took place against the national backdrop of the popular Republican president Ronald Reagan having been reelected in 1984. John Breaux, a popular Democratic congressman, ran against Henson Moore, a popular Republican congressman. Polls conducted deep into the campaign showed Moore leading Breaux by a considerable margin. At just about the time it was widely believed Breaux was not going to win reelection to a second term, a news story broke that the state's Republican Party leadership had plans to conduct a statewide effort to remove African American voters from the rolls of registered voters. This news energized African American voters to turn out to vote at a very high level in support of Breaux. It also caused a fair number of white voters, who probably were going to vote for Moore but who were repulsed by this effort, to vote for Breaux. There is no doubt that the overwhelming support that Breaux received from an energized African American electorate was responsible for his election.

In the 1990 U.S. Senate election, the incumbent Democrat Johnston received a very strong challenge from former Klansman David Duke. Although Duke received 60 percent of the white vote, Johnston won the election with overwhelming support from an energized African American electorate.

In the 1987 gubernatorial race, Edwards placed second in the open primary election behind Buddy Roemer, a U.S. congressman from north Louisiana. Edwards decided to drop out of the race, and Roemer became governor. In 1991, Edwards ran for governor for the fifth time. This time he placed first in the open primary and entered into a runoff against David Duke. Edwards won the election with strong support from African American voters. In 1995, in a historic gubernatorial election, former U.S. congressman Cleo Fields from Baton Rouge made the runoff against Republican state senator Mike Foster. Fields was the first African American to run in a runoff election in Louisiana history. Although Fields received substantial support from African American voters, he lost the election by a landslide margin.

The substantial increase in black voter registration also resulted in increased numbers of black elected officials. In 1968, there were thirty-six black elected officials in Louisiana. Ten years later, in 1978, the number of black elected officials in Louisiana had increased to 333. As Jewel L. Prestage and Carolyn Sue Williams indicate (1982, 306), practically all of these were local officials and most were elected from predominately black constituencies.

It is a trend in American politics that the higher level, more prestigious elected offices are the most difficult for blacks to win. Louisiana was no exception in this regard. The first black elected to the state legislature, Ernest "Dutch" Morial, was elected to the Louisiana House of Representatives in 1967. After Morial resigned to accept a judgeship, he was replaced in 1971 by Dorothy Mae Taylor, the first black woman ever to serve in the Louisiana legislature. In 1972, seven other blacks were elected to the state Senate. In 1974, Sidney Barthelemy became the first black ever elected to the state Senate. By 1980, the number of blacks elected to the state legislature had increased to twelve—ten in the House and two in the Senate (Prestage and Williams 1982, 306–307). Additionally, in 1977, Morial made history for a second time when he was elected the first black mayor of New Orleans.

The 1970s represented a watershed period for black officeholding in Louisiana. During this decade, blacks were able to win elections to both houses of the Louisiana legislature and to the mayorship of the largest city in the state. In the 1980s, the number of blacks elected to the state legislature more than tripled. The city of New Orleans has had a continuous history of black mayoral leadership since Dutch Morial's historic mayoral election in 1977. Morial served two terms as mayor and was prohibited by the city's charter from serving beyond two terms. Morial unsuccessfully attempted to have the voters amend the city's charter so that he could run for a third term.

Morial was succeeded by Sidney Barthelemy, who was a former president of the New Orleans City Council and Morial's chief nemesis on the city council. Barthelemy, New Orleans's second black mayor, also served two mayoral terms. Barthelemy was succeeded by Dutch Morial's son Marc Morial, who was a Louisiana state senator prior to his election as mayor. All three of these African American mayors, except Barthelemy in his election to his first term, won because of overwhelming support from African American voters. In his election to his first term as mayor, Barthelemy ran a deracialized campaign in which he received a majority of the white and a minority of the African American vote (see Perry 1990c). In this election, Barthelemy defeated the strong African American candidate William Jefferson, who was a U.S. congressman representing the Second Congressional District, which includes most of New Orleans. Jefferson was the first African American elected to the U.S. Congress from Louisiana since Reconstruction.

CONCLUSION

In the last half century, Louisiana politics has been revolutionized in two ways. First, the Republican Party, which was virtually noncompetitive in Louisiana elections, has emerged to almost parity with the once-dominant Democratic Party. Second, African Americans, who compose almost one-third of the population, have risen from formal suppression to positions of power. This chapter provides a context and a current snapshot of these ongoing revolutions. In sum, Republicans have won several statewide offices including the governorship, control the state congressional delegation, and have made dramatic gains in the legislature. The party still must contend with conflicts within before becoming the dominant party in the state. African Americans have gained tremendous ground in breaking registration barriers and winning local offices and congressional seats, but have yet to overcome the patterns of the past by winning a statewide office.

With the successes of Republicans statewide in the early 2000s, African American strength weakened somewhat as members of statewide winning coalitions. However, African Americans have enjoyed some stunning successes in local elections, with African Americans becoming mayors of Baton Rouge and Shreveport in addition to New Orleans. The most striking success was in 2008, when Baton Rouge mayor "Kip" Holden won reelection with 71 percent of the vote in his majority-white constituency.

After the hurricanes and the lopsided loss of the presidential candidate Barack Obama in the state, African American successes have waned somewhat. However, with some dramatic local wins and the generalized positive feeling from the national win of President Barack Obama, African American efficacy and optimism are likely to grow.

REFERENCES

Bolner, James, ed.1982. *Louisiana Politics: Festival in a Labyrinth*. Baton Rouge: Louisiana State University Press.

Hadley, Charles. 1985. "Dual Partisan Identification in the South." *Journal of Politics* 47:254–268.

Kousser, Morgan J. 1974. *The Shaping of Southern Politics: Suffrage Restriction and the Establishment of the One-Party South, 1880–1910*. New Haven, CT: Yale University Press.

Perry, Huey L. 1983. "The Impact of Black Political Participation on Public Sector Employment and Representation on Municipal Boards and Commissions." *Review of Black Political Economy* 12 (Winter):203–217.

———. 1990a. "Black Politics and Mayoral Leadership in Birmingham and New Orleans." *National Political Science Review* 2:154–160.

———. 1990b. "The Evolution and Impact of Biracial Coalitions and Black Mayors in Birmingham and New Orleans." In *Racial Politics in American Cities*, ed. Rufus P. Browning, Dale Rogers Marshall, and David H. Tabb. White Plains, NY: Longman.

———. 1990c. "The Reelection of Sidney Barthelemy as Mayor of New Orleans." In *Racial Politics in American Cities*, 2nd ed., ed. Huey L. Perry, Rufus P. Browning, Dale Rogers Marshall, and David H. Tabb. New York: Longman.

Prestage, Jewel L., and Carolyn Sue Williams. 1982. "Blacks in Louisiana." In *Louisiana Politics: Festival in a Labyrinth*, ed. James Bolner. Baton Rouge: Louisiana State University Press.

2

THE RIM SOUTH STATES

6

Virginia

From Red to Blue?

Mark J. Rozell

For the Democratic Party, the 2008 elections represented the culmination of a major shift in Virginia politics. By winning Virginia in the Electoral College, Barack Obama became the first Democrat to prevail in a presidential contest in that state since the Lyndon Johnson national landslide in 1964. Johnson barely won in the state, and in 1976 Democrat Jimmy Carter won every southern state except Virginia.

Obama carried the state by a comfortable margin, winning 52.7 percent of the popular vote to John McCain's 46.4 percent. And in an open seat U.S. Senate campaign that year featuring two former governors as the major party nominees, Democrat Mark Warner crushed Republican Jim Gilmore 65.0 percent to 33.8 percent.[1] The Democrats picked up three seats in the House of Representatives: two in which relative newcomers defeated previously solid incumbent GOP members, and a third open seat where there also was a party switch from Republican to Democrat.

Virginia offers an ideal environment in which to study the changing politics of the South. Once the capital of the confederacy, it is the first state in the nation to have elected a black governor. Infamous for its massive resistance to public school integration in the 1950s and still subject to Justice Department approval of its legislative redistricting because of a poor history of protecting minority voting rights, the state is undergoing a profound demographic transformation that is changing the nature of racial politics and partisan competition.

Once a part of the "solid [Democratic] South," in the 1990s Virginia became a Republican-dominated state, before moving back to being

Democrat-dominated again in the new century. At one point in the 1990s, the GOP controlled the state legislature and the three top statewide offices (governor, lieutenant governor, and attorney general). Yet in 2001, the Democrats broke a string of Republican gubernatorial victories and then won the governorship again in 2005. The Democrats have taken back control of one house of the state legislature and also now hold both U.S. Senate seats and a majority of members of the House of Representatives.

The Democratic Party that is dominant in the state today is nothing like the party during the era of the Solid South. Indeed, for many years a Democratic political machine stymied constructive change and kept the party distant from its national organization and leaders. By the 1980s, Virginia Democratic leaders were pointing the way toward a more centrist philosophy that would better promote the party's chances of winning the presidency in the 1990s. Today the Democratic Party at the state and national levels does not look all that different anymore, and the governor of the Commonwealth, Tim Kaine, even serves as chair of the Democratic National Committee.

More than in most states, many residents of Virginia are strongly aware of their political heritage, both good and bad. Citizens and leaders wage heated political fights over proposals to build homes or retail establishments on undeveloped lands that were once sites of Civil War battles. Although demographic changes have altered the electoral landscape, much of the culture of Virginia remains conservative in the old sense: enamored of tradition and resistant to change.

At times the cultural resistance to accept change has opened the state to ridicule. When Congress approved a national holiday to honor Martin Luther King Jr., the state legislature responded by declaring that date Jackson-Lee-King Day to also honor Confederate heroes Stonewall Jackson and Robert E. Lee. Black members of the state legislature responded on that celebrated date by carrying picture posters of their preferred honorees: Jesse Jackson, Spike Lee, and Martin Luther King Jr. In 2001, after seventeen years, the combined holiday practice was discontinued and Virginia celebrated Martin Luther King Jr. Day. Lee-Jackson Day became a separate day of observance in the Old Dominion.

The capital city of Richmond was mired for several years in a bitter debate over where to place a statue to a black hometown hero, former tennis star Arthur Ashe, who had died from AIDS. The city council and residents initially could not agree to place the statue on historic Monument Avenue, which honors Confederate heroes with imposing statues. The city first agreed to place the statue at a public park, but then, in light of heavy criticism, ultimately honored Ashe with the Monument Avenue location.

The historically all-male, state-supported Virginia Military Institute attracted national attention when it fought a seven-year-long legal battle with the U.S. Department of Justice to maintain the school's single-sex status. In June 1996, the Supreme Court mandated that VMI admit women. Emotions ran deep regarding the Court's decision. In January 1997, GOP state senator Warren Barry addressed the legislative chamber and declared that women had no place at VMI because they were "physiologically different" from men, their presence in the military caused sexual harassment, and "aggressive warrior" men shouldn't be forced "to live in a social slumber party." Most Republican members and some Democrats applauded the speech (Hsu 1997).

For decades the state legislature resisted calls to retire the official state song "Carry Me Back to Old Virginny." Although the lyrics had long been justifiably criticized for being racist, lawmakers defended its standing in a bow to tradition. Finally, in 1997 the state legislature struck a compromise in which it approved a measure to give the song "emeritus" status and to commission the search for a new official state song.

Former GOP governor Jim Gilmore opened wounds with his declaration in 1998 of a Confederate History Month. NAACP leaders strongly protested, and some threatened to encourage an economic boycott of the state. Gilmore earned some praise from black leaders when he championed separate official celebrations for Lee-Jackson and for King. Yet others weren't satisfied because they would have preferred to drop the official day recognizing the southern Civil War heroes altogether.

In 2009, after many years of failed attempts, the state legislature and the governor agreed on a measure to ban smoking in restaurants and bars. The traditional tobacco-growing state and home to Philip Morris Company thus became the first state of the Old South to enact such a ban. Yet the ban was able to be passed only because it provided for significant exceptions to allow smoking in private clubs and in ventilated rooms or outdoor patios at restaurants and bars.

These controversies are among many that are illustrative of the modern contradictions of Virginia politics resulting from the reverence for tradition and the need for change. Virginia has progressed enormously in the modern era yet in many ways it remains a bastion of old-style southern politics.

THE CHANGING POLITICS OF RACE AND PARTY COMPETITION

In his seminal work *Southern Politics in State and Nation*, written over half a century ago, V. O. Key described Virginia as a "political museum piece."

He added that, "of all the American states, Virginia can lay claim to the most thorough control by an oligarchy" (Key 1949, 19). At that time, the Democratic political machine of Harry F. Byrd dominated state politics. Byrd served as governor of Virginia from 1926 to 1930 and as U.S. senator from 1933 until he retired in 1965. He assembled his machine from the county courthouse organizations of the landed gentry, who preferred stability over economic growth and who were fiercely committed to racial segregation.[2]

The machine succeeded in part by restricting participation; in 1945, just 6 percent of the eligible adult population voted in the gubernatorial primary, which, in a one-party state, was the only election that mattered (Sabato 1977, 110). Frank Atkinson described how the state literacy requirement restricted participation by whites as well as blacks. He noted that prospective registrants had to answer extraordinarily difficult questions; they were asked, for example, how many people signed the Declaration of Independence, or to name the counties in the Twenty-seventh Judicial District. One college graduate who failed the test received a postcard saying "Yo hav fald to rechister" (Atkinson 1992, 15).

Although the Democratic Party had a minority faction of "antiorganization" members, Key described them as "extraordinarily weak, [having] few leaders of ability, and [being] more of a hope than a reality" (Key 1949, 21). Republicans were few and far between, and their candidates had no hope of winning a general election. In this way, Virginia resembled many other southern states—overwhelmingly conservative, overwhelmingly Democratic. During the 1950s, Virginia's Democratic machine led a massive resistance to school desegregation, choosing to actually close the public schools rather than obey a federal court order.

Like other southern states, Virginia supported Democratic presidential nominees throughout the early part of the twentieth century. The state's electorate defected to the Republicans only in 1928, when the Democrats nominated a Roman Catholic, Al Smith, who opposed prohibition. But Byrd himself feuded with Franklin Roosevelt and Harry Truman and dissented from the growing Democratic support of greater civil rights for blacks. Byrd openly expressed his contempt for "Trumanism" and signaled to state Democrats that it was acceptable to vote Republican at the presidential level.

In the 1944 presidential election and thereafter, Virginia supported Republican presidential candidates in every election except the Lyndon Johnson landslide of 1964. In their classic study of southern politics, Earl and Merle Black show that in the period between 1952 and 1964, Virginia was more supportive of Republican presidential candidates than any other southern state (Black and Black 1987, 266). Many of the conservative Democrats of the Byrd machine were more comfortable with Republican presidential candidates than with their more liberal Democratic opponents. In the post-Byrd era, Virginia remained solidly Republican at the presidential level. In 1976, Virginia was the only southern state to back GOP nominee Gerald Ford over Jimmy Carter. When many other southern states were backing Democrats Bill Clinton and Al Gore in 1992, 1996, and 2000, Virginia backed George Bush, Bob Dole, and George W. Bush.

After World War II, the population growth in the southwestern coal mining counties, the naval activity around Norfolk and Newport News, and the growing number of government workers in the northern Virginia suburbs of Washington, DC, changed the demographic makeup of the state and weakened the Byrd machine. The influx of black voters and the elimination of the poll tax after passage of the Voting Rights Act further weakened the machine. Byrd-machine candidates faced intraparty challenges; most notably, incumbent Democratic senator A. Willis Robertson, father of Rev. Marion G. "Pat" Robertson, lost a primary election in 1966.

As the national Democratic Party moved to the left, many of the more conservative members of the Byrd machine turned to the Republican Party. Moreover, the influx of relatively affluent professionals in northern Virginia and of pro-military citizens in the Norfolk region provided growing numbers of Republican voters. In 1969, with the Byrd machine in disarray, Virginia elected as its first Republican governor a progressive on race issues who drew attention by enrolling his daughter in the predominantly black Richmond public schools. The Republicans won again in 1973 with a candidate who took a less progressive stance on race issues, and again in 1977 with a moderate candidate.

By the late 1970s, Republicans held both the state's U.S. Senate seats and nine of Virginia's ten seats in the U.S. House of Representatives. Virginia moved toward the Republican ranks more rapidly than did other southern states. Between 1951 and 1980 Virginia elected more Republican governors than any other southern state (Sabato 1983, table 4-7).

THE 1980s ERA OF DEMOCRATIC DOMINANCE

The period of Republican control ended in 1981, when Democratic lieutenant governor Charles S. "Chuck" Robb defeated Attorney General J. Marshall Coleman for the governorship. A former marine married to former president Lyndon Johnson's daughter, and the lone Democrat elected to statewide office in 1977, Robb won the governorship as a fiscal conservative with progressive views on race and social issues. Robb's philosophical positioning proved to be an ideal combination for the evolving Virginia electorate.

Robb's victory and gubernatorial leadership had a profound impact on state politics. He presided over a booming state economy and used revenues from the economic upturn to increase spending for education. Robb could have easily won a second term, but the state constitution prohibits gubernatorial succession.

Nonetheless, Robb had established for the state Democratic Party a winning strategy: to court the Byrd Democrats and some Republicans with strong appeals to fiscal conservatism, and to energize the moderate and liberal wings of the Democratic Party with progressive appeals on race, education, and social issues.

The 1980s, the Reagan-Bush era, were the heyday of success for the Virginia Democratic Party at the state level. In the 1981, 1985, and 1989 elections, Democrats swept all three statewide offices (governor, lieutenant governor, and attorney general).

In 1985, the incumbent attorney general Gerald Baliles, like Robb before him, ran as a fiscal conservative with progressive views on race and social issues. He easily defeated a more conservative opponent. Most significantly, Virginia attracted national attention for electing a black and a woman to the other state offices. State senator L. Douglas Wilder, a grandson of slaves, confounded analysts by handily winning the lieutenant governor race, making him the first black elected to statewide office in Virginia. State delegate Mary Sue Terry won the office of attorney general with 61 percent of the vote, making her the first woman elected to state office in Virginia.

The significance of Wilder's victory in 1985 to racial politics in Virginia cannot be understated. At the time Wilder was substantially more liberal than the leadership of the state Democratic Party. It was no secret that such figures as Governor Robb had serious reservations about Wilder's electability, and some even tried to recruit other leading Democrats to challenge him for the nomination. But when Wilder won the nomination, Robb and other Democrats solidly backed his candidacy, despite predictions that a black candidate would sink the entire statewide ticket. Political scientist Larry Sabato was widely quoted in statewide media when he boldly stated that Wilder's odds of winning were worse than 100 to 1 and declared the statewide ticket with a black and a woman "too clever by half." The comments exacerbated an already overheated climate regarding the impact of Wilder's race on the elections, and at the candidate's urging, campaign manager Paul Goldman turned up the heat again when he angrily denounced the political scientist as "in danger of becoming the Dr. Schockley of Virginia."[3]

Wilder's victory permanently put to rest the question of whether a black could win statewide office in Virginia. When others went out of their way to draw attention to Wilder's race, he campaigned throughout the state as a traditional southern politician and even ran televised ads in rural communities featuring a rotund white sheriff with a thick accent offering his strong support for the Democrat.

What made many Democrats and analysts uncomfortable about Wilder was his unabashed liberalism and preference to play by his own rules and not be guided by the leadership of other public figures. Wilder openly criticized the national Democratic Leadership Council, a group of prominent party moderates then led by Robb, as a pseudo-Republican organization. He was openly critical at times of Governor Baliles's leadership and policy priorities. Wilder and Robb openly feuded with each other with a testy exchange of letters in which Robb characterized the lieutenant governor as not a good team player and Wilder vented his anger at Robb for allegedly taking too much credit for the lieutenant governor's victory.

Although Wilder was at times openly disdainful, Robb left office in January 1986 with enormous popularity—so much so that in 1988 incumbent GOP senator Paul Tribble chose to step aside rather than be challenged by Robb. The Republicans, resigned to their fate, nominated a weak candidate who had never held elected office.

The GOP did nonetheless make a bold move by nominating a black minister, Reverend Maurice Dawkins, to challenge Robb. Dawkins claimed that he could put together an electoral majority by appealing to both Republicans and Democratic-leaning blacks with his philosophy of inclusive conservatism. At a post–nominating convention press conference, reporters asked him how he could seriously believe that a conservative Republican would attract the support of blacks. He responded that the black community is not monolithic and quipped, "we're a lot like white folks in that regard."[4]

Dawkins campaigned vigorously in black churches throughout Virginia, trying to promote a message of self-reliance and an anti-welfare state. Ultimately his conservative message was a difficult sell in the black community. He attracted only 16 percent of the black vote (and just over 30 percent of the white vote) and 29 percent overall against the popular former governor.[5]

In 1989 Wilder led the statewide Democratic ticket as the gubernatorial nominee. Although many party leaders continued to harbor reservations about his electability, they uniformly backed his candidacy. Despite his clear victory in 1985, many critics speculated that his race would prohibit him from winning the governorship of a former confederate state.

Wilder's candidacy attracted substantial national and international attention because he stood to become the nation's first elected black governor.[6] That a grandson of former slaves stood to accomplish this goal in the state that was the capital of the Confederacy made his possible election all the more intriguing.

What became clear during the campaign was that despite all of the at-tention paid to Wilder's race and—a year after the odious George H. W. Bush presidential campaign ads featuring a menacing-looking black crim-inal, Willie Horton—the possible temptation for the GOP candidate Mar-shall Coleman to subtly inject racial appeals, neither candidate drew strong attention to that factor. Indeed, during the campaign and especially during his term as governor, Wilder was more likely to endure criticism from prominent black leaders for downplaying race or for not having been a leader in the civil rights movement than from opponents for ex-ploiting race for political gain.

Wilder's victory was by the slimmest margin for a statewide race in Vir-ginia history. With a record turnout of nearly 1.8 million voters (66.5 per-cent of registered voters), Wilder won by only 6,741 votes.[7] On election night, exit polls projected that Wilder would win by a margin of at least 5 percent, and some news stations early on stated that he had won com-fortably, only to backtrack later on as the precincts reported a too-close-to-call election throughout the night. Journalists and pollsters later on said that many of the voters had lied in exit polls in order to appear racially progressive. That explanation, although credible, angered many citizens who felt that by injecting racial motivations to voting patterns, the state's accomplishment in electing a black governor had been tainted. The state's flagship newspaper, the *Richmond Times-Dispatch*, ran a political cartoon featuring a cigar-chomping white man with a Ku Klux Klan outfit telling the exit pollster that he just voted for Wilder.

Despite the closeness of victory and speculation that racially motivated voting nearly cost him the election, the national media celebrated Wilder's win as a historic achievement. The three national newsweeklies prominently featured stories on Wilder's victory with the titles: "The End of the Civil War" (*U.S. News and World Report*), "The New Black Politics" (*Newsweek*), and "Breakthrough in Virginia" (*Time*).[8]

The state Democratic Party surely had much to celebrate from its sweep of statewide offices in the three 1980s elections. In large part this success could be attributed to the party's use of convention nomina-tions, which led to the selection of electable centrist candidates. That stood in contrast to the party's poor showing in the 1970s, when such candidates as liberal populist Henry Howell prevailed in primary nom-inations. A string of statewide defeats convinced the party that it could nominate better candidates in conventions than in primaries—a judg-ment that proved correct.

Yet there was evidence of a Republican resurgence at the grassroots level as the party worked vigorously to recruit good candidates for local offices. The Republicans in the 1980s had continued their steady, incre-mental gains in membership in the Virginia General Assembly, enough so that by 1989 party members could discuss with credibility the possibility of someday taking control of one or even both legislative chambers. In 1967 the Democrats controlled thirty-four of forty Senate seats and eighty-five of one hundred seats in the House of Delegates. By the end of the 1980s, the GOP had picked up four seats in the Senate and twenty-five in the House, giving it ten of forty and thirty-nine of one hundred seats respectively. It appeared that a few good election cycles could give the GOP control of at least one legislative chamber for the first time since Reconstruction.

Aiding the GOP cause, Wilder had a troubled governorship during a period of economic recession. The era of state budget surpluses and economic growth had ended, and Wilder had to govern during a period of government retrenchment. State agencies and employees had become accustomed to better than usual government support from the Democratic administrations of Robb and Baliles and expected more of the same treatment from Wilder. With entirely premature thoughts of national office, Wilder committed his administration to a no tax increase pledge and vowed to cut government spending to keep the state budget balanced, as required by Virginia law. He consequently angered traditional Democratic constituency groups, especially in education and social services, as he promoted program cuts and state salary freezes.

Table 6.1. Party Composition of Virginia General Assembly, 1971–2007

	House			Senate		
	Dem.	*GOP*	*Ind.*	*Dem.*	*GOP*	*Ind.*
1971	73	24	3	33	7	0
1973	65	20	15	34	6	0
1975	78	17	5	35	5	0
1977	76	21	3	34	6	0
1979	74	25	1	31	9	0
1981	66	33	1	31	9	0
1983	65	34	1	32	8	0
1985	65	33	2	32	8	0
1987	64	35	1	30	10	0
1989	59	39	2	30	10	0
1991	58	41	1	22	18	0
1993	52	47	1	22	18	0
1995	52	47	1	22	18	0
1997	51	48	1	20	20	0
1999	47	52	1	19	21	0
2003	38	60	2	16	24	0
2005	40	57	3	17	23	0
2007	44	54	2	21	19	0

As Wilder championed his fiscal conservatism and basked in the praises of such unlikely supporters of the former liberal as the *National Review* editorial board and the libertarian Cato Institute, he planned an ill-fated run for the presidency in 1992. The governor's frequent travels out of state to promote his national profile resulted in an angry Virginia electorate and a popular mocking bumper sticker that read "Wilder for Resident." Wilder further angered Virginians with a very public ongoing feud with Senator Robb and state legislators from the northern Virginia region who believed that his policies were slighting the area of the state that had delivered his election.

Indeed, the geographic base for statewide Democratic candidates is in the northern Virginia communities of Alexandria, Fairfax City, Falls Church City, and Arlington, and along what is known as the "urban corridor"—a densely populated stretch of land from these northern Virginia communities, south to Richmond, and east along the coast in the Hampton Roads-Tidewater region. Excepting the far southwest coal mining communities with a strong labor union presence, the modern Republican base begins west of the urban corridor and covers many of the state's rural areas. On election night in 1989, television maps of voting showed a thin stretch of land along the urban corridor that voted for Wilder while the vast geographic portion of the state chose Coleman. Yet Wilder won with heavy urban support, and Coleman later quipped that he wished that Virginia had a statewide version of the Electoral College.

Although Wilder left office with ebbing popularity, he could credibly claim some important accomplishments. He indeed kept the state budget balanced for four years and never raised the state income tax. He took the leadership in successfully promoting adoption by the General Assembly of a one-gun-per-month-limit bill. That he did so in a state with a strong pro–gun rights tradition was no small feat (Wilson and Rozell 1998).

During Wilder's term, the Democratic-controlled state legislature and the state GOP feuded over redistricting proposals that ultimately resulted in the creation of a black majority district. Consequently, in 1992 Democrat Robert C. Scott of Newport News became the first black elected to Congress from Virginia in over a century. Yet by early 1997, a panel of U.S. District Court judges ruled that the district was unconstitutional because it had been drawn specifically to suit racial considerations (Nakashima 1997).

THE 1990s GOP RESURGENCE

Wilder's governorship nonetheless proved a liability to state Democrats as they sought to extend their string of electoral victories in 1993. The

Democrats nominated their two-term attorney general, Mary Sue Terry, for governor. The GOP nominated former state delegate and one-term congressman George Allen. The GOP campaign quickly seized on public disgust with the feud between Robb and Wilder, as well as the anger toward Wilder for how he conducted his governorship and more anger toward Robb for a series of scandalous allegations about his personal behavior while governor. In his nomination acceptance speech, Allen introduced his theme of asking voters to send a message to the "Robb-Wilder-Terry" Democrats, a refrain repeated throughout the election season.[9] The refrain caught on so well that Terry actually ran television commercials reminding voters that her name was "Mary Sue, not 'Robb-Wilder.'"

Terry ran a spectacularly inept campaign, as she alienated her base by denouncing Clinton's economic policies, refused to accept help from labor union groups, and waited until the final days of the campaign to seek Wilder's support. She lacked presence and performed poorly in the media campaign and in debates. Terry lost in a GOP landslide that gave Allen 58 percent of the vote. In an extraordinary case of ticket splitting in a statewide election in Virginia, voters rejected the GOP lieutenant governor nominee Michael Farris, a former Moral Majority leader. Farris ran 12 percentage points behind the top of the ticket while the attorney general candidate, James Gilmore, easily won with 56 percent.[10] Perhaps more significantly to the GOP, for the first time in the twentieth century the party's candidates for the House of Delegates won a majority of the votes statewide, although the Democrats retained control of a majority of the seats.

In the 1994 Virginia U.S. Senate campaign, the GOP nominated Iran-contra figure Oliver North to challenge incumbent Chuck Robb. Due to widespread reporting of personal scandals, Robb appeared the most vulnerable incumbent Democrat in the nation at the beginning of the year. But because the GOP had nominated probably the only party figure who was even more tainted by scandal, Robb won reelection. What made the race particularly noteworthy was that because the two major parties had nominated controversial candidates, two major figures, Marshall Coleman and Doug Wilder, ran as independents. Ultimately Wilder assured Robb's reelection by dropping out of the race. Coleman stayed in the race as the moderate GOP alternative and pulled 11 percent of the vote.

Also key to Robb's victory was Senator John Warner's opposition to North's candidacy. Warner acted as Coleman's benefactor and convinced the former attorney general to enter and stay in the race. Movement conservatives who backed North fumed that Coleman and Warner were "traitors" to the party and vowed to take revenge on the senator when he ran for reelection in 1996.

Exit polling data by Mitovsky International found that North's base included white born-again Christians and gun enthusiasts. He received about 60 percent of the vote from each of those groups and 81 percent among churchgoing gun enthusiasts. Among the 57 percent who fell into neither category, Robb took 65 percent of the vote. Blacks were key to Robb's victory, giving him over 96 percent of their votes.[11]

Although most of the rest of the nation underwent significant change with the 1994 "Republican Revolution," Virginia opted for the status quo, reelecting its senator and ten of its eleven members of the House. But in 1995, the Virginia GOP determined that the previous year's Republican strategy to nationalize congressional elections offered lessons for state legislative campaigns. Under the leadership of Governor Allen, all but two of the GOP candidates for state legislative offices in 1995 met on the state Capitol steps to unveil their ten point "Pledge for Honest Change," modeled after the "Contract with America."

The goal of the pledge was to have the GOP candidates statewide adopt a unified message that included not only their policy commitments contained in the pledge, but also their plea to the voters to give the governor legislative majorities in the General Assembly. Governor Allen characterized the elections as a referendum on his leadership and staked his future conservative agenda on winning party control of the legislature (Rozell and Wilcox 1995). His effort failed in large part, polls revealed, because the public perceived Allen as pushing too far to the ideological right and believed that legislative majorities would enable him to push such initiatives as easing gun ownership restrictions and limiting abortion rights. Yet the GOP did pick up two state Senate seats to give them twenty of forty seats in the upper chamber, the GOP's best showing since Reconstruction.

In 1990, Republican senator John Warner was such a strong candidate for reelection that the Democratic Party chose to let him run unopposed. His reelection made him the first Republican in Virginia history to win statewide three times. He did not get a free ride in 1996. He faced a serious intraparty challenge from a candidate backed by the Christian Right and then a historically well-financed Democrat in the general election. Warner survived both challenges and earned a fourth term in the U.S. Senate.

That Warner faced a serious challenge for renomination is telling of the divisive nature of the modern Virginia GOP. The Christian Right currently dominates the leadership and activist base of the state GOP. Warner is very popular in the state, but most of the Christian Right despises him largely because he refused to back Michael Farris's campaign for lieutenant governor in 1993 and openly opposed Oliver North in 1994 (Rozell and Wilcox 1996).

In the 1990s, the Republican Party in Virginia mostly relied on convention nominations to choose its statewide candidates. Unlike the Democratic conventions that were tightly controlled affairs, the GOP conventions of the 1990s were open to almost all party activists who wanted to become delegates. The dedicated party activists who tended to be more conservative than rank-and-file GOP voters therefore dominated the party conventions. The conventions enabled a committed group of social movement activists to take control of nominations away from the establishment Republicans, who were more moderate and liked John Warner.

The most important event to Warner's 1996 reelection was probably an April 16 federal court decision to uphold an obscure provision of a Virginia law that enables an incumbent to choose his preferred method of renomination. It was clear that Warner could not win renomination in a party convention dominated by the Christian Right. In fact, given the state party's loyalty rule—that only those who pledged to support the party's nominees and had faithfully done so in the most recent elections would be allowed to participate—it was questionable whether Warner would even be credentialed at his own party's nominating convention. When Warner invoked his right to choose a primary, the state party, led by the chair, challenged the constitutionality of the law that gave the senator that power. When the federal judge upheld Warner's right to an open primary, his renomination was nearly assured.

Former Reagan Office of Management and Budget director James Miller challenged Warner in the primary. Miller had unsuccessfully but credibly challenged North in the 1994 GOP convention. Because of strong Christian Right antipathy toward him, Warner had to take seriously the primary race. The state GOP lacked a tradition of primary nominations and no one could predict turnout. Christian Right activists pledged they would mobilize against Warner.

Perhaps the best evidence of the divide between GOP activists and rank-and-file party voters was the dramatically different results between a state party convention preference poll and the open primary vote. In the former, held just a little over a week before the primary, Miller bettered Warner by a 3:1 margin among the more than two thousand party delegates. But Warner won the primary nomination by a 2:1 margin.

In the general election Senator Warner faced Democrat Mark Warner, a former state party chair with a personal fortune of over $100 million. The Democratic nominee spent over $10 million of his own money to wage a credible campaign against a very popular incumbent. Virginians reelected the senator with 53 percent of the vote. Senator Warner achieved 19 percent of the black vote—a better than usual showing for a Republican. That blacks comprised only 15 percent of the voters in this election and Mark Warner received a significantly lower percentage of black votes than other

Democrats who have won statewide proved important to the senator's re-election. The Democrat Warner was unable to overcome the senator's 58 percent showing among whites.[12]

The 1997 elections continued the move toward GOP dominance in the state. The GOP nominated Attorney General Gilmore, and the Democrats nominated two-term lieutenant governor Donald Beyer. What should have been a competitive race turned yet again into a GOP landslide, as Gilmore proved the much more adept campaigner. The GOP nominee rode to victory mostly on the strength of a single issue appeal: a promise to phase out a very unpopular annual tax on the value of personal property items such as automobiles and boats. With a booming economy and growing state revenues, Gilmore proposed that it was time to eliminate what was commonly called the "car tax." Perhaps most ironically, Beyer, a Volvo dealership owner, miscalculated the populist appeal of the Gilmore proposal, first opposing elimination of the tax and then support-ing a modified version of the idea later on.

The GOP swept the two other statewide races as well in 1997. Retired tobacco company executive John Hager won a close election to become lieutenant governor. State Senator Mark Earley handily won the attorney general campaign.

Perhaps most significantly, in 1997 the GOP picked up two additional seats in the House of Delegates, giving the party a fifty-to-forty-nine ad-vantage (with one independent). With a twenty-twenty tie in the Senate and a GOP lieutenant governor to break votes, the party had effective con-trol of the state legislature and complete control of the executive branch for the first time in the modern era. Additional gains by the GOP in the 1999 legislative elections gave the party clear majorities in both houses. Most important, the GOP earned control of redistricting in the state.

In 2000, former GOP governor George Allen defeated incumbent Dem-ocratic senator Charles Robb. The GOP therefore controlled all three statewide elective offices, controlled both houses of the state legislature, had a majority of the U.S. House delegation, and held both U.S. Senate seats. The GOP realignment in Virginia appeared to be complete.

VIRGINIA POLITICS IN THE NEW CENTURY

In 2001, the GOP looked to sustain its dominance of state politics. That ef-fort ran into the successful gubernatorial campaign of former U.S. Senate candidate Mark Warner, who defeated GOP nominee Mark Earley 52.2 percent to 47.0 percent. Perhaps most significantly, Warner won 50.8 per-cent of the rural vote in the state, the stronghold of the GOP. The multi-millionaire Warner spent a substantial sum from his personal fortune to finance the most expensive statewide campaign in Virginia history. But money alone was not the story of his victory. Warner looked back to the 1980s model of Chuck Robb and other Virginia Democrats who won statewide by running right-of-center campaigns. Indeed, Warner ran as a pro–Second Amendment, anti-tax candidate, leading many Republicans to argue that the only reason the Democratic Party had won was that its nominee effectively ran as a Republican.

That explanation of the election result was not altogether wrong. The election also was characterized by huge ticket-splitting, as the GOP handily won the race for attorney general and picked up a remarkable twelve seats in House of Delegates races. Hence, the GOP had some basis for claiming that the 2001 elections were not at all a repudiation of the party or its principles.

Warner became a very popular governor, and as his governing successes became better known, by the end of his term many in the party were touting him for future national office. Such talk of a Warner national campaign began seriously after Democratic presidential nominee John Kerry lost the 2004 campaign and many analysts said that the party needed to look in the future toward more moderate candidates, preferably from the South. Warner considered a 2008 presidential run, but under pressure from national party leaders he stepped aside and instead ran for the U.S. Senate seat opened by the retirement of John Warner.

Warner's 2001 victory was the beginning of a complete turnaround of the Democratic Party's fortunes in the state. In 2005, the Democrats won the governorship again, as Lieutenant Governor Tim Kaine defeated the Republican attorney general Jerry Kilgore. In 2006, in a stunning political development, first-time candidate Jim Webb narrowly defeated incumbent GOP senator George Allen. In 2007, the Democrats picked up enough seats to take back control of the state Senate. And then the remarkable success of the party in the presidential and congressional campaigns in 2008 sealed the reputation of Virginia as having shifted from "red to blue."

Yet despite this dramatic shift, it is premature to call Virginia a "blue," or Democratic-leaning, state. At this writing, going into the 2009 state elections, the GOP retains control of the lower house of the General Assembly. Although the Republicans lost the governorship in 2005, the party won the other two statewide offices of lieutenant governor and attorney general. The attorney general winner, Robert McDonnell, became the party choice for governor, and most observers believe that he has a credible chance to win. Also, there is little doubt that broader national trends against the GOP and the former Bush administration had a huge impact on Republican fortunes in Virginia in 2008. It is entirely conceivable that under different circumstances, the GOP can stage a political comeback in the Old Dominion. Indeed, some of the GOP's recent losses in the state appear more to be functions of self-destruction than electoral realignment. Earley and Kilgore ran terrible campaigns in 2001 and 2005, and in 2006 a widely publicized comment by George Allen that many perceived as racist completely upended his reelection bid.

CONCLUSION

The Virginia political landscape has undergone significant changes in the modern era. As recently as the heyday of the Reagan era in the mid-1980s, it was almost unimaginable to discuss the possibility of Republican control of the General Assembly and the executive branch. Yet in the 1990s Virginia transitioned to a truly competitive two-party state. The GOP succeeded in a steady march to take control of the state, and political demographers often attributed this development to the swelling ranks of new voters in the fast growing exurban communities in such places as Loudoun County and Prince William County, and the propensity of these communities to lean Republican.

Demographic changes, especially the phenomenal population growth of the Washington, DC, suburbs of northern Virginia, have altered state politics forever. Whereas rural legislators for years chaired crucial committees in the General Assembly and routinely blocked legislation favorable to northern Virginia, today a bipartisan alliance of members representing the "urban corridor"—the stretch of land from northern Virginia down Interstate 95 to the city of Richmond and east to the Norfolk-Tidewater area—exercises substantial influence over state policy and spending priorities. Much of this change is attributable to population shifts that have given a larger percentage of legislative seats to urban and highly populated suburban areas.

These changes have also given rise to a political environment more conducive to minority group interests than ever before, although most analysts of state politics would agree that much remains to be done. The black community now comprises 17 percent of the state's population, and no Democrat is able to win statewide office without a very substantial percentage and turnout of black voters.

Black candidates have seen their fortunes improve dramatically in the state. The first black elected to the House of Delegates since Reconstruction was William Ferguson Reid in 1968. The following year Douglas Wilder was elected to the state Senate in a special election. Today there are five black state senators and twelve delegates (table 6.2). Of course, Douglas Wilder's statewide elections in the 1980s were historic achievements.

The modern GOP is making an increased effort in the state to reach the black community. When the state party chair in 1994 said that he didn't

Table 6.2. Percentage of Blacks in Virginia General Assembly, 1965–2009

	House	*Senate*
1965	0	0
1970	2.0	2.5
1975	1.0	2.5
1980	4.0	2.5
1985	7.0	7.5
1990	7.0	7.5
1995	8.0	12.5
2000	10.0	12.5
2005	11.0	12.5
2009	12.0	12.5

favor spending a lot of time cultivating black support for the GOP campaign because it was not "cost-effective," many party members openly criticized the comment and made it clear that they did not share this view. Although success has been minimal, the Christian Right movement in the state GOP has actively reached out to the black community to try and forge alliances on social issues where conservative white evangelicals and many blacks share similar views. In one successful endeavor, Christian Right and black church leaders throughout the state formed a coalition to fight a proposal for the legalization of riverboat gambling.

As in the rest of the South and the nation, black voters remain loyal to the Democratic Party. The increasingly progressive new state population and efforts by both parties to reach out to blacks are signs of the political evolution and maturation of a state with a poor historical record on racial issues. The civil rights era brought profound changes for blacks in Virginia in protecting their basic rights under the law in voting, education, employment, and housing. Today much of the politically active black community is pursuing state policies that will help to alleviate vast disparities in spending in school districts and promote better educational opportunities at all levels and stronger social services.

Virginia also has seen a vast increase in the Latino population in recent years. In some counties this growth has been dramatic. In Prince William County, for example, the Latino population tripled in the 2000–2006 period. Yet the percentage growth in Latino population is not matched by a comparable growth in voting or political power. Indeed, in Prince William County, anti-immigrant backlashes have resulted in many of the nation's harshest policies toward illegal immigrants. Yet the growth in the Latino population in Prince William County and other areas of the state portends some significant shifts in the future for Virginia politics, perhaps pushing the state another step away from its former status as a Republican "red" state.

NOTES

1. Results provided by the State Board of Elections.
2. For an excellent biography of Byrd and an analysis of his lasting impact on Virginia politics, see Ronald L. Heinemann 1996.
3. For a detailed description of these events and of Wilder's campaign, see Dwayne Yancey 1988 (especially pp. 59, 103–104).
4. Press conference attended by author, June 11, 1988, Roanoke, VA.
5. Results provided by the State Board of Elections.
6. The nation's only previous black governor had been appointed to the office. Lieutenant Governor P. B. S. Pinchback of Louisiana, a Republican, held the office of governor for a month in December 1872–January 1873 while the elected governor underwent an impeachment trial.
7. Results provided by the State Board of Elections.
8. All three issues were dated November 20, 1989.
9. Republican nominating convention attended by author, June 5, 1993, Richmond, VA.
10. Results provided by the State Board of Elections. For a detailed analysis of the 1993 statewide elections, see Mark J. Rozell and Clyde Wilcox 1996, chapter 4.
11. Mitovsky International 1994 exit poll data.
12. "Virginia Senate Exit Poll Results," allpolitics.com, November 6, 1996.

REFERENCES

Atkinson, Frank. 1992. *The Dynamic Dominion: Realignment and the Rise of Virginia's Republican Party Since 1945*. Fairfax, VA: George Mason University Press.

Black, Earl, and Merle Black. 1987. *Politics and Society in the South*. Cambridge, MA: Harvard University Press.

Heinemann, Ronald L. 1996. *Harry Byrd of Virginia*. Charlottesville: University Press of Virginia.

Hsu, Spencer S. 1997. "Fairfax Senator Decries Coeducation at VMI." *Washington Post*, January 10:B1, 4.

Key, V. O., Jr. 1949. *Southern Politics in State and Nation*. New York: Alfred A. Knopf.

Nakashima, Ellen. 1997. "House District in Va. Ordered Redrawn." *Washington Post*, February 8:A1, 10.

Rozell, Mark J., and Clyde Wilcox. 1995. "Governor Allen's Big Chance." *Washington Post*, October 29:C8.

———. 1996. *Second Coming: The New Christian Right in Virginia Politics*. Baltimore: Johns Hopkins University Press.

Sabato, Larry. 1977. *The Democratic Party Primary in Virginia: Tantamount to Election No Longer*. Charlottesville: University Press of Virginia.

———. 1983. *Goodbye to Goodtime Charlie: The American Governorship Transformed*, 2nd ed. Washington, DC: Congressional Quarterly Press.

Wilson, Harry, and Mark J. Rozell. 1998. "Virginia: The Politics of Concealed Weapons." In *The New Politics of Gun Control*, ed. John Bruce and Clyde Wilcox. Lanham, MD: Rowman & Littlefield.
Yancey, Dwayne. 1988. *When Hell Froze Over*. Dallas: Taylor Publishing.

7

◄◈►

North Carolina

Tar Heel Politics
in the Twenty-first Century

Charles Prysby

In 2004, Republicans in North Carolina did very well in the federal elections. The GOP presidential candidate, George W. Bush, won the state with over 56 percent of the two-party vote. In the U.S. Senate election, Republican Richard Burr captured the seat held by Democratic senator John Edwards, who did not run for reelection but was on the ballot as the Democratic vice-presidential candidate. Burr's victory gave Republicans control of both U.S. Senate seats, as Elizabeth Dole retained Republican control of the seat held by retiring senator Jesse Helms in 2002. Republicans also won a majority of the U.S. House seats in 2004. However, Democrats did better in elections for state government. They maintained control of the governorship, won six of the other nine Council of State offices, and retained their majority status in both houses of the state legislature. In 2004, North Carolina was a competitive two-party state, but one in which Republicans had an advantage in federal elections and Democrats an advantage in state elections (Prysby 2005). This pattern of competition had characterized the state over the previous decade, and there was every reason to think that this pattern would prevail in 2008.

Four years later, North Carolina looked much different. Democrats did better in 2008 than they had in any recent previous presidential election year. Starting at the top of the ticket, they won the presidential election for the first time since 1976. Barack Obama's narrow victory in that contest was accompanied by Democrat Kay Hagan's defeat of Senator Dole and by the Democratic pickup of one U.S. House seat, which, when added to a House seat the party had gained in 2006, gave the Democrats eight of the thirteen congressional seats in the state. Democrats continued their control over state government by winning the gubernatorial election, capturing most of the Council of State offices, and maintaining their majority in both houses of the state legislature. The Democratic victory in the gubernatorial election was achieved in spite of some unfavorable circumstances. The incumbent Democratic governor, Mike Easley, was ineligible to run for a third term. The Democratic candidate, Lieutenant Governor Bev Perdue, was considered a lackluster campaigner. The Republican candidate, Charlotte mayor Pat McCrory, was a moderate and pragmatic Republican and probably their strongest gubernatorial candidate in years. Nevertheless, Perdue was able to defeat McCrory.

Early in 2008, Tar Heel Republicans were optimistic. Based on previous election results, McCain seemed likely to carry North Carolina, even if he lost nationally. Senator Dole was considered likely to win reelection. Sixteen years of Democratic governors, combined with recent news stories of scandals or government mismanagement by various state government officials, convinced many Republicans that voters wanted a change in Raleigh and that this gave the GOP gubernatorial candidate a good opportunity for victory. Instead, Republicans suffered defeats across the board, producing great Republican disappointment. North Carolina was still a competitive state in 2008, but it now was one that leaned more toward the Democrats. The question is whether this outcome was simply a result of a very favorable year for Democrats nationally, due largely to widespread dissatisfaction with the foreign and domestic policies of the Bush administration, or whether the 2008 election results signal new developments in North Carolina politics, developments that are likely to continue to favor the Democrats. This chapter examines these two possibilities by analyzing the changes and continuities in Tar Heel politics.

THE DEVELOPMENT OF PARTISAN COMPETITION

Fifty years ago, North Carolina was dominated by the Democratic Party. In 1960, for example, the Democratic presidential candidate, John F. Kennedy, carried the state by about 4 percentage points even though he barely won the national popular vote. Congressional elections were even more favorable to the Democrats, who won a landslide victory in the U.S. Senate race and captured eleven of the twelve U.S. House seats. State elections were no kinder to the Republicans. Democrats swept the statewide races for the ten Council of State offices (governor, lieutenant governor, and eight other executive offices) by comfortable margins, and the vast majority of the state legislative seats were won by Democrats. North Carolina at that time remained a solidly Democratic state, as it had been throughout the century, albeit one in which Republicans were beginning to show some signs of life.

Democratic domination had long been a feature of North Carolina politics, just as it had been in other southern states prior to World War II (Key 1949). North Carolina, like other southern states, almost always supplied its electoral college votes to the Democratic presidential candidate, regularly elected Democrats to Congress, and routinely put Democrats in complete control of state government (Christensen 2008, 7–108; Eamon 2008; Key 1949, 205–228). The only suspense in North Carolina elections during the era of the "Solid South" was over which Democrats would be elected to congressional or state office. One-party control in the South was a crucial aspect of the system of white supremacy that characterized the region in the first half of the twentieth century, and it also served to limit the political influence of lower-income whites (Key 1949, 531–554; Scher 1997, 53–76). Cracks in the Solid South began to appear in 1948 with the Dixiecrat revolt, and the Republican presidential candidate in 1952 and 1956, Dwight D. Eisenhower, carried some southern states (Bass and DeVries 1976). Even so, Democrats remained extremely strong in state and congressional elections in the 1950s. Only in the 1960s did Republicans begin to make real inroads into Democratic domination of the South (Bass and DeVries 1976). By the 1990s, however, a two-party South was a reality (Black and Black 2002, 328–368; Lublin 2004, 33–65; Scher 1997, 79–159).

The movement in North Carolina from a one-party state to a competitive two-party state was not a pattern of smooth and even Republican growth (Lamis 1984, 131–144; Christensen and Fleer 1999; Prysby 2008). Table 7.1 summarizes election results for a variety of offices from 1960 to 2008. As we can see, Republican electoral success occurred earlier for some offices than for others. For example, Republicans first won the presidential election in 1968 and thereafter lost it only in 1976 and 2008. However, it was not until 1994 that the GOP was able to capture a majority of the seats in one house of the state legislature, and the party was only able to hold that majority through the 1996 election. Moreover, Republican advances were sometimes followed by reversals. Great gains were made by the GOP in 1972, but the 1974 election, coming in the wake of the Watergate scandal, produced substantial loses. Republicans were able to win the gubernatorial election three out of five times in the 1970s and 1980s, but Democrats have been victorious in the five most recent gubernatorial elections, beginning in 1992.

The 1972 election was an early milestone in the development of two-party competition in the state. Richard Nixon won the presidential election by an enormous margin. Led by a popular candidate at the top of the ballot, Republicans captured other key offices. Jesse Helms won the U.S. Senate seat up for election, and James Holshouser won the gubernatorial

Table 7.1. Republican Strength in North Carolina, 1960–2008 (in percentages)

	Presidential Vote	Gubernatorial Vote	U.S. Senate Vote	U.S. House Seats	State House Seats	State Senate Seats
1960	47.9	45.5	38.6	8.3	12.5	4.0
1962			39.6	18.2	17.5	4.0
1964	43.8	43.4	44.4	18.2	11.7	2.0
1966				27.3	21.7	14.0
1968	57.5[a]	47.3	39.4	36.4	24.2	24.0
1970				36.4	20.0	14.0
1972	70.6	51.3	54.0	36.4	29.2	30.0
1974			37.3	18.2	7.5	2.0
1976	44.4	34.3		18.2	5.0	6.0
1978			54.5	18.2	11.7	12.0
1980	51.1	37.7	50.3	36.4	20.0	20.0
1982				18.2	15.0	12.0
1984	62.0	54.4	51.9	45.5	31.7	24.0
1986			48.2	27.3	30.0	20.0
1988	58.2	56.1		27.3	38.3	26.0
1990			52.6	36.4	30.8	28.0
1992	50.5[b]	45.1	52.2	33.3	34.4	22.0
1994				66.7	55.8	48.0
1996	52.5[c]	43.3	53.4	50.0	50.8	42.0
1998			47.9	58.3	45.0	30.0

Year						
2000	56.5	47.1		58.3	48.3	30.0
2002	56.2		54.4	53.8	50.0[d]	44.0
2004		43.5	52.3	53.8	47.5	42.0
2006	49.8			46.2	43.3	38.0
2008	48.3	45.6		38.5	43.3	40.0

Sources: America Votes (Washington, DC: Congressional Quarterly, 1960–1990) and *Statistical Abstract of the United States* (Washington, DC: Government Printing Office, 1960–1992), various editions. The 1992–2008 figures were obtained from the North Carolina Board of Elections.

Notes: The first three columns report the Republican vote, calculated as the percentage of the two-party vote. The last three columns give the percent of the seats held by Republicans following the specified election (e.g., after the 2008 election, Republicans held 40 percent of the state senate seats).

[a] In 1968, Republican Richard Nixon won the state with 40 percent of the total vote; Democrat Hubert Humphrey and American Independent George Wallace received 29 and 31 percent, respectively.

[b] In 1992, Republican George Bush won the state with 43 percent of the vote; Democrat Bill Clinton and Independent Ross Perot received 43 percent and 14 percent, respectively.

[c] In 1996, Republican Robert Dole won the state with 49 percent of the vote; Democrat Bill Clinton and Reform Party candidate Ross Perot won 44 percent and 7 percent, respectively.

[d] Republicans won a bare majority of the state house seats in the 2002 elections, but one Republican legislator switched parties shortly after the election, making the house evenly divided, and this is the percentage reported in the table; in the legislative session, Democrats formed a majority coalition with a group of Republicans.

election, which marked the first time in the twentieth century that the Republicans won either of these offices. Republicans also increased their presence in the state legislature to 30 percent, a great improvement over what they had just a decade earlier. But, as mentioned above, the 1972 gains were followed by significant losses in the 1974 midterm elections. Furthermore, Lieutenant Governor Jim Hunt recaptured the governorship for the Democrats in 1976. By the end of the 1970s, Republicans were about where they were in the early 1960s, except for the fact that Helms held a U.S. Senate seat, which he won again in 1978.

Other key elections occurred in 1980 and 1984. With Ronald Reagan heading the ticket in 1980, Republican John East captured the other U.S. Senate seat, and Republicans increased their strength in both the congressional delegation and the state legislature, although Democrats remained in the majority in both cases. In state elections that year, Hunt was reelected governor, and Democrats won all of the other Council of State races, keeping the Democrats firmly in control of state government. Republicans advanced again in 1984, when Republican James Martin won the gubernatorial election. Hunt, who was ineligible to run for a third term as governor, challenged Helms in a well-publicized U.S. Senate election that year, which Helms narrowly won after an expensive, bitter, and highly negative campaign. Republicans also increased their presence in both the congressional delegation and the state legislature, although still remaining the minority party in both bodies.

Following the 1984 elections, some observers expected the Republicans to become the majority party in the state, but in the next few elections the GOP was unable to consolidate and expand the gains it made in the early 1980s. In 1986, former Democratic governor Terry Sanford recaptured the U.S. Senate seat won by East in 1980, and Democrats won back two U.S. House seats that year. Republicans also failed to make significant gains in the state legislature in the late 1980s. The major Republican victory during the late 1980s was Martin's reelection as governor in 1988. In 1992, Hunt again ran for governor and recaptured that office for the Democrats. Democrats also did well in U.S. House and state legislative races that year, but in the U.S. Senate election, Republican Lauch Faircloth defeated incumbent senator Sanford.

The next major Republican breakthrough came in 1994, when the Republicans took four U.S. House seats from the Democrats, giving the GOP a majority of the state's congressional delegation for the first time in modern history. They also became the majority party in the lower house of the state legislature, also for the first time in modern history. However, in subsequent elections the Democrats were able to reverse some of these gains, despite the fact that the Republican presidential nominee easily carried the state in 1996, 2000, and 2004. Republicans had only a slight edge in the congressional delegation in elections held after 1994, even in the presidential election years, and the GOP lost its congressional majority in 2006, when Democrat Heath Schuler captured the Eleventh Congressional District. Moreover, newcomer John Edwards defeated Senator Faircloth in the 1998 midterm election to retake this seat for the Democrats, although it was recaptured by the Republicans in 2004, as discussed above. In 2008, another Republican incumbent senator, Dole, was defeated by a Democratic challenger, as was previously mentioned. Thus, 1994 was the high-water mark for Republicans in congressional elections, as they held both Senate seats and two-thirds of the House seats after the 1994 elections.

Democrats were particularly successful in preventing Republicans from winning control of state government. After winning three of five gubernatorial elections between 1972 and 1988, the GOP lost the next five. After becoming the majority party in one house of the state legislature in 1994, Republicans failed to achieve that status in either legislative house in any election after 1996. They almost became the majority party in the state House after the 2002 elections, when they won a bare majority of seats, but one Republican legislator switched parties, creating an even split in the state House and eventually leading to a compromise that gave control of that house to a coalition of Democrats and a minority of Republicans. Greater success for the Republican Party in federal rather than state elections is a pattern that has characterized politics in a number of southern states (Aistrup 1996; Lublin 2004, 33–65). What makes this pattern noteworthy in North Carolina is the fact that the major state elections are held in presidential election years, unlike every other southern state. Even with a presidential candidate who was winning the state at the top of its ticket, the GOP was unable to score a single decisive victory in any of the major state elections held from 1992 to 2004.

Many of the developments in North Carolina politics reflect changes throughout the South. While the details and timing of Republican growth vary from state to state, throughout the region Republicans have gained considerably in congressional and state elections in recent decades (Black and Black 1987, 1992, 2002; Lamis 1999a; Lublin 2004; Scher 1997). Years of notable Republican gains in North Carolina, such as 1980 or 1994, were years in which Republicans made substantial gains in many other southern states. Moreover, national as well as regional trends have affected the state. For example, 1994, a year in which Republicans won a majority of the congressional seats in North Carolina, not coincidentally was also a year in which Republicans captured a majority of congressional seats in the region and the country (Klinkner 1996). Similarly, Democratic success in North Carolina in 2008 went hand in hand with Democratic success nationally in the congressional and presidential elections. Much of the change that has taken place in the state would not have occurred absent the forces and changes occurring outside the state. In many cases, years in which Republicans made major gains, such as 1972 or 1984, were years in which the Republican presidential candidate carried the state by a wide margin. However, the situation reversed in 2008; Obama's success in the state may have helped Democrats win other important offices, such as U.S. senator or governor (Prysby 2009).

In the last several elections, North Carolina has been very competitive. Either party appears quite capable of winning major statewide races. For example, even though the Republicans have won five of the last seven U.S. Senate elections, in every case the vote was close. No Senate seat was won with as much as 55 percent of the two-party vote. Similarly, while Democrats have won the gubernatorial elections from 1992 on, the instances where the election did not involve an incumbent governor (the 1992, 2000, and 2008 elections) were fairly competitive races, indicating that a Republican gubernatorial candidate could win under the right circumstances. Incumbent governors have a very strong reelection record in the state, which accounts for the more lopsided Democratic victories in the 1996 and 2004 gubernatorial elections.

U.S. House elections have been more competitive in North Carolina than in many other southern states. Not only has the overall balance of seats been fairly even (neither party has been able to capture 60 percent or more of the seats since 1994), but many districts have been competitive. For example, four of the seats currently held by Democrats are seats that at one time were held by a Democrat, were subsequently won by a Republican, and then were won back by a Democrat in a recent election. Moreover, many of the seat changes that have occurred in the past fifteen years involve the defeat of incumbents, which indicates that the seats truly cannot be considered safe for one party. At least five of the thirteen districts appear to be ones that could change partisan hands, particularly in an open-seat election.[1] Some of the U.S. House seats have been drawn in a fashion that makes them safe for one party, but there are fewer safe seats in North Carolina than in many other southern states.

Even the Council of State (COS) and the state legislative elections have been more competitive than the election outcomes indicate. Republicans have won few of the COS offices, but they often have lost by small vote margins. For example, in 2008, the GOP won only two of the nine COS elections (excluding governor), but in four others the Republican candidate captured more than 45 percent of the vote. Also, while Republicans have almost always failed to win a majority of seats in either house of the state legislature, the Democratic Party's percentage of seats has exceeded its percentage of the popular vote in recent elections. A small shift in the vote could produce a sizable shift in seats.

Recent presidential elections have been less competitive in North Carolina. In 1996 and 2000, North Carolina was about 7 percentage points more Republican than the nation in the two-party vote division. Even in 2004, when Edwards was on the ticket as the Democratic vice-presidential candidate, the state was 5 percentage points more Republican than the nation. However, the state was only about 3 percentage points more Republican than the country as a whole in 2008. Thus, the trend over the past three presidential elections shows the gap between the state and the nation narrowing. Obviously, if this trend were to continue, it would mean that North Carolina would join the group of perennial battleground states.

THE DEVELOPMENT OF PARTY DIFFERENCES

Change in North Carolina politics has involved more than the growth of two-party competition. There also has been a realignment of the two political parties in the state, which is evident in the ideological differences between Democratic and Republican candidates (Prysby 2008). Several decades ago, the two parties were not nearly as ideologically distinct as they now are. The Democratic Party included many conservatives, as was true throughout the South. The Republicans, who were strongest in the western part of the state then, included many moderates. The growth of the Republican Party coincided with its becoming more clearly conservative. Democrats moved in the opposite ideological direction. Older conservative Democrats left office, either through retirement or defeat, or in some cases switched parties. New Democratic candidates and officeholders were generally more liberal. A concomitant realignment of voters contributed to this development. As conservative Democratic voters decreased in numbers and conservative Republicans increased, and as blacks became a significant part of the electorate, the Democratic primary electorate became more clearly liberal, making it more difficult for conservative Democratic candidates to win the nomination. On the other hand, the Republican primary electorate became strongly conservative, ensuring that conservative Republicans would be nominated.

The movement of the Republican Party in a conservative direction was undoubtedly fostered by the success of Jesse Helms (Link 2008). When Senator Helms was first elected to the U.S. Senate in 1972, he became the most visible Republican in the state. He touted his conservatism and railed against liberals (Luebke 1990, 124–136). Each of his reelection campaigns attempted to paint his Democratic opponent as a liberal out of touch with North Carolina values. Helms's 1984 reelection effort against Hunt, who was completing his second term as governor, was a very expensive, hard-fought, and divisive race. Helms attacked Hunt on a number of social issues, including ones with a racial aspect, such as the Martin Luther King Jr. holiday, enacted by Congress in 1983 (Luebke 1990, 137–155). Helms used a similar strategy in his next reelection effort. In 1990, he faced Harvey Gantt, an African American and a former mayor of Charlotte, in another expensive, hard-fought, and divisive race (Prysby 1996). In the final days of that campaign, Helms ran a controversial television advertisement that accused Gantt of favoring racial quotas.[2] Helms's outspoken conservatism did not appear only during elections. In the U.S. Senate, he also was vociferous and unrelenting in his criticism of liberal policies and even the federal government in general, earning him the nickname "Senator No." Although Helms may have represented the right wing of the GOP, his visibility made him very influential in defining the image of Republicans in the state and even in defining modern conservatism nationally (Link 2008).

Helms was the most visible conservative face in the North Carolina congressional delegation, but the other Republican senators have been very conservative as well. Senators East and Faircloth both were ideologically close to Helms, both received substantial help from Helms's organization, the Congressional Club, in their election efforts, and both had very conservative Senate voting records. The more recent Republican senators, Dole and Burr, have not used conservative rhetoric in the way that Helms did, but they have been fairly consistent conservatives in their voting in Congress. Burr had a lifetime American Conservative Union (ACU) rating of 91 percent for the ten years that he spent in the U.S. House before being elected senator in 2004. Senator Dole recorded an ACU score of 91 percent during her years in the Senate.

The two most recent Democratic senators, Edwards and Sanford, were much more liberal in their congressional voting. Senator Edwards had an ACU rating of 10 percent for his single term, and Senator Sanford had an ACU score of 12 percent for his single term. This is in sharp contrast to the voting patterns of earlier Democratic senators, who were much more conservative. For example, the two Democratic senators in 1972 had ACU scores of 67 percent and 100 percent. Moreover, the losing Democratic candidates in recent years—Erskine Bowles in 2002 and 2004 and Gantt in 1990 and 1996—took positions that were clearly more liberal than their Republican opponent (Prysby 1996, 1997, 2004, 2005). Of course, Democratic candidates in North Carolina generally are less liberal than Democrats in other parts of the country, and they often emphasize their more moderate orientations and political independence in their election campaigns.

The sharpening ideological differentiation of the two parties, along with their increasing ideological cohesiveness, is clearly visible by examining the American Conservative Union scores for members of the U.S. House from North Carolina over the past few decades. Table 7.2 presents data on the ACU scores of North Carolina members of Congress for 1972, 1982, 1996, and 2007, a period that spans the post–civil rights era. The representatives in 1972 were elected in 1970, before the 1972 breakthrough election for Republicans. In this year, Republicans were moderately conservative, but so were Democrats, who had an average ACU score that was only about ten points lower than the average Republican score. We also can see that the most conservative Democrats were more conservative than the least conservative Republicans. Partisan differences were greater among the 1982 legislators, who were elected in 1980—the year that Reagan won North Carolina and nearly every other southern state. The difference between Democrats and Republicans in average ACU scores was now thirty points, and there was no overlap between the range of scores for each party. The Democrats overall were moderately conservative, as they were in 1972, but the Republicans were more strongly conservative. The 1996 scores represent the voting patterns of congressmen elected in the Republican landslide of 1994. The Democrats, who now were in the minority, were clearly liberal, with an average ACU score of 12 percent, and the Republicans were extremely conservative. The 2007 ACU scores are the most recent ones available and show a continuation of the patterns of the late 1990s. Republicans are strongly conservative overall, although one (Walter Jones in the Third District) recorded a relatively moderate score of 71 percent. Democrats were quite liberal overall, but two of them (Mike McIntyre in the Seventh District and Heath Schuler in the Eleventh District) posted ACU scores of 44 percent.

Table 7.2. American Conservative Union Scores for U.S. Representatives from North Carolina for Selected Years

	1972	1982	1996	2007
Democratic Representatives				
Number of representatives	7	7	4	7
Mean ACU score	68	62	12	14
Highest score	100	75	30	44
Lowest score	40	47	0	0
Republican Representatives				
Number of representatives	4	4	8	6
Mean ACU score	77	92	98	88
Highest score	90	100	100	100
Lowest score	70	82	90	71

Source: Computed from data available on the ACU Web site (www.acuratings.org).
Note: ACU scores indicate the percentage of times that a member of Congress cast a conservative vote on the set of bills used to form the ACU index in the specified year.

Ideological differences between the parties are extremely clear among the grassroots party activists. A 2001 survey of county party chairs and other members of the county executive committees showed that Republican activists were strongly conservative. More than half called themselves very conservative, and most of the rest said that they were somewhat conservative. Democrats were somewhat more diverse in their ideological identification: about 20 percent claimed to be very liberal, about 40 percent somewhat liberal, and about 30 percent moderate in their ideological orientation (Prysby 2003). Analysis of the responses of activists to specific issue items reveals a similar pattern of polarization. A similar survey in 1991 found the Republicans to be less conservative and the Democrats to be less liberal (Prysby 1995). Thus, during the 1990s, the Democratic and Republican local party leaders were becoming more ideologically cohesive and more distinct. The growing ideological polarization of Democratic and Republican elected officials discussed above was matched and even encouraged by similar polarization among the party activists.

The above developments in North Carolina politics parallel those in other southern states. Throughout the region, similar changes in congressional delegations were taking place. Republican members of Congress were becoming more clearly conservative, while Democrats were becoming more consistently liberal (Berard 2001, 111–142). Accounts of politics in individual states report similar patterns of change in state politics (Bullock and Rozell 2003, 2007; Lamis 1999b). Studies of local party leaders and activists throughout the South indicate that the North Carolina patterns reflect regional changes (Cotter and Fisher 2004; McGlennon 1998; Steed 1998). Moreover, the trends in North Carolina and in the South also characterize national developments. Over the past two decades, the Democrats and Republicans at the national level have become more ideologically polarized, and this phenomenon is visible both among both politicians and voters (Abramowitz and Saunders 1998; Knuckey 2001).

Despite the growing ideological cohesiveness and distinctiveness of the two parties, neither should be considered a homogeneous and united group. Among Republicans, there is a division between those who are conservative on economic issues but more moderate on social issues and those who are very conservative on social issues, this latter group often strongly represented by supporters of the Christian Right (Christensen and Fleer 1999; Luebke 1998, 213–215). Among Democrats, the reliance on a biracial coalition for success sometimes creates tensions over a number of race-related issues (Prysby 2006). Democrats also have been divided between more moderate and more progressive supporters. Divisions within the parties are not just ideological. Regional divisions of various sorts have played a role, as have personal conflicts and rivalries. Party factionalism often reflects several of the above factors, which overlap in reinforcing patterns (Prysby 2003, 2006).

PARTISAN CLEAVAGES AND COALITIONS

There also has been a realignment of voters, one that is consistent with the developments in partisan politics just discussed. The two parties now appeal to distinct groups of voters. Contemporary partisan cleavages in North Carolina are similar to those in the South and in the nation. Race, religion, social class, and gender are demographic factors that consistently differentiate Democratic voters from Republican ones. The relationship that these variables have to voting behavior can be analyzed by examining data from recent exit polls in the state. Tables 7.3 and 7.4 present exit poll data for three Senate elections and three gubernatorial elections from 1998 to 2008. These elections involved different offices, years, and candidates, so the similarities that we find across these elections in the base of support for each party reflect basic differences in voter alignments.

Table 7.3 has the results of the exit polls for the 1998, 2004, and 2008 U.S. Senate elections. These elections were discussed earlier, and the candidates and outcomes can be briefly summarized. In 1998, Edwards defeated the incumbent, Faircloth, to retake this seat for the Democrats. In 2004, Republican Burr defeated Democrat Erskine Bowles, who had been in the Clinton administration, for the seat held by Edwards, who did not run for reelection. Bowles also lost in 2002 to Dole; unfortunately, exit poll data for that race are unavailable. Dole was subsequently defeated by Hagan in 2008, the third incumbent to lose in the last six Senate elections.

Table 7.4 contains exit poll data for gubernatorial elections from 2000 to 2008. In 2000, the Democratic attorney general, Mike Easley, defeated Republican Richard Vinroot, former mayor of Charlotte. Easley then defeated state legislator Patrick Ballantine in 2004 to win a second term as governor. In the 2008 gubernatorial election, discussed above, Perdue continued the string of Democratic gubernatorial victories by defeating Charlotte mayor McCrory.

The data in both tables show that race is the most prominent social or demographic division between the parties. North Carolina blacks vote overwhelmingly for Democrats, a pattern that exists outside the state as well. Republicans receive their votes almost entirely from whites. The 1965 Voting Rights Act expanded the southern electorate and brought previously excluded blacks to the polls. In North Carolina, blacks now comprise between one-fifth and one-fourth of the electorate. For a Democrat to win a statewide election, he or she normally must win the overwhelming share of

Table 7.3.   Exit Poll Results for North Carolina U.S. Senate Elections, 1998–2008

	% Voting for		
Variable	*Edwards (1998)*	*Bowles (2004)*	*Hagan (2008)*
All Voters	52	46	53
Race			
White	41	30	39
Black	91	87	96
Income			
Under $50,000	56	59	58
$50,000 and over	46	35	48
Education			
No college degree	54	49	51
College degree	50	46	52
Gender			
Male	43	41	47
Female	59	50	52
Ideology			
Liberal	84	84	89
Moderate	65	55	64
Conservative	18	21	19
Party identification			
Democrat	86	89	90
Independent	55	47	39
Republican	11	6	10

Source: Voter News Service 1998 North Carolina Exit Poll; National Election Pool 2004 and 2008 North Carolina Exit Polls. No exit poll data are available for the 2002 U.S. Senate election.

Note: Entries are the percentage of voters in the specified category who voted for the Democratic senatorial candidate (Edwards in 1998, Bowles in 2004, and Hagan in 2008). Only the percentages for the Democratic candidates are shown; these were essentially two-candidate races, so the proportion of the vote not going to the Democrat went almost entirely to the Republican.

the black vote plus a sizable minority of the white vote, a challenging but achievable goal. Democrats have been able to fashion a winning biracial coalition in some years. Other times they have not. For example, in 2004, Easley and Bowles both attracted nearly 90 percent of the black vote, but Easley also won 43 percent of the white vote, while Bowles could capture only 30 percent of this group. That difference in support among whites resulted in Easley being reelected governor while Bowles again failed in an attempt to be a U.S. senator.

Blacks have been strongly aligned with the Democratic Party since the civil rights movement of the 1960s. Democrats became clearly identified at the national level as the party that supported civil rights legislation, such as the 1964 Civil Rights Act and the 1965 Voting Rights Act. Some southern Democrats opposed these measures, but these conservative voices within the party quickly diminished over time, and differences between Democrats and Republicans on civil rights and other race-related

Table 7.4. **Exit Poll Results for North Carolina Gubernatorial Elections, 2000–2008**

Variable	% Voting for		
	Easley (2000)	*Easley (2004)*	*Perdue (2008)*
All Voters	52	55	50
Race			
White	50	43	43
Black	87	89	87
Income			
Under $50,000	56	55	64
$50,000 and over	52	47	45
Education			
No college degree	55	48	57
College degree	58	55	53
Gender			
Male	50	46	51
Female	61	57	57
Ideology			
Liberal	83	87	83
Moderate	67	60	65
Conservative	30	38	31
Party identification			
Democrat	87	90	88
Independent	49	59	37
Republican	15	19	9

Source: Voter News Service 2000 North Carolina Exit Poll; National Election Pool 2004 and 2008 North Carolina Exit Polls.

Note: Entries are the percentage of voters in the specified category who voted for the Democratic gubernatorial candidate (Easley in 2000 and 2004; Perdue in 2008). Only the percentages for the Democratic candidate are shown; these were essentially two-candidate races, so the proportion of the vote not going to the Democrat went almost entirely to the Republican.

issues were quite clear by the 1980s. Blacks have responded to these party differences with strong support for the party that they perceive as more committed to racial equality. Moreover, blacks are more likely to be in blue-collar jobs and to have lower incomes, so the appeal of Democrats to working-class and lower-income voters, discussed below, reinforces the tendency for blacks to support Democratic candidates.

Religion probably is second only to race as a politically divisive social factor. It is not included in tables 7.3 or 7.4 because the exit polls did not ask a question about religion in a consistent manner in these years. However, two important patterns appear in various polls taken in recent years. First, among white Protestants, those who are evangelical or fundamentalist Protestants (e.g., Southern Baptists) are more Republican than those who are mainline Protestants (e.g., Presbyterians, Methodists). Second, those who are more religious, which most typically is measured by frequency of church attendance, are more Republican than those who are less religious. Similar divisions do not exist among blacks, however, who are overwhelmingly Democratic regardless of religious orientation. The vast majority of North Carolina voters are Protestants, so the voting patterns of Catholics and other non-Protestant groups are both less important in the state and also harder to examine through exit polls.

The religious divisions among whites reflect the relationship of religion to social issues, such as abortion, gay rights, and separation of church and state. Both religious denomination (evangelical versus mainline Protestant) and religiosity (typically measured by church attendance) affect attitudes on these issues. White Southern Baptists who regularly attend church generally are more conservative on social issues than Methodists or Presbyterians who do not attend church very much. Republican candidates almost always take conservative positions on these issues, which makes them more attractive to highly religious white evangelical Protestant voters (Luebke 1998, 213–215). Some Republican candidates have placed considerable emphasis on social issues. Helms in particular often talked about abortion, homosexuality, pornography, and a general breakdown of morals in society. However, Democrats are not consistently liberal on social issues. For example, in the 2004 gubernatorial election, Easley opposed legalizing gay marriage, supported the death penalty, and avoided taking a position on abortion. North Carolina voters tend to be fairly conservative on most social issues, so it is not surprising that Democratic candidates, at least those who are successful in winning elections, are often moderate or even conservative on these issues.

Differences along social class or socioeconomic status (SES) are present but generally not that strong. Democratic candidates consistently do better among those who are below average in income, but the difference between the below- and above-average groups normally is about 10 percentage points (the average household income of voters in recent elections is about $50,000, so this cutoff point is used in the exit poll tables). The pattern for education is less clear. Differences between those with a college degree and those without are often quite small. In some cases, the Democratic candidate did slightly better among those with college degrees than among those without, a pattern of support that fails to fit the expectation that Democrats do better among lower-SES voters. Moreover, if we isolate those who have an advanced degree, these voters often were even more Democratic than others with a college degree. Income appears to be a more relevant aspect of SES for voting behavior. Socioeconomic status is tied to a number of political issues. Democrats are widely perceived as the party more likely to pursue policies that benefit the less well off, and Republicans generally are thought of as the party more favorable to business and upper-income groups. Despite the prevailing images of the Democrats as the party of the working class and lower income groups and the Republicans as the party of business groups and the rich, the reality is that the parties have been less defined by class differences than by other social and demographic cleavages (Fleer, Lowery, and Prysby 1988).

Gender differences have become significant in the state, just as they have nationally, with women usually about 10 percentage points more Democratic than men. This gender gap is less pronounced among married voters; it is among those who are not currently married that women are substantially more Democratic in their voting behavior. Many people believe that gender differences in voting are primarily the result of so-called women's issues, such as abortion or child care. However, gender differences are a result of a more general liberalism among women on a variety of issues, including defense and economic issues. Also, the gender of the candidate has little effect on gender differences in voting. The 2008 exit poll data illustrate this point. The gender gap was only 6 percentage points in the gubernatorial election, in which a Democratic woman ran against a Republican man. In the Senate election, which featured two female candidates, the gender gap was 10 percentage points, and in the presidential contest, the gap was 12 percentage points.

Age generally has not been an important factor in voting behavior in North Carolina, and the relevant data are not included in the exit poll tables for that reason. Democrats sometimes have done better among younger voters, but other times they have not. What patterns have existed have been inconsistent. For example, in 1996, Democratic governor Hunt did worse among young voters than he did among others, and senatorial candidate Gantt did only slightly better among young voters, even though he was running against Helms, who might have been expected to appeal much more to older voters. In 2008, Democrats did far better among those under thirty than they did among the rest of the electorate. Young voters appear to be more volatile, perhaps being particularly affected by short-term forces because they have not developed more stable partisan attachments. Therefore, we should not conclude that because young voters were strongly Democratic in 2008, they will continue to be strongly Democratic as they age. Nevertheless, the fact that Democrats did so well among the young, coupled with the fact that they also did well among these voters in 2004, suggests the possibility that a new generation of Democratic voters is emerging. If the tentative partisan leanings of this age cohort are reinforced in subsequent elections, they could develop stable Democratic partisan orientations.

Ideological orientations clearly distinguish Democratic and Republican voters. Liberals strongly support Democrats. Self-identified conservatives, who outnumber liberals in North Carolina, support Republicans, although perhaps not as strongly as liberals support Democrats. This leaves moderate voters as the determining force. In a statewide election, the Democratic candidate normally has to capture a large majority of the moderate vote in order to win. In the past three gubernatorial elections, the Democratic candidate has won over 60 percent of the vote of moderates, a sufficient majority to ensure election. In other cases, Democratic candidates have failed to do as well with the moderate vote, which in turn usually results in their losing the election. The ideological cleavages among voters reflect differences between the parties and their candidates. In almost every recent major election in the state, the Republican candidate has been more conservative than the Democrat. Sometimes the differences are smaller, with a moderate Democrat facing a moderately conservative Republican; other times the differences are much larger. But the differences almost always exist.

Finally, party identification is strongly related to the vote, as the exit poll data show. In the past, conservative Democratic voters often voted for Republican candidates for some offices. Presidential elections often featured significant Democratic voter defections. Senator Helms sought and received the votes of "Jessecrats," who were often characterized as older, rural, conservative Democrats. Party identification and ideology are now more closely aligned, so there are fewer conservative Democrats to defect. In each of the past three presidential election years, the Democratic candidates for U.S. senator and governor all received at least 87 percent of the vote of Democrats. Democratic defections in the 2000 and 2004 presidential contests were somewhat higher, but even in these cases, at least 80 percent of Democratic voters cast a ballot for the presidential candidate of their party (Prysby 2002, 2005). Republicans usually are even more loyal in their voting. In recent elections, there have been roughly equal numbers of Democratic and Republican voters, although this was not true in 2008, when Democrats outnumbered Republicans by 42 percent to 31 percent. Independent voters, who usually are around one-fourth of all voters, are the key swing group. Neither party can win statewide office without receiving at least a sizable share of the votes of independents. If the numbers of Democratic and Republican voters in an election are equal, and if defection rates are the same for both parties, a winning candidate will need a majority of the independent vote. In 2008, Obama, Hagan, and Perdue all were able to win with only around 40 percent of the independent vote, but that was a year with high Democratic turnout and few Democratic defections.

CHANGE OR CONTINUITY IN 2008?

The 2008 elections deviated from the pattern established in the 1990s. Does this deviation represent a temporary shift due to unique forces operating in that year, or does it signal a new direction in North Carolina politics? If the Democratic sweep in 2008 was simply a result of the very favorable year nationally for the party, then future elections are likely to be similar to past elections. The GOP can be expected to recover its losses in years that are more favorable to the party nationally. In this sense, 2008 may represent continuity of the basic nature of electoral politics in North Carolina. However, if the 2008 elections indicate more than just the impact of national tides largely associated with the unpopular Bush administration— if they instead indicate more fundamental changes occurring in the state's politics—then 2008 may truly be a year of real change.

Considerable evidence indicates that there was substantial continuity in North Carolina politics in 2008. The Democratic victory can be attributed in large part to national tides, which were very favorable for Democrats. President George W. Bush's approval rating in 2008 never rose above 34 percent and dropped to 25 percent in early October, according to the Gallup Poll. Although John McCain attempted to separate himself from Bush, Obama did his best to tie the two together, and the Republican candidate suffered because of the foreign policy and economic failures of the Bush administration. Moreover, 90 percent of Obama voters also voted for Hagan and Perdue, so it is quite plausible that neither of these Democratic candidates would have won if there had not been a strong Obama vote in the state.

There also was considerable continuity in the underlying sources of voting behavior, as our earlier analysis of exit poll data indicates. Party identification and ideology remain strong predictors of vote choice. Republican candidates for governor and senator in 2008 did very well among conservatives and Republican identifiers, as they have in the past. Democrats were a slightly greater share of the electorate in 2008, and a slightly higher percent of Democrats voted for their party's candidates. These small shifts produced the Democratic sweep. Notably, the major statewide Democratic candidates (Obama, Hagan, and Perdue) all received only about 40 percent of the votes of independents, so Republicans more than held their own among this group of voters. The relationships between voting and demographic factors in 2008 also were very similar to patterns in previous years, with the one exception of age, which was discussed above.

If we examine the outcome of recent presidential elections in North Carolina and compare them to the nation, we find that state election outcomes are linked to the national outcome; Republicans did best in North Carolina when they were doing well nationally. In 1996 and 2000, the state was around 7 percentage points more Republican than the country as a whole. It declined to about 5 percentage points more Republican in 2004 (perhaps because Edwards was on the Democratic ticket). In 2008, it was only about 3 percentage points more Republican. Two conclusions can be drawn from these figures. First, if Obama had won nationally with only 51 or 52 percent of the two-party vote, he would not have carried North Carolina. Second, if North Carolina had been 5 percentage points more Republican, as it was in 2004, McCain would have won the state despite his national defeat. Put another way, the Democratic share of the 2008 two-party presidential vote in North Carolina was 6.4 percentage points greater than it was in 2004. Almost 5 percentage points of that change can be attributed to national change, while about 1.6 percentage points came from the narrowing of the gap between the state and the nation.

On the other hand, the fact that there was only a 3 percentage point gap in the presidential vote between North Carolina and the nation in 2008 did contribute to the Obama victory, so it is important to understand why this happened. One possibility is the extremely vigorous campaign effort put forth by Obama in the state. By all accounts, the extent of the Democratic effort far exceeded what either party had done in any previous presidential election (Prysby 2009). Republicans had a substantial campaign effort too, one that exceeded its effort in previous years, but it lagged far behind the Democratic effort. The Obama and Democratic Party effort appears to have paid off in voter mobilization, which is one reason why Democrats were a larger share of the electorate in 2008 than in 2004 (Prysby 2009). It seems unlikely that Democrats will continue to have such an advantage in campaign organization and activity. Campaign effort may be a short-term force that was very favorable to the Democrats in 2008, but it is one that might well be favorable to the Republicans in another year.

Another reason for the narrow gap between the state and the nation in 2008 presidential voting could be a changing political landscape in North Carolina. North Carolina was one of the fastest growing states over the past several years. Its population has increased by 7.6 percent since 2004. Much of the growth has occurred in the major metropolitan areas, particularly Charlotte and Raleigh-Durham. For example, Mecklenburg County (Charlotte) had a population increase of about 25 percent between 2000 and 2007, and Wake County (Raleigh) had an increase of 33 percent.[3] Obama did extremely well in these areas, capturing 62 percent of the vote in Mecklenburg County and 57 percent of the vote in Wake County. Obama also did well in the other major urban areas (Prysby 2009). Many of the newcomers to these areas are northern immigrants who are often more moderate in their political orientations. A recent statewide poll found that northern migrants to the state were less conservative than native Tar Heels. For example, 28 percent of those now living in the state but born in the North called themselves conservative, compared to 34 percent of native North Carolinians (Vercellotti 2008). Significant differences exist in church attendance, which is related to political attitudes, as was discussed earlier. Only 42 percent of those born in the North said that they were regular church attenders; 55 percent of those born in the state said that they attended regularly (Vercellotti 2008). Similar economic and demographic changes have been cited as sources of change in Virginia politics. These changes are likely to continue in North Carolina, so if they were a contributing factor to Democratic success in 2008, they are likely to provide further support for Democrats.

CONCLUSION

North Carolina continues to be a highly competitive two-party state. It seems likely to remain that way in the near future. Whether Republicans will have an advantage in federal elections, as they did for over a decade prior to 2008, is unclear. Most likely, Republican presidential candidates will do better in North Carolina than in the nation. Even in 2008, when there was an unprecedented Democratic campaign effort in the state, North Carolina was still 3 percentage points more Republican than the country as a whole. Quite possibly, future presidential elections will find this gap to be wider, as it was in the past. But even if North Carolina returns to the Republican column in future presidential elections, it is likely to be highly competitive in other races. There are good reasons why in the past a significant number of Republican presidential voters have voted for Democrats for other offices, and these reasons are likely to remain in future elections. North Carolina Democrats generally are more ideologically moderate than their national counterparts, and North Carolina Republicans are often more conservative than northern Republicans, so for some voters there is no ideological inconsistency in voting for a Republican presidential candidate and a Democratic gubernatorial candidate, for example. Also, state government elections often revolve around less ideologically divisive issues, such as improving education, building roads, and attracting new industry, which may help to explain why Republicans have done better in elections for national office than for state office.

On the other hand, we cannot dismiss the possibility that North Carolina is undergoing real change. There are trends in the state, such as the growth of major metropolitan areas and the migration of northerners to these areas, that may benefit the Democrats in the long run. The disproportionate support for Democrats by young voters in recent elections could indicate an important generational shift that might have lasting effects. It is difficult to assess the speed and the significance of these changes at this time, but similar changes also seem to have influenced Virginia politics. Overall, Obama did better in the more rapidly growing southern states, such as North Carolina and Virginia, than in slower-growing states, such as Mississippi and Alabama.

In some sense, these changes may already have affected North Carolina politics. Recent elections have lacked the intense ideological tone of earlier years. Divisive racial and social issues have not held center stage in these contests. This differs from what Tar Heel voters were used to when Helms campaigned in the state. One interesting episode in 2008 involved the Senate race. Dole ran a controversial ad late in the campaign that linked Hagan to atheists, and the ad appeared to have backfired.[4] Perhaps the divisive social issues of past elections do not resonate as well with the contemporary electorate. Similarly, the victory of Obama may indicate that race is a less divisive factor than it once was in Tar Heel politics. Of course, Republicans and Democrats surely will continue to differ greatly in ideology, but the tone and emphasis of ideological debates may be different.

Of course, exactly how these conflicts play out in future elections will depend on the behavior of specific party leaders and candidates. The influence of prominent individuals in the past, such as Helms for the Republicans or Hunt for the Democrats, suggests that how people behave in office shapes the future nature of politics (Prysby 2006). If the state is changing in its social and economic makeup, how the leaders of the two parties respond to these changes will affect Tar Heel politics. Moreover, it is worth remembering that the future of North Carolina politics cannot be considered apart from national politics. If the next decade is one in which Democrats dominate nationally, retaining the presidency and expanding their current control over Congress, Democrats in North Carolina are likely to prosper. But if instead we see a Republican resurgence nationally, Republicans are likely to advance in the state, especially in congressional elections. Given the highly unpredictable nature of national politics over the past ten years, it would be foolish to predict which of the above scenarios will actually occur in the next decade.

NOTES

Author's Note: I have benefited from discussions about North Carolina politics with numerous individuals over the years, including the following: Ted Arrington, Thad Beyle, Kerra Bolton, Rob Christensen, Seth Effron, Ken Eudy, Scott Falmlen, Jack Fleer, Ferrel Guillory, Jack Hawke, Paul Johnson, Chris McClure, Christopher Mears, Jerry Meek, David Price, Bob Shaw, Caroline Valand, and Jim Van Hecke. I appreciate the willingness of these individuals, as well as others whom I have failed to acknowledge, to share their observations and insights with me. However, I am responsible for all of the facts and interpretations that appear in this essay.

1. The underlying partisanship of a district is best measured by the presidential vote in the district. Using the 2004 presidential vote, which is the most recent set of results currently available for congressional districts, we find five Democratic House seats (districts 2, 7, 8, 11, and 13) that are not solidly Democratic. In each of these districts, Bush received between 52 percent and 57 percent of the two-party vote. The incumbent Democrat in each of these districts may be able to win reelection, but each district could switch in an open seat election, particularly in a good year for the GOP. The other three Democratic seats (districts 1, 4, and 12) probably are safe ones for the party; Bush received less than 45 percent of the vote in each of these districts. The five Republican seats (districts 3, 5, 6, 9, and 10) are all ones won by Bush in 2004 by over 60 percent; each would almost certainly be won by a Republican even if the incumbent failed to run for reelection.

2. This ad, often referred to as the "hands" ad, showed the hands of a white man holding a letter, which he crumpled up. The voice-over indicated that the man had received a rejection letter for a job that he needed and was the most qualified for, and that his rejection was due to the fact that the employer had to hire a minority applicant because of a racial quota. The ad ended with the statement that Helms opposed racial quotas and Gantt did not (Jamieson 1992, 97–100; Luebke 1998, 181–184).

3. The figures on population change were calculated from data presented in "Population Estimates and Projections," Office of State Budget and Management Web site. Accessed on November 29, 2008, at: http://www.osbm.states.nc.us.

4. Late in the campaign, a Dole ad linked Hagan to a prominent atheist who hosted a fund-raising event for Hagan; the ad ended with a picture of Hagan and another woman's voice saying that there is no God (but giving the impression that Hagan was making the statement). Hagan protested vehemently, stating that she was very active in her church and that the ad deliberately misrepresented her position. News coverage of the controversy seemed to benefit Hagan (Zagaroli 2008).

REFERENCES

Abramowitz, Alan I., and Kyle Saunders. 1998. "Ideological Realignment in the U.S. Electorate." *Journal of Politics* 20:634–652.

Aistrup, Joseph A. 1996. *The Southern Strategy Revisited: Republican Top-Down Advancement in the South.* Lexington: The University Press of Kentucky.

Bass, Jack, and Walter DeVries. 1976. *The Transformation of Southern Politics: Social Change and Political Consequences Since 1945.* New York: Basic Books.

Berard, Stanley P. 2001. *Southern Democrats in the U.S. House of Representatives.* Norman: Oklahoma University Press.

Black, Earl, and Merle Black. 1987. *Politics and Society in the South.* Cambridge, MA: Harvard University Press.

———. 1992. *The Vital South.* Cambridge, MA: Harvard University Press.

———. 2002. *The Rise of Southern Republicans.* Cambridge, MA: Harvard University Press.

Bullock, Charles S., III, and Mark J. Rozell, eds. 2003. *The New Politics of the Old South*, 2nd ed. Lanham, MD: Rowman & Littlefield.

———. 2007. *The New Politics of the Old South*, 3rd ed. Lanham, MD: Rowman & Littlefield.

Christensen, Rob. 2008. *The Paradox of Tar Heel Politics*. Chapel Hill: University of North Carolina Press.

Christensen, Rob, and Jack D. Fleer. 1999. "North Carolina: Between Helms and Hunt No Majority Emerges." In *Southern Politics in the 1990s*, ed. Alexander P. Lamis. Baton Rouge: Louisiana State University Press.

Cotter, Patrick R., and Samuel H. Fisher III. 2004. "A Growing Divide: Issue Opinions of Southern Party Activists." In *Southern Political Party Activists: Patterns of Conflict and Change, 1991–2001*, ed. John A. Clark and Charles Prysby. Lexington: University of Kentucky Press.

Eamon, Thomas F. 2008. "The Seeds of Modern North Carolina Politics." In *The New Politics of North Carolina*, ed. Christopher A. Cooper and H. Gibbs Knotts. Chapel Hill: University of North Carolina Press.

Fleer, Jack D., Roger C. Lowery, and Charles L. Prysby. 1988. "Political Change in North Carolina." In *The South's New Politics*, ed. Robert Swansbrough and David Brodsky. Columbia: University of South Carolina Press.

Jamieson, Kathleen Hall. 1992. *Dirty Politics*. New York: Oxford University Press.

Key, V. O., Jr. 1949. *Southern Politics in State and Nation*. New York: Alfred A. Knopf.

Klinkner, Philip A., ed. 1996. *Midterm: The Elections of 1994 in Context*. Boulder, CO: Westview Press.

Knuckey, Jonathan. 2001. "Ideological Realignment and Partisan Change in the American South, 1972–1996." *Politics and Policy* 29:337–360.

Lamis, Alexander P. 1984. *The Two-Party South*. New York: Oxford University Press.

———. 1999a. "Southern Politics in the 1990s." In *Southern Politics in the 1990s*, ed. Alexander P. Lamis. Baton Rouge: Louisiana State University Press.

———, ed. 1999b. *Southern Politics in the 1990s*. Baton Rouge: Louisiana State University Press.

Link, William A. 2008. *Righteous Warrior: Jesse Helms and the Rise of Modern Conservatism*. New York: St. Martin's Press.

Lublin, David. 2004. *The Republican South*. Princeton, NJ: Princeton University Press.

Luebke, Paul. 1990. *Tar Heel Politics*. Chapel Hill: University of North Carolina Press.

———. 1998. *Tar Heel Politics 2000*. Chapel Hill: University of North Carolina Press.

McGlennon, John. 1998. "Factions in the Politics of the New South." In *Party Organization and Activism in the American South*, ed. Robert P. Steed, John A. Clark, Lewis Bowman, and Charles D. Hadley. Tuscaloosa: University of Alabama Press.

Prysby, Charles. 1995. "North Carolina: Emerging Two-Party Politics." In *Southern State Party Organizations and Activists*, ed. Charles D. Hadley and Lewis Bowman. Westport, CT: Praeger.

———. 1996. "The 1990 U.S. Senate Election in North Carolina." In *Race, Politics, and Governance in the United States*, ed. Huey L. Perry. Gainesville: University Press of Florida.

———. 1997. "North Carolina: Republican Consolidation or Democratic Resurgence?" In *The 1996 Presidential Election in the South*, ed. Laurence W. Moreland and Robert P. Steed. Westport, CT: Praeger.

———. 2002. "North Carolina: Continued Two-Party Competition." In *The 2000 Presidential Election in the South*, ed. Robert P. Steed and Laurence W. Moreland. Westport, CT: Praeger.

———. 2003. "North Carolina: The Development of Party Organizations in a Competitive Environment." *American Review of Politics* 24:145–164. Special issue on "Southern Grassroots Party Activists," edited by John A. Clark and Charles Prysby.

———. 2004. "A Civil Campaign in a Competitive State: The 2002 North Carolina U.S. Senate Election." In *Running on Empty? Political Discourse in Congressional Elections*, ed. L. Sandy Maisel and Darrell M. West. Lanham, MD: Rowman & Littlefield.

———. 2005. "North Carolina: Color the Tar Heels Federal Red and State Blue." *American Review of Politics* 26:185–202. Special issue on "The 2004 Presidential Election and Southern Politics," edited by Larry Moreland and Robert Steed.

———. 2006. "North Carolina: Two-Party Competition Continues Into the Twenty-First Century." In *The New Politics of the Old South: An Introduction to Southern Politics*, 3rd ed., ed. Charles S. Bullock III and Mark J. Rozell. Lanham, MD: Rowman & Littlefield.

———. 2008. "The Reshaping of the Political Party System in North Carolina." In *The New Politics of North Carolina*, ed. Christopher A. Cooper and H. Gibbs Knotts. Chapel Hill: University of North Carolina Press.

Prysby, Charles. 2009. "North Carolina: Change and Continuity in 2008." In *The 2008 Presidential Election in the South*, ed. Branwell DuBose Kapeluck, Lawrence W. Moreland, and Robert P. Steed. Fayetteville: University of Arkansas Press.

Scher, Richard. 1997. *Politics in the New South*, 2nd ed. Armonk, NY: M. E. Sharpe.

Steed, Robert P. 1998. "Parties, Ideologies, and Issues: The Structuring of Political Conflict." In *Party Organization and Activism in the American South*, ed. Robert P. Steed, John A. Clark, Lewis Bowman, and Charles D. Hadley. Tuscaloosa: University of Alabama Press.

Vercellotti, Timothy. 2008. "How Southern Is the Old North State?: Public Opinion in North Carolina." In *The New Politics of North Carolina*, ed. Christopher A. Cooper and H. Gibbs Knotts. Chapel Hill: University of North Carolina Press.

Zagaroli, Lisa. 2008. "'Godless' Ad Sets Off War of Words between Hagan, Dole." *Charlotte (NC) Observer*. 30 October. http://www.charlotteobserver.com/politics/story/287745.html.

8

Tennessee

Once a Bluish State, Now a Reddish One

Michael Nelson

The history of chapter titles in the scholarly literature on Tennessee politics offers a history in microcosm of Tennessee politics itself. In 1949 V. O. Key invoked the state's southern and Democratic heritage by calling his chapter about Tennessee "The Civil War and Mr. Crump." A quarter century later, Lee S. Greene and Jack E. Holmes (1972) celebrated the state's transition to racial integration and legislative reapportionment with "A Politics of Peaceful Change." More than a quarter century after that, John Lyman Mason (2003) marked another feature of Tennessee politics: its consistent contributions to the roster of prominent national political leaders. He called his chapter "Politics and Politicians Who Matter Beyond State Borders."

Most chapter titles have weighed in, as this one does, on the question of party competition in Tennessee. "Genuine Two-Party Politics" was the title of both Jack Bass and Walter DeVries's chapter on Tennessee in 1976 and David Brodsky's in 1998. Alexander Lamis joined the chorus, labeling Tennessee a "Composite of All the South" in a 1984 book called *The Two-Party South*. Taking a different tack, Robert Swansbrough and David Brodsky used "Weakening Party Loyalties and Growing Independence" in their 1988 chapter on Tennessee politics. A year later, Philip Ashford and Richard Locker identified the Republican sweep of all three statewide offices in the 1994 elections as "A Partisan Big Bang amid Quiet Accommodation."

Anyone who presumes to join this long and distinguished scholarly procession is well advised to choose his or her own words with care. The title of this chapter toys with the red state/blue state distinction in the election-night maps that the television networks have used in recent years to display which states the Republicans have won (the red ones) and which states have gone Democratic (the blue ones). In truth, although Tennessee has never been purely red or purely blue, it has nonetheless evolved from being a bluish state to a reddish one. One-and-a-half party competition, with the Republicans gradually replacing the Democrats in the dominant position, has typified most of Tennessee's post–World War II political history.

Two features of Tennessee geography help to explain why the state has not been solidly Democratic or solidly Republican even though it has tended one way or the other in different eras. One is the state's location. The labels that scholars have variously used to place Tennessee within the South—"Peripheral," "Rim," "Outer," and so on—all serve to remind that Tennessee is on the northern edge of the South, not embedded within it. Unlike, say, Alabama or North Carolina, Tennessee shares borders with two states that are not generally reckoned as southern, Kentucky and Missouri.

The other geographical feature of Tennessee that bears on its politics is the state's extraordinary length. Tennessee is more than 500 miles long from east to west. A voter in Mountain City, in the state's northeastern corner, lives closer to Canada than to Memphis, which is as far south and west as one can go and still be in Tennessee. With this length comes variety, so much so that the state officially recognizes three "grand divisions" in various ways (including a three-star flag): mountainous East Tennessee, the rolling hills of Middle Tennessee, and the flat fertile land of West Tennessee.

The rest of this chapter consists of a series of seven prose "snapshots" of Tennessee politics in the postwar era. The first one is of 1946, and the rest follow at ten-year intervals through 2006, with a postscript on 2008–2009. Although these snapshots unfold page by page within the covers of this book, they might better be imagined side by side in a row, like a spectrum of colors. Pure blue and pure red do not appear on this spectrum. But looked at in sequence, the flow from bluish on the left to reddish on the right is hard to miss.

SNAPSHOT 1: 1946

Tennessee was never a solidly Democratic state, at least not after Andrew Jackson, a Tennessean, left the White House in 1837. In 1844, Tennessee voted for the Whig candidate for president, Henry Clay, even as the rest of the country was electing Tennessee's former Democratic governor,

James K. Polk, by nearly a two-to-one electoral vote majority. After Reconstruction, observes Dewey W. Grantham (1995), the Republican "challenge to the Democrats gave Tennessee the most consistently competitive politics of any southern state." In the early twentieth century, Tennessee occasionally (1910, 1912, 1928) elected Republican governors. Since 1867, the Second Congressional District has always elected a Republican to the House of Representatives, and the First District has done so since 1880. Indeed, in several elections from the end of Reconstruction until the 1950s, these East Tennessee districts were the only two in the South whose voters sent Republican members to Congress.[1] East Tennesseans also reliably elected Republicans to the state legislature. In 1939, for example, the 17 percent of state House members who were Republicans and the 12 percent of Republican state senators were nearly three times as many as in any other southern state (calculated from data in Scher 1992, 166).

In presidential elections, Tennessee was the only state in the South to support the Republican candidate, Warren G. Harding, against Democrat James M. Cox in 1920. Eight years later it supported Herbert Hoover against his Democratic opponent, New York governor Al Smith. Indeed, in presidential elections from 1900 to 1944, Tennesseans gave a larger share of their votes to the Republican nominee for president than the people of any other southern state in all but two elections, and in those two they were a close second.[2]

One could say, then, that in 1946, at the time of this chapter's first political snapshot, Tennessee was the most Republican state in the South. But a more accurate way of putting it would be that Tennessee was the least Democratic of all the southern Democratic states—bluish in a sea of blue. In the twentieth century through 1946, for example, the GOP's three victories for governor paled in comparison to the Democrats' twenty-one, and all three depended on deep but temporary divisions within the Democratic Party. The same could be said of the two (out of twelve) presidential elections in which Tennessee voted Republican. And never were Democratic divisions so serious as to affect Senate elections, which Democratic candidates won without exception. To be sure, GOP strength was unflagging in the Smokies of East Tennessee, which had stoutly resisted secession and generally supported the Union during the Civil War. But these "Mountain Republicans" nearly marked the extent of Republican influence in the state.[3] To call them the GOP's base would be a misnomer because little was built on it. As V. O. Key (1949, 75) wrote at the time, "Tennessee in a sense has not one one-party system but two one-party systems," with the one-party Republican East considerably smaller than the one-party Democratic Middle and West.

Indeed, Key found that one of the firmest props of the statewide Democratic majority in Tennessee in this era was the reluctance of East

Tennessee Republicans to see their party grow. The "Tennessee Republican high command contemplates victory in state races with a shudder," Key wrote (1949, 78), with only mild hyperbole. As the established Republican leadership saw it, growth might mean losing control of the party apparatus to new members. Even worse, it might mean losing the political patronage that Middle and West Tennessee Democratic leaders allocated to their East Tennessee Republican peers in exchange for mild acquiescence to statewide Democratic control. Tennessee politics, Key (1949, 79) observed, was akin to "monopolistic competition" between two firms, each of which preserves its position by allowing the other to dominate a portion of the market without fear of challenge.

As for the state's Democratic Party, it was controlled in large measure by E. H. Crump, the conservative, pro-business Democratic boss of Memphis and surrounding Shelby County. From the 1910s to the early 1950s (the longest period of control by any urban machine politician in the twentieth century), Crump dominated his city with patronage, contracts, "efficient government, a clean city, and other blessings, but all without freedom or liberty" (Key 1949, 63). In 1932, Franklin D. Roosevelt called him "a good Tammany Hall Tennessean"; twelve years later *Time* featured him on its cover as "the most absolute political boss in the U.S." (Dowdy 2006, 68, 111).

In 1932, Crump extended his span of control to include the state government. His approach was simple: he would personally choose candidates for statewide office and, by persuading Memphians to cast their votes for them almost unanimously, give his slate a virtually insurmountable lead in the Democratic primary that, in the absence of serious Republican competition, was tantamount to election. In 1936, for example, the Crump-endorsed candidate for governor, Gordon Browning, won the Democratic primary on the basis of the 59,874 votes he received in Shelby County. Two years later, having fallen out with Crump, Browning's Shelby County vote shrank to 9,315, costing the governor his bid for reelection. Crump's most reliable allies during his long period of statewide control were Kenneth McKellar, a Memphis Democrat who served in the Senate from 1917 to 1953, and B. Carroll Reece, the First District's Republican House member from 1920 to 1946.[4] McKellar saw to it that Crump controlled most of the federal patronage in the state, and Reece distributed the Republican jobs that Crump allotted to East Tennessee in return for keeping the GOP quiescent in statewide elections.

SNAPSHOT 2: 1956

The first decade after World War II was marked by significant changes in Tennessee politics. Crump died in 1954, but his control of the state predeceased him by several years. With the end of the Crump regime, several Tennesseans emerged as nationally influential political leaders, an unprecedented development since the Jackson-Polk era of a century before, but one that has persisted ever since. And the state went Republican in two presidential elections, this time in ways that, unlike Harding and Hoover's flukish victories in the 1920s, augured a new era of competition for Tennessee's eleven electoral votes.

Lots of fingerprints were on the weapons that slew the Crump machine. Returning veterans eager for change, northern migrants unaccustomed to boss rule, rising labor unions impatient with pro-business conservatism, the gradual waning of organizational vitality that comes with the passage of time, and his own bad choices were among the causes of Crump's rapid decline in statewide influence. In 1948, matters came to a head. Crump opposed President Harry S. Truman's bid for reelection in favor of South Carolina governor Strom Thurmond, the anti–civil rights States' Rights Party nominee. Thurmond ran well in Memphis and nearby counties in West Tennessee, an area whose climate, economy, and history resembled the four Deep South states that he carried on Election Day. But Thurmond won only 14 percent of the statewide vote in Tennessee. Crump's abandonment of his party in the presidential election helped sour the voters on his candidates for governor and senator, both of whom were soundly defeated in the Democratic primary. The Crump era in state politics, if not in Memphis, was over.

The anti-Crump candidate who won the Senate election in 1948, Estes Kefauver, was the first of three Democrats to enter the national political spotlight. Albert Gore Sr., elected to the Senate in 1952 after beating longtime Crump stalwart McKellar in the Democratic primary, and Frank Clement, who was elected governor in 1952 and reelected in 1954, were the others. All three were more liberal than was the norm in Tennessee or the rest of the South, which earned them the attention of Democrats outside the region—so much so, in fact, that *Harper's Magazine* ran an article called "Too Much Talent in Tennessee?" (Dykeman 1955).

Kefauver parlayed a long series of nationally televised Senate hearings on organized crime into a candidacy for the Democratic presidential nomination in 1952. He lost to Truman's anointed successor, Governor Adlai E. Stevenson of Illinois, but not before winning fourteen of seventeen state primaries, making him the century's first southerner to mount a national campaign for his party's nomination (Black and Black 1992, 100). In 1956, Kefauver lost to Stevenson again, then defeated Gore and Senator John F. Kennedy of Massachusetts to win the vice presidential nomination when Stevenson threw the choice open to the convention. Clement was featured at the convention as the keynote speaker, but his florid oratorical style, well suited to courthouse squares in rural Tennessee, did not translate well into the national idiom. "Bombastic cornpone" was one of the kinder descriptions of Clement's long, loud, and melodramatic effort.

The national Democratic Party's interest in Kefauver, Gore, and Clement in 1956 was not coincidental. Two years earlier, when the Supreme Court ruled in *Brown v. Board of Education* that public school segregation was unconstitutional, all three Tennessee Democrats responded in ways that set them apart from most other southern political leaders. Clement made clear that the ruling would be enforced in his state and called out the National Guard when segregationist thugs burned down the high school in Clinton; he was the first southern governor to take such forceful action. Kefauver and Gore were two of only three southern Democratic senators (Senate Majority Leader Lyndon B. Johnson of Texas was the third) who denied their signatures to the Southern Manifesto, a defiant defense of racial segregation signed by nineteen southern senators and ninety-six southern representatives, all of them Democrats.

Because of Tennessee's northern location within the South, the ability of Kefauver, Gore, and Clement to disdain the region's rampant racial conservatism in the 1950s (each survived to win more statewide elections) was not altogether surprising. African Americans in the South tended to be treated the worst in the states where their numbers were greatest. In Tennessee, blacks comprised 16 percent of the population, second lowest to Texas among the southern states. "In the cities there has long been no serious obstacle to Negro voting" in Tennessee, Key noted (1949, 75). Especially in Memphis, where the state's African American population was concentrated, black voters had been a mainstay of Crump's power, and he had acknowledged their support by paying their poll taxes and giving them "a fairer break than usual in public services" (Key 1949, 74). Indeed, during the 1930s, as President Franklin D. Roosevelt sought to detach African American voters from their post–Civil War affiliation with the GOP and bring them into his New Deal Democratic coalition, his aides consulted with Crump about how to build a biracial majority (Dowdy 2006, 88, 113).

As for the state's Republicans in the first postwar decade, they consistently maintained their two East Tennessee seats in Congress but did not add to them. The same was true of their representation in the state legislature. The GOP also continued to lose every election for governor and senator. Sometimes Republican candidates waged strenuous campaigns for statewide office (Reece ran hard for senator and Grand Ole Opry star Roy Acuff for governor in 1948, and each won around one-third of the vote), but sometimes the party ran no candidate at all.

The bright spot for Republicans—and it was bright indeed—was that Tennessee was one of four southern states (Virginia, Florida, and Texas were the others) to support the Republican candidate for president,

Dwight D. Eisenhower, not just in 1952 but also, despite native son Kefauver's presence on the Democratic ticket, in 1956. Although Eisenhower ran best in traditionally Republican East Tennessee, his margin of victory came from the inroads he made among well-educated, middle-class voters in the state's metropolitan areas—the very group that had been growing most rapidly since the war.

Excitement about Eisenhower drew some of his supporters into local and state Republican politics, as did the presence in Washington, for the first time since 1932, of a patronage-rich Republican administration. The long era of monopolistic competition was about to end. The revitalized GOP extended its sights to the middle and western two-thirds of the state, where Democrats had seldom been challenged. Tennessee remained a bluish state in 1956, but Republicans were readying their brushes with red paint.

SNAPSHOT 3: 1966

Richard Nixon extended the Tennessee GOP's winning streak in presidential elections to three in 1960, demonstrating that Republican chances for success in the state did not depend on having a national hero like Eisenhower on the ballot. Yet it was the losing Republican presidential candidate in 1964, the strongly conservative Senator Barry M. Goldwater of Arizona, whose candidacy raised the state's Republican Party to a greater level of vitality than it had ever enjoyed.

To be sure, some Republican progress was achieved in this period independent of Goldwater's influence. Bill Brock, a Chattanooga businessman who had been drawn into grassroots Republican politics by the Eisenhower and Nixon campaigns, secured the GOP's third East Tennessee House seat by winning the Third Congressional District in 1962. More important, the Supreme Court ruled in *Baker v. Carr*, a landmark 1962 case that originated in Tennessee, and in related decisions that legislative districts must be reapportioned immediately and after every census on the principle of "one man, one vote." In Tennessee, which had not changed the boundaries of its state House and Senate districts since 1901, this meant transferring many seats from the state's declining rural counties to its growing metropolitan areas, where the GOP was strongest. Republican representation in the state legislature essentially doubled in subsequent elections, rising quickly to around two-fifths of both houses by the late 1960s.[5]

Goldwater's contribution to Republican progress in Tennessee was both organizational and electoral. Organizationally, he inspired and energized legions of economic conservatives and fervent anticommunists, many of them in the Memphis and Nashville suburbs, to become "New Guard" Republican activists committed to winning elections up and down the ballot (Parks 1966). "For the first time," write William Lyons, John Scheb, and Billy Stair (2001, 200), "many Middle and West Tennesseans began to think of themselves as Republicans, rather than as Democrats who sometimes voted Republican in presidential elections." In electoral terms, Goldwater also established a beachhead for the GOP among racially and socially conservative white working-class voters, previously a mainstay of the Democratic Party (Lamis 1984, 164–165).

In congressional elections as well as in the presidential contest, 1964 was a year of Republican defeats that set the stage for subsequent Republican victories. Senator Gore was up for reelection in 1964, and Kefauver's death in 1963 meant that an election to fill the remaining two years of his term was also on the ballot. Dan Kuykendall, a Goldwater Republican from Memphis, challenged Gore. Howard Baker, an East Tennessee Republican whose father had held the Second District House seat, ran against Representative Ross Bass, a Kefauver Democrat, to finish Kefauver's term. Both Republicans lost, but Kuykendall's 46 percent and Baker's 47 percent were by far the strongest showings by any Republican senatorial candidates in the state's history.

Two years later, in 1966, Kuykendall ran for Congress in the Ninth District (Memphis and Shelby County) and unseated the Democratic incumbent, making him the fourth Republican in the state's nine-member House delegation, and the only one from outside East Tennessee. Baker ran against former governor Clement, who had beaten Senator Bass in the Democratic primary, for a full Senate term in 1966. He won handily (56 percent to 44 percent) to become the first elected Republican senator in the history of the state.

SNAPSHOT 4: 1976

For a time during the decade portrayed in this fourth snapshot, Tennessee politics flashed redder than it ever had, and for a time it flashed bluer than at any time since the 1940s. Underlying this apparent volatility, however, was the continuing trend toward a more Republican Tennessee. To be sure, each party was usually successful when a strong national or regional tide was running strongly in its favor, or when an even moderately popular incumbent was running for reelection. But as the country and, especially, the South grew more Republican during the latter third of the twentieth century and the early 2000s (Nelson 2005), Tennessee Republicans were more likely to benefit from external tides than the state's Democrats. What's more, the state GOP tended to do well in elections when no national or regional trend was at work or when no acceptable incumbent was running.

None of this was apparent in 1968, when the only statewide election was for Tennessee's electoral votes for president. Although the Republican candidate, Richard Nixon, defeated Democratic vice president Hubert H. Humphrey by nearly 10 percentage points, he won only 38 percent of the vote in doing so. The most popular third-party candidate in Tennessee in more than a century,[6] former Democratic governor George C. Wallace of Alabama, won 34 percent to finish second, running best among the same socially conservative working-class whites whom Goldwater had drawn to the Republican ticket in 1964. Clearly, if the Republicans could win these voters back, they could prevail in future statewide elections.

Two years later they did. Nixon's chief political goal as president was to bring Wallace supporters into the Republican fold. The first application of his "southern strategy" came in the midterm elections of 1970. The strategy was moderately successful in most of the South, but spectacularly so in Tennessee. In the Senate election, the conservative Republican challenger, Representative Brock, pounded the liberal incumbent Gore on gun control, school prayer, activist judges, school busing, and a host of other social issues. In the open-seat gubernatorial election, a dentist and local Republican leader from Memphis, Winfield Dunn, opposed liberal Democratic lawyer-businessman John J. Hooker. Both Republican candidates were able to add several West Tennessee cities and counties to their party's East Tennessee base, and both were elected, Brock by 51 percent to 47 percent and Dunn by 52 percent to 46 percent. The GOP now controlled all three major statewide offices.

Republican progress continued in 1972. Nixon carried Tennessee with 68 percent, accomplishing his goal of winning over nearly every Wallace voter. Liberal South Dakota senator George S. McGovern won 30 percent, barely more in the two-candidate 1972 election than the 28 percent Humphrey had received in three-candidate 1968. Baker won an easy re-election to the Senate, proving that his first-ever Republican victory in 1966 had not been a fluke. And even though Tennessee lost one seat in the House of Representatives after the 1970 census, Robin L. Beard's victory in a district that straddled Middle and West Tennessee grew the Republican delegation from four to five, outnumbering the Democrats for the first time since Reconstruction.

Tennessee's new pattern of Democratic success when regional or national political trends were running strongly in the party's favor was never more apparent than in the next two elections, 1974 and 1976. The Watergate scandal and Nixon's resignation in disgrace made the 1974 midterm elections a Democratic triumph nearly everywhere in the country. Former representative Ray Blanton, a conservative West Tennessee

Democrat, built on the statewide recognition he had secured in his 1972 Senate campaign against Baker and was easily elected as governor. He beat Nixon White House staff member Lamar Alexander by 55 percent to 44 percent. In the state legislative elections, the Democrats regained much of the ground they had lost since the mid-1960s, winning a sixty-three to thirty-five majority in the House and a twenty to twelve majority in the Senate. Tennessee's U.S. House delegation swung from five to three Republican to five to three Democratic when Marilyn Lloyd unseated the Republican incumbent in the Chattanooga-based Third District, and Harold Ford, a state legislator, defeated Kuykendall in Memphis's Ninth District. Ford became Tennessee's first African American member of Congress.

In 1976, the tide that propelled Tennessee Democrats was less national than regional. With strong southern support, the party nominated former Georgia governor Jimmy Carter for president. In a very close election against Nixon's successor, President Gerald R. Ford, Carter carried Tennessee and every other southern state except Virginia, the best showing in the region by far of any Democratic presidential candidate since Franklin D. Roosevelt in the 1930s and 1940s. Carter's 56 percent majority in Tennessee brought Senator Brock's Democratic opponent, state party chair James Sasser, in on his coattails with 53 percent of the vote.[7]

Harold Ford's 1974 election to a term in the House (and to ten subsequent terms) was the most visible success by an African American political leader in Tennessee during this decade. But it was hardly the only one. The Voting Rights Act of 1965 had enfranchised fewer new African American voters in Tennessee than in most other southern states because the racial barriers to voting had always been lower. But the act also required states to abandon practices that made it difficult for black voters to elect black candidates. When Tennessee complied by changing from county-wide to district-based elections for state legislature, the number of black state representatives rose from one in 1964 (A. W. Willis Jr. of Memphis) to thirteen by 1977, and the number of black senators rose from none to two.[8] Ford's election to Congress was facilitated by the state's redrawing of the Ninth District's boundaries to maximize the number of African American voters.

These victories aside, the underlying trend toward a more Republican Tennessee was also a trend away from the party that African American voters overwhelmingly supported. A few Republican politicians actively sought to build biracial coalitions—Baker, for example, ran 6 percentage points behind Nixon statewide in 1972, but 5 percentage points ahead of him in heavily African American Memphis. But most Republican office-seekers saw little hope of peeling black voters away from their Democratic loyalties and more to be gained by continuing to cultivate white working-class Wallace voters. Not surprisingly, perhaps, every

African American elected to state or federal office in Tennessee has been a Democrat.

SNAPSHOT 5: 1986

During the nineteenth and, more recently, the mid-twentieth century, the Tennessee political leaders who strode onto the national stage were all Democrats.[9] Tennessee Republicans made their first appearance in 1977, when Howard Baker was elected Senate minority leader by his Republican colleagues (the first southerner ever to hold this position) and Bill Brock became chair of the Republican National Committee. Brock is widely credited with reviving the GOP's dispirited fundraising, candidate recruitment, and organizational apparatus, both in Washington and at the grassroots. In doing so, he forged the model that successful chairs of both national parties would try to emulate for decades to come. Baker united the divided and demoralized Senate GOP into an effective political force during the Carter years.

Reelected to the Senate by a fifteen-point majority in 1978 against Jane Eskind, a wealthy Democratic businesswoman, Baker emerged as one of the early favorites for the Republican presidential nomination in 1980. Unfortunately, Baker was bucking two strong national trends: his party was becoming more conservative than he was, and, disillusioned by the Vietnam War, Watergate, and a bloated federal bureaucracy, the country had begun looking to the states rather than to Washington for its presidents. Governors won seven of the eight presidential elections from 1976 to 2004; senators won none. Both trends worked strongly in favor of Ronald Reagan, the GOP's leading conservative and a two-term governor of California. Baker dropped out of the race after finishing fourth in the New Hampshire primary.

Reagan was elected president in a landslide. In a mirror image of 1976, when Carter carried every southern state but one, Reagan carried all but one in 1980, Carter's home state of Georgia. Although Reagan had long coattails in the South, Tennessee Republicans were unable to take advantage of them because no statewide offices were on the ballot and every incumbent House member ran for reelection against a weak challenger. Still, the addition of twelve new Republican senators transformed Baker from minority leader to majority leader, increasing his power and prominence.

Baker's reelection to the Senate in 1978 was accompanied by Republican Lamar Alexander's election as governor. A recent Supreme Court decision, *Buckley v. Valeo*, had authorized candidates to spend as much of their own money as they wanted on their own campaigns. The main effect in Tennessee was to enable wealthy, self-financed candidates to buy nominations but not elections. Alexander, like Baker, faced an opponent with a bottomless checkbook, Democratic banker Jake Butcher. In losing to Blanton in 1974, Alexander had been widely perceived as a preppy, country club Republican. In 1978, he shed that image by donning a red-and-black flannel shirt and walking 1,022 miles through the state to visit with voters in their homes, churches, and workplaces (Langsdon 2000, 388). Alexander benefited from widespread revulsion with the scandal-plagued Blanton administration. (Among other things, the governor had been selling pardons to violent criminals.) The Republican won an easy 56 percent to 44 percent victory.

Focusing on public education and economic development in ways that earned him national as well as statewide acclaim, Alexander was a popular governor—not the first in Tennessee history, but the first to be constitutionally eligible to seek a second four-year term. Until the state constitution was amended in 1953, governors were elected for two years and, as long as they sat out a term every eight years, could be reelected without limit. The 1953 amendment provided for a single four-year gubernatorial term. Just before Alexander took office, the constitution was amended again to allow the governor to seek a second four-year term.[10] In 1982, he was handily reelected with 60 percent of the vote against the Democratic mayor of Knoxville, Randy Tyree.

While Governor Alexander bucked a strong national Democratic tide to win in 1982, Senator Sasser rode it. Sasser, who had worked the grassroots hard during his first term, was reelected against an aggressive challenger, five-term Republican representative Robin Beard, by 62 percent to 38 percent. Democrats also won the House seat that was restored to Tennessee after the 1980 census, expanding their ranks in the nine-member congressional delegation to six.

Like Sasser's reelection in 1982, Democratic victories in the next two elections confirmed the rule that Tennessee Democrats do well when a reasonably popular Democratic incumbent is on the ballot, or when a strong national or regional tide runs in their favor. Nationally, Reagan won a landslide without coattails in 1984; indeed, the GOP lost two Senate seats in the election. One of them was in Tennessee, where Baker retired, having interpreted his failure to win the presidency in 1980 to mean that he could only seek it successfully if unencumbered by the responsibilities of office. (In any event, he decided not to try again in 1988.) The Democrats united behind Al Gore Jr., a four-term representative from the rural Fourth Congressional District. Gore had distinguished himself in Washington by mastering important but relatively non-ideological issues like organ transplants, infant formula, and single-warhead nuclear missiles. When no prominent Republican stepped forward to challenge Gore, the nomination went to Victor Ashe, a state legislator from Knoxville.

Why was Gore spared a strong opponent for an open Senate seat? His own stature (he was already being talked about as a future president) is part of the answer, but only part. Two other, more deeply rooted aspects of Tennessee politics are also relevant. One is constitutional: in Tennessee, unlike other southern states, hardly any statewide offices are filled through popular election. Tennessee's lieutenant governor is elected by the state Senate; its comptroller, treasurer, and secretary of state by the entire legislature; and its attorney general by the state supreme court. Other executive officials are appointed by the governor. These positions provide springboards for serious gubernatorial and senatorial candidacies elsewhere in the South, but in Tennessee, membership in the U.S. House performs most of that function by default. If, as in 1984, none of a party's House incumbents are willing to risk their seat in pursuit of higher office, the party is usually left with a weak nominee for governor or senator. Ashe campaigned hard in 1984, but his lack of a statewide reputation lost him the election to Gore by 61 percent to 34 percent.

A second deeply rooted feature of Tennessee politics that helps to explain Gore's rise to prominence in 1984 is cultural. Tennessee is one of five states (all of them southern) with a dominant "traditionalistic" political culture (Elazar 1966, 92–94, 110).[11] One of the ways that Tennessee's traditionalism manifests itself is in a deferential attitude toward "an established elite which often inherits their 'right' to govern through family ties" (Elazar 1966, 93; see also Nelson 1998). Gore, the son of a former senator, obviously benefited from this attitude. So, two years earlier, had both candidates for the Fourth District House seat: Republican Cissy Baker, the daughter of Howard Baker (himself the son of a Tennessee congressman), and the winner, Jim Cooper, the son of former Democratic governor Prentice Cooper. Subsequent elections witnessed John Duncan Jr.'s succession to John Sr.'s Second District seat in 1988, and Harold Ford Jr.'s succession to Harold Sr.'s Ninth District seat in 1996, not to mention the 1988 election of Bob Clement (his father was Governor Frank Clement) to the House from the Fifth District.[12] With few exceptions, these candidates were treated as heirs apparent and faced no serious competition for their party's usually coveted nominations for open House seats.

In 1986, Tennessee Democrats did not need to rely on tradition. Instead, they rode the national and regional tides that ran strongly in their party's favor. In the South, Democrats defeated four one-term Republican senators, and nationally the party regained control of the Senate. In Tennessee, Ned McWherter, a conservative Democrat from the rural northwestern part of the state and the longtime speaker of the state House of Representatives, won the gubernatorial election against former Republican governor Winfield Dunn by 54 percent to 46 percent. In the early 1970s, Governor Dunn had alienated traditionally Republican East Tennessee by vetoing a bill to establish a medical school in the region. The legislature passed the bill over Dunn's veto, but the bad feeling toward him never ebbed. Republican James Quillen, who had represented the First Congressional District since 1962 (and after whom the new medical school was named), bore an especially long grudge. Dunn lost Quillen's district to McWherter while Quillen was winning it by more than two-to-one, and Dunn nearly lost the rest of East Tennessee, something no reasonably strong Republican candidate for statewide office had ever done.

The end of 1986 marks the modern apex of the Democratic Party in Tennessee. The governor and both senators were Democrats, as were six of nine members of the state's House delegation, twenty-three of its thirty-three state senators, and sixty-one of its ninety-nine state representatives. But looked at as part of the entire decade, these Democratic victories appear less like a blue landscape than as blue highlights against a reddish backdrop. Not only did Reagan carry the state in 1980 and 1984—the sixth and seventh times the Republican presidential nominee had won Tennessee in the last nine elections—but the excitement he generated in the state allowed the GOP to close the gap in voters' party identification. In 1981, when Reagan took office, 42 percent of Tennesseans identified themselves as Democrats, compared with only 25 percent Republicans. Four years later, the gap had nearly vanished, shrinking from 17 percentage points to 3 percentage points (Lyons, Scheb, and Stair 2001, 194). Throughout the decade, Republicans constituted a larger proportion of the state legislature in Tennessee than in any other southern state (calculated from data in Scher 1992, 166–167). An index of state partisanship devised by Earl Black and Merle Black (1987, 311) for the period 1965–1985 showed that in Tennessee (but nowhere else in the South), the GOP had won a majority of recent presidential, gubernatorial, and senatorial elections. In what seemed their recent darkest moment, Republicans were poised for the breakthrough that was soon to come.

SNAPSHOT 6: 1996

The decade portrayed in this sixth snapshot was the most eventful in the modern political history of Tennessee, starting with Gore's first quest for the Democratic presidential nomination and ending with the full flowering of the state's growing Republican majority.

Gore's presidential candidacy in 1988 was an effort to cast him in a role that others had created and that no one else was stepping forward to perform. In the aftermath of Reagan's crushing defeat of former vice president Walter F. Mondale of Minnesota in 1984, Democratic leaders across the South had decided that they wanted "southern moderate" to replace "northern liberal" as the shorthand description of the party's next nominee for president. They agreed to cluster virtually all of their states' 1988 presidential primaries on the second Tuesday in March, just two weeks after the New Hampshire primary. By creating "Super Tuesday," southern Democrats hoped to attract a popular southern moderate into the race, then anoint him as the nominee (Black and Black 1992, 260–271).

Super Tuesday fulfilled one of its intended purposes—Gore declared his candidacy—but not the other. To be sure, Gore won the primaries in Tennessee and three neighboring states: Arkansas, Kentucky, and North Carolina. But Jesse Jackson, an African American minister and liberal activist, won Virginia and the four Deep South primaries, and Massachusetts governor Michael S. Dukakis, a liberal and a northerner, swept the two biggest states, Texas and Florida. Gore's candidacy foundered—no surprise, considering that he was a thirty-nine-year-old, first-term senator—and Dukakis's flourished. Election Day in November brought the very outcome that southern Democratic leaders had tried to avert by creating Super Tuesday. Dukakis lost every southern state to Vice President George Bush, a Texan, by a landslide. In Tennessee, Bush ran just as strongly as Reagan had in 1984, winning 58 percent of the vote.

Bush's victorious candidacy for president did not prevent Sasser from winning an easy reelection to a third Senate term in 1988; nor did Gore's defeat hurt him when he ran for a second term in 1990. Both senators executed to perfection the textbook strategy for an incumbent seeking reelection: tend assiduously to constituents' interests and raise so much money that no serious opponent will emerge as a challenger. Neither Bill Anderson, the young East Tennessee lawyer who ran against Sasser, nor William Hawkins, the former economics instructor who challenged Gore, brought anything like a statewide reputation to their races. Nor did either GOP candidate raise more than a tiny fraction of the funds needed to run an effective campaign. Sasser was reelected with 65 percent of the vote in 1988, and Gore with 68 percent in 1990.

Governor McWherter was also reelected without serious opposition in 1990; Republican Dwight Henry, a first-term state representative, campaigned hard but with few resources, and secured only 37 percent of the vote to McWherter's 61 percent. Indeed, since the change in the state constitution that allows governors to serve two four-year terms, every governor has been reelected without serious challenge: the Republican Alexander in 1982, the Democrat McWherter in 1990, the Republican Don Sundquist in 1998, and the Democrat Phil Bredesen in 2006. Tennessee's governors have had every incentive to move toward the center of the political spectrum, in part because, as in other states, the challenges a governor faces are less ideological than managerial, and in part for a reason peculiar to Tennessee, the so-called Wilderbeast.

Until its extinction in 2007, the Wilderbeast was a bipartisan, centrist coalition in the state Senate that took its name from John Wilder. From 1971 to 2006 (longer by far than any other state political leader in the country), Wilder was elected by his colleagues as speaker of the Senate and thus, under Tennessee's unusual constitution, as lieutenant governor. Wilder was a Democrat who prided himself on working well with governors of both parties. In advance of the 1987 legislative session, when a majority of Democratic senators declared their intention to replace him with a more partisan leader, Wilder forged a coalition consisting of every Senate Republican and enough Democrats to secure reelection. In return, he consistently appointed both Republican and Democratic supporters to chair all the Senate's committees. The long existence of the bipartisan Wilderbeast encouraged Tennessee's governors to operate in a similarly centrist—and popular—way.

Although Gore chose not to run for president again in 1992, he ended up on the ticket anyway as Arkansas governor Bill Clinton's vice presidential running mate. Clinton's choice of Gore defied the canons of traditional ticket-balancing: like Clinton, Gore was a politically moderate Southern Baptist baby boomer from an adjacent southern state. But, as a senator, an environmentalist, a Vietnam veteran, and a staunch family man, Gore balanced the pro-development, skirt-chasing, draft-avoiding governor in more subtle and, it turned out, more politically meaningful ways (Nelson 1993).

Tennessee was one of four southern states that Clinton and Gore carried against President Bush in 1992. Clinton received 47 percent of Tennessee's popular vote to Bush's 42 percent, with 10 percent going to independent candidate Ross Perot. It is far from certain that Clinton would have won Tennessee without Gore: a Mason-Dixon poll showed Gore adding 7 percentage points to Clinton's own support in the state, well above the margin by which he carried it (calculated from data in Brodsky and Swansbrough 1994, 160).

No statewide elections were on the Tennessee ballot in 1992. Every House member ran and was reelected, enabling Democrats to maintain their six-to-three majority in the state's delegation. Part of Tennessee's traditionalistic political culture is expressed in its deference to incumbents. Just as no incumbent governor of Tennessee has been seriously challenged for reelection since the two-term limit replaced the single gubernatorial term, so was no incumbent House member defeated from 1974, when Ford unseated Kuykendall, to 2008, when David Davis, a first-term incumbent from the Republican First District, was narrowly defeated in the Republican primary by Johnson City mayor Phil Roe.

Carter in 1980 is the only reelection-seeking president not to carry Tennessee since Herbert Hoover in 1932. Even in 1994, when a Republican governor replaced a Democrat, two Republican senators replaced two Democrats, and the state's House delegation went from six to three Democratic to five to four Republican, only one incumbent, Senator Sasser, was defeated. All the other changes in party control came through open-seat elections.

Nationally and throughout the South, the 1994 elections were a triumph for the GOP, which took control of Congress for the first time in forty years and, for the first time ever, won a strong majority of southern House and Senate seats. Tennessee, with its complete turnover from Democratic to Republican control of statewide offices, led the way. Sasser ran exactly the wrong sort of campaign, offering himself to the voters for a fourth term by boasting of his Washington connections and declaring that he was his party's consensus choice to be the new Senate majority leader. But 1994 was not the year for candidates to stress their clout as Washington politicians, and Sasser lost by 56 percent to 42 percent to Republican Bill Frist, a prominent heart surgeon and political newcomer who branded Sasser the "personification of an arrogant, imperial Congress" and led audiences in chants of "Eighteen years is long enough!" (Black and Black 2002, 268).

Gore's elevation to the vice presidency placed the remaining two years of his term on the 1994 ballot as well. The Democrats nominated Representative Jim Cooper to oppose Republican Fred Thompson. Thompson was a curious figure. Although he had spent most of his career as a backstage Washington lawyer and lobbyist, he was best known as an actor in popular movies like *Marie* and *The Hunt for Red October*. Thompson saved his best performance for his Senate campaign, when he "parked his Lincoln, shucked his lawyer attire, donned blue jeans, cowboy boots, and a western-style khaki shirt, and rolled out what would become the symbol of his campaign, a red extended pickup truck. . . . The transformation to 'Ol' Fred' was one of the most remarkable political makeovers in years" (Ashford and Locker 1999, 211). Thompson carved up the reserved, intellectual Cooper, winning by 60 percent to 39 percent. In the House elections, two young conservative Republicans, Zach Wamp and Van Hilleary, won the open Democratic seats vacated by Cooper and the retiring Marilyn Lloyd, respectively.

The Tennessee GOP also fared well in elections for state office. Republican representative Don Sundquist, who represented the long congressional district that connects the Nashville and Memphis suburbs, defeated the largely self-financed Phil Bredesen, the mayor of Nashville, by 54 percent to 45 percent. In the state legislative elections, the Republicans won a narrow seventeen-to-sixteen majority in the Senate. They left the Wilderbeast intact, however, and, despite a Democratic redistricting plan that jammed twelve Republican incumbents into six districts after the 1990 census, won forty of ninety-nine seats in the House of Representatives.

Ironically, one casualty of the Republican sweep in 1994 was the presidential candidacy of former governor Lamar Alexander. Alexander had been striking grassroots chords around the country by promising to shake up Washington with reforms like mandatory term limits for members of Congress. Clinton's political advisers regarded him as the president's most formidable rival in 1996 (Morris 1997, 266). But the GOP sweep in the 1994 congressional elections took the wind out of Alexander's sails. Clearly the elections showed Washington could be shaken up without imposing term limits; besides, now that the Republicans were in charge, their interest in changing the rules of the game had flagged considerably. Alexander ran third in the 1996 New Hampshire primary, then dropped out of the race soon afterward in favor of the eventual nominee, former Senate Majority Leader Bob Dole of Kansas.

Clinton and Gore carried Tennessee again in 1996, but this time just barely. Nationally, Clinton's popular vote margin rose from 6 percentage points against Bush in 1992 to 9 percentage points against Dole in 1996. But in Tennessee, Clinton's victory margin fell by more than half, from 5 percentage points to 2 percentage points. In the Senate election for a full six-year term, Thompson put the tires back on his red pickup and easily defeated Democratic lawyer Houston Gordon by 61 percent to 37 percent. Foolishly, Gordon attacked Thompson for being "an accomplished actor" (Swansbrough and Brodsky 1997, 189), making the same mistake that all of Reagan's opponents had made with equal lack of success. Hilleary and Wamp added to the majorities they had received in capturing their House seats from the Democrats in 1994, each of them winning reelection by more than 10 percentage points.

SNAPSHOT 7: 2006

The 1998 elections in Tennessee were relatively uneventful. Like all of his recent predecessors, Sundquist was easily reelected as governor, winning 69 percent of the vote against weak opposition. No current Democratic leader sought the party's nomination, forfeiting it to a cantankerous figure from the 1960s, John J. Hooker, who won 30 percent of the vote. All nine House members ran again and, in keeping with state tradition, all were reelected. In 2000, a similar pattern prevailed. The same nine House incumbents ran and won the same easy victories. Senator Frist, with 65 percent of the vote, won a landslide reelection against a token Democratic opponent, former state party treasurer Jeff Clark, who received 32 percent.

Only in the 2000 presidential election were politics in Tennessee anything but usual, but in this case the exception was far more significant than the rule. With Clinton barred from running again by the Constitution's two-term limit, the Democratic Party nominated Gore to succeed him. As vice president, however, Gore had neglected Tennessee and, although he located his national campaign headquarters in Nashville, he seldom campaigned there until just before Election Day. Personal and political history apparently reassured Gore that he could take Tennessee for granted; he had never come close to losing an election there and, during the previous seventy-five years, the only presidential candidates not to carry their home states were the most severe landslide losers: Republican Alfred M. Landon of Kansas, who won only two states in 1936, and McGovern of South Dakota, who carried only one in 1972. Even Goldwater in 1964, Carter in 1980, Mondale in 1984, and Dukakis in 1988, all of them far weaker candidates than Gore, had won their own states.

The Republican nominee for president in 2000, Governor George W. Bush of Texas, conceded nothing to Gore. Bush campaigned ardently throughout Tennessee, advertised extensively on the state's radio and television stations, and brought in surrogates like movie star and National Rifle Association president Charlton Heston to remind Tennesseans of Gore's unpopular support for gun control. Bush carried Tennessee handily, by 51 percent to 47 percent. For more than a month after the election, the eyes of the nation were riveted on Florida, where Gore hoped that recounts would turn the state in his favor and win him the presidency. But if Gore had carried his own state, the outcome in Florida would have been irrelevant. Tennessee's eleven electoral votes would have raised Gore's national tally to 277, more than enough to win the election.

While Bush was taking advantage of Tennessee's ever more reddish political coloration, Sundquist was squandering it. As a candidate for governor in 1994, Sundquist had opposed enacting a new state income tax and, when strolling toward reelection in 1998 in a one-sided race, he had said nothing to suggest a change of mind. Voters were therefore astonished (and Republicans apoplectic) when, in 1999 and afterward, Sundquist made an income tax the centerpiece of his second term.

After Representative Hilleary's Fourth Congressional District was redistricted to favor the Democrats in 2002, Hilleary sought and won the GOP nomination for governor on an anti-tax platform. Sundquist said that his fellow Republican would be "a horrible governor" (Barone and Cohen 2003, 1476). Despite these deep divisions within the party, Hilleary ran a close second against former Nashville mayor Phil Bredesen, a Democrat and another income tax opponent. Raising money from a broad base of donors this time, Bredesen won the election by 51 percent to 48 percent, and conservative Democrat Lincoln Davis won Hilleary's redistricted House seat.

Another open seat election, this one for senator, provided Tennessee Republicans with their major victory in 2002. When Senator Thompson decided to retire, former governor Alexander declared his candidacy for the Republican nomination. The state GOP had moved steadily rightward since the early 1980s, when Alexander was governor, and Representative Ed Bryant, the conservative Republican who had filled Sundquist's seat in Congress when Sundquist ran for governor, challenged Alexander for the nomination. But President Bush, who took a much more active role in recruiting Republican candidates in 2002 than presidents usually do, made clear that he preferred Alexander (Nelson 2004). Alexander did his part by centering his campaign on a host of conservative issues. He defeated Bryant in the primary by 54 percent to 43 percent, then polished off another political veteran, Democratic representative Bob Clement of Nashville, in the general election by an almost identical margin: 54 percent to 44 percent.

Alexander's victory was one of several that helped the Republicans regain control of the Senate in 2002. Shortly after the results were in, Senator Trent Lott of Mississippi, who was slated to become majority leader, remarked offhandedly that the country might have been better off if segregationist third-party candidate Strom Thurmond had won the 1948 presidential election. In the media firestorm that followed, Bush quietly made clear to Senate Republicans that he would rather they choose someone else as majority leader. With White House encouragement, Senator Frist entered the race and was unanimously elected. Frist was a relatively junior senator, but he had earned his partisan spurs by successfully chairing the National Republican Senate Committee during the 2002 elections.

Although no statewide offices were on Tennessee's ballot in 2004, the presidency was. The Democrats nominated a northern liberal, Senator John F. Kerry of Massachusetts, to challenge Bush. Kerry chose a southerner, North Carolina senator John Edwards, for vice president, but, strangely, made no effort to win North Carolina, much less Tennessee or any other southern state except Florida. Bush carried Tennessee handily, by 57 percent to 43 percent. The GOP also drew within four seats of a majority in the ninety-nine-member state House of Representatives and won a seventeen-to-sixteen majority in the Senate. When the legislature gathered in January 2005, most Republicans were ready to replace Wilder as speaker with one of their own, but the votes of two defecting GOP senators enabled Wilder to win reelection by a margin of eighteen to fifteen.

In 2006, Bredesen, like other recent governors, was handily reelected, defeating Republican state senator Jim Bryson by 69 percent to 30 percent. The GOP maintained its majority in the state Senate, however, and this time it deposed Wilder by electing a Republican speaker, Ron Ramsey. No seats changed parties in elections to the U.S. House, but two new members replaced retiring incumbents. One of them, liberal Democratic state senator Steve Cohen of Memphis, a white candidate, was elected in the majority-black Ninth District, which had been controlled by Harold Ford, *père et fils*, since 1974. Cohen won the Democratic primary, which is tantamount to election in Memphis, with 31 percent of the vote against a crowded field of African American candidates.

Memphis's seat in the House had become open in 2006 because the incumbent, Harold Ford Jr., decided to run for the U.S. Senate when Senator Frist fulfilled his 1994 pledge to step down after two terms.[13] Ford, who was bidding to become the first African American senator ever elected by southern voters, faced Republican Bob Corker, a wealthy businessman who had been a successful mayor of Chattanooga. Ford's strategy was to roll up huge majorities among black voters in Memphis and Nashville and keep Corker's statewide majority of white voters below 60 percent by taking a variety of conservative positions on economic, national security and, especially, moral issues. "What Tennesseans will get," Ford said on *Fox News Sunday*, "is a Jesus-loving, gun-supporting believer that family should come first, that taxes should be lowered, and that America should be strong" (Baker 2006).

Corker responded effectively with a two-pronged strategy (Nelson 2008). One prong was to brand himself the true Tennessean running against a Washington insider who—as part of his congressman father's household and then as a congressman himself—had not lived in Tennessee full time since he was nine years old. The other prong was to tie Ford to his controversial family. On October 7, Corker raised the issue by attacking the "machine-type politics" employed by the long-controversial "Ford political machine" in Memphis (Zuckman 2006). As if to remind East and Middle Tennesseans why they did not like the Fords, Harold's uncle John Ford resigned from the Tennessee Senate after the U.S. attorney indicted him for taking bribes, and his aunt Ophelia Ford was expelled from the Senate when her election to fill John's seat was ruled fraudulent.

Unknown to Corker, national Republican operatives added a third prong to his campaign strategy by playing the race card in an ad paid for by the Republican National Committee. Referring to a pre–Super Bowl party sponsored by *Playboy* magazine that Ford had attended in 2005, the ad featured a scantily clad blond woman. "I met Harold at the Playboy party," she said flirtingly, then winked and added, "Harold, call me." The ad's evocation of the white South's primal fear of black men having sex with white women could not have been less subtle, which made Corker's renunciation of the ad as "tacky" a wild understatement. Late polls showed Corker pulling into the lead. Although Ford ran better than any Democratic nominee for senator in Tennessee since Gore in 1990, Corker prevailed on Election Day by 51 percent to 48 percent.

POSTSCRIPT: 2008–2009

Two prominent Tennesseans, Bill Frist and, after Frist dropped out of the race, Fred Thompson, sought the 2008 Republican presidential nomination. But, like Howard Baker and Lamar Alexander before them, neither came close to winning it. Because Frist dropped out on November 28, 2006, and Thompson withdrew on January 22, 2008, no Tennessee Republican was on the ballot when the state held its presidential primary on February 5. Instead, former Arkansas governor Mike Huckabee narrowly defeated Senator John McCain of Arizona by 34 percent to 32 percent. Among Democrats, Illinois senator Barack Obama chose not to campaign in Tennessee, conceding the state to Senator Hillary Rodham Clinton of New York. After winning the Democratic nomination, Obama again wrote off Tennessee, visiting only once to participate in the second presidential debate in Nashville on October 7. Not surprisingly, McCain carried Tennessee handily, by 57 percent to 42 percent.

For the first time since 1869, Republicans also won control of both houses of the state legislature, expanding their Senate majority to nineteen to fourteen and securing a razor-thin fifty-to-forty-nine majority in the House of Representatives. Because their edge in the House was so small, suspense attended the election of a speaker when the legislature gathered on January 13, 2009. Forty-nine Republicans voted for their party's nominee, Jason Mumpower. But in a surprise move, all forty-nine Democrats voted for sophomore Republican Kent Williams, whose vote for himself secured his election. Williams had secretly promised to award House Democrats nearly half of all committee chairmanships. In the U.S. House elections, Democrats retained their five-to-four majority, but Tennessee's long record of fealty to incumbents was interrupted when Phil Roe unseated David Davis in the First District's Republican primary.

CONCLUSION

As these prose snapshots of Tennessee politics since the 1940s show, Tennessee has been transformed from a bluish state to a reddish one—that is, from being basically but not entirely Democratic to being basically but not entirely Republican. The Republicans have held onto East Tennessee while broadening their base to include the Memphis and Nashville suburbs and, increasingly, rural West Tennessee as well. But the Democrats usually can prevail when a national (1974, 1982, 1986) or regional (1976) tide runs in their favor. In addition, the state's traditionalistic political culture fosters an attitude of deference to incumbents and to established political families, sometimes to the advantage of Democrats.

Although Tennessee has grown steadily more Republican in recent decades, it has done so at a slower pace than most other states in the South. Once the least blue state in the solidly blue South, it has become one of the least red states in an increasingly red South. Until the 1960s, for example, Tennessee was one of the few southern states that elected Republican members to the House of Representatives. Since 2002 it has been one of the few that sends more Democrats than Republicans. Until the 1960s, too, Tennessee gave Republican candidates for president their highest level of support in the South. It still tends to support Republicans—even rejecting native son Al Gore in 2000—but some other southern states do so by greater margins. In 2004 Bush won Tennessee by a landslide, but not by as big a landslide as in Alabama, Georgia, Mississippi, South Carolina, and Texas. In 2008, Tennessee was McCain's fourth-best southern state, outpaced by Alabama, Arkansas, and Louisiana.

NOTES

1. Of the eighty victories Republicans won in southern House elections during the first half of the twentieth century, fifty (twenty-five apiece) were in Tennessee's First and Second Congressional Districts (Black and Black 2002, 59).

2. In 1900, Tennessee was second to North Carolina by 1 percentage point, and in 1928 it was second to Florida by 1 percentage point.

3. For reasons grounded in local politics during the antebellum period, the Highland Rim, a thin line of counties running north to south along the eastern edge of West Tennessee, also opposed secession and later supported Republicans.

4. Reece resumed his First District seat in 1950 after serving as chair of the Republican National Committee and running for senator.

5. Under circumstances akin to the freakish victories of Republican gubernatorial candidates in 1910, 1912, and 1928, the GOP controlled the state House of Representatives by a one-vote margin from 1969 to 1971.

6. In the four-way election of 1860, John Bell, a prominent Tennessee political leader, won the state handily as the Constitutional Union Party nominee.

7. As evidence of Carter's coattails, Sasser was one of only four congressional Democrats in the country to run behind Carter (Barone and Ujifusa 1981, 1028).

8. Only modest gains have been made since then. African Americans have occupied three state Senate seats since 1982 and did not win a fourteenth seat in the state House of Representatives until 2000.

9. Andrew Johnson, who succeeded to the presidency when Abraham Lincoln was assassinated in 1865, was a Jacksonian Democrat placed on the ticket when the GOP rebranded itself the National Union Party for the wartime election of 1864.

10. The state constitution bars only third consecutive terms. Although it has yet to happen, a governor could serve two terms, sit out for one or more terms, and be elected again.

11. Respect for family and tradition is part of the reason Governor Alexander's economic development policy was able to attract more tradition-valuing Japanese corporations to Tennessee than to any other state east of California (Barone and Ujifusa 1991, 1143).

12. When Clement left the seat to run for senator in 2002, Cooper, who had moved to Nashville after losing a Senate race in 1994, won it.

13. For a fuller account of the 2006 Senate election, see Nelson 2008.

REFERENCES

Ashford, Philip, and Richard Locker. 1999. "Tennessee: A Partisan Big Bang Amid Quiet Accommodation." In *Southern Politics in the 1990s*, ed. Alexander P. Lamis, 193–226. Baton Rouge: Louisiana State University Press.

Baker, Jackson. 2006. "Center Stage." *Memphis (TN) Flyer*, November 2.

Barone, Michael, and Richard E. Cohen. 2003. *The Almanac of American Politics, 2004*. Washington, DC: National Journal.

Barone, Michael, and Grant Ujifusa. 1981. *The Almanac of Americans Politics, 1982*. Washington, DC: Barone and Company.

———. 1991. *The Almanac of American Politics, 1992*. Washington, DC: National Journal.

Bass, Jack, and Walter DeVries. 1976. *The Transformation of Southern Politics*. New York: Basic Books.

Black, Earl, and Merle Black. 1987. *Politics and Society in the South*. Cambridge, MA: Harvard University Press.

———. 1992. *The Vital South: How Presidents Are Elected*. Cambridge, MA: Harvard University Press.

———. 2002. *The Rise of Southern Republicans*. Cambridge, MA: Harvard University Press.

Brodsky, David M. 1998. "Tennessee: Genuine Two-Party Politics." In *The New Politics of the Old South: An Introduction to Southern Politics*, ed. Charles S. Bullock III and Mark J. Rozell, 167–184. Lanham, MD: Rowman & Littlefield.

Brodsky, David M., and Robert H. Swansbrough. 1994. "Tennessee: Favorite Son Brings Home the Bacon." In *The 1992 Presidential Election in the South*, ed. Robert P. Steed, Laurence W. Moreland, and Tod A. Baker, 157–168. Westport, CT: Praeger.

Dowdy, G. Wayne. 2006. *Mr. Crump Don't Like It: Machine Politics in Memphis*. Jackson: University Press of Mississippi.

Dykeman, Wilma. 1955. "Too Much Talent in Tennessee?" *Harper's Magazine* 210 (March): 48–53.

Elazar, Daniel J. 1966. *American Federalism: A View from the States*. New York: Thomas Y. Crowell.

Grantham, Dewey W. 1995. "Tennessee and Twentieth-Century American Politics." *Tennessee Historical Quarterly* 54 (Fall): 210–229.

Greene, Lee S., and Jack E. Holmes. 1972. "Tennessee: A Politics of Peaceful Change." In *The Changing Politics of the South*, ed. William C. Havard, 165–200. Baton Rouge: Louisiana State University Press.

Key, V. O., Jr. 1949. *Southern Politics in State and Nation*. New York: Alfred A. Knopf.

Lamis, Alexander P. 1984. *The Two-Party South*. New York: Oxford University Press.

Langsdon, Phillip. 2000. *Tennessee: A Political History*. Franklin, TN: Hillsboro Press.

Lyons, William, John Scheb II, and Billy Stair. 2001. *Government and Politics in Tennessee*. Knoxville: University of Tennessee Press.

Mason, John Lyman. 2003. "Tennessee: Politics and Politicians Who Matter Beyond State Borders." In *The New Politics of the Old South: An Introduction to Southern Politics*, 2nd ed., ed. Charles S. Bullock III and Mark J. Rozell, 177–194. Lanham, MD: Rowman & Littlefield.

Morris, Dick. 1997. *Behind the Oval Office*. New York: Random House.

Nelson, Michael. 1993. "The Presidency: Clinton and the Cycle of Politics and Policy." In *The Elections of 1992*, ed. Michael Nelson, 125–152. Washington, DC: CQ Press.

———. 1998. "Foreword." In *Tennessee Governments and Politics: Democracy in the Volunteer State*, ed. John R. Vile and Mark Byrnes, ix–xi. Nashville, TN: Vanderbilt University Press.

———. 2004. "George W. Bush and Congress: The Electoral Connection." In *Considering the Bush Presidency*, ed. Gary L. Gregg II and Mark J. Rozell, 141–159. New York: Oxford University Press.

———. 2005. "The Setting: George W. Bush, Majority President." In *The Elections of 2004*, ed. Michael Nelson, 1–17. Washington, DC: CQ Press.

———. 2008. "Tennessee Senate: (Almost) All in the Family." In *The Sixth Year Itch: The Rise and Fall of the George W. Bush Presidency*, ed. Larry S. Sabato, 307–320. New York: Pearson/Longman.

Parks, Norman L. 1966. "Tennessee Politics Since Kefauver and Reece: A 'Generalist' View." *Journal of Politics* 28 (February): 141–168.

Scher, Richard K. 1992. *Politics in the New South: Republicanism, Race, and Leadership in the Twentieth Century*. New York: Paragon House.

Swansbrough, Robert H., and David M. Brodsky. 1988. "Tennessee: Weakening Party Loyalties and Growing Independence." In *The South's New Politics: Realignment and Dealignment*, ed. Robert H. Swansbrough and David M. Brodsky, 76–93. Columbia: University of South Carolina Press.

———. 1997. "Tennessee: Belle of the Presidential Ball." In *The 1996 Presidential Election in the South*, ed. Laurence W. Moreland and Robert P. Steed, 183–196. Westport, CT: Praeger.

Zuckman, Jill. 2006. "Senate Quest a Historic Path." *Chicago Tribune*, October 17.

9

———◆———

Arkansas

Deep Blue and Bright Red at the Same Time?

Andrew Dowdle and Joseph D. Giammo

In many ways, the 2008 elections highlighted the electoral peculiarities of the state of Arkansas. In a year where the presidential election generated excitement nationally, turnout in the state barely budged from its 2004 level. And while the Democratic presidential nominee received the highest percentage of the national vote that the party's standard-bearer has garnered in more than four decades, Barack Obama's finish in Arkansas was the fourth lowest by any Democratic nominee since it became a state.

However, just as shockingly, in a year where its presidential nominee was soundly defeated, the Democratic Party managed to maintain a level of dominance over statewide offices that few Southern states have seen since the days of the 1960s. Democrats boasted a supermajority with more than 70 percent of the seats in both houses of the state legislature and three of the state's four seats in Congress. In the case of its U.S. Senate race, Mark Pryor was the only incumbent unchallenged by an opponent from the other major party. And while it is always hazardous to predict the future, recent evidence suggests that Republicans face a steep challenge in 2010. In one recent poll, for example, 74 percent of respondents said they approved of the performance of Mike Beebe, the Democratic governor up for reelection in 2010, while only 9 percent disapproved (Parry and Schreckhise 2008).

Just eight years earlier, few individuals would have predicted this statewide Democratic dominance. Like most of the South, Arkansas looked like it was either moving into the Republican column at both the national and state levels, or at least becoming a two-party state (Wekkin 1998, 2003). Ironically, the presidency of Bill Clinton saw a significant growth in the ability of Republicans to compete below the presidential level. This surge was noticeable almost immediately in the first major statewide election after Clinton's 1992 victory. In July 1993, a special election was held to fill the lieutenant governorship, which was vacant after Jim Guy Tucker was elevated to the governorship following Clinton's inauguration. Mike Huckabee beat Nate Coulter in a close contest (Blair and Barth 2005).

At the onset, it was easy to dismiss Huckabee's victory as an aberration. Some observers felt Coulter ran a poor campaign. Others cited anger with Clinton over certain issues, such as gays in the military, that had temporarily energized Huckabee's base in a low-turnout election, along with Huckabee's heightened name recognition from his unsuccessful 1992 Senate race (Blair and Barth 2005). After all, Republicans had won isolated victories in the past. Winthrop Rockefeller won the 1966 and 1968 governor's races against a Democratic Party split over the issue of civil rights. Frank White captured the governorship in 1980. Still, both Rockefeller and White lost their respective reelection bids in 1970 and 1982, and neither had been able to break the Democratic monopoly over the vast majority of state and local offices.

It soon became evident that the 1990s were going to be different. Huckabee won reelection to a full term in 1994 by a much wider margin, and, after Tucker's 1996 resignation due to his role in the Whitewater scandal, became governor. Not only did Huckabee win reelection in 1998 and 2002, but in 1996, Tim Hutchinson became the first Republican since the 1870s to win a U.S. Senate race in Arkansas. This growth was also mirrored in state legislative races, where the Republican vote shares in contested state House and Senate races jumped from 35.7 percent and 37.2 percent, respectively, in 1990 to 48.2 percent in state House races and 49.0 percent in state Senate races by 2000 (Wekkin 2003).

Though Arkansas looked like it was trending away from its historical one-party dominance, it slowly began to revert to the traditional pattern. This reversion was largely due to a state Republican Party that became a top-down party after 2000. In large part, this occurrence mirrored the popularity of George W. Bush in the state. In 2000 and 2004, Bush's coattails provided a significant boost for Republican candidates (Dowdle and Wekkin 2006).

This reliance on Bush was problematic for three reasons. First, it left Republican candidates vulnerable in years when Bush was not on the ballot (Dowdle and Wekkin 2006). The year 2002 was the perfect example, with Hutchinson losing his reelection bid to Mark Pryor. Though it is easy to credit the presence of a strong challenger and scandal for Hutchinson's defeat, neither explains Huckabee's narrow 2002 win over what some consider a weak opponent. Winthrop Rockefeller, the popular Republican lieutenant governor and son of the former governor, also won by a much smaller margin. Second, the lack of stronger second-tier candidates made it more difficult for Republicans to find quality challengers even when Bush was running. The Democrats were able to run Pryor, the son of a popular former governor and senator and the state's attorney general, in 2002. On the other hand, the Republicans had to rely on Jim Holt, a state senator with little name recognition or support outside of the Republican stronghold of northwest Arkansas, as their challenger to Blanche Lincoln in 2004 (Dowdle and Wekkin 2006). Third, the continued success of the party depended in large part on Bush's approval ratings remaining high, something that would create further challenges for the GOP two years later.

These problems were clearly illustrated during the 2006 elections. Mike Huckabee was leaving office after ten years in the governor's mansion, creating a vacuum at the top of the ticket that was only exacerbated by the tragic death of Winthrop Rockefeller from a rare blood disease. This would have created problems in any year for a party that had failed to broaden its base of quality candidates from which to draw on during the decade in which it controlled the top office in the state, but was disastrous in a year in which concerns about the war in Iraq, a series of scandals involving congressional Republicans, and the drop in Bush's popularity combined to reverse the GOP's electoral fortunes nationally. While the party did nominate a candidate, Asa Hutchinson, who had both congressional and executive branch experience, and who managed to raise a respectable $3.4 million for his campaign (Hutchinson 2006), he was soundly defeated by Mike Beebe, the state's attorney general and a former state senator, who not only had the advantage of having won a statewide contest before but also a fund-raising advantage of more than $3 million (Beebe 2006).

The problems for the party were only magnified further down the ballot, where the smaller pool of elected officials from which Republicans could draw quality candidates would be expected to create even greater problems. Beebe's nearly 15-percentage-point margin of victory over Hutchinson was, along with a nearly identical margin for Democratic candidate Bill Halter over Jim Holt in the lieutenant governor's race, the smallest for any Democrat running for statewide office.[1] Democrats running for attorney general, secretary of state, and treasurer all won by more than 20 percentage points. The Republicans did not even field candidates in the races for auditor and land commissioner. Meanwhile, the Democrats maintained their twenty-seven-to-eight seat margin in the state Senate and widened their margin in the state House from 72–28 to 75–25. These 2006 results would augur a troubling trend for Republicans in 2008.

SOUND AND FURY, SIGNIFYING NOTHING:
THE 2008 PRESIDENTIAL PRIMARIES IN ARKANSAS

Throughout 2007, another unusual occurrence seemed to be the driving force in the 2008 Arkansas election. Despite the 1992 and 1996 candidacies of Bill Clinton, Arkansans usually played a peripheral role in presidential contests. At the start of 2008, however, most observers thought that the year's elections would be heavily influenced by two candidates with ties to Arkansas: former governor Mike Huckabee on the Republican side, and Hillary Clinton as part of the Democratic field.

In many ways, their respective campaigns began as polar opposites. Clinton was the clear front-runner through 2007. While Clinton's lead in popular support varied during the year, the typical margin ranged from 15 to 25 percent in the polls. Huckabee, on the other hand, looked like a lower-tier candidate through much of 2007. Until Thanksgiving, Huckabee polled in single digits in public opinion polls of likely Republican caucus and primary voters. Both Arkansas candidates saw dramatic reversals of fortune as 2007 ended and 2008 began. Senator Obama, Clinton's closest Democratic rival, began to successfully challenge her lead in the "money primary" that occurs before the start of the Iowa caucus (Adkins and Dowdle 2008). Obama also began to whittle down Clinton's lead in the popular polls after the organizational skill of his campaign produced a surprise win in Iowa that left Clinton in third place behind John Edwards.

Huckabee, on the other hand, began to gain momentum at the end of 2007. A weak pool of GOP opponents, his ability to utilize soft news, and a lack of serious competition for grassroots social conservative support all boosted his campaign. After his surprise win in the Iowa caucus, Huckabee was also to win primaries in five other states, with losses by narrow margins in Missouri, Oklahoma, and South Carolina. However, he had limited success in terms of establishing support outside of the South and the Border States.

The prospects for both candidates faded despite doing well in their respective parties' Arkansas presidential primaries. Clinton won 70 percent of the Democratic primary vote, while Huckabee captured 60 percent with strong showings statewide. Huckabee won each of the state's four congressional districts by at least a 5:2 margin over John McCain. Interestingly enough, Clinton also won each of the state's four congressional districts. She did beat Obama by less than a 2:1 margin in the state's Second District, which is home to Little Rock, the state's largest city, and which has a slightly larger than average African American population (19.4 percent compared to the state's average of 15.6 percent). What might have been more ominous for Obama was his poor showing in rural areas where Democratic presidential nominees tended to be somewhat competitive in recent general elections. The majority of residents in the Second Congressional District and the Fourth Congressional District, whose population is nearly one-quarter African American, live in rural areas and voted for Clinton by more than a 3:1 margin.

Both Huckabee and Clinton suffered another round of disappointments when their parties held their national conventions. While both candidates were mentioned as possible vice-presidential nominees, Huckabee was not vetted by McCain, and Joe Biden was selected by Obama instead of Clinton. Those decisions put an end to the national 2008 aspirations of both candidates and their supporters, as well as to the chances of another Arkansan ending up on the national ticket.

MR. IRRELEVANT? ARKANSAS AND THE 2008 PRESIDENTIAL GENERAL ELECTIONS

To say that Arkansas ran counter to the national trends in the 2008 presidential general election is a mild understatement. Not only did Obama fail to carry the state, his share of the vote when compared to John Kerry's 2004 performance dropped from 44.5 percent to 39.0 percent. This failure relative to 2004 was widespread, as Obama ran behind Kerry's vote percentage in seventy-two of the state's seventy-five counties.

This overwhelming statewide Republican tilt at the presidential level is in many ways unrepresentative of Arkansas historically at the presidential level. While Jimmy Carter did lose the state in 1980, it represented his eighth-strongest finish in terms of popular vote share that year. And though Al Gore lost the state by fifty thousand votes, much of the deficit can be accounted for by the fact that he lost the heavily Republican-leaning Third Congressional District by fifty-two thousand votes. Arkansas could boast two of the six counties nationwide (i.e., Logan and Van Buren counties) that had voted for the winner in every presidential election from 1960 to 2004 (Kraushaar and Mahtesian 2008). Not only did both vote for McCain in 2008, but the percentages garnered by the Democratic nominee dropped precipitously from 2004 to 2008. Kerry tallied 39 percent of the Logan County vote and nearly 45 percent in Van Buren County. Obama's respective totals were 29 percent and 32 percent. To be fair, there were three other states (Louisiana, Oklahoma, and West Virginia) where Obama's raw vote totals trailed behind Kerry's. However not only was Obama's fifty-five thousand vote drop in Arkansas the largest of the four states, it came close to the aggregate total decline of sixty-three thousand votes from the other three states combined.

Much of this decline can be credited to a collapse in support for the Democratic nominee in rural areas (Brown 2008). An examination of CNN exit polls for the state showed that among rural voters, who make up about 45 percent of the state's electorate, support for the Democratic nominee dropped from 48 percent in 2004 to 33 percent in 2008.[2] While there was no clear winner between Bush and Kerry in rural eastern Arkansas, McCain won the region by 15 percent. On the other hand, Obama actually outran Kerry in the state's two most populous counties, traditionally Democratic Pulaski County and the Republican stronghold of Benton County, though the jump was less than 0.5 percent. The only county in which Obama outperformed Kerry by a larger margin was Crittenden County, part of the Memphis metropolitan area, where Obama ran nearly 2.5 percentage points ahead of Kerry's 2004 finish (56.68 percent to 54.10 percent).

Some of Obama's problems can probably be linked to the "guns and God" issues that he referenced in a comment made in April in San Francisco. Obama's and Kerry's vote percentages were almost identical among voters who were not white evangelicals. Among those white evangelical voters, however, Kerry outperformed Obama by a 29–20 percent margin. In a state where this group is a majority of the electorate (i.e., 53 percent in 2004 and 56 percent in 2008), losing nearly a third of the Democratic Party's 2004 support makes overcoming the evangelical deficit an even more difficult task. And while there were no state-level polls for Arkansas measuring support among gun owners, national exit polling suggests that McCain ran as strong or stronger among households possessing firearms as Bush did in 2004. Equally striking was McCain's appeal across all age groups. While Obama benefited from overwhelming support among eighteen-to-twenty-nine-year-old voters nationwide, McCain managed a 49–49 split among young voters in Arkansas, while carrying every older age group.

Partisanship, ideology, and pocketbook issues seemed to play a much smaller role in explaining Obama's poor showing relative to Kerry's 2004 finish. While McCain drew 21 percent of the Democratic vote compared to Bush's 18 percent, the 93 percent support of Republican voters was lower than Bush's 97 percent mark. The absence of Hillary Clinton on the ticket may have helped depress white Democratic support, since only 68 percent of these voters supported Obama. Bush and McCain both garnered 82 percent of conservative support, while Kerry outdrew Obama among liberals by a small margin, 79–76 percent. The differential impact of material, noncultural issues within the state is highlighted by the fact that McCain won not only those Arkansas voters who were concerned about the national economy but also those who were not worried, while Kerry managed to win a majority who were concerned about the economy in 2004. By contrast, McCain only won 38 percent of voters nationwide who were worried about the state of the economy.

Arkansas was also an outlier when compared to the national surge in voter turnout. Initial estimates were that turnout had barely surpassed 50 percent of eligible voters. The low numbers were not due to poor registration, as these same figures suggested that the turnout rate among *registered* voters was below 60 percent. A number of experts concluded that poor turnout among the state's white conservative Democrats, due to their lack of enthusiasm for either ticket, led to this poor showing (Brown 2008).

THE 2008 CONGRESSIONAL AND STATE RACES

While the race between Obama and McCain only provided further evidence that Arkansas has become a securely red state in the Electoral College, Democrats maintained their significant advantages at the congressional and state levels in the 2008 elections. Arkansas' five congressional elections were collectively perhaps the least interesting in the nation during this election cycle. After comfortable wins for all four incumbent representatives in the 2006 elections, neither party put forth a challenger in any of the House districts in 2008. Most striking, however, was the fact that no Republican candidate ran against Mark Pryor in his first bid for reelection to the Senate. Neither Pryor nor Blanche Lincoln had won overwhelming victories in the previous two Senate races in Arkansas in 2002 and 2004, receiving roughly 54 percent and 55 percent of the vote, respectively. This might have been interpreted as giving a Republican candidate at least some realistic possibility of victory, especially in a presidential election year; however, the landslide defeats that the party suffered in statewide elections in 2006, coupled with the relative lack of quality depth from which to draw a candidate, appeared to combine to prevent any Republican from entering the race, leaving Pryor to win comfortably. Interestingly, the Green Party placed more candidates on the ballot (four) in the congressional elections than did the Republican Party (one).

The lack of contested races continued in the elections for the state legislature, where once again the state's strict term limits seemed to encourage potential candidates to wait for a seat to open up rather than run against an incumbent. In the one hundred state House contests, seventy-two candidates ran completely unopposed, while an additional six found a major-party candidate facing only third-party opposition. The remaining twenty-two races, in which a Democratic and Republican actually squared off against one another, only resulted in three seats changing hands. In all three cases, term limits had left an open seat, which Republican candidates managed to secure. The state House races, however, made the state Senate races look contentious. Eighteen of the thirty-five seats were up for grabs, but in seventeen of them incumbent party candidates were unopposed. The only race in which there was opposition saw a Republican incumbent, Gilbert Baker, defeat a Democratic challenger, Joe White, in what is considered to have been the most expensive state legislative race in the state's history, with combined spending by the two candidates nearing $800,000 (Baker 2008, Hale-Shelton 2008, White 2008). Given that donors on both sides had so few choices of candidates in contested elections to donate to, this should not be a surprise. Overall, then, the new legislature, with a seventy-two-to-twenty-eight Democratic majority in the state House and a twenty-seven-to-eight Democratic majority in the state Senate, remained substantively unchanged by the election.

The 2008 elections in Arkansas were also notable for the success of three constitutional amendments and a ballot initiative, all of which passed with comfortable margins. Given the different ideological leanings of these amendments, as well as Arkansans' historical propensity for shooting down actions that would increase the power of government or cost the state more money, both politicians and analysts were surprised by these results (Frago and Wickline 2008). The first proposed amendment dealt with cleaning up some of the language in the constitution concerning elections and removing the language denying the right to vote to any "idiot or insane person." The second called for a limited budget session of the legislature in even numbered years and limited all appropriations to a single year. The third authorized the creation of a state lottery to fund college scholarships. The proposed initiative, which drew at least as much attention as any of the amendments, prohibited individuals who are "cohabitating outside of a valid marriage" from adopting children or serving as foster parents. This initiative, which was sponsored by the Family Council Action Committee, represented a carefully worded reaction to court rulings keeping a similar proposal that specifically prohibited same-sex couples from adopting or becoming foster parents off the ballot (Family Council Action Committee n.d., Wickline 2008).

It would be tempting to look at this amendment as a contributing factor in the outcome of the presidential campaign, in the same way that a measure opposing same-sex marriage has frequently been cited as a contributing factor in Bush's victory in the state in 2004. The idea, of course, was that Christian conservatives, drawn to the polls to vote against gay marriage, also voted for Bush over Kerry. Just as that interpretation of 2004 appears to have been erroneous (Dowdle and Wekkin 2006), such an interpretation also appears problematic in this cycle. First, while the initiative was passed by a significant margin (57 percent to 43 percent), it was a smaller margin than McCain's victory over Obama in the state (59 percent to 39 percent). The opposite should be true if McCain was riding what would essentially be the coattails of the initiative. Second, the constitutional amendment authorizing a lottery was also an important issue for many religious leaders in the state, drawing strong opposition not only from the same groups that would be expected to favor the adoption and foster care ban, but also the same group that sponsored it (Blomeley 2008). That amendment, however, drew significantly more support than either the adoption and foster care ban or McCain. Finally, while the exit polls do indicate that McCain supporters were strongly in favor of the proposed initiative, Obama supporters were essentially split on the issue (Arkansas Exit Poll 2008).

ONE-PARTY DOMINANCE, BUT WHICH PARTY ON WHICH LEVELS?

Overall, the results of the 2008 elections in Arkansas illustrate an electorate that continues to defy simple categorization. The state strongly supported the Republican presidential nominee in what was nationally a very pro-Democratic year, while at the same time maintaining Democratic majorities of more than 70 percent in the state House, state Senate, and in the congressional delegation. Voters supported changes to the state's constitution that will allow the government more opportunities to meet and act, and that authorized the creation of a state-sponsored lottery, both positions that would point to a liberalizing trend in the electorate. At the same time, though, they voted to prevent single, cohabitating individuals (and therefore same-sex couples) from adopting children or becoming foster parents, which points strongly in the other direction. While explaining these differences remains a challenge, they certainly indicate that Arkansans seem to view the choice between the two major parties differently at the national and state level, and to view issues through more than one ideological lens.

This bifurcated view of politics, however, may not be an unreasonable one. The Arkansas Democratic Party seems to have avoided the realignment that has dramatically shifted the political landscape of other southern states over the past forty years, creating Republican majorities in states that could once be counted on to overwhelmingly support Democrats. Either because it has avoided that realignment, or perhaps as a way to avoid one, the state party remains significantly more conservative than the national Democratic Party. Two of the three Democrats representing Arkansas in the House, Marion Berry and Mike Ross, are members of the Blue Dog Coalition, a group organized around principles of fiscal conservatism (Blue Dog Coalition n.d.). The state's two Democratic senators also find themselves in the more conservative wing of the national party. Blanche Lincoln's official website discusses her commitment to balancing the budget, reauthorizing TANF, the reform of the welfare system that requires recipients to work in order to be eligible for benefits, crime victims' rights, and the right of private citizens to own firearms. Mark Pryor's official website lists lower taxes, a balanced budget, increased defense spending, and health care reform focused on tax credits as some of his legislative priorities. Clearly, these are not the issue positions most commonly associated with the Democratic Party nationally. The congressional delegation reflects a similarly conservative bent among many other Democratic elected officials in state and local office.

This disparity between the state and national parties may help to explain, then, how a state in which 45 percent of respondents in the 2008 exit poll identified themselves as conservative, 41 percent identified themselves as moderate, and only 14 percent identified themselves as liberal so consistently elects large Democratic majorities at the state level. A fairly conservative state Democratic Party puts the state's Republican Party into the position of trying to compete for what might otherwise be its own base, while at the same time trying to still win over voters from the significant group of self-described moderates in the state. At the same time, this disparity can help to explain why national Democratic candidates suffer by comparison in Arkansas. Self-identified Democrats who might never even consider voting for Republican candidates for state or local offices must see the national Democratic Party as a completely separate entity from the one they are familiar with closer to home. As long as the state and national Democratic parties remain ideologically distinct, Arkansas' pattern of being reliably red at the presidential level and reliably blue below that seems unlikely to change.

CONCLUSION

In many ways, the summary for the 2008 elections could have been written months before the actual election occurred. In small part, the results of the 2008 nomination contests made the presidential election in Arkansas a foregone conclusion. While early polls showed Clinton would be competitive against any Republican nominee, her absence on the ticket ensured that Arkansas would remain a red state on the presidential map.

More importantly, the absence of major party competition in almost every major contest froze the rest of the state in political amber. It is correct to point out that neither party made serious efforts to challenge the other's incumbents. However, the effect is particularly detrimental to the Republican Party for two reasons. Obviously the lack of competition made it impossible for the GOP to challenge the Democratic Party's dominance in state politics in 2008.

Of equal concern to the Republicans is the effect this election will have on future contests. The party has always suffered from a shortage of quality challengers with some political experience. In this case, that problem severely hampers its prospects for 2010. In most Southern states, a midterm election where a U.S. senator, three-quarters of the House delegation, a sitting governor, and the rest of the statewide officers are Democrats would present multiple targets of opportunity to the state Republican Party. In Arkansas, there are real questions as to whether the Republican Party will be able to field candidates with any chance of running competitive campaigns against these incumbents.

NOTES

Authors' Note: The authors would like to thank Ann Clemmer and Gary Wekkin for their helpful comments.

1. State and county ballot totals for 2004, 2006, and 2008 are from the Arkansas Secretary of State's website at http://www.arelections.org.
2. All of the 2008 Arkansas exit poll data cited in this chapter come from CNN's 2008 Arkansas exit poll (http://www.cnn.com/ELECTION/2008/results/polls/#ARP00p1) unless otherwise indicated. The 2004 Arkansas exit poll data cited in this chapter come from CNN's 2004 Arkansas exit poll (http://www.cnn.com/ELECTION/2008/results/polls/#ARP00p1) unless otherwise indicated.

REFERENCES

Adkins, Randall E., and Andrew J. Dowdle. 2008. "Continuity and Change in the Presidential Money Primary." *American Review of Politics* 28:319–341.

Arkansas Exit Poll. 2004. CNN's Election Center 2004. http://www.cnn.com/ELECTION/2004/pages/results/states/AR/P/00/epolls.0.html.

———. 2008. CNN's Election Center 2008. http://www.cnn.com/ELECTION/2008/results/polls/#ARP00p1.

Baker, Gilbert. 2008. Financial Disclosure Form #4304. Arkansas Secretary of State's Office. http://www.sos.arkansas.gov/elections/ce/index.php?do:getFilings=1&id=4304.

Beebe, Mike. 2006. Financial Disclosure Form #1087. Arkansas Secretary of State's Office. http://www.sos.arkansas.gov/elections/ce/index.php?do:getFilings=1&id=1087.

Blair, Diane D., and Jay Barth. 2005. *Arkansas Politics and Government*, 3rd ed. Lincoln: University of Nebraska.

Blomeley, Seth. 2008. "All Sides in State Lottery Question File Briefs Before Supreme Court." *The Arkansas Democrat Gazette*. October 8: Section B.

Brown, Amy Jo. 2008. "Voters Cast Record Though Turnout Doesn't." *The Arkansas Democrat Gazette*. November 6: Section B.

Blue Dog Coalition. n.d. Membership List. http://www.house.gov/ross/BlueDogs/Member%20Page.html. Accessed 11/8/08.

Dowdle, Andrew, and Gary D. Wekkin. 2006. "Arkansas: The Post-2000 Elections in Arkansas: Continued GOP Growth or a Party That Has Peaked?" In *The New Politics of the Old South*, 3rd ed., ed. Charles S. Bullock III and Mark J. Rozell. Lanham MD: Rowman & Littlefield.

———. Forthcoming. "It Was Bush, Stupid: Moral Values and Candidate Effects in Arkansas Elections, 2000–2004." *Midsouth Political Science Review*.

Family Council Action Committee. n.d. "About the Adoption Act." http://adoption act.familycouncilactioncommittee.com/index.asp?PageID=2.

———. n.d. "FAQ." http://adoptionact.familycouncilactioncommittee.com/index .asp?PageID=4.

Frago, Charlie, and Michael R. Wickline. 2008. "Passage of All Five Ballot Issues Stuns Some." *The Arkansas Democrat Gazette*. November 6: Section A.

Hale-Shelton, Debra. 2008. "Baker Defeats White in Pricey Senate Race." *The Arkansas Democrat Gazette*. November 5: Section B.

Hutchinson, Asa. 2006. Financial Disclosure Form #1063. Arkansas Secretary of State's Office. http://www.sos.arkansas.gov/elections/ce/index.php?do:get Filings=1&id=1063.

Kraushaar, Josh, and Charles Mahtesian. 2008. "Five Things to Watch Tonight." Politico.com. http://www.politico.com/news/stories/1108/15226.html.

Lincoln, Blanche. "Issues." Senator Blanche Lincoln Official Website. n.d. http://lincoln.senate.gov/leg_issue.htm.

Parry, Janine A., and William Schreckhise. 2008. *The Arkansas Poll, 2008 Summary Report*. Fayetteville, AR: The Diane D. Blair Center of Southern Politics and Society, University of Arkansas.

Pryor, Mark. "Issues." Senator Mark Pryor Official Website. n.d. http://pryor.senate .gov/issues/.

Wekkin, Gary D. 1998. "Arkansas: Electoral Competition in the 1990s." In *The New Politics of the Old South*, ed. Charles S. Bullock III and Mark J. Rozell, 185–203. Lanham, MD: Rowman & Littlefield.

———. 2003. "Arkansas: Electoral Competition and Reapportionment in the 'Land of Opportunity.'" In *The New Politics of the Old South*, 2nd ed., ed. Charles S. Bullock III and Mark J. Rozell, 195–222. Lanham, MD: Rowman & Littlefield.

White, Joe. 2008. Financial Disclosure Form #4046. Arkansas Secretary of State's Office. http://www.sos.arkansas.gov/elections/ce/index.php?do:getFilings= 1&id=4046.

Wickline, Michael R. 2008. "Campaign Focus: Voters Getting Say on Lottery, 4 Others." *The Arkansas Democrat Gazette*. November 2: Section B.

10

Oklahoma

Red State Rising

Ronald Keith Gaddie and John William Shapard

These presidential elections are killing us.

—Ivan Holmes, Oklahoma Democratic Party Chairman,
November 6, 2008

The ongoing realignment of the South continued full force in Oklahoma as Republicans seized total control of the legislature and won all statewide contests in 2008. The 1994 election initiated a dramatic increase in Republican electoral strength. By 2004, the Republicans controlled both U.S. Senate seats, all but one congressional seat, and the state House of Representatives. In 2006, Republicans tied the state Senate while losing most of the statewide constitutional offices on the coattails of a moderate Democratic governor, but then in 2008 stormed back to take the Senate and also a commanding majority in the House. The principal catalyst for political change has been social conservatism, and in particular the continued mobilizing effort of evangelical Protestants. Democrats remain competitive in certain parts of the state, and when economic issues are predominant. This conservatism has combined with a favorable local economy to shift the political debate firmly into a conflict between social conservatism and chamber of commerce conservatism, with little room for liberal or progressive politics.

THE EXPATRIATE SOUTHERN STATE

Oklahoma was originally part of the Louisiana Purchase. Most of present-day Oklahoma was set aside from the purchase as Indian Territory. During the 1820s, the first southerners came to Oklahoma, as the Five Civilized Tribes (the Cherokee, Chickasaw, Choctaw, Creek, and Seminole) were forcibly removed from Florida, Georgia, and Alabama to the Indian Territory. Once there, the tribes established five Indian nations that ruled as republics under written constitutions (Morgan, England, and Humphreys 1991). During the Civil War some Indian tribes, most notably the Cherokees, sided with the Confederacy. Many tribes owned slaves, and the potential costs of abolition to the tribes were great. The Oklahoma tribes sent delegates to the Confederate Congress and served in the southern armies.[1]

After the end of the Civil War, the Civilized Tribes underwent a reconstruction as harsh as that of the rest of the South. Indian participation in the rebellion gave the Federal government sufficient justification to seize the central and west Oklahoma lands from the tribes and to then open the territory to white settlement. In the remaining Indian territories, tribes were forced to free their slaves and to offer the freedmen membership in the tribes. In response to the emancipation of the blacks, the tribes passed segregation laws that created all-black townships and placed limitations on the black freedmen that resembled those of the Jim Crow laws.

In the 1880s, the Bureau of Indian Affairs declared the tribal reservation system to be an abysmal failure (see Gaddie and Buchanan 1998). This evaluation was reached by the Dawes Commission, apparently under some influence from development interests that sought to open the Indian Territory to white settlement. The lands of the Civilized Tribes were broken up, and each tribal member was granted a 160-acre homestead. The territory was partitioned into two territories: Oklahoma Territory, which took in the northern and western parts of the state, and Indian Territory, which covered an area roughly south of a line running from the northeast corner of the state, through Tulsa and Oklahoma City, and on to the Texas border. This partition is reflected in the settlement patterns and subsequent political behavior of the state. White settlers in the Indian Territory were largely expatriate southerners from Texas, Arkansas, and Mississippi. A journey through the southeast corner of the state, commonly referred to as "Little Dixie," reveals that many of the towns and counties take their names directly from Mississippi locales.

So is Oklahoma really southern? Oklahoma stands at the fringe of the South, both in the study of southern politics and in the mind-set of Oklahoma. Oklahoma—then Indian Territory—was not a state at the time of the Civil War, but many of the events and cultural factors that structure Oklahoma politics are distinctly southern (Price 1957; Ewing 1953). As in many southern states, the GOP has enjoyed dramatic growth in adherents and has sustained electoral success in contests at all electoral levels. Unlike the Deep South, however, the Republican growth in Oklahoma is a product of the intriguing catalyst of religious social conservatism. Most southern state studies show that Republican growth can be linked initially to race (Carmines and Stimson 1989; Lamis 1988; Black and Black 1992). Race, though, is not such a divisive issue in Oklahoma. Only 7.5 percent of the state population is black; however, Native Americans outnumber blacks, and Hispanics are the fastest growing minority in the state, leaving Oklahoma with a white population comparable to Alabama's.

The unique specter of fear of black political and economic empowerment is a historic footnote to Oklahoma's early segregationist history. Tulsa was host to one of the most vicious, deadly race riots in American history eighty-five years ago, and, until the 1960s, many small cities and towns were formally segregated by illegal "sundown" laws. Oklahoma did not resist national government efforts to integrate public schools or accommodations. By the 1970s, the wave of integration was viewed with ambivalence, as Oklahoma boomed and culturally diverse Oklahomans (one in four, when asked, will claim Native blood) looked to the sky as oil prices soared. Subsequent to the economic collapse of the oil industry in the 1980s, religion, specifically the growth of the Christian Right, emerged as a major catalyst in the GOP upswing in Oklahoma.

RACE POLITICS

Oklahoma is unique among the southern states for its diverse nonwhite population. It is also the state where minority voters have the least direct impact on the politics of the state. Bullock and Gaddie (2006, 4) describe the state thus: "set aside as an Indian Territory and populated by the Cherokee, Chickasaw, Choctaw, Seminole, and Muscogee, the Sooner State was almost three-fourths white as of the 2000 census. It has a black population substantially less than any of the states that seceded, 7.5 percent. Indeed, African Americans are slightly outnumbered by Native Americans (7.7 percent). Hispanics constitute a sizeable remainder of the non-Anglo, white population at 5.2 percent in the 2000 census." Nonetheless, over 90 percent of the electorate is usually Anglo white, followed by black voters and then American Indians.

Oklahoma's record on race relations is not clean, as we noted in the introduction, and that legacy extends to voting rights. The first instance of a Jim Crow voting law being stricken is an Oklahoma case, *Guinn v. United States*. The original Oklahoma Constitution allowed "anyone entitled to vote prior to January 1866 or that person's lineal descendants to register and vote without passing a literacy test" (Bullock and Gaddie 2006). The U.S. Supreme Court subsequently ruled that fighting the grandfather clause ran afoul of the Enforcement Acts of 1870. Oklahoma's legislature continued to discriminate against a number of its African

Americans, providing only a twelve-day registration window, from April 30 until March 11, 1916, for those who had not voted in 1914 to register. The law stood until invalidated by the Supreme Court two decades later.[2]

School desegregation was controversial in the 1970s and led to white flight from the Oklahoma City school system. More recently, immigration politics have reached the forefront of the political debate in the state, as Republicans and Democrats in the legislature defied the will of the business community by imposing sweeping sanctions on businesses employing illegal immigrants, and by denying undocumented aliens access to a broad array of public services.

Voting Rights Act Coverage: Oklahoma did not trip the Section 4 trigger of the 1965 Voting Rights Act and therefore is not subject to election law preclearance. The language amendments made to the Voting Rights Act in 1975 do extend to Oklahoma elections. Section 203 of the Voting Rights Act requires provision of foreign-language ballots. In the 1990s, Adair County provided Cherokee-language ballots, and currently Texas County and Harmon County provide Spanish-language ballots. There is a strong expectation that additional rural Oklahoma counties and also the major urban counties will eventually fall under Section 203(c).

Minority Voter Participation: Surveys conducted by the U.S. Bureau of the Census after each federal election provide the best resource for figures on minority participation rates in Oklahoma. The registration and turnout figures generated by these surveys are self-reported and thus subject to inflation (Abramson and Claggett 1986). Table 10.1 shows black and white registration and turnout rates from 1980 to 2004 (Bullock and Gaddie

Table 10.1.   Race and Registration in Oklahoma (in percentages)

	Registration		Turnout	
	Black	*White*	*Black*	*White*
1980	51.9	67.7	44.5	61.1
1982	59.2	63.3	44.9	47.5
1984	60.7	72.6	43.5	62.6
1986	58.5	68.4	29.9	51.3
1988	59.8	66.5	53.0	57.6
1990	51.6	69.2	29.2	52.0
1992	65.5	75.5	52.4	69.3
1994	49.8	68.5	31.5	49.8
1996	67.1	71.3	52.0	60.5
1998	60.3	65.1	31.8	41.6
2000	57.4	69.5	44.5	59.3
2002	54.2	69.3	36.4	50.8
2004	61.8	71.4	54.7	62.6

Source: From Bullock and Gaddie (2006), 3.

2006). African American registration most closely approached that for whites in three election years, while in seven other election years the difference equaled or exceeded 10 percentage points. Throughout the quarter century chronicled in the table, white voting rates exceeded African American turnout. Beginning with 1988, a majority of Oklahoma's African Americans report having voted in presidential elections, except in 2000 when the figures slumped to 44.5 percent. Participation among African Americans is substantially lower in midterm elections.

Minority Officeholding: Table 10.2 enumerates African American officeholders from 1969 to 2001. In the initial enumeration, Oklahoma had twenty-five blacks in elective office, mainly on school boards. In the 1970s, Oklahoma experienced a substantial increase in black officeholders, mainly in municipal offices. In the 1980s a second burst occurred. As with the gains of the early 1970s, the new additions came in cities, which by 1984 had sixty-three African Americans holding office, and black candidates started to win occasional county offices. Black officeholding peaked at 123 in 1993, and as of the most recent enumeration in 2001, black officeholders numbered just over 100, mainly in municipal offices and on school boards.

Table 10.2. Historic Black Officeholding in Oklahoma

Year	Total	County	Municipal	School Board
1969	25	0	1	19
1970	36	0	12	19
1971	61	0	35	18
1972	62	0	35	19
1973	67	0	43	18
1974	66	0	40	20
1975	68	1	42	20
1976	67	1	41	20
1977	69	0	46	18
1978	68	0	45	18
1980	77	0	50	21
1981	85	0	43	20
1984	122	2	63	23
1985	122	2	91	22
1987	117	2	84	23
1989	115	2	81	25
1991	122	3	90	21
1993	123	3	92	21
1997	102	2	74	19
1999	105	1	79	16
2001	105	1	74	21

Source: Bullock and Gaddie (2006), table 4.

Oklahoma was a trailblazer of sorts in electing minorities to major office. In 1994, J. C. Watts, a former OU quarterback, was elected to the U.S. House as one of two black Republicans in Congress; he had previouly been the only black Republican elected statewide in the South (as Corporation Commissioner). Watts represented a 7.5 percent black district. Gaddie and Buchanan (1998) and Bullock and Gaddie (2006) note that in Watts's initial congressional campaign, he took "less than a third of the vote of (largely white) rural Democrats in the southern part of the state" but that by his last election, Watts was "carrying an estimated majority of those votes." Exit polling performed by the University of Oklahoma in 1996 found Watts garnering about four in ten black votes in his congressional district (Gaddie and Buchanan 1998).

Native Americans in Congress: In 2003, Oklahoma had the most heavily Native American congressional delegation in the United States. Two of five members elected from Oklahoma—Representative Brad Carson (D-CD2) and Representative Tom Cole (R-CD4)—were enrolled members of recognized Indian nations. Carson, from Claremore, is a member of the Cherokee Nation; his father had been a Bureau of Indian Affairs (BIA) attorney and Carson grew up on or near reservations in four states. He left the House in 2004 for an unsuccessful bid for the U.S. Senate. Cole is a member of the Chickasaw Nation and is now the only Native American serving in Congress.

POLITICAL GEOGRAPHY

The geographic settlement patterns of Oklahoma play a prominent role in explaining the politics of the state. After the Oklahoma Territory was opened to white settlement, the western and northern tier of counties was settled by Midwesterners and plainsmen. The southern and eastern counties were settled by southerners from Texas, Mississippi, and Arkansas. Democrats dominated politics in the state after co-opting the progressive and socialist movements. The west and north continued as a Republican redoubt.

As the urban centers of Oklahoma grew, the political geography of the state took on a tripartite shape familiar to Oklahoma political observers. If one draws a line from the northeastern corner of the state to the southwestern corner, it would pass through the urban centers of Tulsa, Oklahoma City, and Lawton. To the north and west of this line and outside of these cities is predominantly Republican, and contains about 10 percent of the state population. To the south and east of the line is predominantly Democratic, the "Little Dixie" region that contains about 20 percent of the state population. The remaining 70 percent of Oklahomans live in the urban corridor that encompasses the major cities of the state (Morgan, England, and Humphreys 1991).

For years the growth of the suburban corridor has not altered the partisan differences that exist between the two major urban counties (Oklahoma and Tulsa) and the rest of the state. Kirkpatrick, Morgan, and Kielhorn (1977) observed that, in the 1960s, the major urban counties voted substantially more Republican than the rest of the state in major statewide elections. As indicated in table 10.3, the average urban/rural difference in gubernatorial elections was over 9 percentage points through 2002. The GOP won a majority of the urban core counties' vote on six of ten occasions but did not carry the rural vote between 1966 and 1994, and lost it again in 2002. The urban vote constituted the margin of victory for the last three Republican governors, none of whom won an outright majority of

Table 10.3. The Cities and Republican Success (in percentages)

Year	State	OKC/Tulsa	Out-State	Difference
Vote for Governor				
1962	55.2	61.2	52.5	+8.7
1966	55.7	65.3	51.0	+14.3
1970	48.1*	57.9	43.3	+14.6
1974	36.1	45.5	31.4	+14.1
1978	47.2	53.9	43.9	+10.0
1982	37.6	47.5	32.6	+14.9
1986	47.5*	54.5	44.0	+10.5
1990	36.2	43.0	32.9	+10.1
1994	46.9*	59.0	40.3	+18.7
1998	57.9	61.9	55.8	+6.1
2002	42.6**	48.2	39.6	+8.6
2006	33.5	37.8	31.3	+6.5
Vote for President				
1964	44.3	51.3	40.7	+10.6
1968	47.7*	52.9	44.9	+8.0
1972	73.7	76.3	72.2	+4.1
1976	49.9*	58.8	45.1	+13.7
1980	60.5	66.1	57.5	+8.6
1984	68.6	72.3	66.6	+5.7
1988	58.4	64.0	54.6	+9.4
1992	42.6*	48.9	39.1	+9.8
1996	48.2*	54.1	45.1	+9.0
2000	60.3	61.8	59.5	+2.3
2004	65.6	64.3	66.3	−2.0
2008	65.6	60.3	68.8	−8.5

Source: Kirkpatrick, Morgan, and Kielhorn (1977); Morgan, England, and Humphreys (1991). Figures since 1990 computed by authors from data provided by the Oklahoma State Board of Elections.
*GOP plurality win
**GOP plurality loss

the vote until Frank Keating was reelected with 57 percent of the vote in 1998. The difference in the rural/urban vote was generally between 10 and 14 points for every election between 1966 and the mid-1990s. A huge gap (18.7 percent) was evident in 1994, but in subsequent elections it declined, notably in the last three gubernatorial elections. The urban/rural split in Oklahoma had become even less pronounced in presidential races, but recently reemerged with a realigning twist. In 2004 President Bush ran more strongly in out-state regions than in the state's metro areas, and Senator McCain enhanced this pattern in 2008.

PARTY DEVELOPMENT

The Democratic Party dominated state politics from the first state elections in 1907 until the 1990s. The only exceptions to Democratic hegemony were the two Republicans elected governor in the 1960s and one again in the 1980s, and the brief Republican control of the state legislature from 1920 to 1922. At the presidential level the Democrats faded earlier; Lyndon Johnson is the only Democrat to carry Oklahoma since 1952.

The reputation of Oklahoma politics is conservative, but its heritage is populist. The territorial and early statehood Democratic Party rode to dominance on a progressive platform, following the southern Democratic habit of co-opting the Populists. Soon after statehood, a series of economic depressions hit Oklahoma. Many Oklahomans supported socialist candidates; by 1914 there were numerically more socialists in Oklahoma than New York State, and a Socialist candidate for governor pulled nearly 20 percent of the vote. This socialist presence cost the Democrats control of the state legislature in 1920, as well as a U.S. Senate seat and three congressional districts. The Democrats regained control of the legislature in 1922, and by the time of the New Deal realignment the GOP was thoroughly devastated. In the late 1950s, over half of the legislative seats in the state still went to Democrats without contest (Hale and Kean 1996). The Republican journey into the wilderness of Oklahoma politics lasted until 1962 with the election of Henry Bellman as the first-ever Republican governor.

The 1960s were a better time for the GOP. In 1962, Henry Bellmon was elected the first Republican governor of Oklahoma. (The 1958 GOP gubernatorial candidate had won just 19 percent of the vote and lost every county in the state.) As the decade proceeded, Republicans won a congressional seat, and Barry Goldwater ran ahead of his national average, although Johnson carried the state for president. In 1966, Republican Dewey Bartlett succeeded Bellmon as governor (at that time Oklahoma governors were limited to a single term). Bellmon was subsequently elected to the Senate in 1968, and he was joined in the Senate by Bartlett in 1972.

Below the level of major statewide offices, success by the GOP was at best fleeting. Like many southern states, Oklahoma was forced to reapportion the state legislature and congressional districts to accommodate the one-man, one-vote standards set in *Baker v. Carr* and *Wesberry v. Sanders*. Rural interests had traditionally been overrepresented in the legislature due to guarantees of representation for each county. This malapportionment helped to perpetuate the Democratic domination of both chambers. After reapportionment, the Democrats continued to hold substantial majorities, especially in the rural areas, while Republicans were elected almost entirely from the populous metropolitan counties. This initial era of Republican emergence did not lead directly to a competitive party, but it did break ground for the coming realignment of Oklahoma politics.

In the 1980s, Republican registration surged and the GOP won more seats in the legislature. Bellmon returned for another term as governor in 1986, and Don Nickles, a thirty-one-year-old Republican businessman from Ponca City, succeeded Bellmon in the Senate in 1980. The GOP held two U.S. House seats from 1986 forward, when James Inhofe was elected to represent Tulsa.

A systematic electoral eradication of Democrats started in 1994. Entering the election year the GOP held one Senate seat, two House seats, and no major state office. After the November election, Republicans held both U.S. Senate seats, five of six U.S. House seats, and had recaptured the governor's mansion. Moreover, the political force of the evangelical right movement and its influence within the Republican Party, and the state more generally, was undeniable—an influence that, if not still growing, persists today. In 1996, the last Democratic congressional seat was captured by the Republicans after incumbent Bill Brewster retired and was succeeded by former incumbent (and former Democrat) Wes Watkins.

MODERN PARTY ORGANIZATIONS

I don't belong to an organized political party; I am a Democrat.

—Will Rogers

The Democratic and Republican Party organizations in Oklahoma are decidedly different in their degree of organization, unity, and in their relationships with the national parties. The state Democrats resemble the Democratic parties of so many southern states: fractured, teeming with internal conflict, and only loosely linked to the DNC. The Oklahoma Republican Party has been centrally organized since the 1960s, and the state party has sought to follow the "grassroots" development model advanced by former RNC chairman Haley Barbour. More recently, the Christian conservatives have firmly established themselves in the party.

Oklahoma spent decades as a "modified one-party state" (Kirkpatrick, Morgan, and Kielhorn 1977; Hale and Kean 1996). Republicans nonetheless have demonstrated consistent national election strength for almost fifty years, even as the Democrats dominated state and local politics. Henry Bellmon, the first Republican governor of Oklahoma, sought to overcome the political anemia of the GOP in the 1950s by actively organizing the party at the county level. Bellmon's "Operation Countdown" emphasized candidate recruitment and voter mobilization. He even ventured into the "Little Dixie" region of the state. Bellmon's grassroots efforts won him the governorship in 1962, as well as the moniker of "father" to the modern Oklahoma GOP. In the 1980s, Republicans reinvigorated this strategy, using sophisticated data analysis and polling to target campaigns outside of the GOP strongholds. Grassroots mobilization of Republicans, especially evangelicals, has served to further invigorate the GOP.

For years the state Republican Party was characterized by a bifactionalism between "moneybags" elements from Tulsa (also called country-club Republicans) and "grassroots" elements from the small towns of the western plain and panhandle (Hale and Kean 1996). Bellmon typified the country-club GOP, advocating smaller government and lower taxes; it is widely acknowledged that he has no patience for social-issue conservatives. The emergence of the Christian Right as a force in the party has reoriented this factionalism to set traditional Bellmon Republicans against the Christian Right. For the present, though, intraparty disputes have been muted by the success enjoyed by the GOP. The state Republican organization is a modernized organization that has developed a stable of technically savvy political consultants who are highly effective at campaign advertising, fundraising, and voter targeting and mobilization. A series of state party chairmen, from Tom Cole (now a congressman) through Chad Alexander and Gary Jones, have sought to balance competition among the country-club and social-conservative elements, and have also sought to keep the state party organizations strong in the face of growing legislative party leadership. However, a new dispute is unfolding as nativist interests vested in the GOP come into conflict with the business interests of Oklahoma City.

The Oklahoma Democrats are decidedly less organized. Until 1990, the state party did little to organize with the national party. There is minimal paid staff. The Democratic National Committee still does not see Oklahoma as a critical state, and consequently national party funds and support are not readily forthcoming. The most notable exception to this generalization was the rush of interest in Brad Carson's 2004 campaign for the U.S. Senate, when it looked winnable and like control of the U.S. Senate might hinge on the outcome.

Financial difficulties were resolved by recent party chair Lisa Pryor and co-chair Ben Odom (both former candidates), but recent leadership comes from the grassroots and has little organizational or financial savvy. The main organizational efforts for Democrats come from spotty local organizations or the state legislative campaign committees.

The decentralized state Democrats are beset with internal factional divisions. A mix of urban liberals and unionists, Little Dixie state legislators, and county elected officials compose the principal factions. The traditional factions have been joined more recently by an emerging netroots movement that defies the conventional profile of the netroots movement in that it is largely middle-aged.

Republican state chairs took advantage of the organizational groundwork laid by Henry Bellmon to develop grassroots organizations and strategies that exploit the division among state Democratic voters. This model of Religious Right mobilization and sophisticated targeting of congressional and state legislative races has paid electoral dividends. The state Republican Party has exploited its financial model of funding candidates through the statewide coordinated campaign (called the Victory Fund) and used the state legislative caucus and House and Senate PACs to direct expertise and money to potentially competitive state legislative districts. Battles over control of the Victory Fund and other party resources continue between federal, state legislative, and grassroots organization Republicans.

Democrats, meanwhile, continue to be caught in factional infighting between different constituency groups. In 2004, they ousted a state party chairman, Jay Parmley, over his support of Howard Dean as DNC chair and replaced Parmley with former state Senate candidate, teacher, and grassroots organizer Lisa Pryor. Pryor reestablished the financial solvency of the party. The most recent party chairman, Ivan Holmes, comes from the grassroots of the party but has had difficulty establishing a financial base for the party.

THE LEGISLATURE

In 2008, the Republican party won complete control of the Oklahoma state legislature, ending eighty-six years of Democratic dominance. The growth of Republicans in the Oklahoma legislature is indicated in table 10.4. In 1962, the last election preceding the court-ordered reapportionment of state legislative seats to comply with one-man, one-vote, the GOP held 24

Table 10.4.   Party and Race in the Oklahoma Legislature (in percentages)

| | Republican | | Black | |
Year	House	Senate	House	Senate
1965	17.2	18.5	2.5	2.0
1975	24.8	18.8	2.9	2.0
1985	31.7	35.4	2.9	4.2
1995	35.6	27.8	2.9	4.2
1997	35.6	31.3	2.9	4.2
1999	39.6	31.3	2.9	4.2
2001	47.5	37.5	2.9	4.2
2003	47.5	41.7	2.9	4.2
2005	56.4	45.8	2.9	4.2
2007	56.4	50.0	4.0	4.2
2009	60.4	54.2	4.0	4.2

Source: *Oklahoma Almanac* 1995–1996; National Conference of State Legislatures (2001, 2003, 2005, 2007, 2009).
Note: There are 101 members of the Oklahoma House and 48 members of the Oklahoma Senate.

of 129 House seats (18.5 percent) and 5 of 44 Senate seats (11.3 percent). The reapportionment of seats produced a loss of two seats in the House and a gain of five in the Senate. By 1991 the GOP House caucus had increased to 32 of 101 seats, with a pair of brief setbacks after Watergate and during the 1982 recession. In 2000 and 2002, Democrats managed to barely hang onto their majority status in the state House of Representatives. Republicans gained the majority in 2004, capturing 57 of the 101 seats in the House. In 2008 they enhanced that number to 61 seats. In the Senate, Republicans achieved a 24–24 tie in 2006, and a 26–22 majority in 2008.

The state House of Representatives became a center of excessive drama with the rise of Republican leadership. A party purge of professional staff and efforts to alter the calendar of business slowed legislation in the 2005 legislative session. Senate Democrats and the governor exploited Republican inexperience in budget negotiations. In 2006, the term-limited speaker, Todd Hiett, sought another office, and his personal fundraising operation created conflict with the efforts of the incoming speaker-designate, a young attorney named Lance Cargill. Cargill subsequently became the center of an ethics investigation regarding campaign fundraising, and was ousted as speaker over strong-handed conduct with his caucus and the revelation of repeated delinquent state taxes. Cargill was eventually succeeded by Tulsa Republican Chris Benge, who had support of both party caucuses.

The state Senate was a study in civility and moderation by comparison. Party-line behavior had protected the governor from controversial legislation, and when the tied chamber was achieved in 2006, Democrats and Republicans secured a power-sharing arrangement that split everything—committee seats, co-chairs, co-presiding officers—and also ensured that controversial legislation would not see a vote on the floor. This did not stop Democrats and Republicans from getting together in 2008 to pass one of the most restrictive abortion laws in the United States over the governor's veto. The Republican takeover of the Senate after the 2008 elections led to the ascendancy of the first Republican president pro tempore, Glen Coffee, who proceeded to force through a set of rules that centralized control of debate and legislation in the hands of the presiding officer.

As the state legislature became more competitive in terms of parties, it remained a largely white, male institution. There has been little variation over time in black representation in Oklahoma (see table 10.4). Currently, there are six black state legislators in Oklahoma: four state House members and two state senators. (Former Member of Congress and Corporation Commissioner J. C. Watts has been the only other prominent African American officeholder). All but one black state legislator were elected from Tulsa and Oklahoma county districts that are predominantly urban, center-city districts. Additionally, women make up 11.9 percent of the House and 10.4 percent of the Senate, which are some of the lowest percentages of female representation in the South or the nation (see also Wyman 2005).

THE OKLAHOMA ELECTORATE

With low prosperity indicators and Democratic registration figures still above 50 percent, on paper Oklahoma would appear to be a Democratic state. However, the state has steadily moved to the Republican Party, if not in voter registration then in actual ideology and votes cast.

The profile of the 2008 Oklahoma electorate reveals a conservative population (46.1 percent conservative, 41.0 percent moderate) that is still nonetheless heavily Democratic by registration. It is a religious electorate, with over 28 percent of persons attending church more than once a week and another 29.9 percent attending weekly. The income of the likely voters in the electorate is high relative to the state in general—a median of about $57,000 compared to a Census Bureau median of about $43,000 in the general population. The potential electorate was also composed largely of persons with less than a college education (see table 10.5). The Oklahoma electorate, while whiter than the rest of the South, is also poorer, less educated, more conservative, and more religious than the rest of the nation.

Table 10.5. Profile of Likely Voters in Oklahoma

Party (n = 7,111)	Percent	Education (n = 6,345)	Percent
Democrat	51.9	<High School	3.4
Republican	42.1	High School grad	22.9
Independent	6.1	Tech/VoTech	7.5
		Some College	24.4
		College grad	22.1
Ideology (n = 7,111)		Post-Grad study	7.4
Liberal	9.1	Post-Grad degree	10.8
Moderate	41.0	Refused	1.5
Conservative	46.1		
Don't know/Refused	3.8		
		Income (n = 6,344)	
		<$15,000	7.0
Church Attendance (n = 7,111)		$15,000–25,000	11.3
Several times a week	28.1	$25,000–40,000	16.4
Once a week	29.9	$40,000–55,000	14.6
Monthly	21.6	$55,000–70,000	14.0
Several times a year	13.6	$70,000–100,000	13.4
Annually	4.3	$100,000–150,000	8.0
Never	1.3	$150,000+	4.7
Don't know/Refused	1.2	Refused	10.6

Source: TvPoll.com, September 1–November 1, 2008 (inclusive).

Oklahoma's conservatism, and subsequent Republican leanings, is in large part a product of the state's firmly ensconced Religious Right. The role of Christianity in the state of Oklahoma cannot be overstated. This is a state where prayer only recently was excluded from sporting events, where a gay marriage prohibition amendment was supported by 75 percent of the voters, where stores cannot sell beer with more than 3.2 percent alcohol, and where tattoo parlors were illegal until 2007. Throughout the state, polling indicates that most Oklahomans describe themselves as evangelical or fundamentalist Christians. In 2004, exit polling placed the proportion of self-identified evangelicals at 44 percent (almost double the national electorate average of 23 percent). Oklahoma appears to be significantly more religiously conservative than most of the South. The average proportion of the electorate self-identifying as evangelical in the other southern states is 33 percent, and only Arkansas (at 53 percent) shows higher numbers of evangelicals in their electorate (Gaddie 2004).

The power of religious identity in the politics of the state is evident in recent polling. Exit poll data gathered after the 2004 and 2008 elections (see table 10.6) show how strongly those who claimed to be conservative white Protestants and those who defined themselves as evangelical fa-

Table 10.6. **Dimensions of the Oklahoma Electorate in 2004 and 2008 (in percentages)**

	Bush	*McCain*
Total Vote	66	66
Sex		
Male (48%/45%)	67	66
Female (52%/55%)	64	64
Partisanship		
Democrats (40%/41%)	32	33
Republicans (43%/44%)	96	95
Independents (16%/14%)	66	64
Age		
18–29 (19%/19%)	62	60
30–44 (27%/30%)	69	61
45–59 (28%/37%)	65	71
60+ (26%/14%)	66	—
White Evangelicals		
Yes (44%/44%)	77	79
No (56%/56%)	56	48
Economy Voters (17%/55%)	22	61

Source: CNN Exit polls
Note: *n* = 1,577 for 2004, 869 for 2008.

vored the Bush candidacy. Amongst the evangelical Protestants, 90 percent answered that they had voted for President Bush, of evangelicals, 77 percent backed the president's reelection. Exit poll questions asking respondents to explain their vote choice recorded that the greatest concern for Oklahomans in the presidential election was the issue of morality. Those who viewed morality as the top concern voted overwhelmingly, 90 percent, for Bush. Of further interest was a question asking about candidate qualities. While strong leadership was the number one response, 15 percent of those who were asked answered that they felt a candidate's religious affiliation was the most important characteristic, and these respondents voted 94 percent in favor of Bush.

The Church Gap: The Oklahoma electorate is structured by a churchgoing gap. Registered Republicans are the most frequent churchgoers. Almost a majority of persons going to church more than once a week are Republicans (+3.5 percentage points over Democrats in the same group) while those who go to church monthly or less are generally around 20 percentage points more Democratic than Republican (see table 10.7). Church attendance and ideology are closely related. Nearly two-thirds of those who attend services most often are conservative, while a majority of those with weekly or less attendance identify as moderate. Those who attend monthly or less are twice as likely to be liberals as those who attend several times a week.

Table 10.7. Church Attendance and Voter Identification

| | Church Attendance | | | | |
	Several Times a Week	Once a Week	Monthly	Several Times a Year	Annually
Party					
Democrat (%)	46.20	51.10	56.40	53.80	59.70
Republican (%)	49.70	44.40	34.90	37.40	33.30
Independent (%)	4.20	4.60	8.60	8.80	6.90
n =	1,999	2,129	1,538	967	303
Ideology					
Liberal (%)	5.60	8.70	10.10	15.00	10.30
Moderate (%)	27.10	39.60	51.30	51.40	53.60
Conservative (%)	63.30	48.60	35.50	29.30	27.80
DK/Refused (%)	4.00	3.10	3.10	4.20	8.30
n =	1,998	2,129	1,537	966	302

THE REPUBLICAN TWENTY-FIRST CENTURY IN OKLAHOMA

Republican presidential candidates have won Oklahoma's electoral votes in every election since 1968. In 2008, John McCain ran 21 percentage points ahead of his national showing. As in many southern states, Republican presidential candidates run ahead of other Republicans in rural, traditionally Democratic counties. Aistrup (1996) observed that the persistence of Republican success up the ticket in rural localities eventually leads to GOP success down-ticket in those areas. Southern voters have usually found it far easier to first break with the Democratic Party at the national level, where the policy stands and personal values of the party candidates are often at odds with southern tradition and values. The breaking of the southern Democratic linkage at the state and local level requires greater effort, especially if the values of Democratic candidates comport to the beliefs and values of the Democratic electorate (Heard 1952). The great success of candidates Bush and McCain in the nonmetropolitan areas should open up even more avenues for Republican success in Oklahoma.

Democrats have continued to dominate statewide constitutional offices through the first decade of the twenty-first century, and that success is owed to understated moderation. In 2002, the GOP vote split over the entry of renegade Republican lawyer Gary Richardson as an independent. The Democratic nominee, rural state senator Brad Henry, enjoyed support from the core Democratic constituencies—unions, teachers, and lawyers—and also enjoyed the benefits of an active grassroots effort in the rural counties to oppose a measure banning cockfighting in Oklahoma. While the effort to defeat the cockfighting measure would fail, the get-out-the-vote effort in rural Oklahoma fused with local Democratic Party organizations to create a strong turnout for the party's nominee. GOP nominee Steve Largent (a former NFL player and GOP congressman) failed to ignite the GOP electoral base, allowing Henry to exploit his rural advantage for a six-thousand-vote win. Henry exploited the formula for success of so many other southern governors—taming legalized gambling and enacting a lottery, both to fund education—which helped him with swing voters and further emboldened the Democratic base. Henry pulled 43.7 percent of the vote in 2002 to win by less than seven thousand ballots statewide, or about three votes per precinct (Copeland, Cruise, and Gaddie 2006).

The 2006 Election: Brad Henry's reelection bid demonstrated the power of political moderation and economic prosperity for a Democratic incumbent. Henry's initial term had focused on relatively noncontroversial issues such as early-childhood education, establishing a lottery, and expanding Indian gaming while ensuring the state received a share of revenues from the gaming tribes. The Democratic state Senate kept controversial issues off of his desk by not allowing social issue bills or tort reform proposals to exit committee, and Henry found common ground with Republican speaker of the House Todd Hiett to cut taxes. Brad Henry's four-year record of moderate governance drove his approval rating into the mid-70 percent range throughout the latter part of his term.

Henry's popularity caused most major Republicans to pass on the governor's race. The only major opponent, longtime congressman Ernest Istook (R-Warr Acres), had recently been ousted as an Appropriations subcommittee chair and had to endure a competitive primary against Tulsa oil man Bob Sullivan. Istook won nomination but his candidacy never found traction. Henry's reelection bid over Istook was virtually assured from the moment Henry filed. Istook was unable to raise substantial funds to challenge Henry, unwilling to concede control of his campaign to others, and unable to get voters to bite on the primary issue that GOP messaging testing indicated would work against Henry: illegal immigration reform.

Entering the week of reelection, Henry enjoyed a 78.1 percent approval rating and just a 20.0 percent disapproval rating. The last trial heat ballot before the November election showed Henry leading Istook by 30 percentage points, with 6.6 percent undecided. With undecideds allocated, a 66.7 percent to 33.3 percent result was expected. Henry defeated Istook 66.5 percent to 33.5 percent and won seventy-four of seventy-seven counties (everywhere except the panhandle). Eighteen months after reelection, Henry still enjoyed an approval rating of 74.2 percent.

The more exciting races were down-ticket. Democrats reclaimed the open lieutenant governor's seat. Three-term incumbent Mary Fallin (R-Oklahoma City) was elected to the U.S. House, and state representatives

Jari Askins, the Democratic minority leader, and Todd Hiett, the Republican speaker, battled in an expensive and divisive campaign that was ideologically charged. Polling consistently showed Askins narrowly leading the sometimes-controversial Hiett throughout the late fall. The final 50.1 percent to 47.5 percent margin for Askins was the closest of several statewide contests. Democrats came out of the election with eight of the nine statewide contests on the ballot.

The Henry election demonstrates the continuing crossover appeal of a Democrat who can point to successful job performance while staying away from controversial social issues. In Oklahoma, a solid majority of the electorate attends church at least once a week. Those churchgoers are more conservative and Republican than the rest of the electorate. But in 2006, Brad Henry captured a solid majority of every category of churchgoer. Down-ticket, in the open lieutenant governor contest, Democrat Jari Askins led among all but the most-frequent churchgoers and the small monthly-attendance crowd—and she pulled a bare majority of the vote (see table 10.8).

The 2008 Presidential Primary: Oklahoma voted for the eventual winners in the 2008 presidential primary. Oklahoma is an early primary state, going on the first week of February. On both the Republican and Democratic side, there was substantial volatility in the primary during the four weeks following the Iowa caucus (see table 10.9). An initial poll taken two days after the Iowa caucus showed a tight race between John Edwards and Hillary Clinton, while Republican Mike Huckabee, who had been campaigning in Oklahoma, held a solid 2:1 lead over John McCain. After the New Hampshire primary cleared part of the field, the Democratic primary was still a two-person fight while Republican Mike Huckabee's numbers came back to earth and John McCain picked up ground. On the eve of the February primary, John Edwards's departure from the field left Hillary Clinton with a solid lead over Barack Obama, while Huckabee, McCain, and a rising Mitt Romney battled for the winner-take-all GOP delegation.

Table 10.8. Church Attendance and Vote Choice in 2006 (in percentages)

	Governor		Lt. Governor	
	Henry (D-I)	*Istook (R)*	*Askins (D)*	*Hiett (R)*
More than once a week	**52.2**	39.9	36.8	**56.9**
Once a week	**67.1**	26.5	**46.8**	43.3
Several times a month	**75.6**	20.0	**60.9**	32.6
Once a month	**50.0**	30.0	40.0	**55.0**
Several times a year	**58.8**	35.3	**48.8**	44.0
Never	**71.4**	25.5	**58.6**	27.3

Table 10.9. Oklahoma Presidential Primary Polls (in percentages)

	1/07/08	*1/20/08*	*2/01/08*	*Result*
Democratic Primary				
Clinton	33.7	34.9	47.2	54.7
Edwards	28.5	25.7		10.2
Gravel	1.2	0.4	6.0	
Kucinich	1.2	2.3		0.6
Obama	16.4	15.3	26.1	31.2
Richardson	3.0			1.7
Don't know	15.9	21.3	20.7	
Republican Primary				
Giuliani	9.5	9.8		0.7
Huckabee	39.3	29.6	29.1	33.4
Hunter	1.8	0.4		0.1
McCain	18.0	25.0	35.6	36.6
Paul	2.2	4.8	2.1	3.3
Romney	8.9	12.8	22.9	24.8
Thompson	10.4	11.0		0.6
Don't know	10.0	6.7	10.4	

Source: TvPoll.com, January 7–February 1, 2008 (dates inclusive).

The final result on February 5 ratified the opinion polls, with Clinton registering a 23-percentage-point victory over Obama (the departed Edwards still took 10 percent of the vote). McCain edged Huckabee and outstripped Romney, as most of the undecideds broke toward the former Baptist preacher from Arkansas. The Clinton campaign had strong support from establishment Democrats, women, and older voters, while Edwards appealed to conservatives and moderates, men, and rural voters. The aging, conservative, white electorate offered little fertile ground for Obama.

The 2008 General Elections : Early trial heats for the presidential campaign indicate that Oklahoma voters were destined for a Republican preference in November (see table 10.10). Despite the lack of intensity for McCain in the primary electorate and strong support for Clinton, most Oklahoma voters indicated they would decisively pick McCain over either Clinton (64.7 percent to 27.4 percent) or Obama (65.6 percent to 24.4 percent). George W. Bush retained a higher approval rating in Oklahoma than most anywhere in the United States throughout 2008, indicating little cost to John McCain for running on a "stay the course" campaign theme.[3]

Over the last two months of the presidential campaign, the Oklahoma electorate was largely unmoved by campaign events. John McCain held a solid double-digit lead among the conservative Oklahoma electorate. The

Table 10.10.   Presidential and U.S. Senate Campaign Tracks for 2008

	President (%)		U.S. Senate (%)			
	McCain (R)	Obama (D)	Inhofe (R)	Rice (D)	Wallace (I)	n
January 16	—	—	61.0	19.0	—	500
September 6	65.9	27.8	57.1	29.1	3.5	893
September 13	69.1	26.8	56.5	30.0	4.3	859
September 20	65.8	26.2	54.9	33.3	1.6	667
September 27	67.5	26.5	55.9	35.5	2.6	904
October 4	65.4	29.0	52.4	39.7	2.1	802
October 11	62.9	31.8	53.1	39.5	1.9	737
October 18	63.6	32.3	52.8	39.5	3.9	763
October 25	61.6	34.7	51.2	40.9	3.3	720
November 1	63.1	33.0	55.2	38.8	2.8	766

Source: TvPoll.com, September 6–November 1, 2008 (dates inclusive).

results of the last nine weeks showed little change in the status of the race. John McCain pulled between 61 percent and 69 percent support from likely voters, while Democrat Barack Obama polled from just over 26 percent to just under 35 percent of the vote. Undecideds narrowed after October 11. Going into the election, the final poll with allocated undecided voters indicated a 65.6 percent to 34.4 percent McCain victory (the final margin was 65.6 percent to 34.4 percent).

CONGRESSIONAL ELECTIONS

Oklahoma elects five U.S. House members and two U.S. senators. All but one of these seats are reliably Republican, and in the 1990s Republicans briefly dominated the entire legislative delegation, holding all six House seats and both Senate seats. The decennial census led to the loss of a House seat by the state of Oklahoma in 2002; a court redistricting placed 40 percent of state Democrats in a single eastern district. The consequence was the election of one congressional Democrat—Dan Boren, son of former U.S. senator David Boren—and four Republicans. Only one member of the congressional delegation has been in power since before 2001, and the delegation is among the weakest in Democrat-dominated Washington. The two incumbent U.S. senators, Jim Inhofe and Dr. Tom Coburn, are among the most colorful and controversial lawmakers in Washington.

2004 Senate Election: Coburn, a former congressman who quit DC, was elected to an open U.S. Senate seat in 2004 to succeed retiring assistant majority leader Don Nickles. A strong set of Republicans lined up for the office: Oklahoma City mayor and Republican Party establishment favorite Kirk Humphreys, iconoclast Corporation Commissioner Bob Anthony, and former U.S. Representative Dr. Tom Coburn. The set of contenders on the Democratic side was not as strong, but the list featured the young and successful Second District Member of Congress Brad Carson, who easily captured his party's nomination, and a scandal-ridden Democratic insurance commissioner. Republican Party leadership generally lined up behind Humphreys, but his campaign went downhill almost from the start while Coburn picked up steam as he went along. Coburn's campaign was greatly aided by support from the Washington-based Club for Growth. In the end, Humphreys found himself attempting the nearly impossible task of getting to the right of Coburn and just plain failing; the presumptive nominee took just 25 percent of the vote while upstart former congressman Coburn carried over 60 percent of the vote. Within twenty-four hours of the polls' closing, there was a great show of Republican unity aimed at putting the primary bitterness behind them and uniting against Carson.

The general election contest featured two candidates who had represented the same congressional district, but the outcome would be heavily influenced by outsiders. Both the politics of the election and early polling suggested that the seat was a possible pick-up for the Democratic Party. Because it was widely believed going into the 2004 campaign that control of the U.S. Senate would turn on one or two outcomes, the race took on substantial national importance. The race was easily the most expensive in the state's history, with about $10 million spent in hard money and about $2 million spent in soft money and independent expenditures, including nearly $1 million by the Club for Growth (Gaddie et al. 2005).

Carson gained early momentum as a gun-toting, NRA-backed conservative Democrat. He also had initial success painting Coburn as an extremist who would not even bring Oklahomans their share of the federal largesse. Coburn promised voters that he would feed at the trough with the rest of the Senate and turned his attack on Carson. Coburn and his allies did everything they could to tie Carson to Washington liberals like John Kerry, Hillary Clinton, and Ted Kennedy. Heading into these attacks, the race was a dead heat. But the ads, one of which featured "Dancing Brad" with liberal Democrats pulling his strings and the tag line: "Putting DC Democrats Ahead of Oklahoma Values," proved to be very effective. The ad saturated the state's media markets, and those who saw the ad were more favorable to Coburn by about 10 percentage points (Gaddie et al. 2005). In the end, Carson could not overcome being saddled with the "sins" of his party, especially in a presidential election year, and Coburn won with 52.8 percent of the vote to Carson's 41.2 percent.

2008 Senate Campaign: By comparison, the 2008 U.S. Senate campaign in Oklahoma was an entertaining contest that, while largely determined from the start, proved to be exciting in terms of candidate contrasts and campaign events. Incumbent Republican Jim Inhofe (age 74) sought a third full term in the U.S. Senate. His opponent, thirty-five-year-old state senator and former Christian missionary Andrew Rice, was seeking to ride a wave of increased discontent with the Bush administration to defeat the Republican incumbent. Jim Inhofe's campaigns are legendary in Oklahoma, largely for the biting negative campaign commercials crafted by his nephew and media consultant Freddy "Hollywood" Davis. Past advertisements had used humor to belittle the misdeeds and mala-propisms of Democratic opponents, and the liberal state lawmaker from Oklahoma City provided ample fodder, being attacked by Inhofe as too liberal on abortion, too soft on crime, and too strong a supporter of gay rights. For example, an advertisement illuminating Rice's ties to a group advocating gay marriage was accompanied by a visual of two grooms atop a wedding cake. Rice countered by critiquing Inhofe's ties to big oil, his unwillingness to support tax breaks for working people, and his failure to support giving body armor to deployed troops.

Early positioning in the Senate race had placed Rice as the only credible Democrat seeking to displace Inhofe. Polling in January of the election year revealed the challenger running 40 percentage points behind the incumbent (see table 10.10). However, the summer primary revealed that the new challenger had a lot of connecting to make with the Democratic base. Running against gadfly candidate Jim Rogers, Rice garnered 58 percent of the vote and lost eighteen counties. This inauspicious start did not dampen the enthusiasm of the campaign, but it laid stark the challenge before Rice with Democratic voters. Immediately after the primary, Rice trailed Inhofe by nearly 30 percentage points. This gap remained through early September, then the race tightened as the campaign turned negative and the autumn fiscal crisis unfolded. The race narrowed to 13 percentage points on October 4 and then stayed in the low double digits through Election Day. Final polling indicated a 56.8 percent to 39.9 percent win for Inhofe; Inhofe prevailed 56.7 percent to 39.2 percent, with 4.1 percent going to independent candidate Stephen Wallace.

These most recent rounds of elections demonstrate the eroding division between the politics of the state and national politics. National political organizations entered state party politics in an effort to influence primary elections, and, according to the data collected by the Center for the Study of Electoral Democracy, the national parties and their surrogate organizations targeted the general election in the state as well. The state is generally "red" and, as we will see, getting redder and redder further and further down ticket. It becomes increasingly difficult for state Democratic candidates to avoid the politics of their national party, and, at the same time, it becomes difficult for the Republican Party establishment to avoid the evangelical realignment of their grassroots, which threatens the control of the party organization and message.

CONCLUSION

The emergence of the Republican Party as the majority party of Oklahoma continues unabated. The Republican electorate of the Sooner State resembles the electorate of so many other southern states—white, Anglo, and Protestant, and with a set of issue concerns associated not with the poverty of the pocketbook so much as the poverty of leadership, values, and the soul. This new electorate and its focus presents a very real challenge for state Democrats, who are searching for a viable organizational and issue basis with which to compete for political power.

The challenge for the Democrats is daunting. For decades the Democrats' ability to hold state power was predicated on their status as the majority party and the ability to provide access, goods, and services based on that majority status. Now rural Oklahomans, who still provide the foundation for the legislative Democratic Party, find that in the state House they are not the majority. Rural Oklahomans are regularly voting for Republicans at the national and congressional level. At some point, if legislative Republicans are willing to take care of the needs and concerns of the dwindling rural Oklahoma electorate, they can compete for votes in these constituencies.

The other challenge that vexes Democrats the South over is how to get past the religious impediment with white voters. White evangelicals make up a greater share of the Oklahoma electorate than in virtually any other southern state, and their vote has become increasingly homogeneous. When Democrats have succeeded statewide in Oklahoma since 1994, it has either been in lower-level statewide offices with incumbents or because of rifts in the GOP that fractured the vote, such as in the case of the election of Governor Henry in 2002 and 2006. When Republicans are united and able to activate their evangelical base, the likelihood of a Republican victory is almost certain, absent the presence of Democratic incumbents.

NOTES

1. As early as the 1840s, white settlers were anxious for the lands of Oklahoma, and white settlement occurred around the trading posts that would become Tulsa, Sallisaw, and Poteau. The federal government attempted to keep white settlers

out, but strategic male settlers would often flee their encroaching settlements for Fort Smith, Arkansas, because it was known that the cavalry would not displace women settlers found alone. (Oral history interview with Senator Larry Dickerson, July 16, 1998, conducted by Keith Gaddie.)

2. *Lane v. Wilson*, 307 U.S. 268 (1939).

3. Bush approval in 2006 and 2008, Oklahoma:

	Bush 11/06	Bush 1/08	Bush 11/08*
Strongly/somewhat approve	56.7	53.8	44.0
Strongly/somewhat disapprove	42.1	45.6	55.0
Unsure	1.2	0.6	1.0

*2008 Election Exit Poll

REFERENCES

Abramson, Paul R., and William Claggett. 1986. "Race-Related Differences in Self-Reported and Validated Turnout in 1984." *Journal of Politics* 48:412–422.

Aistrup, Joseph. 1996. *The Southern Strategy Revisited*. Lexington: University Press of Kentucky.

Black, Earl, and Merle Black. 1992. *The Vital South: How Presidents Are Elected*. Cambridge, MA: Harvard University Press.

Bullock, Charles S., III, and Ronald Keith Gaddie. 2006. *An Assessment of Voting Rights Progress in Oklahoma*. Washington, DC: American Enterprise Institute Policy Series.

Carmines, Edward, and James Stimson. 1989. *Issue Evolution*. Princeton, NJ: Princeton University Press.

Copeland, Gary W., Rebecca J. Cruise, and Ronald Keith Gaddie. 2006. "Oklahoma: Evangelicals and the Secular Realignment." In *The New Politics of the Old South*, 3rd ed., ed. Charles S. Bullock III and Mark J. Rozell. Lanham, MD: Rowman & Littlefield.

Ewing, Cortez A. M. 1953. *Uniparty Politics in the South*. Norman: University of Oklahoma Press.

Gaddie, Ronald Keith. 2004. *A Fish, a Flag, and a "W" Tag*. Invited presentation, Southeastern Oklahoma State University, Durant, OK, December 6.

Gaddie, Ronald Keith, and Scott E. Buchanan. 1998. "Oklahoma: Realignment in the Buckle of the Bible Belt." In *The New Politics of the Old South: An Introduction to Southern Politics*, ed. Charles S. Bullock III and Mark J. Rozell. Lanham, MD: Rowman & Littlefield.

Gaddie, Ronald Keith, with Jennifer Christol, Charles Mullin, Katherine Thorne, and Benjamin Wilson. 2005. "Issue Advocacy in the 2004 Oklahoma Senate Election." In *Soft Money and Issue Advocacy in the 2004 Elections*, ed. David Magleby, Kelly Patterson, and Quin Monson. Washington, DC: Pew Charitable Trusts.

Hale, Jon F., and Stephen T. Kean. 1996. "Oklahoma." In *State and Party Profiles*, ed. Andrew M. Appleton and Daniel S. Ward. Washington, DC: Congressional Quarterly Books.

Heard, Alexander. 1952. *A Two-Party South?* Chapel Hill: University of North Carolina Press.

Kirkpatrick, Samuel A., David R. Morgan, and Thomas Kielhorn. 1977. *The Oklahoma Voter.* Norman: University of Oklahoma Press.

Lamis, Alexander. 1988. *The Two-Party South.* New York: Oxford University Press.

Morgan, David R., Robert E. England, and George G. Humphreys. 1991. *Oklahoma Politics and Policies.* Lincoln: University of Nebraska Press.

Price, H. D. 1957. *The Negro in Southern Politics: A Chapter of Florida History.* New York: New York University Press.

Wyman, Hasting. 2005. *Southern Political Report* 662 (October 10).

11

Florida

Political Change, 1950–2008

Michael J. Scicchitano and Richard K. Scher

In the last half of the twentieth century, Florida experienced profound changes in its population. These changes have largely been driven by a massive migration of retirees seeking a warmer climate and younger persons seeking employment opportunities. The population of Florida more than tripled between 1960 and 2008. This migration substantially changed the demographic character of the state. The percentage of white residents, for example, has grown steadily since 1900, and the percentage of African Americans has consistently declined. While the rest of the country has gotten younger, Florida's population has aged, and the state now ranks first in the percentage of the population that is sixty-five and older (about 18 percent). In addition, the percentage of the population that is of Hispanic origin has nearly doubled since 1970; the state now has nearly four million Hispanic residents, about one-fifth of the total.

The change in the demographic characteristics of Florida has not been politically neutral; indeed, because of it, the political character of the state has undergone profound changes. This chapter will help us to understand better the nature of the changes to Florida's political system. It will then provide a detailed description of the partisan changes that have occurred in Florida from 1980 to 2008. Finally, we will examine the impact of demographic changes and party registration on Florida elections for both state and national offices.

THE CHANGING POPULATION OF FLORIDA

If there is one distinguishing feature of the demographic characteristics of Florida, especially in the latter half of the twentieth century, it is growth. In 1900, Florida was one of the least-populated states in the East, but by 2000 it had become the second most populous state east of the Mississippi, and the fourth most populous nationally. In every decade since 1900, Florida's population has grown by about 30 percent or more. In two of those decades the growth was more than 50 percent. From 1950 to 1960, the population grew by nearly 80 percent. The population growth, however, has not been uniformly distributed across the state. Before 1950, the state's population center was north Florida, and particularly the Jacksonville area. But between 1950 and 1970, population growth was strongest in southern Florida. The central Florida region, with the development of Disney World and other recreational attractions in the Orlando area, has had the highest growth rates since 1970.

The growth in population has largely been fueled by two forces. Like the rest of the nation, Florida has experienced an increase in population from the baby boom generation. The most important reason for the growth rate in Florida, however, has been migration into the state. In the five-year period from 1985 to 1990, for example, nearly 1.5 million people moved into Florida from other states or countries. Between 1990 and 2000, Florida's net in-migration numbered some 1.7 million people. By 2008, however, migration into Florida ceased, and the population reached a steady-state level of 19 million. The flow of new residents stopped because of the collapse of the state's economy in mid-decade.

The tremendous growth that Florida has experienced in the twentieth century, and particularly since 1950, has not maintained the demographic characteristics of the state that existed in 1900. Instead, there have been fundamental changes in the demographic patterns in the state. The most significant changes have occurred among three groups. First, the population of Florida has gotten older. Second, the racial composition of the state has changed, and the percentage of African American residents has declined. Finally, the percentage of Florida residents who are Hispanic has increased. The changes in the age, race, and ethnicity of residents have produced a state that is demographically—and politically—different than it was in 1950.

CHANGES IN AGE PATTERNS

A large number of those migrating to Florida since 1950 have been older people seeking a better climate for their retirement years. The changes in the age of Florida's residents are part of a complex national pattern of aging. Better medical care and nutritional and lifestyle behaviors have permitted people to live longer, while the baby boom produced a surge of younger people that has driven the average age of the population down. Florida did not escape the effects of the baby boom. Still, the state provides an extremely attractive climate for retirees who want to avoid harsh winters in the Northeast and Midwest. Retirees with fixed incomes also find Florida's low taxes and lack of an income tax attractive. As a result of the in-migration of retirees, the age of Florida's population has increased more rapidly than that of other states, and now Florida ranks first in the nation in the number of residents who are sixty-five and older (Smith 1995).

Changes in Race Patterns

At the beginning of the twentieth century, Florida had a large African American population. In 1900, 44 percent of the state was African American and 56 percent was white. The number of African Americans in the state has increased since 1900. This growth, however, has not equaled the growth of whites. Migrants to Florida have mostly been older whites. As a result of the migration patterns, the relative percentage of African Americans in Florida declined consistently between 1900 and 1980. Since 1980, however, the racial composition of the state has stabilized at approximately 84 to 85 percent white and 14 percent African American.

Changes in the Hispanic Population

The last major change in the demographic character of Florida is the large increase in the number of Hispanic residents. From 1970 to 1990, the percentage of Hispanic residents nearly doubled, to about 12 percent of the population. Many Hispanic residents, particularly of south Florida, are of Cuban origin. South Florida continues to attract residents from other locations in Latin America as well. The percentage of Hispanics in Florida should continue to grow in the next century; indeed, the increase in the Hispanic population between 1990 and 1995 was 28 percent (Allen 1997).

PARTISAN CHANGES IN FLORIDA

In the years following World War II, the political character of Florida changed from solidly Democratic to one in which the Republican Party, in many regions, became competitive. The transition to this more competitive political environment was fueled by three forces (Scher 1997,

143–151). The first of these forces was the tremendous in-migration of more conservative, white, middle-class individuals from the North. A second force, related to the first, was the in-migration of large numbers of elderly persons who were also conservative and were more likely to vote for Republican candidates. These new arrivals had a profound effect on Florida politics, especially in the 1980s and 1990s, when the number of new conservative voters became sufficiently large to produce a competitive two-party state. Finally, many traditional Democrats began to question their loyalty to their party, which had become more liberal and "seemed no longer to represent southern interests and concerns" (Scher 1997, 145).

To understand Florida politics, it is important first to examine the changes in party registration in the state in the last two decades. Table 11.1 shows the percentage of the population registered as Democrats, Republicans, and as having no party identification (independents). This table indicates that while the Democrats were clearly the dominant party in 1980, the political landscape was fundamentally different in 2008. In 1980, nearly two-thirds of registered voters were identified as Democrats. By 2000, less than one-half of registered voters were Democrats. During the 1980s and continuing into the 1990s, increasing numbers of voters registered as Republicans and independents. The number of Republicans has increased more than one-third, from less than 30 percent of registered voters to slightly fewer than 40 percent by 2008.

The most significant change in the partisan composition of the Florida electorate has been the substantial growth of independents. By 2008, the percentage of registered independent voters reached 22 percent, one of the highest in the nation. The independents are Florida's swing voters and they are the group that presidential and other statewide candidates assiduously court. They are sufficiently numerous that they literally hold the balance of power in statewide elections. While they are found throughout the state, they are concentrated along the I-4 corridor in central Florida, which contains about one-third of the state's voters.

The rates of change in partisanship in Florida largely mirror the growth of the state's population. The right-hand columns of table 11.1 summarize the changes in the percentages of registered voters for the Democrats, Republicans, and independents every two years between 1980 and 2008. The mid-1980s were a period of tremendous change in the state.

The decline in the percentage of Democrats was most dramatic during that period. From 1980 to 1992, Democrats experienced an average loss of 2 percentage points per biennium, with the greatest change in 1986 and 1988, when the combined decrease was 7 percent. The growth in the number of Republicans was greatest in these two years. By the middle of the 1990s, it appeared that the decline in Democratic strength had slowed; in

Table 11.1. Partisan Identification in Florida, 1980–2008

	Dem. (%)	Rep. (%)	Ind. (%)	% Change in Identification Dem.	Rep.	Ind.
1980	65.8	28.8	5.4			
1982	63.0	30.8	6.2	−2.8	+2.0	+0.8
1984	61.0	32.8	6.2	−2.0	+2.0	0
1986	57.1	36.2	6.7	−3.9	+3.4	+0.5
1988	54.0	39.0	7.0	−3.1	+2.8	+0.3
1990	52.2	40.6	7.2	−1.8	+1.6	+0.2
1992	50.1	40.9	9.0	−2.1	+0.3	+1.8
1994	49.5	41.8	8.7	−0.6	+0.9	−.03
1996	46.8	41.5	11.7	−2.7	−0.3	+0.3
1998	44.9	40.1	15.0	−1.9	−1.4	+3.3
2000	43.3	39.2	17.5	−1.6	−0.9	+2.5
2002	42.7	38.9	18.4	−0.6	−0.3	+0.9
2004	41.7	38.0	20.3	−1.0	−0.9	+2.5
2006	40.4	37.7	21.8	−0.9	0	+0.8
2008	41.4	36.8	21.7	+1.0	−0.9	−0.1

Source: Florida Statistical Abstract.

1994, the decrease was only about one-half of a percentage point. In 1996, however, there was another large decline in the relative number of Democrats—nearly 3 percent. The Republicans did not, however, benefit from this decline, since the Republican registration also dropped slightly. Independents, though, gained slightly that year, and in 1998 their numbers increased by 3 percent. Research indicates that the "motor voter" law contributed significantly to these changes (Mortham 1995). It is evident that partisan registration in Florida is still changing, and it is unclear when it will stabilize.

These data on changes in the registration pattern should not be interpreted as indicating that changes in party registration are uniform across Florida. There are still areas where Democratic or Republican registration is relatively stable. The patterns of these concentrations of party strength in Florida are complex. Democrats are still very strong in some traditional rural and small-town areas, and in metropolitan counties where there are concentrations of African American and low-income residents, particularly in central and south Florida. It is of interest that Miami-Dade County also includes concentrations of Cubans, who generally have voted Republican. In Orange County (Orlando), however, the in-migration of other Hispanics, mainly Puerto Ricans and Mexicans, has tilted this formerly Republican stronghold into a heavily Democratic one. In general, however, Republicans tend to be concentrated, as in other states, in the more suburban sections of metropolitan areas, where voters are largely white and higher-income, although some heavily white rural areas have also become Republican.

It should also be noted that if one looks at party registration by county, one sees that by the twenty-first century, Democrats had become increasingly concentrated, if not isolated. By 2008, more than 60 percent of the state's Democrats lived in only ten metropolitan counties; 80 percent lived in just twenty counties. What this means is that while Democrats can continue to have a major impact on statewide races and even win some, for congressional and state legislative races—determined by districts—it will be hard for them to achieve a majority of the congressional delegation or of either chamber of the state legislature. There are simply too many Democrats in too few places to expect otherwise.

The changes in party registration are not, of themselves, important. What is important is the impact of party registration changes on state and national elections in Florida. The following sections provide a detailed analysis of the change in election patterns for both national and state executive and legislative offices.

PRESIDENTIAL AND CONGRESSIONAL ELECTIONS

The Presidency

The presidential elections in Florida were the first to demonstrate the emerging strength of the Republican Party. Figure 11.1 provides a summary of the results of presidential contests in Florida. From 1920 to 1948, Floridians generally voted for Democratic presidential candidates. The only exception was the 1928 election, in which the state supported Herbert Hoover by a substantial margin over Al Smith, a Catholic from New York. In 1932, however, Floridians abandoned Hoover and voted for Franklin D. Roosevelt by a 3:1 margin. Starting with the Dwight D. Eisenhower election in 1952, a majority of Floridians voted for Republican presidential candidates. Since 1952, Democrats have carried Florida only four times, each time with a southern candidate. In 1964, Lyndon Johnson, in the course of a tremendous national victory, won Florida by only a 2.3 percent margin. Jimmy Carter, from adjacent Georgia, also won a narrow victory over the incumbent Gerald Ford in 1976. Voters abandoned Carter in 1980 and gave a substantial majority to Republican candidate Ronald Reagan.

In 1992 Democrat Bill Clinton ran a close second to the incumbent George Bush, but many potential Clinton votes were siphoned off to the independent candidacy of Ross Perot. Clinton was able, in 1996, to best Republican candidate Bob Dole in Florida. In this case, however, Clinton managed to position himself skillfully on several issues of importance to

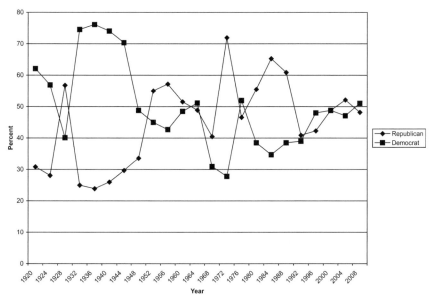

Figure 11.1. Summary of U.S. Presidential Elections

Floridians. Clinton was able to frighten elderly Florida voters with the warning that Dole, as a result of the large budget cut he promised, might be a threat to the health services and other benefits they received from the federal government, especially Social Security. Another important issue for Clinton in Florida was immigration. Dole's tough stands against illegal immigration and in favor of cutting benefits for illegal immigrants cost him substantial votes among Hispanics, especially Cuban Americans. Instead of strongly supporting the Republican candidate as they had done in 1992, Hispanics in Florida split their vote almost evenly between Dole and Clinton (Schneider 1996). In 2000, of course, the Florida vote was almost exactly equally divided between Democrat Al Gore and Republican George W. Bush; the U.S. Supreme Court decided the race when it stopped vote recounts in *Bush v. Gore*, giving the state to Bush by 537 votes. In 2004, however, John Kerry proved no match for the incumbent Bush, losing the state by four hundred and sixty-one thousand votes. In 2008, the tables turned as Barack Obama handily defeated John McCain by two hundred and thirty-six thousand votes.

U.S. Senate Elections

While presidential elections in Florida have resulted in a rapid transition in favor of Republican candidates, the U.S. Senate contests are a more accurate indicator of the gradually changing nature of partisanship in the state. Figure 11.2 provides a summary of the U.S. Senate elections from 1920 to the latest election in 2006. The Democratic Party clearly dominated the U.S. Senate elections at least into the late 1950s. From 1920 until 1962, only one Democratic candidate won by a margin of less than 40 percent of the vote. That was Park Trammell, an incumbent who faced a strong challenge in 1928, a year in which Republican presidential candidate Herbert Hoover won Florida. Trammell returned in 1934, however, to win an uncontested election. Changes in the nature of U.S. Senate elections began to appear by the late 1950s and early 1960s. During this period, Florida's U.S. Senate seats were held by two strong incumbents, George Smathers and Spessard L. Holland. Holland, a former governor, eventually served four terms, while Smathers served three. Smathers retired in 1968, but would have been reelected had he run for a fourth term. Both Holland's and Smathers's reelection margins for their third terms, in 1958 and 1962, respectively, were about 40 percent. While these are solid election victories, they are by less than the typical margin for the previous four decades. Holland won by less than 30 percent in his last reelection campaign in 1964. The dividing line in Florida U.S. Senate elections is between the 1964 and 1968 contests. The first Republican senator in at least a half century was elected in 1968 in an election for the seat Smathers had vacated. From 1968 until 1994, Republicans had tight first-election tries. Dick Stone, a Democrat, and Paula Hawkins, a Republican, won by about 3 percent of the vote in their first (and only) victories. Connie Mack, a Republican, won by less than 1 percent in his first Senate victory in 1988. Once elected, some candidates were able to build support and win more substantial victories. Lawton Chiles's second and third victory margins were each about 25 percent, and Bob Graham, a popular former governor, achieved his second victory by more than 30 percent. None of these reelections, however, was as strong as the Democratic victories from 1920 to 1950. Connie Mack, a Republican incumbent, won his second reelection by more than 40 percent in 1994. However, in a strong Republican year, Mack faced a weak opponent in the relatively inexperienced Hugh Rodham, who had the advantage (or liability) of being the brother of First Lady Hillary Clinton. In 2000, a well-known state Democrat, Bill Nelson, narrowly defeated a discredited Republican, Bill McCollum, who was one of the House floor managers during the Clinton impeachment proceedings. In 2004, Republican Mel Martinez defeated former Florida Commissioner of Education and University of South Florida president Betty Castor in a hard-fought, vicious campaign by a mere eighty-three thousand votes out of over 4 million cast. On the other hand, incumbent senator Bill Nelson easily won his reelection bid in 2006, with a one-million-vote margin (60 percent of the vote) over former Florida secretary of state Katherine Harris. Nonetheless, it is clear that the Democratic Party will no longer

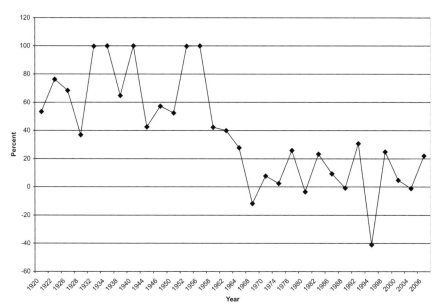

Figure 11.2. Democratic Margin (in percentages)

dominate the U.S. Senate elections in Florida as it did from 1920 until 1950. Instead, both Democratic and Republican candidates will face tough initial election campaigns. Only as incumbents will they be able to build more substantial election margins.

U.S. House Elections

The U.S. House elections in Florida largely mirror the results that are evident in the Senate elections. Table 11.2 summarizes the results of the U.S. House elections in Florida from 1950 to 2008. The table presents the year, the number of Democratic and Republican victors, and the average victory margin for Democratic and Republican senators. The last column in the table lists the percentage of House seats held by Republicans.

Democratic candidates dominated Florida U.S. House elections from 1920 to 1950. The first Republican was elected only in 1954, when William Cramer won the First Congressional District by a very tight 1.5 percent margin against a one-term incumbent who had narrowly been elected in 1952. Cramer was the only Republican congressman from Florida from 1954 until 1962 and was able to expand his victory margin to about 17 percent. While the election of this single Republican candidate hardly represented an overwhelming change in Florida congressional elections, it was

Table 11.2. U.S. House of Representative Elections in Florida, 1950–2008

	Dem. Seats	Avg. Dem. Margin (%)	Rep. Seats	Avg. Rep. Margin (%)	Rep. Seats (%)
1950	6	84.5			
1952	8	58.4			
1954	7	87.3	1	1.5	12.5
1956	7	48.2	1	12.7	12.5
1958	7	82.4	1	17.6	12.5
1960	7	64.6	1	16.8	12.5
1962	10	49.4	2	16.4	16.6
1964	10	73.7	2	21.1	16.6
1966	9	76.4	3	54.5	25
1968	9	38.5	3	74.5	25
1970	9	56.8	3	31.4	25
1972	11	39.1	4	50.4	26.6
1974	10	72.9	5	32.5	33
1976	10	67.2	5	29.0	33
1978	12	55.6	3	53.0	20
1980	11	39.1	4	44.6	26.6
1982	13	48.4	6	28.3	31.6
1984	12	53.5	7	67.6	36.8
1986	12	41.0	7	45.3	36.8
1988	10	64.9	9	52.7	47.4
1990	9	36.1	10	58.7	52.6
1992	11	63.3	12	62.8	52.2
1994	8	69.4	15	85.0	65.2
1996	8	70.7	15	70.1	65.2
1998	8	85.7	15	93.0	65.2
2000	8	78.4	15	74.3	65.2
2002	7	50.3	18	34.1	72
2004	7	66.6	18	41.3	72
2006	9	71.7	16	22.5	60
2008	9	45.5	16	21.6	60

Source: Florida Department of State election results.

certainly an indication of more substantial changes to come. In the years that followed, the number of Republicans elected to Congress from Florida continued to grow. The size of the Florida congressional delegation has increased to reflect the increase in population, but the percentage of Republican-held seats does not merely parallel the increase in the number of congressional seats. By the 1980s, Republicans held one-third of the seats, and by the 1990s, they had surged to control more than 60 percent of the Florida delegation. Moreover, the size of the victory margin of Republican candidates has increased to rival that of Democratic candidates.

The number and percentage of total seats, however, do not accurately reflect the growing strength of the Republican Party in Florida. Congressional districts, of course, were drawn by the Democratic officials who still held a majority of the legislature (the districts in 1992 were drawn by a three-judge federal panel after legislators could not agree on a plan). Table 11.2 shows that, interestingly, the number of Republican congressional seats increased after redistricting allocated more seats to rapidly growing areas. Republicans held only one seat in the 1950s, two to three seats in the 1960s, three to five seats in the 1970s, six to nine seats in the 1980s, and twelve to fifteen seats in the 1990s. Both of the House seats that Florida gained as a result of the 2000 census were won by Republicans in 2002 and 2004. Following the 2008 elections, Republicans held a sixteen-to-nine edge in the congressional delegation.

GUBERNATORIAL AND STATE LEGISLATIVE ELECTIONS

The Gubernatorial Elections

The elections for governor of Florida largely mirror the results for U.S. Senate and House elections. Table 11.3 lists the party of the victorious candidate as well as the percentage of victory margin for gubernatorial elections in Florida from 1920 to 2006.

Again, we see that Democratic candidates for governor dominated the elections from 1920 until the mid-1950s. The first Republican governor was Claude Kirk, who was elected in 1966. The next Republican, Bob Martinez, was elected in 1986. Both were one-term governors. By 1960, however, the victory margins of Democratic governors were less than 20 percent, substantially smaller than the 56 percent average for the preceding forty years. The margin of victory for subsequent Democratic victors was only 15 percent. The gubernatorial elections from 1970 to 1998 were won

Table 11.3. Gubernatorial Races in Florida, 1920–2006

Year	Victor's Party	Victory %	Year	Victor's Party	Victory %
1920	D	60	1966	R	14.8
1924	D	65.6	1970	D	10.2
1928	D	22.0	1974	D	13.8
1932	D	33.2	1978	D	22.4
1936	D	61.8	1982	D	11.2
1940	D	100	1986	R	29.4
1944	D	57.8	1990	D	9.2
1948	D	66.8	1994	D	13.0
1952	D	49.6	1998	R	10.6
1956	D	47.4	2002	R	12.8
1960	D	19.7	2006	R	7.1
1964	D	19.7			

by three relatively popular Democratic candidates who each served two terms—Reubin Askew, Bob Graham, and former three-term senator Lawton Chiles. Martinez, the sole Republican elected governor after the 1966 Kirk victory, won an open-seat election against a relatively unknown opponent, Steve Pajcic, who received the nomination after a divisive Democratic runoff. Pajcic was viewed by voters as a liberal, which made defeating Martinez difficult (see Black and Black 1987). Martinez was not able to win reelection against the popular and well-known Chiles. Chiles, after a first term in which he was not viewed as very successful, won an extremely narrow victory against Jeb Bush, son of the former president. Bush was well financed and was able to benefit from running in a year in which the Republican Party was generally successful across the nation. In 1998, Jeb Bush won with a margin of 11 percentage points over the Democratic lieutenant governor, Buddy MacKay. In 2002, Bush handily won reelection against his opponent, 56 percent to 43 percent. The 2006 gubernatorial elections were also a debacle for Democrats, with Republican Charlie Crist winning by a margin of greater than 7 percentage points over a weaker Democratic opponent.

While Democrats largely dominated gubernatorial elections in Florida from 1970 to 1994, this dominance is substantially different from that evident in the 1920–1960 period. The victories from the late 1970s to the 1990s were generally narrow Democratic victories won by capable and popular candidates. It is likely that in the next several elections, the office will alternate between parties.

An interesting feature of Florida government is the election of cabinet officers. In most systems of government, the executives appoint, typically with the approval of the legislature, officials to run most cabinet offices. In Florida, the cabinet positions of secretary of state, attorney general, comptroller, treasurer, and commissioners of education and agriculture were elected positions. But in 2000, constitutional revisions to the cabinet went into effect. The secretary of state and commissioner of education positions were removed from the cabinet; now the governor appoints them. The comptroller and treasurer slots were combined into a chief state fiscal officer. Currently the cabinet consists of the attorney general, commissioner of agriculture, and chief state fiscal officer; the governor continues to sit with this smaller body.

While many states have multiple elected officials in the executive branch, Florida was unique both in the number and the range of such officials' duties, which were constitutionally and statutorily assigned. As a result, the cabinet served as a collegial governing board for the executive branch (Scher 1994). It is very easy to imagine the difficulty of governing in a system in which the chief executive officers of major departments are not controlled by the governor. It is even more difficult to govern when these individuals are from the opposite party. In 1986, Republican governor Bob Martinez's cabinet offices were all held by Democrats. In 1990, concurrently with the election of Democrat Chiles, two Republicans held cabinet slots, and in 1994 three of the cabinet positions were filled by Republicans. Governor Bush, who won in 1998, held a Republican majority on his cabinet. Following the 2006 statewide elections, one cabinet member is a Democrat (state fiscal officer) while the others are Republican.

Florida House and Senate Elections

The changing nature of partisanship and elections in Florida is also evident in the races for the state legislature. To understand the changes in Florida state legislative elections, it is important first to examine the partisan registration in House and Senate districts. Table 11.4 presents the mean number of Democratic, Republican, and independent party registrations in the Florida House and Senate districts. Data are available only for 1988–2008, but even this short time span clearly demonstrates the changes in partisanship in Florida.

In 1988, the number of registered Republicans was substantially smaller than the number of Democrats. By 2000, however, the number of registered Republicans had increased to approach the number of Democrats. Moreover, by 1996, independents and Republicans together outnumbered the registered Democrats. The percent change for each party differs significantly. While the rate of change from 1988 to 2008 is about 44 percent for Democrats, it is a much more substantial 72 percent for the Republicans.

Table 11.4. Average Party Registration in State House and Senate Districts, 1988–2008

	House Districts			Senate Districts		
	Dem.	*Rep.*	*Ind.*	*Dem.*	*Rep.*	*Ind.*
1988	27,200	19,595	3,511	81,602	59,010	10,534
1990	26,062	20,395	3,582	78,743	61,212	10,748
1992	27,654	22,274	4,550	82,964	66,824	13,651
1994	27,054	22,892	4,376	81,137	68,676	13,192
1996	31,064	25,575	7,734	93,212	82,727	23,212
1998	30,765	27,438	10,299	92,293	92,314	30,898
2000	31,692	28,585	12,661	95,755	85,756	38,235
2002	32,991	29,992	12,787	98,973	89,976	38,360
2004	35,509	32,437	15,716	106,528	97,310	47,149
2006	39,607	24,373	16,283	105,481	106,019	49,098
2008	39,237	33,869	17,426	115,552	101,621	52,578
% increase 1988–2008	44.3	72.8	396.3	41.6	72.2	399.1

Source: Florida Department of State voter registration statistics.

The increase in the number of independents, though starting from a relatively small number, is a surprising almost 400 percent. While some districts still have a strong Democratic majority, the trend since 1988 is for rapidly increasing numbers of Republican and especially independent registrations.

Another perspective on the changing nature of partisanship is provided by table 11.5, on state Senate and House districts. This table lists the number of Florida House and Senate districts in which the Democrats have a majority of the party registrations. In 1988, the Democrats had a majority of those choosing a party in 86 of the 120 House districts (71.6 percent) and 29 of 40 Senate districts (72.5 percent). By 2008, Democrats had fallen way behind, holding registration majorities in only 36.6 percent of state House districts and 35 percent in the Senate districts. The registration numbers clearly indicate that races for state legislative seats were no longer competitive after the 1990s.

In addition to examining the party registration in each district, it is important to examine the party composition of the Florida House and Senate. The percentages of Democratic and Republican membership in the legislature are presented in table 11.6.

This table demonstrates that there has been a significant change in the party composition of the Florida legislature. In 1976, both the House and the Senate were about 75 percent Democratic. Since 1976, there has been a consistent decline in the number of Democratic legislators and a corresponding increase in the number of Republicans. The percentages of the Democratic and Republican members of the House and Senate were about equal in the 1990s. In 1996, for the first time since Reconstruction, Republicans took control of the Florida House. As expected, Republican

Table 11.5. Florida Legislative Districts with Majority Democratic Registration, 1988–2008 (in percentages)

	House (120 Districts)	*Senate (40 Districts)*
1988	71.6	72.5
1990	65.8	67.5
1992	64.2	67.5
1994	60.8	57.5
1996	55.0	52.5
1998	55.0	52.5
2000	53.3	50.0
2002	45.0	48.0
2004	44.0	45.0
2006	42.5	42.5
2008	36.6	35.0

Source: Florida Department of State voter registration statistics.

Table 11.6.   Partisan Makeup of Florida State Legislature, 1976–2008 (in percentages)

	House (120 seats)		Senate (40 seats)	
	Democrats	Republicans	Democrats	Republicans
1976	76.6	23.3	72.5	25.0
1978	74.2	25.8	72.5	27.5
1980	67.5	32.5	67.5	32.5
1982	70.0	30.0	80.0	20.0
1984	64.2	35.8	80.0	20.0
1986	62.5	37.5	62.5	37.5
1988	73.3	26.7	57.5	42.5
1990	61.7	38.3	57.5	42.5
1992	54.2	40.8	50.0	50.0
1994	59.2	40.8	47.5	52.5
1996	49.2	50.8	42.5	57.5
1998	42.0	58.0	43.0	58.0
2000	35.8	64.2	37.5	62.5
2002	35.8	64.2	35.0	65.0
2004	32.5	67.5	35.0	65.0
2006	29.2	72.5	35.0	65.0
2008	36.6	63.6	35.0	65.0

Sources: Florida Department of State general election returns; National Conference of State Legislatures; HR 2002 & 2004, www.myfloridahouse.gov/legislators; Sen. 2002-Clark's Manual 2002–2004; Sen. 2004-www.flsenate.gov.

domination of both chambers rose following reapportionment in 2002 and increased in 2004; following the fall 2008 elections, Democrats held only 37 percent of the House and 35 percent of the Senate, while Republicans held 63 percent and 65 percent, respectively.

RACE AND POLITICS IN FLORIDA

Florida provides an interesting opportunity to examine the impact of federal legislation and court decisions that make it possible for minorities to participate fully in the electoral process. The Voting Rights Act of 1965, extended in 1970, 1975, and 1982, effectively eliminated the roadblocks that states and local governments had erected to minority participation in elections. The 1986 *Thornburg v. Gingles* decision gave a clear indication that states should create minority legislative districts whenever possible. The Florida situation is unique from several perspectives. First, legislative districts for African Americans must be created in a state in which the percentage of blacks has declined throughout the century, apparently stabilizing at about 14 percent. Clearly, crafting legislative districts for African

Americans in a declining population is no easy task. The second issue relates to the rapid increase, especially in south Florida, in the size of the Hispanic population. Both African Americans and Hispanics want to maximize their number of districts. Moreover, Hispanics in Florida, in contrast to those in many other states, are conservative and tend to vote Republican. The creation of Hispanic districts, therefore, further increases the number of Republicans in the legislature. The third issue relates in a somewhat different fashion to the population changes that Florida is experiencing. With the declining number of Democratic voters, the creation of districts for African Americans means that many traditional Democratic (African American) voters will be concentrated in these districts. This will further reduce the number of Democrats and increase Republican strength in adjacent districts.

Finally, it is important to understand that Florida's concentration of three distinct groups—white, African American, and Hispanic—has produced fierce electoral competition. The groups strive to promote candidates who share their race or ethnicity. This competition is particularly keen in the Miami-Dade County area, where all three groups exist in strength. The partisan conflict usually is evident at two levels. The competition between African Americans and whites to promote their Democratic candidates can be evident at the primary level. Hispanics, traditionally Republicans, enter the fray during the general election, when their candidate will oppose the primary winner. In recent years, however, Republicans have also been involved in significant internecine ethnic conflict in local primaries.

One example of racial conflict is the commission races in the city of Miami. M. Athalie Range became the first African American city commissioner in 1965. She was followed by a succession of African Americans who occupied her seat. In 1996, however, the seat was won by a Hispanic man. In fact, the thirteen commission seats in Miami as of 2005 were occupied by seven Hispanics, four African Americans, and two whites; the chair of the commission is Hispanic, but the vice-chair is African American. There is a keen sense of frustration among blacks, who feel that the rise of Hispanic political power symbolizes the "unfulfilled promise" of a better life for African Americans in the Miami metropolitan area (Navarro 1997).

This pattern of race- and ethnic-based electoral conflict may, however, be changing. In the 1996 Miami mayoral (nonpartisan) election, white and Hispanic voters formed a coalition to promote a single candidate. With the increase in the number of younger Hispanic voters who are less conservative, these coalitions may become increasingly common. It is worth noting that Bill Clinton did extremely well among younger Cubans in 1996 (Fiedler 1996). However, Democrat Al Gore did not fare as well among Cubans in 2000, probably as a result of the Elian Gonzalez affair that year. John Kerry, however, did manage to win Miami-Dade County in 2004, but by a razor-thin forty-eight thousand votes.

To aid in understanding the increase in African American representation in the Florida legislature, table 11.7 presents the percentage of African American House and Senate members from 1976 through 2004. It is clear from the table that the number of African American legislators has increased substantially since 1976. In 1976, there were only a handful of African American members in the House and none in the Senate. By 2008, the percentage of African American members in the House was stable at about 13 percent, and in the Senate the percentage was stable at about 17 percent. It is also interesting that the changes in the number of African American legislators are largely related to redistricting. African American members of the House jumped from 3.3 percent to 9.2 percent following the redistricting in the 1980s. The percentage of African Americans in the Senate jumped from zero to 5 percent. The change following the 1992 redistricting primarily affected the Florida Senate, where African American membership jumped from 5 to 12.5 percent.

THE 2000, 2004, AND 2008 PRESIDENTIAL ELECTIONS

The 2000 presidential election in Florida became a national, even an international, cause célèbre. A statistical tie, the final official results showed that George W. Bush received 537 votes more than Al Gore. However, what is less well known is that official county totals showed that Gore actually won the state by 202 votes on election day; it was the 739-vote margin that Bush

Table 11.7. African American Membership in the Florida Legislature, 1976–2008 (in percentages)

Year	House (120 seats)	Senate (40 seats)	Year	House (120 seats)	Senate (40 seats)
1976	2.5	0	1994	10.0	12.5
1978	3.3	0	1996	11.6	12.5
1980	3.3	0	1998	10.7	12.5
1982	9.2	5.0	2000	13.3	15.0
1984	9.2	5.0	2002	13.3	15.0
1986	9.2	5.0	2004	13.3	17.5
1988	10.0	5.0	2006	14.2	17.5
1990	11.6	5.0	2008	13.3	17.5
1992	11.6	12.5			

Sources: Joint Center for Political and Economic Studies; Florida Department of State general elections returns; www.myfloridahouse.gov; www.flsenate.gov; Clark's Manual 2002–2004.

gained from federal absentee ballots that accounts for the final 537-vote official difference.

While a number of aspects of the 2000 election deserve mention, space limitations will permit just three. In the first place, the entire presidential election came down to the Sunshine State. Not since 1876 has Florida played such a key role in determining the identity of the next president. Indeed, even late into the twentieth century, Floridians had generally decided their presidential preference early on, to the extent that the presidential contenders largely ceased campaigning there by mid-to-late September, as they felt the matter was already resolved for or against them. Beginning in 1992 and then again in 1996, Florida became less predictable, however, and by 2000 it was impossible to foretell the outcome of the election ahead of time (or, for that matter, for a long time after it was over!). It may be, then, that as Republicans and Democrats achieve virtual parity in electoral registration, and as independent voters become still more numerous and thus hold the balance of power, Florida (which will have twenty-seven Electoral College votes in the next election) will become more central, more valuable, and possibly more unpredictable to presidential contenders.

Second, African American voters played a key and unprecedented role in making the 2000 presidential election as close as it was in Florida. Not only did black voters turn out in record numbers, but they voted in most counties at above 90 percent for Democrat Al Gore, roughly 5 to 8 percent higher than their usual support for Democratic presidential candidates. Moreover, black voters are still upset because of seemingly nonsystematic but nonetheless troubling evidence of disenfranchisement, discarding of ballots in black precincts, and a higher rate of problem ballots in black precincts than in white ones, due in many instances to the heavy reliance on older voting technologies in the black precincts. If black voters continue to show anger and frustration and are willing to come to the polls, it is entirely likely that their vote might well prove determinative in future elections.

Finally, the 2000 election showed a significant shift in the distribution of Florida voters. Whereas for much of the state's history elections were decided by votes in north Florida and the panhandle, this is no longer the case. Some 73 percent of all the ballots in the 2000 presidential contest were cast in the twenty-six Florida counties lying on or south of I-4 (a major transportation artery running through the geographic middle of the state, from Daytona Beach on the east coast to Tampa Bay on the west coast); Florida has some sixty-seven counties in all. What this means is that the geopolitical center of gravity of the state has shifted to the central and southern sections of the state. Indeed, with the exception of heavily populated Duval County (Jacksonville) in the northeast, the remainder of the northern tier of the state is almost politically irrelevant as far as statewide elections are concerned. Future presidential candidates, as well as those for governor, U.S. senator, and the remaining state cabinet positions, will have to direct their campaigns to the major population centers of the state, leaving voters elsewhere largely out of the campaign loop.

Republicans did much better in the 2004 presidential election than four years earlier. The impact of 9/11, uncertainty about the future, the fear of terrorist attacks, ambiguities about Democrat John Kerry, and the very negative campaign that Republicans waged all appear to account for the four hundred and sixty thousand vote margin of victory for the GOP.

However, as they did in other states, Republicans engaged in a new and effective political strategy. They appealed very strongly to the Religious Right/Christian conservatives, who are numerous and powerful in Florida. Both Vice President Cheney and President Bush made trips to carefully identified counties in Florida, even majority Democratic ones, where they found sizable pockets of evangelical and fundamentalist Protestant voters. These visits proved productive. Turnout in "smaller" rural counties was much higher than normal, and Republican vote totals rose considerably as well. The result was to augment Bush's overwhelming advantage in suburbs and along I-4 in central Florida, to dilute the Democratic vote, and to propel Mr. Bush to an easy victory in the Sunshine State. Democrats had no comparable strategy to mobilize their voters, but fortunately for them rapid changes made 2008 more promising.

By mid-2007, the Florida economy began to collapse. Relying too heavily on real estate, mortgage, and banking sectors, the state was devastated by the national deterioration of these industries. As these sectors fell, they dragged other important elements of the state's economy with them—especially the tourism and service sectors. Florida's unemployment figures doubled in less than a year, to nearly 8 percent. The state was in deep financial trouble.

Coupled with these serious woes was Floridians' disillusionment with the Iraq war and, more generally, the George W. Bush administration. The Republican presidential nominee, Senator John McCain, gained little traction in the state, including among some of his most stalwart supporters, Cubans in Miami. Even the Christian Right and other Republican social conservatives were at best lukewarm to him; they appeared to prefer Sarah Palin.

The Democratic nominee, Barack Obama, originally trailed Senator Hillary Clinton in the polls, but by late summer 2008, he was in a strong position in Florida. His message of bipartisanship and hope resonated strongly across a range of state population groups, especially African Americans, students and other young people, disaffected Republicans, Hispanics (including younger professional Cubans), the economically marginal, and independents.

In the end, Obama won Florida by more than a quarter million votes out of eight million cast (up a half-million from 2004). Most significantly, the I-4 corridor delivered the Sunshine State to him. Some 69 percent of his two hundred and thirty-six thousand vote margin over McCain came from that part of the state, undoubtedly because of its heavy concentration of independent voters.

CONCLUSION

The political situation in Florida has been one of the most dynamic of any southern state. The trend toward increasing numbers of Republican and independent voters means that Democratic candidates are no longer assured victory. Elections will be increasingly competitive and will be won by the candidates who have the most resources and make the most effective appeals to voters. It is unclear at this time if current trends will continue and Republicans will come to dominate Florida politics. Another scenario is that there will be a partisan balance, and elective offices will alternate between parties. It is also likely that the increasing independent vote will have a decisive influence on the outcome of state and even local elections.

REFERENCES

Allen, Diane Lacey. 1997. "Hispanics in Florida." *Gainesville (FL) Sun*, November 2:1D.
Benton, J. Edward, ed. 2008. *Government and Politics in Florida*, 3rd ed. Gainesville: University Presses of Florida.
Black, Earl, and Merle Black. 1987. *Politics and Society in the South*. Cambridge, MA: Harvard University Press.
Colburn, David R. 2007. *From Yellow Dog Democrats to Red State Republicans: Florida and Its Politics since 1940*. Gainesville: University Presses of Florida.
Fiedler, Tom. 1996. "Rewriting the Book on Florida." *Miami Herald*, November 6:16A.
Mortham, Sandra. 1995. "The Impact of the National Voter Registration Act of 1993 on the State of Florida." Tallahassee, Florida, Secretary of State. November 15. http://election.dos.state.fl.us/reforms/nvra.htm.
Navarro, Mierya. 1997. "As the Population Shifts, Many Florida Blacks Say They Feel 'Left Out.'" *New York Times*, February 17:16A.
Scher, Richard K. 1994. "The Governor and the Cabinet: Executive Policy Making and Policy Management." In *The Florida Public Policy Management System*, ed. Richard Chackerian. Tallahassee, FL: Askew School of Public Administration and Policy and Florida Center for Public Management.

———. 1997. *Politics in the New South*, 2nd ed. Armonk, NY: M.E. Sharpe.

Schneider, William. 1996. "Immigration Issues Reward Democrats." *National Journal*, November 30:2522.

Smith, Stanley K. 1995. "Population Growth and Demographic Change." In *The Economy of Florida*, ed. J. F. Scoggins and Ann Pierce. Gainesville, FL: Bureau of Economic and Business Research.

12

——◦——

Texas

The Lone Star (Wars) State

James W. Lamare, J. L. Polinard, and
Robert D. Wrinkle

Once upon a time, a long time ago, in a galaxy far, far away, there was a place called Texas. The Force was with a group called Democrats. It was rumored that in some states a dark side called Republicans was in power, but most Texans had never seen a Republican, so it was difficult to know whether or not they actually existed. The Force also was with White People. There were, of course, African Americans (they were called "Colored" or "Negro" then, at least in polite company) and Mexican Americans (they were called Latin Americans then), but they had none of the Force. At election time, if an African American or Mexican American attempted to vote as an individual, it was an act of courage rather than citizenship. It was, however, common "to vote" the minority groups, as in "don't forget to vote your Mexicans next week." Indeed, in South Texas so many trucks brought Latino farm workers to the polls that the growers would tie different-colored ribbons to the truck beds, so that after the workers had marked the correct ballot, they would return to the correct vehicle.

And the Force was only with Men. Although the colorful Miriam "Ma" Ferguson was elected in 1924, she was viewed widely as a stand-in for her ethically challenged husband, who had been booted out of the governor's office in 1917. Women played little role in the politics of this Texas of another era.

But that was in a galaxy far away, and long, oh so very long, ago.

We are sixty years removed from the Texas that native son V. O. Key examined for his classic study of southern states (Key 1949). No single

267

factor, such as race or oil and gas or conservatism or Key's "modified class politics," can describe the politics in Texas today.

Having said that, one characteristic of Texas politics has not changed in 60 years: the state remains a one-party state. The difference today, of course, is the party. In Key's day, Texas was solidly Democratic. There were thousands of Texans alive in the 1960s who had never met an actual Republican (or at least one out of the closet). Loyalty to the Democratic Party was so deeply embedded in Texas's political culture that a great many partisans were aptly described as "yellow-dog Democrats," voters who would rather vote for a yellow dog than any Republican.[1]

Today, Texas is Republican. Including the 2008 elections, no Democrat has won a statewide race since 1994. No Democrat currently holds a statewide office.

Perhaps ironically, the transition from Democrat to Republican is inextricably linked to the state's past, particularly to the roots of its history as a frontier state and to its history of racial politics.

Part of the legacy of the Texas frontier ethic has been the state's basic conservatism. Until the last two decades, electoral competition as well as legislative conflict broke along ideological rather than partisan lines; with few notable exceptions, the only elections that really counted were between conservative and liberal Democrats in the spring primaries. For the most part, conservatives won these battles. Public policy fights in the state legislature similarly were between conservative and liberal legislators rather than Democrats and Republicans. Even when Republicans began to contest and win state legislative seats, the conservative Democratic leadership in the statehouse and Senate often would appoint GOP conservatives to committee chairs rather than reward the few Democratic liberals.

There still are elements of ideology trumping partisanship. In the announcement of new committee assignments following the 2008 elections, the Speaker of the state House, Joe Strauss (R-San Antonio) did name some Democrats as chairs of standing committees.

Texas also is a former state of the Confederacy, and race (and ethnicity) has always played a role in the state's politics. Historically, blacks in North and East Texas, and Mexican Americans in South and West Texas, found themselves on the outside looking in when it came to political power. Today, although African Americans and Mexican Americans have won statewide elections and have representation in the state legislature and the congressional delegation, their representation is not proportionate to their percentage of the population. And no African American or Mexican American has held the top three posts in the state: governor, lieutenant governor (which many consider the most powerful political position), and speaker of the house.

We turn now to a detailed examination of the changing politics of party competitiveness, the impact of the 2001 and 2003 redistricting processes, and the politics of race in Texas.

PARTY POLITICS

It is difficult, if not impossible, to separate the politics of contemporary partisanship in Texas from the politics of race. Shortly after Lyndon Johnson signed the 1964 Civil Rights Act into law, he predicted, correctly as it turned out, that he had just ensured the end of the Democratic Party's electoral lock on the South. Certainly race has been a major factor in the Republican upsurge in Texas. As the national Democratic Party became identified as the party representing the interests of African Americans and other racial and ethnic minorities, white Texans increasingly considered the Republican Party as a viable alternative. The subsequent passage of the 1965 Voting Rights Act, which, among other things, sounded the death knell to race-based literacy tests, further contributed to the Democratic Party's image as the party of minorities, and the 1975 inclusion of Texas as one of the jurisdictions covered by the Voting Rights Act cemented this image and accelerated white flight from the Democrats (Burka 1986).

Ideology also contributed to the emergence of the Republican Party in Texas. The nomination of liberal George McGovern as the Democratic Party's presidential candidate in 1972 increased the perception that the party was controlled by the liberal wing of American politics, and this, too, hastened the exodus of conservative white Texans to the GOP (Dyer and Haynes 1987; Dyer, Leighley, and Vedlitz 1997). Furthermore, the appeal of Ronald Reagan's message during the presidential campaigns of 1980 and 1984, according to the then chairman of the state GOP (George Strake), made "it so easy . . . to court conservatives into the Republican Party" (Robison 2004, 2). During Reagan's stint in the White House, some fifty-eight Democratic Texas officeholders switched parties to become Republicans.

Within the electorate, for most of this period there was a steady growth of identification with the Republican Party, paralleled by a significant loss of support for the Democrats. In 1964, Democratic identification stood at 65 percent, eight times greater than Republican affiliation (8 percent). By 1974, the gap had narrowed some, but Democratic identifiers still trumped Republicans by about 4:1. The divide between the parties had closed dramatically by 1984, with one-third of Texans identifying as Democrats and 28 percent calling themselves Republicans. By 1994, the inevitable occurred: more Texans affiliated with the Republicans than with the Democrats. A decade later, this shift became more pronounced: 38 percent called themselves Republican while only 26 percent called themselves Democrat. Texas had completed the transition to a predominantly Republican state.

Demographic patterns also spurred Republican growth in Texas. Texas is a Sun Belt state with a steady influx of immigrants from other states. Many of these new Texans come from traditionally Republican states, with research suggesting that nearly one-fourth of Texas's Republicans are not native to the state (Dyer, Vedlitz, and Hill 1988, 164). Republican strength lies mainly among younger, higher SES, white non-Hispanic Texans, who reside in the more upscale suburbs and satellite communities that encircle the state's largest metropolitan areas. The Democrats draw their support predominately from older, native, lower SES, rural Texans and the state's largest minority groups, a point discussed more fully below (Dye, Gibson, and Robison 1997, 767).

In ideological terms, the more things change, the more they stay the same—at least in Texas. For over a generation, the number of Texans—calling themselves liberal, conservative, and moderate has remained relatively constant, with the ratio of conservatives to liberals also stable at 2:1.

Within the Republican Party there are variant conservative ideological perspectives (such as between the economic conservatives and the social conservatives) and varying degrees of commitment to conservatism. Lately, the Christian Coalition, a group that strongly opposes gay marriage and abortion, has, through a great deal of organizational effort, taken command of the state GOP (Lamare, Polinard, and Wrinkle 2002). Its social conservative message is clear, loud, and appealing.

Given the ideological landscape of Texas, for candidates of both major parties, electoral "victory is gained by trying to convince the electorate that a candidate is more conservative than his opponent" (Champagne and Collis 1984, 142). The difference for the past decade, of course, is the party with which these conservatives now identify.

Voting patterns have paralleled these partisan and ideological trends. Following Reconstruction, no Republican was elected to statewide office until John Tower broke through in 1961 to replace Lyndon Johnson in the U.S. Senate. Ironically, Tower was elected with the help of liberal Democrats who refused to support Tower's more conservative opponent (Gibson and Robison 1995, 195). Although Texas Republicans would win very few other elections at any level in Texas over the next twenty years, Tower's 1961 election is cited as the beginning of the two-party system in Texas (Davidson 1990, 21).

Throughout the Democratic Party's domination at most levels of Texas politics during the 1960s and 1970s, there were Republican gains, most noticeably Bill Clements's 1978 victory in the governor's race. By the end of the 1970s, the GOP was positioned to compete seriously for elective office.

From 1960 to the mid-1980s, the percentage of Texans who identified themselves as Republicans had been steadily, if gradually, increasing (from 8 percent in the early 1960s to 28 percent by the mid-1980s), while the Democrats were on a down elevator, with the Democratic percentage of the population dropping below 38 percent by 1984. In 1980, a Republican occupied the governor's office, a Republican was the state's senior U.S. senator, and Ronald Reagan, beloved by the conservatives in Texas, had just been elected president. The future was now for the GOP.

Well, not quite. Democrats surprised the Republicans in 1982 by recapturing the governor's mansion, sweeping the statewide offices, and maintaining strong majorities in both houses of the state legislature. The 1982 Democratic win can be attributed in part to a ticket that included both liberals and conservatives at the top spots, thereby holding both constituencies in the party, and by the united opposition to the dour Clements. In retrospect, however, this would be the last hurrah for the Democrats in the twentieth century. In the 1984 elections, Ronald Reagan easily carried Texas, Phil Gramm became the second Republican from Texas elected to the U.S. Senate, and, perhaps more importantly, Republicans gained seats in both the state Senate and state House. Republicans also made significant inroads in county elections, winning twice as many seats as they had held prior to the election.

Helped in part by the Republican presence at the top of the ticket, first of Ronald Reagan in 1984 and then of favorite son George Bush in 1988, the GOP upsurge continued throughout the 1980s. Changing party loyalties continued to manifest themselves, both in the sense that some Democrats became Republicans (realignment) and in the sense that some Democrats moved away from the Democratic Party (dealignment) without aligning with the GOP. The net result was that by the 1990s, party identification was virtually identical between the two parties.

The trend established in the 1980s continued through the 1990s. Although the Republicans would suffer some difficult losses, the most visible being the defeat of GOP gubernatorial candidate Clayton Williams at the hands of Democrat Ann Richards in 1990 (or, more accurately, at the mouth of Williams, whose verbal gaffes in the last weeks of the campaign helped snatch defeat from the jaws of victory), they continued to gain seats in almost every other venue. At the federal level, for example, Texas has supported the Republican candidate for president in every election since 1976. With the election of Kay Bailey Hutchison in 1993, Republicans occupied both of Texas's seats in the U.S. Senate and continue to do so today.

At the state level, George W. Bush, son of the former president, defeated incumbent Ann Richards in 1994 to become the second Republican governor of Texas since Reconstruction. The 1994 election also ushered in a Republican sweep of the three seats on the Texas Railroad Commission, which, because of its jurisdiction over the oil industry, is perhaps the most important elected administrative agency in the United States. The GOP also gained a majority on the fifteen-person State Board of Education. The state's elected commissioner of agriculture went to a Republican, while the other elected statewide executives remained Democrats.

However, the handwriting was on the wall. In 1996, Republicans swept every statewide election and, for the first time in 125 years, obtained a majority in the state Senate. The GOP also made a strong showing in races for Texas's House of Representatives, winning 68 of 151 seats that year. By 1998, almost two-thirds of the state's district courts were occupied by Republicans. Nearly 1,100 elected county positions were Republicans. In total, the GOP won more than 1,500 elections at the federal, state, and local level in 1998.

In 2002, following redistricting favoring the GOP, the Republicans captured control of both houses of the state legislature for the first time since Reconstruction, winning 88 of the 150 seats, and cemented that control in 2004. Although the state legislature remains less partisan than the U.S. Congress (following the 2008 elections, the GOP leadership named a small number of Democrats as committee chairs), the state House and Senate are governed by Republicans.

Seven election cycles have turned since the last time Democrats scratched on a statewide office. Indeed, in the 2000 elections, the Libertarian Party contested more statewide offices than the Democrats did.

Nothing changed with the 2006 and 2008 elections. No Democrat broke the GOP stranglehold; currently all statewide offices, including both Texas supreme courts (one for civil, the other for criminal cases), are held by Republicans. Texas is a one-party Republican state.

The only fly in the GOP ointment remained the congressional delegation. Although the GOP had made some gains in the national House seats, following the 2002 congressional elections Democrats still controlled a majority of the congressional delegation.

But not for long!

THE 2003 REDISTRICTING FIGHT

Like most states, Texas redistricts its state and congressional legislative seats once every ten years, following the U.S. census. The census report in 2000 was good to Texas: The state was informed it had picked up two congressional seats, increasing the size of the delegation from thirty to thirty-two.

The Texas effort to redistrict, however, was an exercise in futility. Under the best of circumstances, redistricting is a bitterly fought partisan endeavor. The shape and composition of the district, whether state House, state Senate, or congressional districts, quite simply can determine the outcome of the election in that district. Thus, the stakes are high, as each representative views redistricting as a question of survival rather than good government.

The 2001 Texas legislature charged with drawing the new lines was not up to the task. Although the Democratic-controlled House and GOP-controlled state Senate worked on their respective redistricting chores, the outcome was dismal. The House passed a redistricting bill that died in the Senate. Still, that was better than the Senate effort. The Texas Senate Redistricting Committee produced a bill that could not muster enough support in the chamber to be sent to the House.

By Texas law, this meant the Legislative Redistricting Board (LRB) would take its turn at bat. The LRB, made up of the lieutenant governor, attorney general, land commissioner, state comptroller, and house speaker (the latter was the only Democrat on the LRB), managed to produce redistricting plans for the state House and Senate.

The House plan, however, ran afoul of the Department of Justice, which denied preclearance as required by the Voting Rights Act. A three-judge federal court subsequently adopted a plan that would be in place for the 2002 elections.

The Senate plan produced by the LRB was precleared by the DOJ (although both the Mexican American Legislative Caucus and the Mexican American Legal Defense and Education Fund [MALDEF] challenged the plan unsuccessfully in the courts) and was approved by the three-judge federal court.

These would be the redistricting plans that Texans would use for the remainder of the state legislative and state Senate elections through the decade. The 2002 and 2004 elections ratified the assessments of the partisan impact of the new districts: the GOP maintained control of both the state House and Senate.

THE TEXAS THREE-STEP:
ARDMORE, ALBUQUERQUE, AND AUSTIN

It was a very different matter for congressional districting. The 2001 legislative session was unable to agree on how the thirty-two congressional districts should be drawn; the legislative session finished without new districts in place for the 2002 elections. The LRB's jurisdiction is limited to the state House and Senate seats, so it was not a player in the congressional districting process. That task fell to a three-judge federal district court. The court produced a plan that awarded the two new congressional seats to Republicans and protected the incumbents in the remaining thirty seats.

Despite the overall GOP tenor of the state and the fact that the three-judge court's congressional redistricting map suggested a majority of the thirty-two seats contained GOP majorities, when the dust settled from the 2002 elections, Democrats held seventeen of the thirty-two seats. In part this was due to some congressional districts where the voters chose GOP candidates in the statewide gubernatorial and U.S. Senate races, but voted for their Democratic congressional incumbent as a way of protecting their seniority and the goodies that accrue from that seniority. That is, these districts were predominantly Republican in population, but the GOP voters were making a conscious decision to split their ticket when it came to the congressional representative on the ballot.

Enter the U.S. House Republican leader, Texan Tom DeLay. DeLay saw two benefits in breaking with the tradition of redistricting only once during a ten-year cycle. Redrawing the congressional lines in 2003 would not only produce a GOP congressional delegation from Texas, but, anticipating picking up at least five Republican seats from the redistricting, DeLay would immunize continued GOP control of the U.S. House against any Democratic gains in the 2004 elections.

Democrats cried foul, but the state attorney general declared that the state legislature had the authority to redistrict in 2003 and the battle was joined. The Democrats won the early battles by going to the political equivalent of scorched earth. In a conversation one of the authors had, the comment was made that "the Democrats have gone to the mattresses," a reference to the famous line from *The Godfather*. Actually, it was more accurate to say they moved the mattresses. When the state House scheduled floor action on redistricting, over fifty House Democrats fled to Ardmore, Oklahoma, thereby denying the House leadership a quorum. The Democrats stayed in Ardmore until the time ran out for both the regular session and the redistricting bill in early June 2003.

That did not settle the matter. The governor, Republican Rick Perry, called the legislature into special session on June 30, 2003, with the express charge of redistricting the thirty-two congressional districts. The session was unsuccessful due to an unusual rule in the Texas state Senate. In effect, to get a bill to the floor of the Senate requires a two-thirds vote. The Senate was split nineteen to twelve in favor of the GOP, so, if the Democrats could keep at least eleven of their own in the fold, they could prevent any redistricting bill from getting to a floor vote. This worked for the first special session.

The governor then called a second special session. Now it was time for the Senate Democrats to hit the road. Taking a cue from their colleagues in the state House, eleven of the twelve Senate Democrats took off for Albuquerque (perhaps a step up from Ardmore in terms of creature comforts). So much for the second special session.

The legislative game, which had been entertaining not only Texans but also the nation (the peripatetic Democrats were the source of numerous one-liners on the late-night television shows), finally ended with a third special session. The lieutenant governor, who presides over the state Senate, tossed the two-thirds rule, and one of the Democratic senators defected. The legislators stayed in Austin. The result was a congressional redistricting bill designed to give the GOP at least twenty-two of the thirty-two seats.

The bill was precleared by the Department of Justice and narrowly (2–1) withstood a challenge before the three-judge panel in the fall of 2003.[2] The 2004 congressional elections were held under the new plan, and although the Republicans did not defeat all of the targeted Democrats, they won twenty-one of the thirty-two congressional seats.[3] In 2008, the redistricting continued to pay dividends to the GOP, which emerged from November's election with a twenty-to-twelve margin in the congressional delegation.

THE POLITICS OF RACE

In his classic study, Key suggested race played less of a role in Texas politics than in many other southern states. Instead, Key saw Texas politics as dividing along class lines that closely tracked political ideology (Key 1949, 261). No one familiar with Texas politics, however, would suggest that race and ethnicity are neutral factors in the state's political chemistry.

Paralleling the emergence of the Republican Party in Texas, increased African American and Mexican American political influence largely is a development of the past thirty years. This increased influence in large part is a function of two factors: population patterns and the impact of the Voting Rights Act.

Although the percentage of African Americans who make up the overall Texas population has been decreasing for two decades—it now stands at 11.3 percent—the concentration of this population in urban centers enhances its political influence. Over eight out of ten African Americans in Texas live in metropolitan areas; blacks make up at least 25 percent of the population in several of Texas's larger cities, a figure that translates into political power at election time.

The Mexican American population has been growing steadily, and the percentage of the overall Texas population that is Latino (almost all of which is of Mexican origin) likewise has increased accordingly. Mexican Americans currently constitute 35 percent of the state's population and are by far the largest minority group in Texas.

The increasing urbanization of the black population and the increasing numbers of the Mexican American population have coincided with the utilization of the Voting Rights Act to increase the political power, and representation, of these minority groups. First, the VRA served to register thousands of eligible minority citizens. Then, beginning in the mid-1970s and accelerating through the 1980s, the VRA was used to successfully challenge the at-large voting structures of dozens of city councils and school boards, and the district boundaries of state legislative districts, state Senate districts, and congressional districts.

The result of these legal challenges was the creation of hundreds of electoral districts designed to enhance minority voting power. A quick glance at the data shows how successful these efforts were. In 1970, there were 29 African Americans serving in elective office in Texas; by 1993 this figure had increased to 472. In 1974, there were 540 Latino elected officials in Texas; twenty years later, there were 2,215.

The electoral success of the racial and ethnic minority candidates has been primarily at the local levels. This is significant, first because these offices have a direct impact on the population, and second, these offices are training grounds for movement to higher offices. In a very real sense, the VRA has produced an invisible revolution at the municipal and school board levels that almost certainly will begin to be manifested at higher offices of the state government in the near future.[4]

As mentioned earlier, partisan commitment in Texas takes a racial and ethnic cast.[5] Anglos in Texas have steadily become more Republican over the last two decades. In the 1990s and the early part of the first decade of the twenty-first century, while most African Americans and Hispanics continued to affiliate with the Democrats, there was some movement in response to GOP outreach efforts. For example, in 1984 only about 7 percent of Hispanics identified with the GOP (Texas Poll Archives). By 2000, that figure had increased more than threefold, to 23.5 percent (William C. Velasquez Institute 2000, 5).

However, as discussed in more detail below, the recent GOP emphasis on immigration as a wedge issue has had a negative impact on its attempt to attract minority, particularly Mexican American, voters.

Actual voting behavior also reflected these racial and ethnic patterns. In recent elections, Anglos have mostly supported Republican candidates in Texas. Meanwhile, African Americans have remained a core component of the Democratic electoral base, usually with 90 percent of this group voting for Democratic candidates (Shannon 2004). Republican inroads into the Latino vote were discernible from 1998 to 2006. In 2000, for example, George W. Bush gained nearly one-third of the Hispanic vote in his initial election to the presidency, and incumbent Republican U.S. senator Kay Bailey Hutchison garnered 46 percent of this vote in her reelection (William C. Velasquez Institute 2000, 4). In the 2004 presidential race, George W. Bush did well in predominately Hispanic South Texas counties, carrying Cameron County and averaging 41 percent in the counties that sit on the Mexican border (Russell 2005, 80).

Both parties must take cognizance of the turnout patterns for ethnic and racial groups in Texas. As indicated in table 12.1, Anglos still constitute most of the pool of voters in Texas. Although Anglos make up almost a majority of the state's population, they are overrepresented among the eligible (58.7 percent), the registered (63.6 percent), and, more to the point, the actual voters (69.2 percent).

African Americans constitute 11.3 percent of the state's population. This proportion is reflected in the number of Texans eligible to vote (12.3 percent), registered (11.9 percent), and voting (11.8 percent) who are African Americans.

Although slightly over one-third of Texans are Hispanic, only 25.8 percent of the state's eligible voters, 22.3 percent of its registered voters, and 17.1 percent of its actual voters are Hispanic.

The figures of table 12.1, however, fail to disclose fully the changes that are occurring among Texas voters. The decline in the number of Anglos in Texas recorded over the last decade is mirrored in the decrease of non-Hispanic whites as a portion of the state's eligible, registered, and actual voters. In the early 1990s, for instance, Anglos made up three-fourths of the state's voters; by 2006, that figured had dropped to 69 percent. Over this same period, Hispanics have not only gained as a percentage of Texas's population (from 28 percent to 35 percent), but also as a percentage of its eligible voters (from 20 percent to 25.4 percent), its registered voters (from 15 percent to 22 percent) and its actual voters (from 12 percent to 17 percent). The destiny of political parties in Texas may very well be determined by the way these population and electorate dynamics play out—a point that is fully appreciated by candidates and strategists plotting their future in Texas politics.

THE CLOCK IS TICKING

However, the long-range picture suggests a strong ray of hope for the Democrats. The Hispanic vote, enhanced by both the impact of the Voting Rights Act and the maturation of the very young Mexican American

Table 12.1. Voting Participation and Ethnicity, 2006

Ethnic/Racial Background	Percent of Total Population	Percent of Eligible Voters	Percent of Registered Voters	Percent of Actual Voters	Percent of Eligible Voters by Race
Non-Hispanic White (Anglos)	48.33	58.7	63.6	69.2	45.2
Hispanic	35.5	25.8	22.3	17.1	25.4
African American	11.3	12.3	11.9	11.8	36.6

Sources: Texas Quick Facts, U.S. Census Bureau, and William C. Velasquez Institute (www.wcvi.org).

population, is expected to increasingly become the pivotal vote in the state's elections.

Virtually all demographers agree that over half of Texas's population either already is or soon will be comprised of "minorities."[6] Most of this change is the result of the growth of the Latino population (which may constitute almost half of the state's population by 2020).[7]

In 2006, the GOP handed the Democrats a gift by elevating the issue of immigration to the top of their policy agenda. It quickly became clear that the Latino population nationwide, and the Mexican American population in Texas, viewed the GOP focus on immigration as a threat to Latino empowerment.

In the 2006 Texas elections, the Democrats reestablished their hold on the Mexican American vote. Then in 2008, they received well over 60 percent of the Latino vote. The handwriting on the wall is clear. If the Democrats continue to hold more than 60 percent of the Latino vote and retain their 90 percent preference rating among African Americans, they will soon be in a position to return to their glory days of yesteryear.

In the 2008 elections, the Democrats continued to gain House and Senate seats. They currently are just one seat away from parity in the Texas House; the GOP has a seventy-six-to-seventy-four advantage. In the state Senate, the GOP maintains a stronger lead (nineteen to twelve), but, not unlike the national Senate, the Texas Senate's rules generally require at least twenty-two votes to pass legislation. Thus, as long as the Democrats can hold on to at least eleven votes, they can block action.

Perhaps most ominously for the GOP, the state clearly is in flux in terms of party identification. A Gallup poll released in January 2009 reported that party identification in Texas has undergone a sea change. In 2002, 52.4 percent of Texans identified themselves as either GOP or leaning GOP, compared to 39.6 percent of Democrat identifiers. In 2006, a trend toward increased Democratic identification emerged. Then, 50 percent of Texans identified themselves as GOP/leaning GOP, but the Democrat percentages had increased to 42 percent. The results reported in January 2009 show a plurality of the state now identifies as Democrat/leaning Democrat, 43.4 percent to 41 percent.[8] Given the ethnic demographics discussed above, one would expect the next cycle to continue the trend toward a more Democratic state. Figure 12.1 represents the partisan trends for the past forty-five years.

CONCLUSION

As Texas moves into the twenty-first century, two parallel political tracks are visible. One is the partisan track, where the Republican Party continues

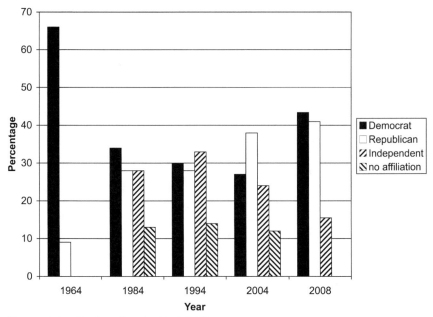

Figure 12.1.   Partisan Trends, 1964–2008

not only to dominate statewide elections, but has cemented its hold on the state through the 2001 and 2003 redistricting processes. Texas arguably has been a one-party GOP state in presidential elections for a generation, and Republicans have won five of the last seven gubernatorial elections. Republicans have swept every statewide office in the last seven election cycles.

However, the recent Democratic gains in terms of party identification suggest the partisan pendulum is beginning to swing in a different direction.

The second track marks the increasing influence of the minority population in the state, particularly of the Mexican American population. The trend here, too, favors the Democrats in the long, and perhaps even in the not-too-short, run.

Demography is destiny. It is only a matter of time, and not very much time at that, until the sociological minority populations are a numerical majority, and these numbers, combined with increased educational and occupational gains, eventually will translate into political power. Both parties know this. Democrats design their strategies to keep the minority voters in the Democratic camp. Republicans, reaching out to the Mexican American vote during the early Bush years, have seen their gains disappear in the dust of the party's focus on immigration. The fence they want to build along the border between Mexico and Texas has become a fence keeping Mexican American voters out of their party.

A decade ago, the two tracks suggested a continued period of GOP dominance in Texas politics. As we turn toward the 2010 elections, glimpses into the future necessarily are more nuanced. At the very least, the Democrats no longer are in free fall and, at best, are poised to compete on a level playing field.

NOTES

Authors' Note: The authors wish to acknowledge the valuable research help provided by Javier Alvarez.

1. Perhaps the best definition of a "yellow-dog Democrat" was overheard by one of the authors at a conference in 2008. The conference speaker said his mother was such a strong yellow-dog Democrat that he once told her he thought she'd vote Democrat even if Jesus Christ ran as a Republican. She responded, "Son, don't be silly; Jesus isn't going to change his party affiliation after all these years!"
2. One of the co-authors of this chapter was an expert witness for the plaintiffs in the redistricting case (*Jackson v. Perry*).
3. The U.S. Supreme Court ordered the three-judge federal court to reconsider its earlier ruling in light of the high court's recent decisions on partisan gerrymandering. In the spring of 2005, the three-judge panel, as expected, declined to alter its earlier decision. In June 2006, the Supreme Court did conclude that one of the new districts was drawn in such a way as to dilute the voting strength of Mexican Americans and ordered the state to redraw the boundaries for the Twenty-third District in order to remedy the situation. For more detailed analyses of the redistricting, see Brown and Wilkens 2004 and Linda Greenhouse, "Justices Uphold Most Remapping in Texas by GOP," *New York Times*, June 18, 2006.
4. For a more detailed analysis of the impact of the VRA, see Polinard et al. 1994, *Electoral Structure and Urban Politics: the Effect of the Voting Rights Act on Mexican American Communities*. New York: St. Martin's Press.
5. See, for example, pp. 718–719 in Shea et al. 2009, *Living Democracy: Texas Edition*, 2nd ed. New York: Longman Publishing.
6. See, for example, U.S. Census Bureau, "Texas Becomes Nation's Newest 'Majority-Minority' State," August 11, 2005, available at www.census.gov.
7. Texas State Data Center, Texas A&M University.
8. "State of the States: Political Party Affiliation," by Jeffrey Jones. Gallup Poll, 2009.

REFERENCES

Brown, Lyle C., and Jerry Wilkens. 2004. "Redistricting and Electoral Results in Texas in the Twenty-First Century." In *Practicing Texas Politics*, ed. Lyle C. Brown, Joyce A. Langenegger, Sonia R. Garcia, and Ted Lewis. Boston: Houghton Mifflin.

Burka, Paul. 1986. "Primary Lesson." *Texas Monthly*, July.

Champagne, Anthony, and Rick Collis. 1984. "Texas." In *The Political Life of the American States*, ed. Alan Rosenthal and Maureen Moakley. New York: Praeger.

Davidson, Chandler. 1990. *Race and Class in Texas Politics*. Princeton, NJ: Princeton University Press.

Dye, Thomas, L. Tucker Gibson Jr., and Clay Robison. 1997. *Politics in America: Texas Edition*. Upper Saddle River, NJ: Prentice-Hall.

Dyer, James, and Don Haynes. 1987. *Social, Economic, and Political Change According to the Texas Poll*. Austin: College of Communication, University of Texas at Austin.

Dyer, James A., Jan E. Leighley, and Arnold Vedlitz. 1997. "Party Identification and Public Opinion in Texas, 1984–1994." In *Texas Politics: A Reader*, ed. Anthony Champagne and Edward J. Harpham. New York: W. W. Norton.

Dyer, James A., Arnold Vedlitz, and David B. Hill. 1988. "New Voters, Switchers, and Political Party Realignment in Texas." *Western Political Quarterly* 41 (March): 164.

Gibson, L. Tucker, Jr., and Clay Robison. 1995. *Government and Politics in Texas*. Englewood Cliffs, NJ: Prentice-Hall.

Herrick, Thaddeus. 1996. "Poll Shows Hispanics Conservative." *Houston (TX) Chronicle*, February 22.

Key, V. O., Jr. 1949. *Southern Politics in State and Nation*. New York: Alfred A. Knopf.

Lamare, James W., J. L. Polinard, and Robert Wrinkle. 2003. "Texas Religion and Politics in God's Country." In *Marching toward the Millennium: The Christian Right in the States*, ed. John C. Green, Mark J. Rozell, and Clyde Wilcox. Washington, DC: Georgetown University Press.

Office of the Secretary of State. 1982. *May Primary Election Analysis*. Austin, TX: Office of the Secretary of State, table 3.

Polinard, J. L., Robert D. Wrinkle, Norman Binder, and Thomas Longoria. 2004. *Electoral Structure and Urban Policy*. New York: St. Martin's Press.

Robison, Clay. 2004. "Reagan Changed Texas." *Houston Chronicle*, June 13.

Russell, Jan Jarboe. 2005. "Grand Opportunity Party." *Texas Monthly*, March.

Shannon, Kelly. 2004. "Republican Shift Means Changing Definition of Texas Democrat." Associated Press Wire, February 27.

Shea, Daniel M., Joanne Connor Green, and Christopher E. Smith. 2009. *Living Democracy: Texas Edition*, 2nd ed. New York: Longman Publishing.

Texas Poll Archives. Scripps Howard Research Center. Abilene, Texas.

Tuell, Sherry Carter. 1995. "Racial Bias Reported in Loans, Jobs: NAACP Poll Hits Texas Problems." *Houston (TX) Chronicle*, February 2.

William C. Velasquez Institute. 2000. "2000 Texas Exit Poll of Latino Voters." Los Angeles: William C. Velasquez Institute.

Conclusion

The Soul of the South

Religion and Southern Politics in the New Millennium

John C. Green, Lyman A. Kellstedt,
Corwin E. Smidt, and James L. Guth

Over the past half century, the South has undergone a major political transformation, changing from a one-party Democratic bastion into a largely Republican region. Many factors have contributed to this change: the civil rights revolution, economic development and migration, and the politicization of "moral" issues. Religious influences have received considerable media attention in recent decades because of the highly visible efforts by the Christian Right to mobilize evangelicals on behalf of the GOP, but the political behavior of other religious groups is also a vital part of the story.

The transformations of the past half century have had the effect of reducing southern distinctiveness. This is especially true with respect to religion, as the linkage between religious communities and partisan behavior has been nationalized: Evangelicals have emerged as the core religious constituency of the Republican coalition in both the South and other regions, and the Democrats have relied everywhere on a "coalition of religious minorities," including unaffiliated or secular voters. White mainline Protestants, the old "Republican Party at prayer," and non-Latino Catholics, long the confessional core of the Democratic Party, have become swing constituencies in the new religious politics (Green et al. 2007).

The critical question here is whether recent Democratic victories, first in the congressional elections of 2006 and then in Barack Obama's historic presidential victory of 2008, have fundamentally altered this new religious order in southern—and American—politics. To answer this question, we review the political behavior of major religious groups in the

South, tracing continuity and change from the 1960s through the 2008 election. We find that traditional Protestantism is still a crucial facet of regional elections, but that it operates in a new context. On the one hand, the "white Protestant alliance" that once buttressed the Democratic "Solid South" has been altered and largely reassembled in the Republican Party, and on the other hand, increased religious diversity has re-created in the South the "coalition of religious minorities" that has long supported northern Democrats. These transformations have provided Democrats a solid, if modest, advantage outside the South, but have also built a southern redoubt for the national GOP, with some vital—and perhaps adverse—implications for Republican fortunes elsewhere.

ELECTORAL ORDER AND SOUTHERN RELIGION

Byron Shafer's (1991, 43–45) concept of an *electoral order* provides a useful tool to discuss the role of religion in southern politics. An electoral order is a stable political relationship between the "social base," "intermediary organizations," and "government institutions." The social base is determined by the politically relevant demographic differences among voters, such as race, class, or religion; intermediary organizations are the formal mobilizers and representatives of such voters, such as political parties, unions, or churches; and government institutions are constituted by the public officials elected by the social base, as mediated by these institutions. At any point in time the electoral order is largely defined by the key social groups supporting the major parties; changes in the nature of that group support can ultimately produce a new order.

According to Shafer (1991, 43), religion is one of the fundamental social bases of the American electoral order, and one that is especially important in the South. Indeed, religion has long been central to the region's distinctive culture and politics (Hill 1983). Scholars have argued that the "religious solid South preceded the political solid South" (Weaver 1968, 98) and have surmised that "the first will apparently outlast the latter" (Reed 1972, 57). Surprisingly, however, scholars of southern electoral politics have largely overlooked religion until recently (Jelen 2006). Indeed, V. O. Key's masterful work (1949) may have set the stage, as its neglect of religion was often replicated in the genre it inspired (e.g., Havard 1972; Lamis 1984). Petrocik's (1987) study of southern party coalitions ignores religion altogether in an otherwise sophisticated analysis. Even Black and Black's monumental two-volume treatise (1987, 1992) gives the topic short shrift, although their more recent work (2002, 2007) partially remedies the defect. With some exceptions (Baker et al. 1983; Kellstedt 1990; Smidt 1983, 1989; Rozell and Wilcox 1996), religion is still not featured in works on southern politics, taking a back seat to race (Carmines and Stimson 1989; Feldman 2005) or economics (Black and Black 1987; Shafer and Johnston 2006).

Religion may have been overlooked because it can be difficult to understand southern religion, which is at the same time unusually homogeneous and remarkably diverse. First, the South has been, and still is, dominated by white Protestants; the concentration of pious "Baptists and Methodists" contrasts sharply with religious diversity in the rest of the country (Hill 1966, 31–39). Thus, some scholars might assume that if religion did not vary much, it could hardly be of political significance. But in reality, southern Protestants are not monolithic, exhibiting numerous and significant variations in belief and practice (Harrell 1991): Baptists differ from Methodists, white Protestants differ from black Protestants, Latinos differ from both blacks and whites, and believers differ from backsliders. And the small but growing non-Latino Catholic population differs from all these. Such complexity may have misled other scholars into ignoring the politics of southern religion out of frustration with understanding its nuances.

Recent social science research offers some conceptual tools that can simplify religious complexity. The first and most basic analytic concept is *religious tradition*, constituted by religious communities that share a distinctive worldview. Religious tradition is measured by grouping those who affiliate with similar denominations, movements, and congregations (Kellstedt et al. 1996a; Steensland et al. 2000; Smidt et al. 2009). Although the best classifications vary slightly, scholars typically recognize four major American religious traditions: evangelical, mainline Protestantism, black Protestantism, and Roman Catholicism. A fifth group, the nonreligious, unaffiliated, or secular population, is analogous to a religious tradition in many respects. Two religious sub-traditions—Latino Protestants and Catholics—have become increasingly important as their numbers have grown over the past two decades. During the past half century, evangelical, mainline, and black Protestants have been the major players in southern politics, while non-Latino Catholics, Latino Christians, and seculars have become more relevant recently.

For analysis of southern politics, the conceptual distinction between white evangelical and mainline Protestants is especially important. Evangelicals are more traditional in belief and practice, stressing "otherworldly" concerns, while mainliners are more modernist, putting greater emphasis on "this worldly" matters (Kellstedt et al. 1996b; Green 2007, Smidt 2007; Smidt et al. 2009). By this definition, most white Baptists in the region are evangelicals, and most white southern Methodists are mainliners. Indeed, the two largest American Protestant denominations, the Southern Baptist Convention (SBC) and the United Methodist Church (UMC), dominate the national evangelical and mainline traditions, respectively, and are especially well represented in the South. Black Protestant churches, on the other hand, constitute a separate religious tradition, shaped by centuries of slavery and segregation (Sernett 1991). Although black Baptists and Methodists share many beliefs and practices with their white counterparts, their institutional locations are separate and their religious worldviews are quite distinct.

Another concept that helps reduce religious complexity is *religious commitment*, the extent of an individual's attachment to faith. Religious commitment can be gauged in many ways, ranging from frequency of church attendance to participation in private devotional practices, but all such indicators help distinguish those who take their faith seriously from those with more nominal attachments (Kellstedt et al. 1996a). Although Southerners are known for strong religious commitment (Reed 1972), their involvement in public and private religious activity is hardly uniform (Stark and Bainbridge 1985). Assessing religious commitment is vital because we suspect that those with stronger commitment are most likely to exhibit the distinctive worldview of their tradition.

Combining religious tradition and commitment allows us to identify several groups that include most southern voters (see table C.1). First, we look at high- and low-commitment white evangelicals, as well as their white mainline counterparts, as we shall find important differences among these large southern religious constituencies. We also examine Black Protestants, Latino Christians (both Protestant and Catholic), non-Latino Catholics, and seculars. Given the small numbers in most surveys, these latter groups cannot be reliably divided by level of religious commitment. And of course, commitment is quite low among seculars.[1] Although the influence of other demographic factors, such as income and gender, is beyond our scope here, statistical controls for these do not substantially alter the religious patterns we find (Kellstedt et al. 1996a; Guth et al. 2006).

These religious groups have been historically related to southern distinctiveness in several ways. First, as historians of religion attest, high-commitment evangelicals have constituted the "soul" of traditional southern religion, while the other three white Protestant groups represent at least some departures from it, both in belief and practice. Second, the remaining groups have been on the margins of southern religion: black Protestants because of the "color line" (the "ethnic line" for Latinos), non-Latino Catholics and seculars because of the "papal line" and "theistic line," respectively.

All four white Protestant groups were allied with the Democratic Party in the electoral order of the old "Solid South." Together they constituted a powerful faction in the national "coalition of minorities" that the party assembled, helping elect Democratic presidents from Grover Cleveland to Bill Clinton and, very often, majorities in Congress. High-commitment evangelicals were the core of this "white Protestant alliance," remaining loyal to a substantial degree even during regional rebellions such as the States' Rights agitation in 1948 and the Wallace campaign in 1968. Indeed, it was low-commitment white Protestants who were most likely to defect to third-party candidates, whether in the past or more recently (Gilbert et al. 1995; Green 1997).

Mainline Protestants were also less firmly anchored to the "Southern Democracy" and more prone to defect to the Republicans, the party of their co-religionists outside the region, as occurred in 1956. Black Protestants, non-Latino Catholics, Latino Christians, and secular voters were largely excluded from this coalition; in response, they sometimes allied themselves with northern Democrats in intraparty battles, and sometimes defected to the GOP in general elections. All four groups, however, made up only a small fraction of the southern electorate.

Our task is to assess how these historic patterns have persisted or changed in recent years. The 2000 presidential election is a convenient marker for the emergence of a new southern religio-electoral order. In contrast to that of the old Solid South, the new order has a remarkable resemblance to electoral structures in the rest of the nation. And this new order appears to be *stable*, meaning that it will not change easily and is likely to provide the context for understanding southern electoral politics for years to come. To anticipate our argument: the new order emerged in full flower in the 2000 campaign, producing Republican victories in both 2000 and 2004, and remained largely intact in 2008, despite Democratic inroads in the Rim South states of Virginia, North Carolina, and Florida. Indeed, despite Democratic advances in 2008, religious alignments differed only marginally from those in 2000 and 2004.

THE RELIGIOUS COMPOSITION OF THE SOUTHERN ELECTORATE

A good place to begin to understand the contemporary role of religion and politics in the South is with the changes in the relative size of religious groups since the 1960s (table C.1). After all, a social group's size sets the upper bounds on its contribution to the electoral order. One source of continuity has been evangelical Protestants, who have accounted for somewhere between one-third to two-fifths of the southern electorate over the period. Note, however, that the proportion of high-commitment evangelicals has risen at the expense of their less faithful brethren. Mainline Protestants, on the other hand, experienced a sharp numerical decline over these decades, reflecting national trends, and accounted for less than 15 percent of the region's population by 2008. Overall, the total number of white Protestants declined from about 70 percent of the electorate in the

Table C.1.   Relative Size of Southern Religious Groups, 1960s–2008 (in percentages)

	1960s	1970s	1980s	1990s	2004	2008
Evangelical						
High Commitment	20	23	23	27	26	30
Low Commitment	13	14	12	9	7	7
Mainline						
High Commitment	25	11	10	10	9	9
Low Commitment	12	8	5	6	6	4
Black Protestant	15	16	19	13	14	17
Latino Protestant	*	*	2	3	3	4
Catholic						
Non-Latino	4	8	5	10	10	9
Latino	*	2	6	4	6	7
Secular	9	6	16	13	14	9
Others	1	3	3	5	5	4
Total	100	101	101	100	100	100

Sources: American National Election Studies (ANES) 1960–1988; National Survey of Religion and Politics (NSRP) 1992–2008.
*Fewer than .5 of 1 percent.

1960s to about 50 percent in 2008. But the core bloc in the "white Protestant alliance," high-commitment evangelicals, has actually grown even as the alliance shrank at the periphery.

The other side of this trend was growing religious diversity. Prior to the Voting Rights Act of 1965, black Protestants constituted only a tiny fraction of the electorate, but by 2008 they outnumbered white mainline Protestants. Non-Latino Catholics, Latino Christians, and "other" religious groups also grew significantly over the period, enhancing their electoral significance. These changes reflect the same forces of economic development and in-migration that historically eroded the national dominance of Protestantism, especially the mainline variety. So, groups once excluded from traditional southern religion expanded as the "white Protestant alliance" changed and contracted. In addition, the social and cultural tensions associated with economic growth and in-migration have intensified the religious commitment of some white Protestants, encouraging the growth in numbers of high-commitment evangelicals. These changes in the electorate's religious composition had vital implications for the southern electoral order.

RELIGION AND POLITICAL BEHAVIOR IN THE
SOUTHERN ELECTORATE

The size of religious groups has obvious implications for their electoral importance, but so does their propensity to exercise the franchise. Groups maximize their influence if their members actually vote, but suffer politically if they do not. Historically, the South has been a low-turnout region, reflecting demographic factors such as lower education levels as well as the historic one-party dominance of the region. In analysis of religious groups, the scholarly literature suggests that higher-status groups, such as mainline Protestants, should get to the polls in greater proportions than lower-status groups, such as evangelicals. Of course, religious commitment may complicate this relationship, as church attendance—more characteristic of evangelicals and black Protestants—encourages turnout (Rosenstone and Hansen 1993, 130).

Not surprisingly, religious commitment has an independent effect on turnout: Since 1960, high commitment was nearly always associated with higher turnout. Although turnout declined across the board from the 1960s through the 1980s and was lower in the South than in the rest of the country, the downturn was smallest among high-commitment groups (including high-commitment black Protestants, Latino Christians, and non-Latino Catholics). Reflecting their high socioeconomic status, mainline Protestants had the strongest turnout, while black Protestants, seculars, and, in particular, Latino Christians had the weakest. Evangelical Protestants and non-Latino Catholics fell in between (American National Election Studies, data not shown).

In table C.2 we take a closer look at the turnout of southern religious groups in presidential elections since 1992.[2] Turnout in the entire South was close to 50 percent in the first three elections, but jumped six points in 2004 and rose again in 2008. Note that the two high-commitment Protestant groups had the highest rates across the period, with the higher-status

Table C.2.   Electoral Turnout among Southern Religious Groups (percent voting)

	1992	1996	2000	2004	2008
Evangelical					
High Commitment	54	52	57	65	57
Low Commitment	45	42	38	51	50
Mainline					
High Commitment	75	70	61	84	81
Low Commitment	56	60	55	60	60
Black Protestant	41	47	50	44	68
Latino Protestant	28	58	30	48	46
Catholic					
Non-Latino	58	54	57	67	79
Latino	31	42	41	50	40
Secular	40	40	43	39	57
Totals	50	52	52	58	61

Source: National Survey of Religion and Politics, 1992–2008.

mainliners in the lead. However, there was some variation over time. Voting among high-commitment evangelicals reached a peak in 2004, when mobilization efforts targeted this group (Guth et al. 2007), but fell off dramatically in 2008. Meanwhile, turnout among black Protestants in the South was quite low from 1992 to 2004, but increased significantly in 2008, with a religiously active African American Protestant heading the national Democratic ticket. Hence, in 2008 the most Democratic group, black Protestants, voted in record numbers, while turnout by their Republican counterpart, high-commitment evangelicals, receded from their own high-water mark of 2004.

Turnout also varied over the period for other groups, but generally increased in 2008, especially for seculars, another component of the Democratic Party coalition. Latino turnout, both Protestant and Catholic, was low throughout the period, but increasing Latino numbers (see table C.1) partly counteracted the poor turnout rates for 2008. In addition, the relatively small non-Latino Catholic population in the South also had record turnout in 2008. For other groups, turnout remained about what it had been in 2000 and 2004. Given the strong support that black Protestants gave to Obama (see table C.3a), their elevated turnout may well have produced the close Democratic presidential victories in Florida, North Carolina, and Virginia.

Group size and turnout tendencies influence the role of religious groups in the electoral order, but their partisan choices are clearly the critical consideration. What voting and partisan changes have occurred among southern religious groups? Table C.3 examines three common measures of political behavior: vote choice in presidential and House elections, and party identification. To make comparisons over time easier, the first two measures are restricted to the Republican share of the two-party vote, with Democratic and third-party voters excluded. For party identification, independent "leaners" are combined with strong and weak partisans, and pure independents are omitted from the table. Each measure reveals very similar patterns, with the presidential vote being the most volatile and party identification being the least volatile.[3]

By the 1960s, high-commitment evangelicals were already deserting the "Southern Democracy." Partly in reaction to John Kennedy's Catholicism in 1960, but also in response to the 1964 and 1968 campaigns of Barry Goldwater and Richard Nixon, just over half of these voters cast GOP presidential ballots during this decade. The Republican vote expanded to about two-thirds in the 1970s and 1980s, slid to about three-fifths in the 1990s, and skyrocketed to over 80 percent in the period from 2000 to 2008. It is truly remarkable that high-commitment southern evangelicals gave John McCain over five-sixths of their vote in 2008, despite their clear lack

Table C.3. Partisanship by Southern Religious Groups, 1960s–2008

	1960s	1970s	1980s	1990s	2000	2004	2008
(A) Republican percent of two-party presidential vote							
Evangelical							
High Commitment	52	65	68	61	80	80	86
Low Commitment	33	67	66	47	39	61	69
Mainline							
High Commitment	56	76	66	65	67	60	59
Low Commitment	60	58	60	58	57	63	48
Black Protestant	10	11	9	3	5	5	7
Latino Protestant	—	—	27	50	38	67	29
Catholics							
Non-Latino	34	62	73	56	58	68	61
Latino	—	54	40	27	40	37	30
Secular	46	60	66	27	46	39	32
Totals	44	55	53	41	56	56	51
(B) Republican percent of two-party House of Representatives vote							
Evangelical							
High Commitment	24	31	38	61	81	78	83
Low Commitment	13	33	36	60	41	57	69
Mainline							
High Commitment	35	38	42	66	66	55	57
Low Commitment	38	37	41	66	67	60	64
Black Protestant	9	7	9	17	8	9	15
Latino Protestant	*	*	*	59	38	56	13
Catholics							
Non-Latino	16	21	61	61	69	62	61
Latino	*	11	13	24	36	19	33
Secular	18	35	40	43	45	48	37
Totals	26	28	33	48	58	55	52

(continued)

Table C.3. (*continued*)

	1960s		1970s		1980s		1990s		2000		2004		2008	
	D	R	D	R	D	R	D	R	D	R	D	R	D	R
(C) Partisan identification (in percent, with independents excluded)														
Evangelical														
High Commitment	69	19	58	28	53	35	40	49	27	56	26	60	25	60
Low Commitment	73	14	51	26	50	30	48	37	37	39	44	41	33	41
Mainline														
High Commitment	56	30	47	41	42	49	35	58	33	50	41	45	37	51
Low Commitment	56	33	50	32	46	41	42	49	32	45	24	58	34	46
Black Protestant	66	11	76	9	80	10	79	10	71	14	73	5	77	11
Latino Protestant	*	*	*	*	50	25	42	38	39	30	54	33	52	24
Catholics														
Non-Latino	64	20	64	19	43	39	46	45	36	46	43	44	32	52
Latino	*	*	66	25	60	23	62	26	57	31	65	18	45	16
Secular	56	22	53	24	50	32	47	29	38	37	35	29	42	22
Totals	63	22	58	25	56	30	51	35	39	42	42	38	41	39

Sources: American National Election Studies, 1960s–1988; National Survey of Religion and Politics, 1992–2008.
*Less than .5 of 1 percent.

of enthusiasm for the GOP candidate—and what many journalists saw as McCain's contempt for them (Guth 2009).

The shift of high-commitment evangelicals to the GOP in presidential elections was accompanied by similar—but delayed—changes in U.S. House vote and party identification. Until the 1990s, high-commitment evangelicals voted overwhelmingly for Democratic congressional candidates and identified with the Democratic Party, albeit at lower rates than in the 1960s. In the 1990s, their vote for GOP House candidates rose to over 60 percent (although higher in presidential years than in off-year elections [data not shown]) and vaulted even more in this century (again, being somewhat lower in off years). In party identification, high-commitment southern evangelicals went from being a very strong Democratic bloc in the 1960s to favoring the GOP by more than 2:1 by 2000. Clearly, they are the new religious base of the Republican Party in the South.

Low-commitment evangelicals also have moved toward the GOP, but less enthusiastically. They gave only one-third of their votes to Republican presidential candidates in the 1960s (and only 13 percent to GOP House candidates), and have exhibited a "saw-tooth" pattern since. In 2004 and 2008, they provided over 60 percent of their votes to Bush and McCain, but still trailed their highly committed brethren. Their House vote has favored the GOP in every year since 1990 except 2000, and their partisanship has moved away from the Democrats since the 1960s, but has not approached the Republican identification of the high-commitment group.

Mainline Protestants with high religious commitment gave their strongest support to Republican presidential candidates in the 1970s, but since then their backing has declined somewhat. Still, their support has been stronger than that of less committed mainliners in every year but 2004 and has generally remained above 60 percent. House voting among mainliners follows the evangelical pattern, with little support for GOP candidates until the 1990s. High-commitment mainliners gave about two-thirds of their votes to Republican House candidates in the 1990s and in 2000, but the percentage has fallen off since then and was surpassed by that of low-commitment mainliners in 2004 and 2008. High-commitment mainline Protestants still identified as Democrats in the 1960s and 1970s, but they moved toward Republican partisanship by the 1980s, a full decade ahead of high-commitment evangelicals. By the 1980s, however, their GOP identification leveled off, just as evangelical movement toward the GOP was getting started. At present, partisan differences between the high-commitment and low-commitment mainliners are not substantial. Both are solidly Republican, but both are more willing to deviate from their partisan ties than high-commitment evangelicals.

The political behavior of black Protestants looks remarkably different from that of white Protestants. Over the entire period, they were solidly Democratic at the ballot box and in partisanship. Although fewer in number than the high-commitment evangelicals, black Protestants now constitute the Democratic Party's base in the South, both in voting behavior and partisanship. And their higher turnout rates in 2008 have made them even more significant players in the southern religio-electoral structure. It would take a shift of seismic proportions to change this attachment in the foreseeable future.

Non-Latino Catholics exhibit a somewhat different pattern, both in comparison with other southern religious groups, and, to some extent, from their co-religionists elsewhere. In the South, they have supported GOP presidential aspirants since the 1970s and have voted for Republican House candidates since the 1980s. Non-Latino Catholics have also become much more Republican in party identification than they were in the 1960s, siding with the GOP since 2000. In this case they resemble southern white Protestant groups more than their brethren elsewhere, who are still marginally Democratic. Remember, though, that non-Latino Catholic influence is limited by the fact that they make up only about 10 percent of the southern electorate. In addition, their historic status as a negative reference group for many southern white Protestants may still inhibit their influence, if to a declining degree.

Latino Christians made up only a tiny part of the southern electorate during the 1960s and 1970s, but their influence has grown with their numbers. Latino Catholics outnumber Latino Protestants by more than a 2:1 ratio, and they are more supportive of Democratic candidates for president and Congress. (In 2004, for example, southern Latino Protestants supported George W. Bush with over 60 percent of the vote.) When ethnic issues such as immigration policy are high on the agenda, however, as in 1996 and again in 2008, Catholic and Protestant Latino communities coalesce behind the Democrats. In 2008, both groups gave Obama more than 60 percent of the vote. In partisanship, both tend to identify as Democrats, albeit Latino Catholics more so than Latino Protestants. With each passing election cycle, the proportion of Latino voters is likely to increase nationally and, in particular, in the South. The results of the 2008 election suggest that the Democratic "coalition of minorities" may literally become a "rainbow coalition" in the future.

Southern secular voters may provide another base for revival of Democratic electoral fortunes. After giving majority support to Democratic presidential candidates in the 1960s, seculars voted Republican in the 1970s and 1980s before veering strongly back to the Democrats ever since, with 2008 being a banner Democratic year. In House elections, seculars remained Democratic over the entire period, although drifting slightly toward the

GOP from time to time until 2008, when they voted more strongly for Democratic candidates. The partisan ties of seculars were strongly Democratic until 2000, when they split about evenly between the two parties. In 2004, however, their partisanship moved back toward the Democrats, and this trend accelerated in 2008. In the religious South, seculars will likely remain a classic "out-group," and attempts to organize them for electoral purposes will continue to be problematic. But their strong attachment to the Democrats and their enhanced turnout rates suggest that they may be an important element in a revived Southern Democracy.

Thus, the transformation of the southern religio-electoral order had twin engines: political change among white Protestants and growing religious diversity. On the first count, a large contingent of high-commitment evangelicals marched into the very core of the GOP, steadily increasing their propensity to vote for Republican presidential and congressional candidates and expanding their identification with the party. Other white Protestants arrived in the same neighborhood by more circuitous paths and in smaller numbers. In fact, most GOP gains among mainliners came before 2000 and have stalled since. The small non-Latino Catholic population has also moved strongly in a Republican direction, although trailing their high-commitment evangelical neighbors. Meanwhile, black Protestants remained overwhelmingly Democratic and became much more politically active in 2008. Although seculars showed some variation, flirting with GOP presidential candidates in the 1970s and 1980s, they were on balance Democratic. Finally, Latino Christians are usually strong backers of the Democratic Party, particularly when immigration issues are paramount, and their growing numbers make them a force to be reckoned with in the future.

RELIGION AND CHANGES IN THE ELECTORAL ORDER

We can summarize the changes in the southern religio-electoral order by looking at the contribution religious groups make to party voting coalitions. As we have stressed, electoral impact is a function of group size, turnout rates, and level of support for candidates of each party. Table C.4 illustrates the combined impact of religious tradition and commitment by examining the major party voting coalitions in the 1960s and then in the three elections from 2000 to 2008. Very similar patterns appear in analyses of House vote and party identification (data not shown). The data in table C.4 starkly reveal the new religio-electoral order, with each party's coalition exhibiting a different core religious constituency (Green 2007, 2009).

Not surprisingly, the new centerpiece of the Republican coalition is the high-commitment evangelical group, reflecting an ironic version of

Table C.4. Religion and Presidential Vote Coalitions in the South, 1960s–2008

	1960s D	1960s R	2000 D	2000 R	2004 D	2004 R	2008 D	2008 R	Change 1960s–2008 D	Change 1960s–2008 R
Evangelical										
High Commitment	22	31	15	47	14	43	8	44	−14	+13
Low Commitment	17	11	9	4	6	7	4	9	−13	−2
Mainline										
High Commitment	17	29	10	16	13	14	10	13	−7	−16
Low Commitment	8	15	6	5	5	6	5	4	−3	−11
Black Protestants	21	3	25	1	27	1	38	3	+17	0
Latino Protestants	0	1	2	1	2	4	5	2	+5	+1
Catholics										
Non-Latino	7	4	11	11	8	13	10	16	+3	+12
Latino	0	*	4	2	6	3	6	3	+6	+3
Secular	5	5	12	8	11	5	10	4	+5	−1
Others	4	1	6	4	9	4	4	3	0	+2
Totals	101	100	100	99	101	100	100	100		

Sources: American National Election Studies, 1960s; National Survey of Religion and Politics, 2000–2008. D = percentage vote for the Democratic presidential candidates; R = percentage vote for Republican presidential candidates. Column percentages may not add up to 100 due to rounding.
*Less than .5 of 1 percent.

"southern distinctiveness." This group grew from less than one-third of the GOP vote in the 1960s to over two-fifths in all three elections in this century. (Note that the 1960s figure for the GOP presidential vote is much higher than the comparable House or partisan percentage, given strong evangelical support for Nixon and Goldwater.) This gain is due to growing numbers, changing partisan preferences, and increasing turnout among high-commitment evangelicals. All other Protestants, but particularly the mainline groups, declined as a proportion of the Republican vote. Given the increasing GOP propensities of each group, much of this change results from reduced numbers and, in the case of low-commitment evangelicals, from relatively lower turnout. Thanks mainly to committed evangelicals, all white Protestants still accounted for 70 percent of the Republican vote in 2008, down somewhat from the 86 percent in the 1960s.

Groups other than high-commitment evangelicals made modest gains in their contribution to the Republican coalition. Non-Latino Catholics also increased substantially their share of the GOP voting bloc to become the second largest component of the coalition, but their absolute proportion was still only modest in 2008. Latino Christians were absent from the 1960s GOP coalition but added a small share to the contemporary totals (as noted above, Latino Protestants gave Bush substantial vote support in 2004). "Other" religious groups also increased their share. In both cases, increased size accounts for the change. On the whole, "southern distinctiveness" remains with white Protestant dominance, but in 2008 with a high-commitment evangelical flavor.

This fact is vividly illustrated by a closer look at the role of that quintessential southern religious institution, the Southern Baptist Convention (SBC). Not only is the SBC the nation's largest Protestant denomination, it is especially prominent in its home region (Reed 1972; Hill 1983; Harrell 1991; Smith 1997). In ANES and NSRP surveys since 1970, Southern Baptists have comprised between 25 percent and 34 percent of the southern white Protestant electorate. If SBC respondents are compared with southern white Protestants as a whole, Southern Baptists identified more closely with the Democratic Party throughout the 1970s, 1980s, and 1990s. In 2004, however, Southern Baptists led all groups in the southern electorate in identification with the Republican Party, and they maintained that leadership role in 2008, although perhaps at a slightly diminished level. Movement toward the GOP has been most pronounced among high-commitment Southern Baptists and especially among young, high-commitment members, where the GOP has a 3:1 margin in party identification (data not shown). We cannot explore here all the possible causes of this change, but cue giving by intermediary groups such as pastors and denominational agencies undoubtedly played a significant role. We have shown elsewhere that SBC clergy moved toward the GOP after 1980, well ahead of SBC laity, reaching a margin of 5:1 in favor of the Republicans by 2004 (Green et al. 2006; Kellstedt et al. 2007).

The Democratic Party's religious coalition has changed even more dramatically than the GOP's. White Protestants accounted for 64 percent of the Democratic vote in the 1960s, but this fell to 27 percent in 2008, a precipitous drop. At present, the core of the Democratic coalition is black Protestants—another ironic version of "southern distinctiveness." This group has almost doubled its contribution to the Democratic totals in the past 40 years, especially with their high turnout in 2008. Non-Latino Catholics, Latino Christians, and seculars all increased their contribution to the Democratic vote over the period. Increasingly, the Democratic Party has become the "party of religious minorities" in the South, just as it has been nationwide.

Thus, by 2000 the southern electoral order had two religious centers of gravity: high-commitment evangelicals for the GOP, led by Southern Baptists, and black Protestants for the Democrats. The former were joined by other white Protestants in most instances and by non-Latino Catholics as well, leaving a new form of "southern distinctiveness" as part of the electoral order. At the same time, the South has become less "distinctive" to the benefit of the Democrats, as black Protestants, seculars, Latino Christians, Jews, and other small religious groups allowed the national Democratic coalition of minorities to extend into Dixie. This religio-electoral order has been in place through three presidential elections and appears to be a stable force in the South for at least the near future. In contrast with the past, the electoral advantage in the region is with the Republicans, although membership in the Democratic religious groups is rising.

THE SOUL OF THE SOUTH

The election of 2008 in the South saw a swing toward the Democrats in both presidential and House voting, with Obama victories in three southern states—Florida, Virginia, and North Carolina. Partisanship had moved in a Republican direction from the 1960s through 2004, but actually moved back a bit toward the Democrats in 2008. A sizable decrease in high-commitment evangelical turnout from 2004 to 2008, a dramatic turnout increase by black Protestants, a sizable turnout increase by seculars, and a larger presence of Latino voters in the electorate (and a change in voting direction by Latino Protestants from 2004) all contributed to the 2008 results. Many of these trends may be short-term factors, however, and may not have significance in future elections.

The 2008 results may suggest to some analysts that the Democratic Party is on its way to reclaim dominance in yet another new "Solid South." But it is far too early to draw such conclusions. After all, the unique factors in the 2008 election may not repeat themselves. For example, black Protestant turnout skyrocketed, while it declined among high-commitment evangelicals. At least some of this difference resulted from the relative attractiveness of the GOP and Democratic presidential candidates to each party's core religious constituency: very high for black Protestants, very low for committed evangelicals (Guth 2009). If such short-term factors reverse in the future, the GOP should retain at least some advantage in the region in the near term.

In the end, what is remarkable about the 2008 election results in the South is how similar they look to those of 2000 and 2004. A religio-electoral order is in place that puts high-commitment evangelicals as un-questioned leaders of the Republican coalition, opposed by black Protestants at the core of the Democratic voting bloc. In this view, religion continues to be at the center of southern politics, but in a different form from a generation ago. In the near future, this new order should continue to dominate the politics of the South, giving the Republican Party a slight advantage, but an advantage that is small enough to give the Democrats frequent electoral opportunities.

Our findings about the electorate do not inform us about other elements in Shafer's electoral order—especially intermediary groups and elites, particularly elected officials. As we suggested in our brief look at Southern Baptists, such groups may play an important part in religious mobilization. Preliminary evidence suggests that in 2008, religious interest groups and state Republican Party organizations did not match their mobilizing efforts in 2004, accounting in part for the lower turnout among high-commitment evangelicals. Still, the Southern Baptist clergy and SBC agencies such as the Ethics and Religious Liberty Commission remain in the hands of strong conservatives, creating enormous potential for education and mobilization of this religious constituency. And media reports from the 2008 campaign confirmed that African American churches remained a key source of Democratic mobilization in the South and elsewhere.

There is circumstantial evidence that the electoral polarization between African American Protestants (Democrats) and highly religious evangelicals (Republicans) is also present among party activists and government officials. For example, increasingly southern congressional delegations pit black Protestants against their evangelical counterparts. The growing presence of evangelicals in the party strengthens the GOP in the South, but, ironically, might hinder it in other regions where the party may need to broaden its base and reduce dependence on its evangelical wing. As the title of V. O. Key's classic work reminds us, "Southern Politics" is always politics in the context of "state and nation." And while many have commented recently on the "evangelical imprisonment" of the GOP, it is also well to remember that just a few years ago, the Democrats' inability to surmount their own capture by secularists and religious minorities was the topic of fervent intraparty debates. In the future, religious politics in the South will still show some regional "distinctives," but will also be an increasingly integral part of national religious coalition-building.

NOTES

1. The following analysis is based on the American National Elections Studies Cumulative File (1960 to 1988) and the National Surveys of Religion and Politics conducted at the University of Akron in 1992, 1996, 2000, 2004, and 2008 (see Kellstedt et al. 1996a for details). The sample size varies by decade for the ANES data (1,890 in the 1960s; 3,648 in the 1970s; 2,994 in the 1980s); the Akron data sets had sample sizes of over 4,000 in each year. The ANES data were made available by the Inter-University Consortium for Political and Social Research; the National Surveys of Religion and Politics were supported by grants from the Pew Charitable Trusts. The authors are solely responsible for the interpretations presented here. Denominational affiliation was coded into religious traditions according to Kellstedt et al. (1996a). Religious commitment was measured by church attendance (high commitment was coded as attending more often than "a few times a year"; low-commitment as attending "a few times a year" or less). Contact the authors for additional details in the coding of religious variables in these data sets. Here, the South is defined as Alabama, Arkansas, Florida, Georgia, Kentucky, Louisiana, Mississippi, North Carolina, Oklahoma, South Carolina, Tennessee, Texas, and Virginia.

2. Like all surveys, the National Survey of Religion and Politics experiences "overreporting" of voting among respondents. The data in table C.2 have been adjusted to correct for this tendency.

3. Traditional distinctions between the "Deep" and "Rim" South also appear in these data. High-commitment evangelicals and black Protestants are more important to their respective party coalitions in the Deep South, while these groups are less important in the Rim South. For more analysis on this point, see Kellstedt and Guth (2008).

REFERENCES

Baker, Tod A., Robert P. Steed, and Laurence W. Moreland, eds. 1983. *Religion and Politics in the South.* New York: Praeger.
Black, Earl, and Merle Black. 1987. *Politics and Society in the South.* Cambridge, MA: Harvard University Press.
———. 1992. *The Vital South.* Cambridge, MA: Harvard University Press.

——. 2002. *The Rise of Southern Republicans.* Cambridge, MA: Harvard University Press.

——. 2007. *Divided America: The Ferocious Power Struggle in American Politics.* New York: Simon and Schuster.

Carmines, Edward G., and James A. Stimson. 1989. *Issue Evolution: Race and the Transformation of American Politics.* Princeton, NJ: Princeton University Press.

Feldman, Glenn, ed. 2005. *Politics and Religion in the White South.* Lexington: University of Kentucky Press.

Gilbert, Christopher P., Timothy R. Johnson, and David A. M. Peterson. 1995. "The Religious Roots of Third Party Voting: A Comparison of Anderson, Perot, and Wallace Voters." *Journal for the Scientific Study of Religion* 34:470–484.

Green, John C. 1997. "The Third Party South." In *The 1996 Presidential Election in the South.*, ed. Laurence W. Moreland and Robert P. Steed. New York: Praeger.

——. 2007. *The Faith Factor: How Religion Influences American Elections.* Westport, CT: Praeger.

——. 2009. "What Happened to the Values Voter? Believers and the 2008 Election," *First Things.* http://www.firstthings.com/article.php3?id_article=6497.

Green, John C., James L. Guth, Corwin E. Smidt, and Lyman A. Kellstedt, eds. 1996. *Religion and the Culture Wars.* Lanham, MD: Rowman & Littlefield.

Green, John C., Corwin E. Smidt, Lyman A. Kellstedt, and James L. Guth. 1997. "Bringing in the Sheaves." In *Sojourners in the Wilderness: The Christian Right in Comparative Perspective,* ed. Corwin E. Smidt and James M. Penning. Lanham, MD: Rowman & Littlefield.

Green, John C., Lyman A. Kellstedt, Corwin E. Smidt, and James L. Guth. 2006. "The Soul of the South: Religion and Southern Politics in the New Millennium." In *The New Politics of the Old South: An Introduction to Southern Politics,* 3rd ed., ed. Charles S. Bullock III and Mark J. Rozell. Lanham, MD: Rowman & Littlefield.

——. 2007. "How the Faithful Voted: Religious Communities and the Presidential Vote." In *A Matter of Faith? Religion in the 2004 Election,* ed. David E. Campbell. Washington, DC: Brookings.

Guth, James L. 2009. "Religion in the 2008 Election." In *The American Elections of 2008,* ed. Janet Box-Steffensmeier and Steven E. Schier. Lanham, MD: Rowman & Littlefield.

Guth, James L., Lyman A. Kellstedt, Corwin E. Smidt, and John C. Green. 2006. "Religious Influences in the 2004 Presidential Election," *Presidential Studies Quarterly* 36:223–242.

Guth, James L., Lyman A. Kellstedt, John C. Green, and Corwin E. Smidt. 2007. "Getting the Spirit? Religious and Partisan Mobilization in the 2004 Elections." In *Interest Group Politics,* 7th ed., ed. Allan J. Cigler and Burdett A. Loomis. Washington, DC: Congressional Quarterly Press.

Harrell, David Edwin, ed. 1991. *Varieties of Southern Evangelicalism.* Macon, GA: Mercer University Press.

Havard, William C., ed. 1972. *The Changing Politics of the South.* Baton Rouge: Louisiana State University Press.

Hill, Samuel S. 1966. *Southern Churches in Crisis.* New York: Holt, Rinehart, and Winston.

———. 1983. "Introduction." In *Religion and Politics in the South*, ed. Tod A. Baker, Robert P. Steed, and Laurence W. Moreland. New York: Praeger.

Jelen, Ted G. 2006. "Reflections on Scholarship in Religion and Southern Politics." In *Writing Southern Politics: Contemporary Interpretations and Future Directions*, ed. Robert P. Steed and Laurence W. Moreland. Lexington: University Press of Kentucky.

Kellstedt, Lyman A. 1990. "Evangelical Religion and Support for the Falwell Policy Positions: An Examination of Regional Variation." In *The Disappearing South*, ed. Robert P. Steed, Laurence W. Moreland, and Tod A. Baker. Tuscaloosa: University of Alabama Press.

Kellstedt, Lyman A., John C. Green, James L. Guth, and Corwin E. Smidt. 1996a. "Grasping the Essentials: The Social Embodiment of Religion and Political Behavior." In *Religion and the Culture Wars*, ed. John C. Green, James L. Guth, Corwin E. Smidt, and Lyman A. Kellstedt. Lanham, MD: Rowman & Littlefield.

———. 1996b. "The Puzzle of Evangelical Protestantism." In *Religion and the Culture Wars*, ed. John C. Green, James L. Guth, Corwin E. Smidt, and Lyman A. Kellstedt. Lanham, MD: Rowman & Littlefield.

Kellstedt, Lyman A., John C. Green, Corwin E. Smidt, and James L. Guth. 2007. "Faith Transformed: Religion and American Politics from FDR to G. W. Bush." In *Religion and American Politics*, 2nd ed., ed. Mark A. Noll and Luke E. Harlow. New York: Oxford University Press.

Kellstedt, Lyman A., and James L. Guth. 2008. "Religion and Political Behavior in the Sunbelt," presented at "Sunbelt Rising: The Politics of Space, Place, and Region in the American South and Southwest," The Huntington Library, San Marino, California, July 18–19.

Key, V. O., Jr. 1949. *Southern Politics in State and Nation*. New York: Alfred A. Knopf.

Lamis, Alexander P. 1984. *The Two-Party South*. New York: Oxford University Press.

Lincoln, Eric C., and Lawrence H. Mamiya. 1990. *The Black Church in the African American Experience*. Durham, NC: Duke University Press.

Petrocik, John R. 1987. "Realignment: New Party Coalitions and the Nationalization of the South." *Journal of Politics* 49:347–75.

Reed, John Shelton. 1972. *The Enduring South*. Lexington, MA: D. C. Heath.

Rosenstone, Steven J., and John Mark Hansen. 1993. *Mobilization, Participation, and Democracy in America*. New York: Macmillan.

Rozell, Mark J., and Clyde Wilcox. 1996. *Second Coming: The New Christian Right in Virginia Politics*. Baltimore, MD: Johns Hopkins University Press.

Sernett, Milton G. 1991. "Black Religion and the Question of Evangelical Identity." In *The Variety of American Evangelicalism*, ed. Donald W. Dayton and Robert K. Johnston. Knoxville: University of Tennessee Press.

Shafer, Byron E. 1991. "The Notion of an Electoral Order: The Structure of Electoral Politics at the Accession of George Bush." In *The End of Realignment?*, ed. Byron E. Shafer. Madison: University of Wisconsin Press.

Shafer, Byron, and Robert Johnston. 2006. *The End of Southern Exceptionalism*. Cambridge, MA: Harvard University Press.

Smidt, Corwin E. 1983. "'Born Again' Politics: The Political Attitudes and Behavior of Evangelical Christians in the South and Non-South." In *Religion and Poli-*

tics in the South, ed. Tod A. Baker, Robert P. Steed, and Laurence W. Moreland. New York: Praeger.

———. 1989. "Change and Stability in the Partisanship of Southern Evangelicals: An Analysis of the 1980 and 1984 Presidential Elections." In *Religion in American Politics*, ed. Charles Dunn. Washington, DC: CQ Press.

———. 2007. "Evangelical and Mainline Protestants at the Turn of the Millennium: Taking Stock and Looking Forward." In *From Pews to Polling: Faith and Politics in the American Religious Mosaic*, ed. J. Matthew Wilson. Washington, DC: Georgetown University Press.

Smidt, Corwin E., Lyman A. Kellstedt, and James L. Guth. 2009. "The Role of Religion in American Politics: Explanatory Theories and Associated Analytical and Measurement Issues." In *The Oxford Handbook of Religion and American Politics*, ed. Corwin E. Smidt, Lyman A. Kellstedt, and James L. Guth. New York: Oxford.

Smith, Oran. 1997. *The Rise of Baptist Republicanism*. New York: New York University Press.

Stark, Rodney, and William Bainbridge. 1985. *The Future of Religion*. Berkeley: University of California Press.

Steensland, Brian, Jerry Park, Mark Regnerus, Lynn Robinson, W. Bradford Wilcox, and Robert Woodberry. 2000. "The Measure of American Religion." *Social Forces* 79:291–318.

Weaver, Richard. 1968. *The Southern Tradition at Bay*. New Rochelle, NY: Arlington House.

Index

About the Contributors

David Breaux is professor and head of the Department of Political Science and Public Administration at Mississippi University.

Charles S. Bullock III is Richard B. Russell Professor of Political Science at the University of Georgia.

Patrick R. Cotter is professor of political science at the University of Alabama.

Andrew Dowdle is an associate professor of political science at the University of Arkansas, Fayetteville.

Ronald Keith Gaddie is professor of political science at the University of Oklahoma.

Joseph D. Giammo is an assistant professor of political science at the University of Arkansas at Little Rock.

Cole Blease Graham Jr. is professor of political science at the University of South Carolina. He specializes in South Carolina and Southern Politics and is often called on by the media for commentary.

John C. Green is Distinguished Professor of Political Science and director of the Bliss Institute of Applied Politics at the University of Akron. He has written extensively on religion and politics in the United States.

James L. Guth is the William R. Kenan Jr. Professor of Political Science at Furman University. His essay, "Religion and Roll Calls: Religious Influences on the U.S. House of Representatives, 1997–2002," received the Paul J. Weber Award for the best paper on religion and politics presented at the 2007 annual meeting of the American Political Science Association.

Lyman A. Kellstedt is a professor of political science emeritus at Wheaton College in Illinois. He has written extensively in the field of religion and politics.

James W. Lamare is professor of political science at Florida Atlantic University, Jupiter Campus.

Laurence W. Moreland is professor of political science at The Citadel.

Michael Nelson is professor of political science at Rhodes College.

Wayne Parent is associate dean of the College of Arts and Sciences and professor of political science at Louisiana State University.

Huey L. Perry is professor of political science and Chancellor's Fellow at Southern University in Baton Rouge, Louisiana.

J. L. Polinard is a professor in the Department of Political Science at University of Texas, Pan American.

Charles Prysby is professor of political science at the University of North Carolina at Greensboro.

Mark J. Rozell is professor of public policy at George Mason University.

Richard K. Scher is the Robin and Jean Gibson Professor of Political Science at the University of Florida.

Michael J. Scicchitano is associate professor of political science at the University of Florida.

Stephen D. Shaffer is professor of political science at Mississippi State University.

John William Shapard is owner and president of Shapard Research LLC, a market research firm, and SoonerPoll, a public opinion survey firm in Oklahoma City.

Corwin E. Smidt is professor of political science at Calvin College.

Robert P. Steed is a professor of political science at The Citadel.

Robert D. Wrinkle is professor of political science at the University of Texas, Pan American.